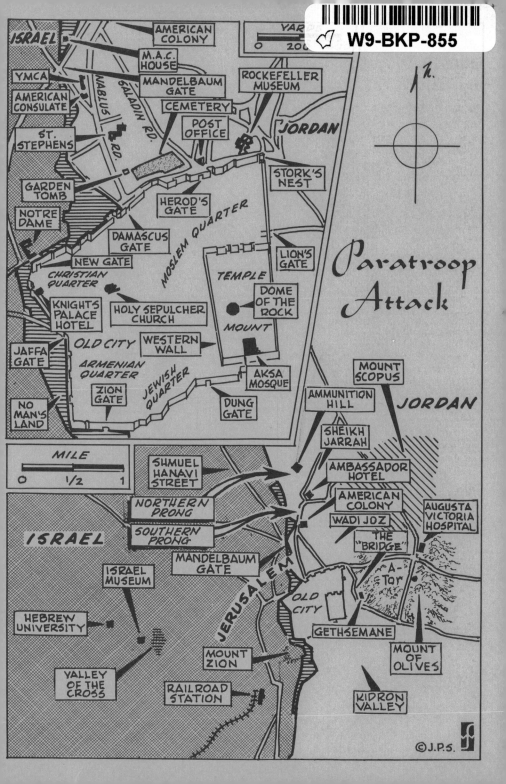

# the battle for Jerusalem

*JUNE 5-7, 1967*

# the
# battle
# for
# Jerusalem

*JUNE 5-7, 1967*

*by*

**Abraham Rabinovich**

*THE
JEWISH
PUBLICATION
SOCIETY
OF
AMERICA
5732-1972*

*to Rachie and Michal*

# contents

# *illustrations*

## illustrations

# FOREWORD

This book is based on some three hundred interviews, most of them carried out in the two years following the Six-Day War. They were conducted in Jerusalem itself and in cities and settlements across the country—among them thirty-five kibbutzim.

Despite the passage of time, the fog of war still clouded the memory of the soldier-reservists who participated in the battle. On occasion they remembered things that never happened, and they were frequently blank about things that did. Time had been telescoped and events distorted by the shock of battle. Whenever conflicting or otherwise uncertain testimony was encountered, an attempt was made to trace other men from the platoon or squad involved until a verified account could be obtained. Of the paratroop brigade which bore the brunt of the fighting, 125 officers and men were interviewed. (All interviews were conducted separately; they lasted from one to four hours.)

Some vivid recollections which could not be substantiated have been reluctantly omitted. In a number of instances, however, I have relied at some length on the unsupported testimony of individual soldiers—particularly those who received official citations—when there were no other survivors in a particular action or their identity was not known. The interviews are supplemented to a limited extent by my own observations as a reporter in Jewish Jerusalem before and during the battle and in the Old City in the first hours after the entry of Israeli troops. In addition, several of the participants walked with me over their part of the battlefield.

For the story of the attack on the Radar position in the Jerusalem Corridor I have relied in part on report in the Israel military magazine, *Ma'archot,* written by the commanding officers involved. Except for some minor points of information, this is the only published account of the battle that I have utilized. At the request of the Israeli Army, all unit identity numbers have been changed, and officers are generally identified only by their first names.

*A.R.*

# the battle for Jerusalem

JUNE 5-7, 1967

The six Israelis cut through an alley just short of the barricaded street intersection that had come to be called Mandelbaum Gate and entered the garden at the rear of a two-story building in no-man's-land. Jordanian officers were waiting for them inside. The building in the heart of divided Jerusalem had once been a school for blind Arab girls, but for almost two decades now it had served as headquarters of the Jordan–Israel Mixed Armistice Commission (MAC). Here every Monday morning officers from the two sides met across a horseshoe-shaped table presided over by a United Nations officer, to discuss problems along the 635-kilometer boundary between their countries— camels or children strayed across the line, a broken sewer pipe in no-man's-land. This, however, was a Sunday morning—May 14, 1967—and the Israelis were on their way to an emergency meeting called by the Jordanians to protest the Independence Day parade scheduled by the Israelis in their half of the city the next day, the nineteenth anniversary of the founding of the state.

Heading the Israeli delegation was Shaul Ramati of the Foreign Ministry, who had recently returned from seven years in a post abroad. Ramati was an old Jerusalem hand who had, in fact, been instrumental in choosing this very building as MAC headquarters. He was surprised to see that the building had been changed from a Jordanian-Israeli meeting ground in which a UN officer had a modest office into a UN headquarters with pictures of U Thant on the walls.

The diplomat had been attached to the regular five-man mili-

3

tary delegation to see to it that there would be no resolution condemning the parade—at least not before the parade got under way in twenty-four hours. Ramati shook hands warmly with the head of the Jordanian delegation, Colonel Mahmud Daoud, whom he had known when the Arab was a young lieutenant in the early days of MAC. He asked Daoud to give his regards to Jamal Bey Toukan, the Jordanian official with whom he had fixed the precise boundaries of Jerusalem's no-man's-land in 1951. The amenities over, Colonel Daoud stated his case. The parade, he maintained, would violate the armistice agreement, since it would tend to confirm the status of Jerusalem as the capital of Israel. Ramati replied that the armistice agreement did not ban parades in Jerusalem. Only fifteen hundred soldiers would participate, and there would be no armored vehicles. The complaint, Ramati said, was "calculated to create artificial tensions."

The crusty New Zealand officer serving as MAC chairman, Colonel Stanaway, seemed to be leaning toward the Jordanian viewpoint. Since Stanaway would cast the deciding vote on any resolution, Ramati determined to keep the meeting going twenty-four hours to delay a vote. It was not until 9:30 A.M. Monday—just as the parade was getting under way from Hebrew University stadium—that the groggy negotiators at MAC House finally rose from their chairs. They had stormed at each other around the clock, taking a break of only a few hours about dawn.

Stanaway had finally managed to draw up a statement which both parties could sign. In it the chairman agreed that the Jordanian complaint was outside the scope of the armistice agreement, but said he could not support the parade because it would increase tensions. Walking back from MAC House, the six Israelis found the head of the parade coming abreast as they reached Jaffa Road, the city's main thoroughfare. A crowd of two hundred thousand persons lined the route, and men held little children on their shoulders.

4

Ramati, unshaven and still carrying his attaché case, stood on tiptoe to see the rows of passing soldiers. It was the first parade he had seen in seven years. He started counting the soldiers to see if there were indeed as few as he had said there would be.

Chief of Staff Itzak Rabin was also making calculations as he watched the last of the marchers file out of the university stadium. The general had been informed of ominous moves in Egypt whose implications could not yet be determined. First word had come the night before, when he and his wife were attending a small gathering at the opulent Jerusalem home of former Venezuelan industrialist Miles Sherover. Also present were General Uzi Narkiss, commander of the Central Area Command, which included Jerusalem, and Yigal Yadin, the eminent archaeologist who had served as General Staff operations officer during the War of Independence in 1948. They were talking about the brigade which Rabin had commanded in the Jerusalem area during that conflict when the phone rang. The caller asked for the chief of staff, and Mrs. Sherover led Rabin to an extension in the study. When he returned a few minutes later he lit a cigarette, listened to find out where the talk had drifted, and then rejoined it. There was no mention of the phone conversation.

The call had been a report from the chief of intelligence that the Egyptian Army had been ordered into a state of alert the following afternoon. Now, twelve hours later, there was nothing new; but Rabin would be going through the events scheduled for the day with an ear cocked for sounds coming across the Sinai Desert.

Only once in every nineteen years do the Hebrew and English calendars coincide. This year, for the first time since the state was founded on May 15, 1948, the anniversary was being celebrated on a May 15. Wood for dozens of campfires had been piled on the slopes above the Valley of the Cross, and the

5

downtown streets were strung with colored lights for the street dancing scheduled for nightfall. Late in the afternoon Arye Hauslich, a news editor at the radio station, was on his way out to attend the mayor's Independence Day party in the municipal rose garden when the teletype clattered with a news bulletin. Hauslich paused to watch the keys strike out a story about Egyptian troops passing through Cairo on their way out to the Sinai Desert. Puzzled as to what it meant, Hauslich included the report among the miscellaneous items to be read at the end of the news broadcast and headed for the party.

In the evening eighteen hundred people crowded into Jerusalem's major auditorium to hear the new songs entered into competition at the Independence Day Song Festival. Those who had heard the vague reports about Egyptian troop movements were not unduly concerned. Alarm along the border was a regular feature that one accepted like the torrid *hamseen* periodically blowing out of the desert. The hit of the evening was not any of the ten official entries but a ballad about Jerusalem especially commissioned for the occasion by the city's vigorous mayor, Teddy Kollek, and composed by one of Israel's leading songwriters, Naomi Shemer. It was called "Jerusalem of Gold." "Captive of her own dream, the city that sits solitary—her heart cleaved by a wall. Jerusalem of gold, and copper and light—to all your songs I am a harp." The song was a skillful blend of images taken from the Hebrew poets, and it was destined to become the anthem of the nation in the weeks ahead.

The singer was a young girl soldier, Shuli Natan, making her first public appearance. She was normally stationed in a rural village where she taught illiterate immigrants from the Atlas Mountains in Morocco to read and write. Dressed in a white cotton dress and accompanying herself on a guitar, Shuli was greeted with such a rousing ovation when she finished that Mayor Kollek asked her to go out and sing the song again. This time the audience joined in the refrain: "No Jew visits the Temple Mount/And the caves in the rock/Keen the winds. No Jew goes down to the Dead Sea/By the Jericho road."

6

Jerusalemites, thousands of whom had danced horas in the streets late into the night, went to bed exhausted from the day's revelries unaware that the greatest crisis since the birth of the nation was already upon them. It had begun on the frontier with Syria, where increasing border incursions and the shelling of kibbutzim had led the month before to an Israeli air strike on Syrian artillery positions. Terrorist raids had only increased, and in the first ten days of May eleven sabotage attempts had been reported, more than in the entire previous month. Prime Minister Levi Eshkol, in a widely reported speech, warned that action "no less drastic" than the April air strike might have to be adopted if the sabotage pattern continued. "Informed sources" —plainly government spokesmen—were predicting in newspapers that a military expedition would be undertaken unless the sabotage campaign was called off. The response came not from the Syrians but from Egypt—the ostentatious parade of troop convoys through the heart of Cairo on Israel's Independence Day.

At first it seemed to Israelis to be merely a routine show of force to demonstrate Egyptian support for her sister Arab state. But President Nasser suddenly demanded the withdrawal of the UN buffer force which had kept the Egypt-Israel border free of incident since the 1956 Sinai campaign, and streams of his planes, tanks, and troops began to take up forward positions in the desert. Israel, which on Monday had casually glanced at the Egyptian troop movements, suddenly found itself staring across the border at an Egyptian force twice the size of that deployed prior to the Sinai campaign. By Friday partial mobilization had begun.

Aaron, the owner of a driving school in downtown Jerusalem, was alerted by phone at noon. A major in the reserves, he commanded the lone tank company assigned to the city's defense. He had been asked to organize it ten years before, after a diversified military career which included membership as a teen-ager in the terrorist Stern Gang and then in the Palmach, the chief strike force of Israel's War of Independence. During

7

the Sinai campaign he had fought as a paratrooper, afterwards completing a tank officer's course. He had been expecting the call-up since the first news of the Egyptian troop movements. His unit was a crisis barometer, always the first to be mobilized in Jerusalem when things got tense. Sometimes this happened four times a year or more. His men grew weary of the repeated alarms which took them away from their jobs and families for a period of anywhere from a few hours to a few weeks. "They cry wolf," Aaron reminded them, "but someday the wolf will come." Ten hours after the phone call ordering him to assemble his unit, Aaron and his men rendezvoused and set out for their encampment in the hills outside the city.

The existence of the tank company was one of the most closely guarded secrets in Jerusalem. Under the armistice agreement tanks were prohibited within ten kilometers of the border and so could not be stationed in the city itself. For a decade now the company's World War II vintage Shermans had been kept hidden in a shed well past the ten-kilometer limit.

Upon arrival at the camp the men began to scramble over the tanks which had lain dormant since their previous call-up six months before. An hour after sunup the Shermans had been fueled and loaded with ammunition and were ready to move. Aaron told his men to lie on the ground and get some sleep.

Jerusalemites had grown accustomed, over two decades, to living in a city divided between two hostile states. After a bitter battle, the War of Independence had left the Jews in control of most of the city. But the Arabs had won the part the Jews treasured most—the Old City and the Western Wall, that remnant of the ancient Temple compound to which Jews for two millennia had turned their faces in prayer. One of the major priorities of the Israel government following the war was to secure the tenuous hold it had won on the western half of Jerusalem and to flesh out the narrow corridor which connected the hill city to the coastal plain. The corridor, with Jerusalem at its tip, stabbed deep into the Jordanian-held bulge on the west bank of the Jordan River. The Arabs had severed this lifeline during the fighting, and the city had come close to being starved into submission before the months-long siege was broken. At that time there had been only four Jewish settlements in the Jerusalem Corridor. Although its rocky hills were poorly suited to farming, the government had nevertheless subsidized new agricultural settlements, and there were now fifty-five, their lights riding the corridor's hills at night like comforting sentinels. In addition, where only one road had linked Jerusalem to the coastal plain in 1948—and that promptly blockaded by the Arabs at Latrun—there were now several.

Within the city itself the primary need had also been for increased population. Many people whose nerves had been worn during the extended siege left the city afterwards, and the prewar Jewish population of 100,000 dropped to 65,000, the same number as on the Arab side of the city. The government undertook a crash program for settling new immigrants in Jerusalem, and in nineteen years the Jewish population had trebled to 190,000, while the population of Jordanian Jerusalem climbed to just 90,000.

The immigrants were distributed along the city border with the same deliberateness that kibbutzim were planted along the country's hostile frontiers. While the Jordanians had laced their border in Jerusalem with bunkers and trenches, the Israelis had put up housing projects—known as *shikunim*. These border *shikunim* were designed like fortresses. One apartment building with walls three times the normal thickness and firing slits on the roof would be placed on the very edge of no-man's-land facing the enemy positions, the other buildings in the project being sheltered in its lee. Windows in the front building were built high in the wall to make it more difficult for a housewife to be picked off by a sniper as she dusted her furniture. Nevertheless, one or more civilians were shot dead along the border almost every year, the Jordanians sometimes stating afterwards

9

that one of their soldiers had gone berserk. The strategic use of residential buildings was most striking in the south of the city, where a string of *shikunim* known as the *Katamonim* were thrown up in a giant arc to shield the new government and university center from the Jordanian-held hills in the direction of Bethlehem.

Despite its growth the city still had the character of a large village rather than a national capital. Sitting on the crest of the Judean Hills, it lacked the cosmopolitan night life of Tel Aviv or the industrious bustle of Haifa, the two cities in the country larger than Jerusalem. In Tel Aviv drivers rarely halted for pedestrians at zebra crossings, and pedestrians paid no attention to red lights. In Jerusalem drivers almost always halted for pedestrians, and the latter waited for green lights even on trafficless streets. The gentle pace suited a city that was one of the most beautiful and serene in the world. Built of the same dun-colored stones as those covering the hills surrounding it, the city was itself part of the landscape which opened out in striking vistas in every direction. Only on holidays would Jerusalem stir. During the week before Passover tens of thousands of Israelis would participate in the four-day hike from the coastal plain to Jerusalem in emulation of the ancient spring harvest pilgrimage. At Christmas, pilgrims would stream through Mandelbaum Gate to the holy places in Jordan. (For many Jerusalemites it had become a custom to drive to the southern edge of the city on Christmas Eve to hear the bells of Bethlehem just four kilometers away.)

With virtually no industry, Jerusalem was basically a university and government town. Despite objections by Jordan and by the UN, which regarded Jerusalem as an international city, the then premier, David Ben-Gurion, had insisted shortly after the founding of the state on shifting government offices from Tel Aviv to remote Jerusalem to make it in fact, as well as in name, the capital of Israel.

The combination of a large immigrant population from primitive Eastern countries, on one hand, and of university and government people, on the other, gave Jerusalem an oddly balanced population. There were proportionally twice as many illiterates as in the other two major cities and one-and-a-half times as many university-educated. The element which gave the city its most distinctive flavor, however, was a third group—the religious community, particularly the Chassidim, whose dress and way of life reflected centuries-old customs from Eastern Europe.

It was from this diverse population that the unit entrusted with the defense of the city—the Jerusalem Brigade—was drawn. Except for a small cadre of regular officers, the brigade was composed entirely of reserves, 85 percent of whom were residents of Jerusalem. Many were from Hebrew University, which, with twelve thousand students, was the largest in the country. The brigade's ranks also included government clerks, immigrant fruit peddlers, and bearded Chassidim. Unlike most other reserve units, the brigade was assigned to a fixed area, the capital and its approaches. If it came to war its soldiers knew they might be fighting within sight of their own homes. Men between twenty and thirty-eight were assigned to first-line battalions which would bear the brunt of any fighting. (Youths between eighteen and twenty were away on regular military service.) Those aged from thirty-nine to forty-five were organized into second-line battalions which would hold stationary defensive positions. Men between forty-five and forty-nine were assigned to Haga, the civil defense organization. Childless women up to thirty-five were also subject to reserve duty, mainly in communication and other technical units, but only a small percentage would actually be mobilized. The commander of the brigade, Colonel Eliezer Amitai, was a regular army officer who had fought in the Jerusalem area during the War of Independence. He had recently returned from a tour of duty as deputy military attaché in Washington and had been given the brigade just three months before.

The brigade was stationed in the twenty-kilometer-long Jerusalem Corridor, which tapered from a width of twenty kilometers at the edge of the coastal plain to seven kilometers outside the city. Because the railroad line through the corridor skirted two Arab villages, the armistice agreement between Jordan and Israel had stipulated that the half of each village abutting the tracks be placed on the Israeli side of the frontier, the other half on the Jordanian side. One of the villages, Bait Safafa, was within the Jerusalem city limits, and a fence separated the two halves, cutting off members of the same family. (When a marriage was celebrated in one half of the village, the wedding party would come down to the fence to accept the good wishes of family and friends on the other side.)

The greatest anomaly of all was the Israeli enclave on Mount Scopus on the Jordanian side of the city. During mandatary times, the two best-endowed Jewish institutions in Palestine—Hadassah Hospital and Hebrew University—had been built atop the historic hill, which was linked to the Mount of Olives by a narrow spur. At the end of the War of Independence, the Jews still held Scopus, but the Arabs controlled the Sheikh Jarrah residential quarter which separated it from Jewish Jerusalem, a kilometer and a half away. Under the armistice agreement, soldiers were banned from the hill, which was declared a demilitarized zone. Only eighty-five Israeli police were permitted to be maintained there and thirty-three civilians, ostensibly to look after the maintenance of the hospital and university. However, Arabs, as well as some foreign observers, maintained that despite the police uniforms and civilian clothing, all the Israelis were soldiers.

Every second Wednesday morning a convoy under UN supervision was permitted by the Jordanians to pass through Sheikh Jarrah carrying supplies and replacements to Scopus. The convoy paused at Mandelbaum Gate where UN officers checked the supplies, opening cans and packages pointed to by officers of the Arab Legion. The Jordanians, who were forbidden to touch the supplies themselves, suspected the Israelis of trying to smuggle weapons onto the hill. The armistice agreement limited the arms on Scopus to the small number of light weapons that had been

12

there when the 1948 war ended. Once a convoy had been held up when a UN officer probing with a rod in an oil drum struck a large metallic object near the bottom which the Israelis refused to let him pull out. (It would subsequently be reported by a foreign journalist that three jeeps had been smuggled up to the hill over the years, as well as recoilless rifles which were mounted on them. This in addition to machine guns, mortars, grenades, and mines which could enable the small garrison to hold out while a relief force tried to cut its way through.)

After the inspection of supplies, the Israeli replacements would board two ancient buses completely covered with armored plate except for the driver's slit. Two Legionnaires carrying weapons took places in the front and rear stairwells; their weapons were empty, but they carried loaded magazines in their pockets. Between each Legionnaire and the unarmed Israelis stood a UN officer. The Legionnaires rode the bus through Sheikh Jarrah and descended before it reached the Scopus enclave. The supplies were driven onto the hill by UN officers in trucks whose Israeli license plates were covered for the brief passage through Arab territory.

For the garrison the boredom and isolation of Scopus duty were tempered only by a breathtakingly beautiful view. On one side of the hill was Jerusalem, on the other the Judean Desert. With binoculars, some of the men could see people going in and out of their own homes in Jewish Jerusalem, which may have made for some interesting domestic situations during the years. The hilltop also served as an excellent military observation post overlooking the road leading up to Jerusalem from Jericho and Amman. The hospital and university buildings became sad-looking shells as weather and age took their toll. (Both institutions had established modern new facilities in Jewish Jerusalem.)

On the entire Israeli Central Front which General Narkiss commanded—an area stretching almost from Haifa to Beer-sheba—it was Mount Scopus that concerned him most as the post-Independence Day tension mounted. Narkiss was confident that the Jerusalem Brigade could hold off any attack the Arabs might muster in the city or corridor, but he did not think that the unit—half of whose men were over thirty-five—could by itself break through the defense line the Jordanians had built up in the city over the past two decades to reach Scopus if it were attacked. Without help, the 120-man garrison on the hill could not long hold out against a determined assault. If the Arabs overran Scopus, Narkiss was afraid that a UN cease-fire might be imposed before the Jews had a chance to retake it.

Narkiss also considered the possibility that the Arabs might attempt a limited attack on an isolated settlement such as Maale Hahamisha in the Jerusalem Corridor or the vital waterworks at Rosh Ha'ayin. He could handle this development with the forces he had. There might also be a full-scale attack aimed at the Netanya waist north of Tel Aviv, where the Arabs had only to drive nine miles to reach the sea and divide Israel in two. The mayors of Tel Aviv and Haifa, Narkiss felt, would undoubtedly press the High Command to post sufficient forces near Netanya to ensure that their cities would not be cut off from each other by a breakthrough there. So serious would such an attack be that the General Staff would immediately take over direct control of the Netanya front, and it was no use for him to worry about it, Narkiss felt.

An attack on Scopus, however, would be his alone to handle, and he did not feel he had sufficient forces to ensure its safety. He requested additional reserves but regarded the prospect of help as remote. If Scopus was attacked, he assumed he would have to rely on his own resources.

These resources were slim indeed. There was relatively less strength deployed on the Central Front now than there had been prior to the Sinai campaign eleven years before. At that time there had been a complete tank brigade posted on the approaches to the Jerusalem Corridor in the event that Jordan entered the war. (It did not.) Now there was only a mechanized

14

brigade, a mixed unit consisting of a battalion of sixty World War II Sherman tanks and two battalions of half-track-borne infantry. Most of the artillery had been stripped from the Central Front and sent south. So few guns and heavy mortars did Narkiss have and so limited was their ammunition that he could not hope to lay down a protective barrage around Scopus sufficient to break up a sustained attack. His only hope lay in the mechanized unit—the Harel Brigade. Deployed near Ramle on the coastal plain, its sixty old Shermans were the only counterbalance Narkiss had to the Jordanian armored brigade consisting of eighty-eight modern Patton tanks posted on the Jericho plains east of Jerusalem.

It seemed likely to Narkiss that the fate of the city would depend on the outcome of a race between the two forces, starting on the opposite sides of the Judean Hills, to Jerusalem crowning the heights. It would be a contest in which the odds heavily favored the Jordanians, whose tanks were faster and closer to Jerusalem. Narkiss estimated it would take the Pattons eight hours to reach Scopus. He was counting on the Shermans to reach the Ramallah-Jerusalem road just north of Scopus in twelve hours, a formidable feat considering the distance and terrain they had to cover, the dense minefields they would have to breach, and the enemy defenses barring the way. (The estimate would indeed prove overoptimistic.) Narkiss was hopeful that despite being outnumbered, the superiority of the Israeli commanders and crews would decide the battle once it was joined. It was a risk, however, and Narkiss knew he would have to rely on the General Staff to provide him with additional forces to extricate the Harel if things became sticky.

Even at his most hopeful estimate, the Pattons would be at Scopus first. For at least four hours the garrison there would have to hold on with its few antitank weapons and whatever artillery support Narkiss could provide.

*   *   *

15

On Monday, five days after Israel's partial mobilization had summoned to uniform essential armored and air force personnel, the top officers of a still-unmobilized reserve paratroop brigade were summoned to a briefing by the brigade commander, a regular army colonel named Mordecai (Motta) Gur. The colonel told them that if Nasser closed the Straits of Tiran to Israeli shipping, it would mean war. The officers listened intently as he pointed out on a map the positions taken up by the Egyptian units in the Sinai and explained the brigade's likely role there if war broke out. To Captain Dan, one of the deputy battalion commanders, the statistics of enemy strength were grim—100,-000 men, 400 planes, 1,000 tanks. But as he looked more closely at the disposition of their forces the grayness began to dissolve. In that deployment Dan saw an imbalance he knew the Israeli High Command would exploit to the fullest.

He got home late at night and was shaken awake by his wife at 10 A.M. with the news that the Straits of Tiran had been closed.

# 2   PREPARATION

Dr. Avshalom heard the news of the Tiran closing when he rendezvoused with the bimonthly Scopus convoy forming up in the Schneller compound, the former orphanage serving as Jerusalem Brigade headquarters. The convoy was going up a day early. It was the eye specialist's second tour of reserve duty as medical officer on the hill, and he had been looking ahead to the isolation with foreboding. The sudden crisis made the prospect even less inviting. The mustachioed commander of the Scopus garrison, veteran Menahem Scharfmann, who knew of Avshalom's distaste for Scopus duty, wasn't very encouraging when he said, "You think you're coming back down in two weeks? Forget it." Scharfmann, however, didn't seem too disturbed. "We're going up in armored buses," he said, "but when we come down it will be in open Egged buses." (Egged was the principal civilian bus line.) Avshalom listened in as Scharfmann briefed those men who were going up to the hill for the first time. The last time the doctor had come up, Scharfmann had said, "If there's trouble, plans exist for getting help to us quickly." This time the garrison commander had a different message. "There used to be a plan to rescue us but this has changed. If something happens, it's not likely they'll have enough forces to help us. We can hold."

In a film showing at Hebrew University that night, Yonkele Rotblit, a reserve lieutenant in the Jerusalem Brigade, was watching *The Longest Day*, a movie about the invasion of Normandy, when someone opened the door and shouted a name. In

17

the darkened room, a figure rose and hurried out. A few minutes later another name was called. Rotblit realized it was general mobilization. As soon as the picture was over he hurried home and found his call-up papers waiting for him.

That night, all through the city, messengers rang doorbells and handed reservists orders to report to their unit assembly point in the morning. If the man was out, a notice was pasted on his doorway. It was a drill the country's 215,000 reservists practiced two or three times a year, sometimes being routed out of bed at 2 A.M. and reporting to an assembly point.

Aaron Shai, a newly married schoolteacher, was at home with his wife when a friend arrived with a wedding gift. She had hardly sat down when the bell rang again. Aaron opened the door to a friend who served in the same unit. Looking at the gift on the coffee table, the friend said, "I came with a wedding present too," and handed Aaron his mobilization papers. After preparing kit bag and boots, Aaron went to bed but found it impossible to sleep. He could hear men calling to each other from the balconies of neighboring houses—"Did you get your notice yet?" On the normally quiet street there was a periodic burr of tires as cars rushed by bearing mobilization couriers. Many of the vehicles were taxis which had themselves been mobilized. Every so often couriers mounted the steps in Aaron's building. The last doorbell to be rung was that of the dentist who lived in the next apartment. It was 3:30 A.M. but the dentist opened up immediately as if he had been waiting. When he said goodnight to the courier and closed his door, Aaron fell asleep.

Attorney Johnnie Hyman had been planning to drive down to Tel Aviv the following morning to represent a defendant in a criminal case, but the sound of the doorbell told him that his legal career was suspended. Johnny's cool, intelligent features suited his role as battalion staff officer as well as it did courtroom counsel. Before he returned to defending accused criminals, he would learn what it is like to kill a man in hand-to-hand struggle.

Around the country the men of Motta Gur's paratroop brigade residing in kibbutzim and rural settlements were being collected that night by mobilized buses. They had been waiting impatiently for this moment. The closing Arab ring had aroused in them the deepest instincts of self-preservation, personal and national. Indifference, pacifism, and factional disputes gave way before a universal conviction that there was only one way out now—by the sword.

In the village of Even Yehuda, a pleasant community of Rumanian and Yemenite immigrants near Netanya, more youngsters than usual had crowded into the clubhouse for the regular Tuesday night folk-dancing session. The instructor was Sara Lapid, a vivacious farmer's wife who had been a passenger on the *Exodus* in 1947 when the British had forced it to return to Germany with its cargo of illegal refugees. She stood in the center of the dance floor and watched the youngsters whirl around her with a frenzy she had never seen, obviously venting the tension they all felt. From time to time a name would be shouted from the doorway, and a young man would hurry out. When the session ended, Sara waited outside for her husband to pick her up. (She still had not learned to drive a car, but her husband would give her a lesson on the tractor which she would manage to operate after his mobilization.) Waiting with her was Naphtali Cohen, a dark-skinned youth of Yemenite descent. A private in Gur's paratroop brigade, Cohen had grown increasingly impatient during the night, as the other youths at the dance were summoned while he remained. "I don't care about dying," he told Sara. "I just want to kill one of them first." To Naphtali's distress, several buses filled with men passed without stopping. He was about to head for home on his motor scooter when a half-empty bus approached slowly as if the driver were looking for a street. Naphtali flagged it down. "Are you looking for Naphtali Cohen?" he asked. To his surprise an officer aboard said yes. Naphtali told a friend to take his scooter home and tell his parents he had gone to

19

join his unit. Spurning the officer's suggestion that he go home himself and say good-bye, Naphtali leapt aboard the bus.

At kibbutz Tsuba in the Jerusalem Corridor, Uri Hermeling had been expecting the call-up since hearing the news of the Tiran closing on Radio Cairo's Hebrew language broadcast at 5:30 A.M. At dinner he and the other kibbutz members belonging to the brigade sat together in the communal dining room. People came over from other tables to wish them well and exchange banter. For Uri it was a good moment. The kibbutz women gave them boxes of candy and fruit before they boarded the bus.

At Kfar Blum, a kibbutz in the Upper Galilee founded by Anglo-Saxons, twenty-one-year-old Bitan was on guard duty when the telephone rang at midnight. The caller, from Gur's brigade, asked him to awaken Yair, a paratroop lieutenant responsible for assembling the men from the unit at the kibbutz. Bitan himself was a paratroop officer, but he had just completed his regular service and had not yet been assigned to a reserve unit. He asked the officer on the phone if he could come along to Gur's encampment. The officer said he would find out and call back. Running to Yair's apartment, Bitan rapped on the door and entered. Yair's bag, he saw, was already packed. "It's finally come," Bitan said. Twenty minutes later the officer from the brigade called back and told him he could come along. Gathering in the mess hall to wait for their bus, the men joked and drank coffee from the urn kept filled for the men on night guard duty. When the bus arrived, they found paratroopers from neighboring kibbutzim already aboard.

In nearby Kfar Szold, Dov Stolar was wakened at 1:30 A.M. and told to join the other kibbutz members from Gur's unit in the mess hall. A bachelor, Stolar normally had a room to himself, but since the crisis began two men had been sharing it with him. Their assigned position on the kibbutz defense perimeter was nearby, and they had to be close to it in the event of a night attack by the Syrians from the adjacent Golan Heights. Stolar

20

was careful not to disturb them as he dressed. On board the bus he found himself sitting next to the man in charge of alfalfa irrigation. Stolar himself was in charge of irrigation in the cotton fields. The two had been planning to swap irrigation pipe Thursday. In the cotton fields the pipes are dragged across the ground, and Stolar's were battered now and no longer suitable for such rough treatment. They could, however, be used in the alfalfa fields where the pipes are lifted by hand. "I don't think we'll be changing pipe this Thursday," said Stolar. In his kit bag he had tucked a copy of *The White Nile*. He thought he might be getting a chance to see how the Egyptians water their cotton before he got back to the kibbutz.

The civilian sector had also begun mobilizing. The day after Major Aaron's tank company was called up in Jerusalem, the heads of government departments in the city began implementation of war plans as detailed as any the military had prepared. (After the war Chief of Staff Rabin would say that no country had ever gone to war with its civilian sector so ready. "Those who prepare for the Sabbath," he was to say, quoting an old proverb, "have what to eat on the Sabbath.")

The threat of war raised in Jerusalem the specter of 1948, when the besieged city had nearly been starved into submission. Per capita consumption had been reduced to nine hundred calories a day—one-third the adequate intake—and when the siege was finally lifted only three days' supply of flour remained. Assured by the military that any future war would be over quickly, officials of the Ministry of Commerce and Industry in 1958 dropped rationing, which had existed since the founding of the state ten years before. In its place they adopted a bold policy of "overflow"—keeping so much food on hand that people would be permitted to buy as much as they wanted. The policy was made possible by the tremendous increase in the country's food production, Israeli food factories already processing far more than they could market within the country. Staples

21

were kept in sufficient quantities in local government warehouses to supply the population for more than half a year, even if Jerusalem was completely isolated.

The water situation had also improved radically since 1948, when the solitary pipe bringing water from the coastal plain was cut by the Arabs for ninety-six days and the city had been forced to survive on stored water sparingly ladled out. Two mains now connected the city with the national water grid, and municipal water officials were confident they could manage even if these were cut. In 1949 large water supplies had accidentally been discovered just outside the city when test borings were made for a small dam at Ein Kerem. This local source could supply the city with most of the water it needed. In addition, all houses in Jerusalem since ancient times had been built with underground cisterns to trap and hold the winter rains. Despite the availability of piped water, the Israelis had continued to require new houses to be built with cisterns—now a reservoir not against drought but against siege. In the event that pumping stations were destroyed and it became impossible to supply piped water, the manager of the municipal Water Department, Peretz Even, decided to use one hundred portable water tanks left over from the 1948 siege. They would be filled from reservoirs and cisterns and distributed to the neighborhoods on trucks. He ordered thirty more such tanks constructed.

As the crisis intensified, Even dispatched men to knock on doors and advise householders to fill empty cisterns with piped water. No public announcement was made for fear of creating panic. Many cisterns were already filled—some had not been emptied since 1948—and samples were taken from these to see if the water was still potable. Even and his staff had staged regular drills over the years in which a deputy would call in hypothetical problems—"The 18-inch pipe has been broken at these coordinates, power is out on the northern line. What do we do?"—and the manager would have to devise emergency procedures on the spot. These exercises would prove themselves shortly.

22

While provision for basic supplies seemed adequate for almost any emergency, there was one glaring omission in the city's preparedness—adequate shelter space. In its eagerness to provide quick housing during the years of massive immigration, the Housing Ministry had ignored a Jerusalem municipal ordinance requiring all new buildings to be built with shelters. The city found itself now with no shelters for 40 percent of its population —about seventy-five thousand people. Half the schools—those built before 1948—had no basements. Following the closing of the Straits of Tiran, volunteers turned out in the thousands to begin digging trenches next to shelterless apartment blocks and schools.

The urgency of the situation even overcame the maddening bureaucracy of government agencies. At the city engineer's office the bespectacled chief clerk, Pinhas Yaari, watched the fabric of routine unravel about him as the staff became swamped with inquiries from the public about shelter preparations. Despite his diffident appearance, Yaari had already demonstrated an unusual ability to maneuver in the midst of chaos. During World War II, while he was a laborer in a German work camp on the Russian front, he had somehow persuaded the guards to let the religious Jews in camp work extra hours during the week so they could have the Sabbath as a day of rest. Now, with his superiors having disappeared into uniform, he took it upon himself to order the department's ten phone lines used only for incoming queries, all other work being dropped. In consultation with engineers, Yaari drew up a list of answers to the most common questions being phoned in. Most of the four thousand calls received were from people in buildings without shelters asking what to do. They were advised to choose the lowest room in their house and to block its windows with sandbags. An engineer was quickly dispatched to provide some direction on the spot. One resident of the Anglo-Saxon *Shikun* was visited within three hours of his call by an engineer carrying a plan of the house. After a quick but thorough look at a ground-floor room, the engineer said, "This will serve for anything but a

23

direct hit. The beams will provide support if you're hit upstairs. Fifty sandbags along that wall will do the trick." With a parting "Be healthy," the engineer moved on to the next address.

At the request of the Foreign Ministry, the municipality dispatched two engineers to advise embassies and consulates in the city on shelter preparation. The engineers found that the Latin Americans, who had never experienced war, didn't know where to begin. The Europeans, on the other hand, already had their basements properly sandbagged and stocked with provisions.

The municipality ordered a fleet of trucks to begin dumping sand from a quarry onto street corners throughout the city, to enable the population to sandbag their homes. Burlap sacks were acquired from sugar factories and made available at nominal cost in groceries. The sight of a line of housewives moving antlike through the streets, their arms stiffly holding pails of sand, prompted Aviva Yeriel to call the other women in her apartment building together for a meeting. Aviva, a veteran of the Palmach and now a mother of four, told her neighbors it was time to prepare the building for war. Most of their husbands had already been called up, and the remainder were likely to go any hour. The women decided to clean out the shelter and stock it with water. They might be spending weeks there, and Aviva volunteered to whitewash the walls and hang some cheerful curtains. Her oldest daughter, fourteen-year-old Tolly, said she would paint some murals. The women agreed to ask the remaining men to install an electrical outlet in the shelter so water could be heated for the infants.

Similar meetings were going on in virtually every apartment building in the city. At the Journalists' *Shikun* one of the men brought burlap materials from the central market, and the women got together to sew sacks which they and the *shikun* children filled with sand. The sandbags were piled at the entranceways.

Unknown to the thousands of people living along the city

24

border, plans existed to evacuate them in the event of war. An organization known as PESACH (an acronym made up of the Hebrew words for evacuation, welfare, and burial), whose existence was known only to those assigned to it, began preparing thirty-six schools and other public buildings as evacuation centers. These would be able to accommodate up to twenty thousand people for several months. There would be no evacuation, however, until war was clearly imminent to avoid panic and the problem of caring for twenty thousand people prematurely turned into refugees.

The task of preparing Jerusalem's schoolchildren for the possibility of war was carried out skillfully. Each morning in class the teachers discussed the news, to alleviate anxiety which might develop from rumor. Homework was kept to a minimum so as not to add to the stress.

At the Geulim School in the poor neighborhood of Baka, all the children were given defense tasks. The girls in sewing class turned burlap sacking into bags. These were filled by the rest of the students with sand from the school playground, even the first-graders joining in the effort. Air-raid drills were held, and the children were asked to bring blankets and candy to be stocked in the shelter. Older children were assigned to care for younger children during the drills.

At Hebrew University the job of organizing the campus for war fell on the chairman of the Bible Department, Professor Shmaryahu Talmon, a reserve infantry captain. Although he had been teaching there for years, Talmon now found himself discovering the "innards" of the university for the first time. At a meeting with the heads of the science departments, he learned that there was enough explosive material on hand to destroy a good part of the campus if touched off by a shell. He ordered the material removed to a more remote area and sandbagged. He also ordered the swimming pool filled as a water reserve. Talmon was amused at the sight of some of his scholarly colleagues lugging sandbags and fire hose to the library, where they had been posted as members of the emergency fire brigade.

More than 1,000 foreign students at the university—including Africans and Asians—had gone off to work on kibbutzim and farms around the country as volunteers to replace men who had been mobilized. Another 350 were asked to remain in the campus dormitories and work in hospitals, factories, and other institutions in Jerusalem itself. Two enthusiastic American students, who had painted a rented car in camouflage and equipped themselves with helmets, made themselves available to Talmon as couriers. In the Physics Department twenty-two of the lab assistants had disappeared into uniform. At the request of security authorities, the remaining three devised a makeshift liquid-air plant capable of producing oxygen to supply the city's hospitals in the event that Jerusalem was cut off.

A few nights after the closing of the Straits of Tiran, Chaim Yavin, a broadcaster specializing in educational documentaries, was called out of the class he was attending at the university to answer a phone call. It was from an official at Kol Yisrael (Voice of Israel), the government radio station, asking him to report immediately to the main studio at Queen Helena Street. Before the night was over, he and a dozen colleagues had been given a quick lesson in operating a tape recorder and were dispatched to front-line units as war correspondents. The radio had already become the most important element of cohesion in the country. The six high-pitched beeps announcing each news bulletin could be heard in banks, schools, cafes, and trenches. Hanoch Givton, Kol Yisrael's director, felt that a steady voice was required to put the situation in perspective and ward off despondency. He thought of General (in the reserves) Chaim Herzog, former head of intelligence who had given a well-received broadcast on Vietnam after a visit to that country. (Dublin-born Herzog was the son of a former chief rabbi of Israel and brother of Dr. Jacob Herzog, an aide to Prime Minister Eshkol.) On Saturday night

26

after the closing of the straits, Givton called Herzog at home and asked him to serve as military commentator. Herzog's daily broadcasts were to exercise an immense calming effect on the public.

At the same time, Kol Yisrael's Arabic network was attempting to produce precisely the opposite effect on its listeners in the surrounding Arab countries. If it came to war, the Arabs were told, the results would be even more disastrous for them than the Sinai campaign. A Nasser speech just prior to that conflict, in which he had said Egypt was ready for war, was rebroadcast. "What assurance do you have that he is any more ready now?" Kol Yisrael asked.

## 3  WAITING

For nineteen years the border dividing Jerusalem had been manned day and night by two opposing armies. The Jordanian soldiers had watched Jewish Jerusalem expand steadily, housing developments spilling over the hills to the west. There had been far less urban growth on the Jordanian side of the city, but the Israeli soldiers had been able to see the Arab Legion add trench systems, bunkers, and fortified blockhouses to their defenses over the years.

The tactical balance was fairly even along the city line which stretched for seven kilometers in a north-south line. In the center was the anchor of the Jordanian line, the kilometer-square wall of the Old City itself. Except for some lower courses dating from before the birth of Jesus, the wall was fairly modern by Middle Eastern standards. It had been built by the Turks four hundred years before on the ruins of ancient battlements. Although Renaissance European cities of the same time were built with walls suitable for defense against cannon, Jerusalem's was a medieval construction that hardly acknowledged the invention of gunpowder. Instead of cannon redoubts, it had firing slits for crossbows, for the wall was intended only to keep out bedouin raiders. The isolation of the city had served to spare it any more serious assault until Israel's War of Independence. The Jordanians since then had lined the ramparts facing Jewish Jerusalem with pillboxes and filled in the tall arrow slits with concrete, leaving only small firing holes. Near Jaffa Gate a mouth-shaped segment had been removed near the top of the wall to permit heavy weapons to cover the approaches to Mount Zion. Although the walls of Jerusalem were already an anachronism when they were built four centuries before, the Israelis were to find them a formidable obstacle.

South of the Old City the two armies shared four hills, the Israelis on the western slopes, the Jordanians on the eastern. On the first two hills—Mount Zion and Abu Tor—the Israelis dominated the crest, but the top of the third hill—Jebel Mukaber—belonged to neither. Affording a magnificent view of the Old City two kilometers away, it had been chosen by the British mandatary power in 1933 as the seat of Government House, a three-story structure from which a succession of British administrators had ruled Palestine. Since 1948 it had served as headquarters to the UN command in the Middle East. A large segment of Jordanian and Israeli territory on the hill surrounding the UN compound had been demilitarized. Jebel Mukaber was the only strategic location in all Jerusalem where neither side had a substantial military presence. Two decades of experience along the borders had demonstrated to the Israelis that such vacuums were more a magnet for armed conflict than a buffer. This apprehension would shortly show itself to be justified. The fourth hilltop to the south of the Old City was shared by the Arab village of Sur Bahir and kibbutz Ramat Rachel. The two settlements had enjoyed good relations until the War of Independence separated them in 1948.

North of the Old City the topography was relatively flat. In the kilometer from the city wall to Mandelbaum Gate the opposing blockhouses were sometimes separated by only the width of a narrow street. The "gate," named after the owner of a destroyed house there, was the only crossing point for tourists and diplomats along the Jordan-Israel border. In the kilometer between Mandelbaum Gate and the Pagi neighborhood at the northern end of the city line, a shallow bowl separated the opposing posts by as much as two hundred meters.

In contrast to the solid Jordanian defense positions, the Israeli line was confined to a scattered string of blockhouses—stone dwellings which had been taken over by the military and fitted out with firing slits. Between Mandelbaum Gate and Pagi—a stretch which was to prove the decisive area when war came— the Israelis did not have any blockhouses at all, just two small stretches of open trench. At Pagi itself there was a small block-house and trench, puny compared to the elaborate fortifications the Jordanians had built opposite at Ammunition Hill. The hill dominated a wadi which ran from Jewish Jerusalem to Scopus. The wadi was a logical avenue for an Israeli armored thrust, and to block such a move the Jordanians had built dozens of bunkers and an elaborate trench system on the slopes. For its size, Am-munition Hill was to be the most heavily fortified area Israeli troops would encounter anywhere in the Six-Day War. The Jordanians had fortified Mivtar Hill on the other side of the wadi almost as heavily.

To the south of Ammunition Hill and directly facing the Israeli lines was a large building which during the British Man-date had served as a depot for the training of local police. It was now local headquarters for the United Nations Relief and Works Agency, which provided assistance to Palestinian ref-ugees. But to the Israelis it was still known as the Police Training School, and its white bulk would form a landmark about which bitter battles would flow.

The Jerusalem Brigade troops moving into the line the day after their mobilization had the feeling that they were picking up exactly where their elders had left off when the War of Independence ended two decades before. Looking out the firing slits at Notre Dame Hospice (one wing of which had been a military position since 1948), Aaron Shai, the recently wed schoolteacher, could see two burnt-out Arab Legion armored vehicles in no-man's-land below. They were lying on the spot where they had been knocked out by Molotov cocktails in 1948 as they attempted to break into the Jewish city. Many of the soldiers were the sons of men who had fought for Jerusalem

31

then. Private Gershon Mack's father, a prominent Jerusalem attorney, had fought at the Police Training School in 1948. (Gershon's brother, Hananel, a paratrooper with Gur's brigade, would before long renew the family acquaintance with the Police Training School.) Gershon himself, a law student, was posted on Abu Tor. Shortly after moving onto the line, Gershon was eating an apple on the roof of his blockhouse when a Legionnaire appeared on the roof of a Jordanian blockhouse twenty yards down the hill and motioned him to throw an apple over. If it was a friendly gesture it was the last one Gershon would see on Abu Tor.

No other unit occupied as pleasant an outpost as a five-man squad commanded by Corporal Zvi Paz, an easygoing government clerk who belonged to the "happy ship" school of military leadership. He and his men were assigned to the Lonely House, a two-story building on Jebel Mukaber twenty meters outside the UN's Government House compound. The lookout post commanded one of the most spectacular views in Jerusalem. Two kilometers to the north the crenellated walls of the Old City rode a mountain spur. To the east of the city the Arab village of Silwan clung like a teardrop to the steep slope above the Kidron Valley, tapered at the top, bulging at the bottom. To the west were the multistory buildings of Jewish Jerusalem. The Lonely House enfiladed practically the entire city line and offered its occupants perfect seats for the drama that would soon unfold. Paz and his men had no idea they would be playing a featured role themselves. He had had the same assignment during his reserve stint the previous year. At that time they had merely spent the day in the building, returning to their regular barracks at night. This time they were told they would remain in the Lonely House around the clock. To Paz this was clear indication that war would come.

In the absence of any officers, the squad fell into a leisurely routine. Private Darzi became the chef, specializing in dishes

32

Aerial photograph taken on eve of war shows Government House compound (wooded area in center) where battle for Jerusalem was to begin. Legionnaires entered compound, which was located in demilitarized zone between Jordanian and Israeli Jerusalem, on east (top) road. After passing through compound, they continued on road toward Israeli Jerusalem (at bottom of picture). Off road to right is training farm where Israelis' fire stopped Legionnaire advance. Across road from training farm is Lonely House, whose garrison first spotted Jordanians. Photo shows proximity of the Judean Desert (top).

Lonely House, from which first report of Jordanian advance came. Tree on extreme right marks edge of Government House compound. Village on slope beyond is Silwan. Above it to left, horizontal line marking southeast edge of the Old City wall can be seen. Ridge in distance is Mount Scopus. Continuation of ridge to right is Mount of Olives. Tower on skyline to right marks Russian church on Mount of Olives. Tower visible to left is Augusta Victoria.

View of Old City from northeast. Large dome in center marks seventh-century mosque, Dome of the Rock, on traditional site where Abraham prepared Isaac for sacrifice and where Jewish Temple stood. Smaller dome beyond is part of El Aksa Mosque at southern end of Temple Mount compound. Western Wall is out of sight to right. Outside city wall in foreground is Rockefeller Museum compound, dominated by octagonal tower. Road slanting sharply down to flat-topped shed at lower left is road to Augusta Victoria, where Israeli attack force missed turning the night of June 6, in a fatal error.

Paratroop officer (right) and one of his men beside stone-lined trench leading to Ammunition

BAMAHANE

from his native Iraq. Each day he or one of the others traveled to the main market in town to buy fresh vegetables and other food with which to supplement army issue. Corporal Paz had had the foresight to bring along a pair of slippers and relieved himself of the boots as soon as they arrived. The only drawback to gracious living was the absence of doors and windowpanes, which made for cold nights. But Paz had known from his previous tour to bring along a bottle of cognac.

While two companies held the line, the rest of the brigade fitted out and worked off some of the civilian flab accumulated since the last round of reserve duty. (The accumulation was not much, since every able-bodied citizen in the country under the age of forty-five took to the field annually for a few weeks of reserve training. While doubtless a burden, many looked forward to it as a change in routine and a chance to meet old friends whom they never met the rest of the year.)

The sense of helplessness the men had felt since the crisis began fell away as they hefted their weapons and sensed the massed strength in the camp around them. The types that adapt best to life in the field quickly emerged, expropriating the softest place to lay their sleeping bags and soon having a fire going for coffee. Comrades who had been serving together in the same unit many years brought each other up to date on children born and marriages contracted. Everyday relations between teachers and students, bosses and workers were transformed as they met each other in uniform olive drab. A Hebrew University professor was timidly approached in camp one day by one of his students who asked if the university would postpone the dates of final examinations set for the following month in light of the mobilization. The professor assured the student that the university had dealt with the same problem several times in the past and chided him for his deferential manner. "Don't you have any other worries in your life?" the professor-sergeant asked.

The camps were flooded with volunteers, including men whose idealism must have surprised even themselves. A Jerusalem writer—a dabbler in pornography—who had not reported for reserve duty for seven years turned himself in. He was given a quick trial, spent a few hours in the guardhouse, and was released to join his old unit. In the police lockup downtown a petty thief well known to the cops was let out after clamoring to join his outfit. Several foreign-born faculty members from the Economics Department at the university who had never served in the army managed to get accepted into a second-line battalion whose commander was a friend. The commander of the Jerusalem Reconnaissance Company stopped accepting friends after a while, since the chances of their all coming through alive diminished with each addition.

Some men refused transfer to second-line or civil defense units. Economist Arye Comay, a short, corpulent immigrant from Chile, had reached thirty-nine, the age when reservists are shifted to second-line units. His mobilization papers, however, summoned him to report to his old first-line unit. When he arrived, the company clerk scanned the roster and said there had been a mistake. Comay exploded. "If I hadn't been called, if they thought I was too old and useless, all right. But I'm here now and I'm not going back." The other men with whom Comay had served ten years in the unit joined the argument and said if he was sent away, they were leaving too. After half an hour's debate, the company commander granted Comay permission to stay.

Even for Dennis Silk, a dreamy English-born poet (after years in the reserves he was still not quite sure if two pips on the shoulder meant a first or second lieutenant), the usual pangs he felt at abandoning himself to the military machine were displaced this time by a feeling of relief at having been called. A member of a searchlight crew, he was, to his surprise, ordered not to any of the military camps in the city or the Jerusalem Corridor, but to the Histadrut (labor union) Building in downtown Jerusalem. He found out the reason when he was taken to the roof, which offered an unsurpassed view of the northern half of the city line. Inside a shed, amid orange peels and other litter, were two large projectors. The men camped in the corridors for a few days until Dennis discovered that the key to his crumbling stone hut on Abu Tor fitted all the office doors in the building. Instead of sleeping on the cold floor, the men found rooms with rugs and easy chairs. Dennis himself looked for the secretary-general's office, which he figured would have the most comfortable couch. He settled for an office with an English typewriter on which he began composing a "political-mythological" poem about a merchant in Cairo, a peddler of dreams named Nasser.

Probably no armed force in history, including the Foreign Legion, was as international in origin as the Israeli Army, whose soldiers hailed from more than sixty countries. None of the army's units was more diverse in makeup than the Jerusalem Brigade. Besides English poets and Chileans, the brigade included in its ranks men born in the wilds of Kurdistan, the slums of Casablanca, New York's Lower East Side, and remote villages in India. They had had to adapt to the army's tough standard of training and the egalitarian code of behavior which remained from the pre-Independence, underground days. There was no saluting except on rare formal occasions, and men and officers called each other by first name. (The armored corps, which had instituted the saluting discipline of conventional armies, was an exception.)

As the days passed, Jerusalem's landscape was transformed by tents and gun positions. On the Friday night after the closing of the Straits of Tiran a battalion of heavy mortars was ordered to set up its batteries in the Valley of the Cross, one of the most peaceful retreats in Jerusalem, and to have them camouflaged by dawn. A bulldozer was appropriated from a road construction site in the adjoining Anglo-Saxon *Shikun* to dig the mortar pits. The sound of its engine breaking the Sabbath stillness after midnight startled the residents into wakefulness. Some imagined enemy tanks were upon them. By dawn the valley was still again,

39

but hidden beneath camouflage netting were a dozen powerful mortars. An observer in a light plane reported that one net which had been secured to an olive tree was too conspicuous. It was lowered to conform to the shape of the slope. From the air, at least, the valley now seemed empty except for the Monastery of the Holy Cross, whose massive walls gave it the appearance of a medieval fortress. (According to Christian tradition, the tree from which the true cross was made grew here.)

On a slope adjacent to Hebrew University a second-line battalion had made camp within a stand of pine trees. Its ranks included a number of university professors and students who generally chose to slip into the university cafeteria at lunchtime instead of waiting on their unit's chow line. After training each day, wives and children arrived with food baskets to share with the men the last hours of daylight, when the sun lays an intense golden light upon Jerusalem. The families departed at nightfall, and each company drew around its own campfire. The men sang and some of them told stories, the Asian Jews being particularly adept at the art. The commander of one company was Chaim Guri, a journalist and one of the nation's leading poets. Each evening in front of the fire he gave his men a commentary on the day's political developments. Although some of them were only two hundred yards from home, they adhered to a strict pass schedule of just two brief home visits a week. Passes were given more liberally at the mortar encampment in the Valley of the Cross. A sergeant who could see his apartment in the Anglo-Saxon *Shikun* from his mortar position was able to stroll home every day for a bath and hot meal.

The men of the Jerusalem Reconnaissance Company were deprived of these amenities, their camp being located in the hills outside the city. The all-volunteer unit, half of whose members were former paratroopers, was the brigade's prime strike force. Drawing heavily on Hebrew University, it was perhaps the most intellectual combat unit in the entire army. Seventy percent of its members were either university graduates or students, a good number of the latter being masters degree and Ph.D. candidates. The unit commander, Major Yussi, was a roughhewn geologist who had brought several colleagues from his institute into the unit, his own boss serving as a sergeant.

In the first days after mobilization, the men just test-fired their weapons and stood by for action. When it became apparent, however, that war would not come quickly, a rugged training program was begun. The men practiced leaping from half-tracks while they were in motion, facing forward and dropping backwards out the rear door. They scaled sheer cliff faces on ropes and broke into small groups to make their way cross-country at night on map-reading exercises. The first evening they built campfires and sat around them singing late into the night. After the second day of training nobody had the energy to make a fire, and the men quickly fell off to sleep. The third night the sound of snoring was heavy. But morale was so high that men pestered their officers for more training.

Spirits plunged abruptly in the recon camp and throughout the country on the night of May 28, when Prime Minister Eshkol made a surprise address to the nation after a five-hour cabinet meeting. Instead of the decisive pronouncement his listeners were waiting for, Eshkol merely said that efforts to resolve the problem by international pressure would continue. Worse than his message was his delivery. His voice seemed to tremble, and at one point he stuttered badly. To many, he seemed badly frightened. In order to revive morale, Major Yussi sent an officer into town to buy food for a party and some kind of sporty headgear for every man in the outfit. The officer returned with a supply of ladies' hats designed like jockey caps. They were the only kind which the storeowner had in quantity, he explained. There were blue and white caps for the officers and red and white caps for the men. The effect on morale was instantaneous. Several score men were suddenly running through the camp with jockey caps on their heads, and a soccer game was organized, one team wearing hats, one team bare-

41

headed. Jeeploads of men in jockey caps were to become a familiar if puzzling sight in Jerusalem. "Do you see all those soldiers with red and white hats?" one of the men heard a woman say one day when he went into town to buy a pair of boots. "The army doesn't have enough helmets, and these poor boys have to wear girls' hats." When people asked what kind of unit they were, one man took to muttering, "We're in missiles." The company got the pick of the entertainment groups which visited the army camps almost nightly. One night songwriter Naomi Shemer came. Spotlighted by truck headlights she sang her "Jerusalem of Gold." Although only ten days passed since Shuli Natan had first sung it publicly, the soldiers were already familiar with it, and a strong chorus of voices joined Naomi's from the darkness.

The recon camp had been set up next to Major Aaron's tank encampment and the two companies—which would be fighting alongside each other shortly—challenged each other to soccer matches. One day Mayor Kollek visited Aaron's company. He found the men lined up in front of their Shermans. Are you ready, the mayor asked. In reply, Aaron barked an order: "On the tanks, mount." The men scrambled up the hulls and disappeared into the turrets. In an instant, engines roared and the shed filled with white smoke. Kollek applauded delightedly.

The large-scale mobilization the day the straits were closed had not been total, and those not called up felt embarrassment rather than relief. Some donned khaki when they went out, and others stayed off the street altogether. On Saturday night, four days after the closing, Ariel Fisher—a young economist at the Bank of Israel—took his fiancée to the movies. Reading his watch in the light from the screen, he pulled a transistor radio from his pocket at 8:30 and switched on the news. All around him in the darkened theater he could hear other radios going on. The announcer reported that an Israeli half-track had gone over a mine near the Gaza Strip, wounding seven soldiers. Ariel, a

42

sniper who was to fire one of the last shots in the battle of Jerusalem, told his girl he would probably be mobilized the next day. He found his call-up papers when he got home.

The Jerusalem Brigade sniper platoon was commanded by one of the oldest lieutenants in the Israeli Army, forty-five-year-old Yehuda Ben-Moshe, a German-born translator who had once run unsuccessfully for a seat in the Knesset. He had learned his military craft at a sniper school during the War of Independence. As Ben-Moshe's men assembled on the outskirts of the city they were joined by the man who had set up that school, Alex Eliraz, now a retired lieutenant colonel. Although a grandfather, Eliraz had come up to find a combat role in Jerusalem, an objective in which he would succeed. He traveled along the city line with Ben-Moshe, choosing with an expert eye sniper's perches for the platoon's two-man teams. Private Ariel Fisher and his partner were dropped off at a border tenement in Musrara. They knocked on a door on the first floor and asked the woman if they could camp in her apartment. She turned the living room over to them and provided them with beds. From the front window they had a clear view across no-man's-land to a Legionnaire position atop a hotel just outside the Old City's Damascus Gate. Taking care not to show themselves, the two snipers settled down in their new home and waited for the war to begin.

As the second week of mobilization dragged on, the edge of expectancy among the troops gradually dulled. It seemed to many that the matter would be settled without fighting. After Eshkol's speech, the feeling took hold that the government was no longer master of events. Ranking officers estimated that every extra day the enemy had for preparations meant two hundred more Israeli dead when the battle was finally joined. ("Let's attack or go home," became the predominant sentiment.)

The long wait upset the calculations of the quartermaster corps, which had not expected the men to require more than the

43

one uniform they had been issued when mobilized. When the likelihood of a blitzkrieg began to fade, the army purchased all stocks of uniforms available in factories and distributed them to the men in the field. The new uniforms revealed a disconcerting tendency to pop their trouser buttons where they would most be missed. Arye Comay, the portly Chilean, was unable to find a uniform in his size and continued to wear his civilian clothing. When his officer started calling him "Sir," however, Comay asked his wife to buy him a set of khakis. The ebullient Comay took on the role of commissar, analyzing developments daily for the men in the unit. He expressed disagreement with the overwhelming majority, who felt that if war came, Jordan would stay out of it, as it had during the Sinai campaign. "Hussein will have to fight or lose his life or his throne," said Comay.

The Eshkol speech had cast gloom over Motta Gur's paratroop camp on the coast. The following night Gur took over the microphone after the visiting entertainers had finished. "We're in for a long wait," he told his men. "You can cry, you can shout, but there's nothing you can do about it." The brigade had been kept together since mobilization and subjected to only light training since a combat jump was expected imminently. Now the battalions were split up, each going to a different campsite for intensive training.

The three battalions differed markedly from each other in character. The Eighth was the veteran unit in the brigade, and many of its men had been with it since it was organized ten years before. It was a strongly knit family presided over by Lieutenant Colonel Yussi, a pleasantly dispositioned farmer from Tel Adashim, a moshav on the approaches to Nazareth. At forty, Yussi was the oldest officer in the brigade and probably spoke the best Yiddish of all its senior officers, a language foreign to most of the younger sabras. He was an industrious officer and beloved by his troops.

The battalion turnout was 10 percent larger than its official strength, as scores of former paratroopers showed up demanding a place in the unit. Among them were the halt, the lame, and the partially blind. (One ex-officer with only one eye was to fight with another battalion on Ammunition Hill, there to be wounded in the leg.) Some volunteers were over thirty-five. Yussi decided who could stay, sometimes asking the battalion doctor for advice. Although the unit had had a regular practice jump just two months before, the men greeted each other with raucous good humor as if after a long absence. "I told you guys to leave this outfit, but you wouldn't listen to me."

After Eshkol's speech, the battalion officers decided some diversion was in order. They informed Gur that the wife of Kotcha, one of the company commanders, had given birth and requested army funds for a party. The bearded Kotcha, a superb natural clown, played the part of the proud father. But when Gur ordered a present purchased for the mother, Kotcha protested that such extravagance wasn't really necessary. The Ramat Gan municipality, which had officially adopted the paratroop corps, enthusiastically agreed to cater a party on a secluded Mediterranean beach not far from the paratroop encampment. The joyous bout of singing and dancing around the campfires did much to dispel the tension of the long wait.

The Seventh Battalion was a brand-new outfit, formed just three months before. Where many of the men in Yussi's battalion were in their late twenties and early thirties, the men of the Seventh were fresh out of regular service, most of them twenty-one or twenty-two. They were all so new that officers did not know their men's names. Lieutenant Yair of Kfar Blum requested permission to have Lieutenant Bitan, the night guard at the kibbutz who had wakened him with the mobilization order, assigned to his platoon. In his fellow kibbutznik he would at least have one man whom he knew personally and upon whom he was sure he could rely. (It was to Bitan that Yair would turn to effect the most dramatic flag-raising in the battle of Jerusalem.)

Commanding the battalion was Lieutenant Colonel Uzi, a

former kibbutznik. He had graduated from Hebrew University and spent two years in Chicago studying engineering, a profession he now practiced in Tel Aviv. With his physician wife and their children he had just moved into an American-style ranch house in a fashionable suburb, a far cry from the spartan communal life he had shared in kibbutz Tel Yosef. Uzi had made his mark in the paratroopers as a platoon leader during a retaliation raid on an Arab camp in the Gaza Strip in 1956. The attack had been stopped by well-placed Arab Bren guns, which killed Uzi's company commander and brought down more than a score of paratroopers. Gathering a squad, Uzi cut his way through a side fence and fought his way into the heart of the camp, opening the way for the rest of the attack force. He was wounded in the process and cited for valor.

The third battalion, the Sixth, was about three years old. The men were still young, mostly about twenty-four, but had been together long enough to be whipped into a tight unit. This was the battalion which would draw the toughest assignment in the battle to come. Its commander, Lieutenant Colonel Joseph, a handsome farmer from moshav Herut in the coastal plain, had a generous, straightforward nature. While the Israeli Army had perceptibly stiffened its protocol in the nineteen years of its existence, Joseph was a throwback to the days of the Palmach, the band of brothers who had been at the spearhead of the Israeli Army in the War of Independence. When his men had to dig trenches, Joseph would take off his shirt and dig alongside them, not for a token half hour but for the whole day. "He's got the best heart I know," said one fellow officer. His family had been among the leaders of the Haganah, the principal underground force in the preindependence period. He himself was a deeply believing Zionist who would break his usual reticence with foreign reporters only to urge them, if they were Jewish, to settle in this land which had been promised them. He had been severely wounded during the retaliation raid against Jordanian forces in Kalkilye in 1956 and had missed out on the Sinai campaign, which broke out the following month.

Unlike his battalion commanders, Colonel Gur was a city boy. Born in Jerusalem and raised in the town of Rehovoth, he had joined the Haganah as a teen-ager and worked his way quickly up the ranks of the regular army through his exploits in the field. At the age of twenty-seven he commanded the paratroop battalion that fought the savage Mitla Pass engagement during the Sinai campaign. He afterwards studied at the French War College and headed the Israeli Staff and Command Training School. He was an urbane figure with political instincts and a gift of easy eloquence. His ample self-confidence had sometimes been demonstrated in battle tactics whose audacity had also brought him criticism. But his combination of daring and intelligence marked him for high position.

As for the paratroopers themselves, they were the elite of the nation's youth. Unlike the paratroop corps in the United States and other nations, which fill their ranks largely with men from the underprivileged classes seeking status or higher pay, the Israeli paratroopers were attracted largely by old-fashioned notions of duty. Although the kibbutz population constituted only 4 percent of the nation's total, 80 percent of the officers in the brigade and 50 percent of the men were from kibbutzim. The kibbutznikim in the unit—strapping, sunburned, self-confident young men—were the sons and grandsons of the European immigrants who had founded the settlements.

Many of the nonkibbutznikim in the brigade were university students or graduates. Although they had not been weaned on the soil, their sense of national duty had been well nurtured in the youth movements. In high school they served in Gadna, a paramilitary training program for both boys and girls. For two weeks in their junior year they had gone to summer camp to drill and shoot. Some had gone on to specialized training as snipers or air cadets. Despite this background, the youthful Israelis had not developed any rampant militarism or cult of killing.

The fate of European Jewry had made these young sabras conscious of their special role as Jewish soldiers in a Jewish state. Lieutenant Ophir Fenegar, a platoon commander in the Sixth

47

Battalion, had expressed it in a letter written to his future wife during his regular military service a few years before. Fenegar, a talented young painter from kibbutz Givat Haim, wrote the letter after reading *The House of Dolls,* a novel about the concentration camps. "I feel that from all this horror and helplessness there arises within me a tremendous will to be strong, strong to the point of tears, strong and keen as a knife, composed and terrible and dangerous. This is what I want to be. I want to know that never again will those vacant eyes stare from behind electrified fences. They will not do so only if I am strong, only if we are all strong—strong, proud Jews. Only if we never again allow ourselves to be led to the slaughter. Whenever I see a terrified Jew, a picture or a word that reminds me of this, I regret every minute that I wasted in the army without taking the fullest advantage to become more efficient." Ophir would test his strength on a smoky dawn on Jerusalem's Ammunition Hill.

A fellow platoon leader in the Sixth destined to share that dawn with him—blond, blue-eyed Yoav Tsuri—did not, like others, look forward to the testing. He had seen battle and was frightened and repelled by it. He had come back from the retaliation raid against the Syrian position at Nuqueiba with a wounded man on his back and a lingering depression. But on Ammunition Hill it would be upon Yoav that the greatest challenge would fall. A son of kibbutz Afikim, the quiet youth was a natural leader but he preferred solitude. When he was three, his parents had lost him while taking a Sabbath walk through the cornfields. They found him wandering contentedly in a neighboring row. "Sometimes its nicer to be alone," he told them. He had grown into a golden youth, capable and modest. In the kibbutz, youths are organized into committees from an early age to plan their own sports and cultural and social activities, and Yoav's voice had always been dominant in his group. He became swimming champion of the Jordan Valley but then decided not to compete anymore and swam only for pleasure. Upon reaching military age he followed the path of many other

48

kibbutz youngsters, volunteering for the paratroopers and completing the rugged officer's course. But he preserved unashamedly his civilian mentality. He would preserve it until the madness of battle enveloped him on Ammunition Hill.

A week after mobilization a tall figure appeared late one night in the woods near Ramle, where the Harel Brigade had made camp. Identifying himself as Colonel Uri Ben-Ari, he asked that the battalion commanders be wakened. The three officers who were roused had heard only a few hours before that Ben-Ari had been appointed the new brigade commander. After a brief exchange of greetings, Ben-Ari ordered the officers to have their units ready to roll in forty minutes. In moments the camp came alive as the groggy men rolled sleeping bags, stripped off camouflage netting, and lashed equipment to tanks and half-tracks. When the battalion commanders reported their units ready, Ben-Ari cast an unhappy look at his watch. The men could unpack the equipment and get back to sleep. But the drill would be repeated, he promised, until it could be done faster.

The appointment of Ben-Ari placed on the Central Front one of the most respected armor commanders in Israel. During the Sinai campaign he had led the Seventh Brigade—then the only regular armored brigade in the army. (All others were reserve units.) The Seventh had seen more action than any other brigade, breaking through the center of the Egyptian line and arriving first at the Suez Canal. The tall, handsome Ben-Ari—the riding crop he usually sported adding to his dash—seemed to have a brilliant future in the army. But a personal controversy after the war led to his resignation and the beginning of a new career as a publisher.

Now, eleven years older and graying at the temples, Ben-Ari once again had a brigade to command. This time, instead of the prime armored unit poised on the most crucial front, he had been given a collection of the oldest tanks in the army deployed on the front where the chances of action were most remote. If

49

the Jordanians did become active, however, the defense of Israel's heartland would depend in a good measure on these old Shermans which comprised the core of Narkiss's general reserve. While Colonel Gur knew exactly where his paratroopers would be jumping in Sinai and Colonel Amitai knew that his Jerusalem Brigade would play a defensive role in the city, Ben-Ari could not be certain where on the long Central Front he might be employed. A Jordanian thrust could come anywhere. Among other possibilities was an attack on the country's only international airport at Lod, hardly ten kilometers from the border, or on one of the military air bases in the area. Ben-Ari's chief concern was the two brigades of Pattons the Jordanians had brought across the Jordan River—one near Jericho threatening Jerusalem and one farther north. Every day he went out on reconnaissance, sometimes by jeep, sometimes in a spotter plane.

While his mission was primarily defensive, he was also prepared to chip off some small Jordanian salients from which the Israelis had failed to dislodge the Arab Legion during the War of Independence. The principal one was at Latrun, where the Jordanians in 1948 had blocked the only road linking Jerusalem to the rest of the country. The Israelis had since built alternative roads, but Latrun, where several hundred men had died, was still a bone in their throat. Ben-Ari assigned his single tank battalion to take Latrun if the Jordanians, by some long chance, provided sufficient provocation.

Ben-Ari also had two battalions of half-track-borne infantry. He dispatched the commander of one of these units, Lieutenant Colonel Yigal, to the Jerusalem Corridor to scout the Arab position at Sheikh Abdul Aziz, overlooking the main Jerusalem road. Ben-Ari himself had commanded the Palmach unit which captured it in 1948, but the position had been lost later. There was an outside chance he might get another crack at it.

The tank battalion had returned from its annual reserve training just before Independence Day and the men had had just ten days at home before they were recalled. When the tank commander, Lieutenant Colonel Zvika, was informed that his battalion was facing two brigades of Pattons, he dispatched one-third of his crews—the best in the unit—for a ten-day course in handling Pattons. If their Shermans were disabled, they would use captured enemy equipment. Zvika had little doubt that there would be captured enemy equipment.

Tourists had been pouring out of the country since the beginning of the crisis, urged on by their embassies. Some foreign faculty members at universities disappeared without saying good-bye to their colleagues. At a gathering of Westerners at one faculty apartment a woman gasped, "This is our last hour." At Jerusalem's largest hotel, the King David, hundreds of tourists who had come for Independence Day clamored for airline bookings. In one day the hotel's room occupancy fell from 85 percent to one percent.

By June 4, however, the influx of foreign journalists had brought occupancy back up to 40 percent. Many of the newsmen lugging typewriters and cameras through customs knew each other from Vietnam and other battlefields. The image of descending vultures was hard to shake off. Among Israeli civilians there was a growing sense of isolation. An American journalist asking a woman for directions on a Jerusalem street was met by a distant stare. "Haven't you gone home yet?" the woman said. When the American said he had just arrived, she nodded slightly and pointed out his destination.

How well the civilian population would hold up under the growing strain was a major concern to Israeli leaders. Haga officials got a warning of what they might expect when a transformer exploded one night in an immigrant quarter in the southern part of the city and local residents fled to the shelters. "Don't you know the war has started," a woman screamed at a Haga officer who told them they could go back to bed.

Panic of a different sort hit the entire city with the closing

51

of the Straits of Tiran—a run on food supplies that swept store shelves clean in a few hours. Driven by the specter of the prolonged 1948 siege, some women bought a dozen loaves of bread and carried away supplies of sugar and flour that would last them a year. Food officials began to wonder if their policy of unlimited purchasing would hold up.

Even the prodigious amount of supplies laid in by the government would soon give way under this kind of pressure. Officials of the Ministry of Commerce and Industry decided to play their hand with poker casualness since they felt any display of concern would only increase the panic. They announced that government warehouses would be kept open through the night, so that grocers could restock. The ministry publicized the announcement by the manager of the Bait Hakerem supermarket that he would give away a free key chain with the purchase of every three kilos of sugar—as if he were trying to encourage people to buy more.

The director of the ministry's Jerusalem district office decided to make the city's main marketplace—Mahane Yehuda—the chief proving ground. He ordered groceries not to refuse any purchase request, no matter what the quantity. Instead of the grocers having to go to the warehouses, he took supplies to them on trucks loaned by the Jerusalem Brigade. A shopper entering a grocery found it so crammed with food that wherever he turned he bumped into a sack of flour, coating his trousers white. It seemed to him as if the officials were laughing at him and his fellow consumers by this display of opulence. This was precisely the feeling the ministry had hoped to inspire, and after three days the buying returned to normal.

Except for the rush on food, the population of the city responded to the crisis with remarkable spirit and coolness. From kindergarten tots who helped fill sandbags to the eighty-year-old man who volunteered to donate blood, there was hardly a person in the city who did not contribute to preparing Jerusalem for what might come.

A focal point for volunteers was the headquarters of Magen David Adom (MDA), the Israeli equivalent of the Red Cross. To accommodate them all, MDA limited volunteers to six hours of work a day instead of the normal eight. One group of boys objected to their shortened hours and climbed back in through a window to resume making bandages. Housewives stood in line to wash the building's floors, and thousands waited to give blood. So many people showed up for first-aid courses that they were shortened from sixteen hours to eight. Two old ladies arrived one day wheeling a baby carriage containing a fifty-kilo sack of sugar which they offered.

With almost all the able-bodied men under arms, the burden of physical work was taken up by women and schoolchildren. High school boys and girls wearing post office caps were seen now on the streets, bags of mail on their shoulders and quizzical looks on their faces as they studied house numbers along the routes they had taken over. Hundreds of youngsters were assigned to trench-digging (one meter deep, sandbags piled two high on each lip). Tolly Yeriel scoured the city with her high school chums looking for useful work. "Most of the girls are volunteering as operating room nurses," she told her mother. "I know they'll pass out with the first incision." Tolly was delighted to find that the keepers at the zoo had been mobilized. She and her friends got the job of feeding the animals two hours a day.

At army camps around the city, neighborhood women came each day to wash the soldiers' laundry. An English tourist with a car offered her services as a chauffeur and was soon driving food officials on inspection trips to groceries.

A group of girls from Hebrew University's school of social work visited families along the city border. They found that immigrants from Morocco, Iraq, and other Arab countries had for the most part not read the Haga posters telling them how to prepare their shelters and what to do when the siren sounded. The girls passed on the instructions verbally.

The hard-pressed manager of the Bait Hakerem supermarket

discovered the value of volunteers during the height of the panic buying. He had been working till 3 A.M. since the crisis began and was so exhausted he prayed he would be mobilized. When he finally received his call-up papers he reported to camp, but was told the order had been rescinded since he was needed at his civilian post. Returning to the store, he sent one of his few remaining workers to the Hebrew University dormitories down the street to see if he could find four or five students. The worker returned with ten, mostly Americans, who worked through the night filling small sugar bags from large sacks and stocking the shelves. They refused the manager's offer of payment.

The largest source of adult manpower remaining in the city were the yeshivot—rabbinical academies—whose students were exempt from the draft. Of the two thousand volunteers who turned out each day for trench-digging in shelterless areas, five hundred were yeshiva students. On the Sabbath after the Tiran closing, the Haga commander in Katamon was amazed to see a group of yeshiva students being marched to a digging site by two bearded rabbis. The prohibition of labor on the Sabbath is one of the severest injunctions of Judaism, but the rabbinate had declared the current crisis one of *pikuach nefesh* (life or death) in which vital work is not only permissible on the Sabbath but mandatory. The two rabbis stripped off their jackets and joined the students in the trenches with shovels. At the Tnuva Dairy plant at the other end of town, permission had been received from the rabbinate to remain open this day to lay in a store of hard cheese and milk powder for a possible siege. An elderly rabbi appeared and in a symbolic gesture helped push a milk cart.

Not all yeshivot availed themselves of military deferment. At the Rabbi Kook Yeshiva the dining room table where the older students usually sat was empty. Most of them were serving in the elite paratroop or reconnaissance units. On Sabbath morning an officer of a mortar platoon scheduled to be mobilized the next day sent messages to his squad leaders summoning them to a briefing. The officer was new to his unit and had never met the squad commanders before. When they arrived at the rendez-vous point he was astonished to see that one of them was in Chassidic dress and two others were also plainly of the extremely religious. Somewhat embarrassed, the officer said he realized the Sabbath would not be over for a few hours but that it was important they knew immediately where their gun position would be. The Chassid and the others assured him that it was perfectly all right and climbed unhesitatingly into his car, an object it is normally forbidden to even touch, let alone ride in, on the Sabbath.

There was, however, one tiny segment of the Orthodox community which kept aloof from the national effort. The extremist Neturei Karta sect had always refused to recognize the sovereigny of the State of Israel, and its attitude was not changed by the current crisis. A foreign reporter seeking out one of the sect's leaders, Rabbi Amram Blau, found him unmoved by the impending dangers. Israel, he explained, would be truly resurrected only when the Messiah comes and not by a political movement dominated by irreligious men. "Zionist arrogance has incensed Israel's neighbors to their present animosity," he said. What arrogance? he was asked. "The arrogance of creating a state," he said. "The State of Israel uses the name of holy Israel although they are rebels against God and the holy Torah." With the sixty-nine-year-old Blau was his wife, a convert from Catholicism who was twenty-two years his junior. Their marriage several years before had caused a scandal which forced Blau to leave Jerusalem for a while. A handsome woman with a strong face, Mrs. Blau spoke of her experiences in World War II when she lived in Targes, in the south of France. "I'm not frightened by bombing," she said. "When they bombed the factory in town at night I didn't bother to get out of bed." When the reporter asked the rabbi who he would want to win if it came to war, his wife whispered in Yiddish, "Don't say anything that will harm us." Rabbi Blau smiled and said, "I don't pray for anybody's

55

victory. But I would want the Zionist regime to dissolve as a result of such a war."

Despite near-total mobilization, attempts were made to keep civilian life functioning as normally as possible. Movies continued to show regular features to nearly empty houses, and the Israel Museum maintained regular hours, although the only visitors were a scattering of soldiers who came up to the city on official business. The staff began drills in removing material from exhibit cases to the basement, but museum director Yohanan Boehm told his curators that the items would remain on display until fighting had actually broken out. The curators nodded in agreement, but as the tension grew their concern for the safety of exhibits they particularly prized prompted them one by one to take Boehm aside for a confidential chat. "You're perfectly right, of course," they would say. "I understand completely what you're trying to do. But couldn't we just remove this one item for safety's sake?" Boehm's negative answer was firm.

At the university it was decided to keep classes in session despite the argument that it would be unfair to students who had already been called up. Instructors and students, however, found it difficult to concentrate. One economics professor found it possible to discuss abstract themes, but descriptions of specific phenomena from real life seemed hopelessly irrelevant.

Employers found workers unwilling to stay at their jobs if they were not war-connected. One manager was approached by a succession of secretaries asking to leave for a kibbutz to help with the fruit picking now that the kibbutz men were gone. The manager said he understood their need to do something physical but insisted that it was just as necessary to keep life in the cities going on as normally as possible.

Perhaps the greatest disruption in normal life was the lack of transportation. Most buses and almost all taxis had been mobilized along with their drivers. The vehicles were given a coating of mud for camouflage and assigned to military units as troop transports. Many private vehicles had also been mobilized, the owners, if they were not of military age, sometimes going along as volunteer chauffeurs. Bus lines were consolidated, and service was drastically reduced.

Early on Saturday evening, May 27, the duty officer at Haga central headquarters in Jerusalem began receiving reports from sector commanders that wood was being stacked for giant bonfires around the city. It was the eve of Lag ba'Omer, a holiday celebrating the revolt of Bar Kochba against the Romans. The commanders were worried that if an emergency developed and a blackout was imposed, the bonfires would continue to light up the city. The duty officer contacted Colonel Bengal, the Jerusalem Haga commander, who said that the youths should be advised against setting the fires but that no attempt be made to enforce a ban. The duty officer passed on the instructions and went up to the roof. He broke into laughter as he saw fires springing up on all the hills of the city, the youths obviously not to be deterred from their annual bonfire by any passing crisis.

The woman who normally gave advice on etiquette on Kol Yisrael's program for housewives directed herself now to the crisis, treating it as sensibly as she handled other social complications. She advised mothers to let their school-age children play where they usually did and to explain that if the siren went off, they should go to the nearest shelter where an "auntie" would take care of them. The listeners would, of course, be "aunties" to any child that came into their shelters. Small children, she advised, had better be kept in sight.

Pervading the city was a feeling that if war came to Jerusalem it would be a bloody block-by-block battle in which no quarter would be given. Unspoken of but widely envisioned was the image of the Warsaw Ghetto: buildings turned to rubble from which the battle would continue. The municipality secretly began to bulldoze a hillside near Mount Herzl to prepare grave

57

sites. The slope chosen was out of sight of the Jordanian lines to prevent a repetition of 1948 when, at funerals of people killed by shelling, the mourners themselves came under fire at the graveside. Deputy Mayor Axelrod, who was in charge of burial arrangements, was informed that some officials expected two thousand dead in Jerusalem. These were the optimists who assumed that the Jordanians would not attempt aerial bombardment because of the proximity of the Arab and Jewish sections. The pessimists, those who believed the Arabs would attempt to bomb anyway, estimated six thousand dead.

## 4 COUNTDOWN

On Tuesday, May 30—two weeks after Independence Day and one week after the closing of the Straits of Tiran—Jordan's King Hussein flew to Cairo to sign a defense pact with Nasser. In 1956 a similar trip by Hussein had been followed by the Israeli blow in Sinai. This time the Israeli reaction was partial demobilization.

Aviva Yeriel's husband, Jack, got the word the evening of May 31 in the hills on the southern edge of the Jerusalem Corridor where his second-line unit was dug in. Most of them would be released in the morning. As they sat around a fire debating the significance of the move, someone switched on a transistor radio and picked up the calm voice of General Rabin. "I know the waiting is hard, but I can assure you if war comes it will not be fought on our soil." For the first time since Eshkol's disastrous speech three nights before, spirits rose. One of the men started singing "Jerusalem of Gold," and the others joined in.

The demobilization had been ordered not because the crisis was fading or to fool the Arabs about Israeli intent, but because of the economic strain involved in keeping most of the adult male population from their jobs, a cost estimated by some at 20 million dollars a day. The demobilization order affected almost half the brigade's second-line troops. The largest contingent was mustered out Thursday morning, June 1, at Allenby Barracks, the former British Army camp in the southern part of the city. As his men stood in formation on the parade ground, a company commander quoted two sections of the Bible to them: "Put not your trust in princes" and "Israel, trust in the Lord, thy help and thy shield." To the men, the message was clear: Don't rely on other nations to help. Be prepared to be recalled.

The civilian sector, meanwhile, continued to prepare for war. On the same day that partial demobilization went into effect, Hadassah Hospital was advised by the army to prepare for gas victims. The use of poison gas by the Egyptian expeditionary force which had intervened in the Yemen civil war had been well noted by the Israelis. If the Egyptians had used it against brother Arabs, would they hesitate to use it against Israel? The hospital constructed decontamination rooms and prepared to receive gas victims in waves of two hundred. Judging from the Yemen experience, mustard- and nerve-gas injuries could be expected. Shaarei Zedek Hospital sent an urgent wire to its women's auxiliary in New York on Saturday night, June 3, for a manual respirator and suctions. (The equipment arrived in Jerusalem three hours before the shooting started in the city.)

Following Hussein's trip to Cairo, the city's Water Department finally got clearance to fill the ancient Mamilla Reservoir in the center of town. The municipality had been reluctant to fill it earlier because of the probability of leakage and the improbability of war with Jordan. The filled reservoir, which had been cut out of the living rock more than a millennium before, substantially augmented the city's water reserves.

On Tuesday Moshe Dayan toured the city line with Colonel Amitai. The architect of the lightning Sinai campaign, now a member of the Knesset, had no official position in the military hierarchy, but public clamor was growing for his return to active duty. He had just toured the Southern Front, and he stressed to Amitai that in the event of war the Jerusalem Brigade's role would be strictly defensive. If things went badly in the south, Dayan said, it might be impossible to get help to Jerusalem even if Scopus were heavily attacked. A few hours after his tour of Jerusalem, Dayan's appointment as defense minister was announced by Prime Minister Eshkol.

The appointment dominated the conversation at a party for

Jerusalem Brigade officers that night at the President Hotel. It was the best news the army had heard since the crisis began. Shortly before midnight, Major Aaron, commander of the tank company, approached Colonel Amitai and requested permission to leave. (Army protocol had long since reached the point where an officer did not leave a party early without permission from the senior officer present.) At Amitai's nod, Aaron saluted and slipped out of the brightly lit banquet room. That night his tanks would be taken out from cover and given their first test run since mobilization. When Aaron arrived at camp, they were rolled out and driven up and down the surrounding hills for three hours, their drivers pushing them to their limits. By sunup, the old Shermans were back under cover, heated from the exertion but with certificates of good health.

As the week ended, activity increased along the city line. Shots from Jordanian positions were becoming an almost daily occurrence, but Israeli troops manning the line had strict orders not to return the fire. Some of the shooting was aimed at the Israeli aircraft skirting the border to photograph the Arab Legion positions or carrying senior officers on reconnaissance. Sometimes the shots were aimed lower. Arye Comay, the thirty-nine-year-old Chilean, was shifted Thursday to a trench position just north of Mandelbaum Gate. He was standing upright looking at the Jordanian bunkers opposite when Bren gun bullets spattered the dirt a few yards away. He called home that evening from a nearby phone and asked his wife the news. She said the radio had reported the Jordanians firing on a plane near Mandelbaum Gate. He checked his urge to correct the story. The trench, at the edge of the Bait Yisrael neighborhood, would draw considerable fire in the days ahead.

In the main blockhouse at Mandelbaum, the soldiers learned to anticipate such shooting by watching the workmen who were adding an extra story to the Young Men's Christian Association opposite them in Jordanian Jerusalem. (The building was known locally as the Arab YMCA to distinguish it from the Jewish YMCA in Israeli Jerusalem.) Obviously forewarned by the Arab Legion, the workmen were seen to descend the scaffolding every time shooting was about to break out. The commander of the blockhouse, Lieutenant Genzel, posted some men behind the firing slits on the roof of an adjacent front-line apartment building. The blockhouse and apartment building were on one side of a narrow street and the Jordanian blockhouses on the other, hardly twenty meters away. One day Genzel, fearful that the Arabs might try to slip across in the dark and plant explosives against the Israeli buildings, looked for a way to get around a concrete wall which blocked access to the street. A young neighborhood boy came up and asked, "You trying to get to the other side?" The urchin led Genzel into an adjoining building and opened a door giving out into the street. The area, directly opposite the Jordanian posts, was too dangerous during the day, but Genzel resolved to put men there at night if war broke out.

To spotters on the roof of the Histadrut Building no tension was apparent in the leisurely pace of pedestrians on the Jordanian streets of Jerusalem. Civilian males could be seen in abundance there, in contrast to the Israeli side. Waiters hovering over tables in the dining room of the Mount Scopus Hotel, on the approaches to the hill, seemed to indicate that there was still tourist traffic. At night the lights leading into the Jordanian half of the city from Ramallah to the north were sometimes switched off, and through their powerful binoculars the observers on the roof could make out convoys entering the city.

The principal lookout post in the south of the city was a rooftop in kibbutz Ramat Rachel where a four-man detail had been posted. One of the men, Private Grover, had studied the detailed intelligence maps until he became the resident expert on the Jordanian roads. The Canadian immigrant, a biologist, could watch traffic on the two roads between Jordanian Jerusalem and Bethlehem to the south.

62

The Jordanians had years before built bunkers and trenches into the hillside below the Mar Elias Monastery, seven hundred meters away from Ramat Rachel. It was from one of these bunkers that a machine gunner had killed four Israeli archaeologists examining a dig at the kibbutz in 1956. Private Grover could see the Legionnaires there clearly enough to note that they were cleanly shaven every day and wore clean uniforms. Officers in berets could occasionally be seen pointing out the Israeli post to visiting officers. Grover himself received a welcome visit one day from his wife and children, who brought along a woolen knit cap for the cold nights. Bethlehem was in a plain view, only four kilometers away, and on Friday, June 2, Grover saw crowds demonstrating in the streets. He could make out placards bearing the pictures of Nasser, Hussein, and Ahmed Shukeiry, the leader of the Palestine Liberation Organization.

A similar demonstration outside the Old City's Damascus Gate was seen the same day by an Israeli officer on the roof of Notre Dame Hospice in the center of the line. He was close enough to hear the crowds chanting "Nasser, Nasser." Shukeiry himself was seen from the roof of the Histadrut Building, among a crowd of VIPs inspecting the front line just south of the Police Training School. The spotters on the roof had been alerted to his impending visit. Among the officers accompanying him were some wearing the red stripe of the Iraqi Army on their caps.

With the Scopus garrison tracking traffic up the Jericho road from the east and the Histadrut spotters observing traffic from the north, there could be no significant movement into Jordanian Jerusalem without the Israelis knowing it.

It was assumed that the Jordanian intelligence service was tracking Israeli movements through agents behind Israeli lines. The many vehicles in Jerusalem bearing United Nations or consular plates were suspect. In the Valley of the Cross, where the heavy mortars were set up, soldiers one day spotted a man with a camera on the slope above them near the Israel Museum. A mounted policeman nearby cantered up and apprehended the cameraman, who identified himself as a member of the Russian Embassy in Tel Aviv. He was taken to police headquarters and released after his film was confiscated.

Over the weekend, the troops on the line could see the Jordanians opposite them busily fortifying. On the northern flank, a two-meter high concrete wall was being built at the edge of no-man's-land to the right of the Police Training School. A cement truck was on the scene, and an Arab Legion sergeant with a swagger stick under his arm directed the work. Another legion unit was digging trenches on French Hill, which covered the northern approach of Mount Scopus. At Abu Tor, on the southern part of the line, Legionnaires could be heard digging trenches around their blockhouses. From his observation post Private Gershon Mack saw a Legionnaire appear on the rooftop from which a Jordanian had gestured the week before to throw over an apple. This time the Arab looked at Gershon and drew his finger across his throat.

From a lookout post in the Schneller compound, Lieutenant Colonel Yusske, the brigade artillery officer, looked through binoculars at the Arab Legion position at Nebi Samuel five kilometers away and spotted an Arab officer arriving with maps rolled up under his arm. From the businesslike way the officer set the maps down and scanned the Israeli landscape, Yosske knew he was looking at a fellow artilleryman.

The Jordanian preparations were visible from Scopus too. Twice the garrison had heard the Jordanian sirens go off in tests, and an abundance of military traffic was visible in the streets below. The major source of information on what was happening on the Israeli side of the city was the UN officer who visited the hill periodically. The Israelis asked if stores were still open in the city. The officer said they were but that the streets were nearly empty of men. It was the first indication to the garrison that large-scale mobilization had taken place. One day the UN officer told Dr. Avshalom that he had just returned from Beirut, where he had seen his family off to Cyprus. "They'll be back here after the war," he said. Startled, the doctor asked if he was so certain there would be a war. "My colleagues and I have seen these situations around the world," the officer said. "It's reached the point of no return." As the time for the bimonthly convoy scheduled for Wednesday, June 7, approached, the officer told Major Scharfmann that if conditions remained tense the Jordanians might not permit the replacements to pass through their lines. "We might just be able to send up supplies," he said.

Motta Gur was also thinking about the Scopus convoy. His mission in the event of war lay in the south, but if war with Egypt had not broken out by June 7 and the Jordanians tried to stop the convoy, there was a chance, he felt, that his crack brigade might be called upon. A week before the convoy was due to go, Gur drove up to Jerusalem with his intelligence officer, Lieutenant Colonel Arik, for a tour of the city line. The officers, accompanied by Colonel Amitai, entered a trench north of Mandelbaum Gate—the same trench in which Arye Comay was to draw fire the next day—and scanned the formidable Jordanian defenses. They discussed briefly whether a day or night attack was preferable and agreed that a night attack was the best way to get across the open space covered by the Jordanian guns. Gur said if his men were used in Jerusalem he wanted them to ride in half-tracks, which would offer them a measure of protection. Returning to his base, Gur notified his superiors that he planned to send his battalion commanders up to Jerusalem on Saturday so that they could study the city line for themselves. He was told not to bother since there was no chance his brigade would be sent to Jerusalem. The opportunity thus lost was to be sorely missed.

Many of the paratroopers received leave for the Sabbath, the last Sabbath before war. The soldiers' spirits had revived with the appointment of Dayan, but Captain Dan, the deputy com-

65

mander of the Seventh Battalion, found on arriving at his home kibbutz, Ayelet Hashahar, in the Upper Galilee, that the people left behind were worried. "The only thing I'm worried about," Dan told them, "is how we're going to transport back all the tanks and artillery we're going to capture."

In Jerusalem on the Sabbath wives and children descended in the thousands upon the hills surrounding the city where their men were camped. The wooded slopes became a vast picnic site as family groups sat outside the tents under a lovely springtime sky.

Out in the Jerusalem Corridor, the Jerusalem Reconnaissance Company also had guests this day—Chief of Staff Rabin and other officers of the General Staff. The men were drawn up in front of their well-polished vehicles as their company commander, Major Yussi, greeted the general. Yussi told him that they were both graduates of the Kadoori Agricultural School. Rabin asked which graduating class he had been in. When Yussi told him, the general said he had graduated ten years before. "That's what makes me to my regret chief of staff instead of commander of a reconnaissance unit," he said.

After trooping the line Rabin said, "Fellows, gather around." The men broke ranks and crowded around him. "I know it's very hard not knowing if there's going to be a war or not," he said, "But you have to know that staying in this position is as important as fighting. It's a question of nerves—who will break first. We don't want to fight, but as long as they're on our borders we can't go home." Rabin took leave briefly to visit the adjacent tank company. "Have a little more patience," he told an officer there. "Not much." Instead of helmets, the reconnaissance men were all wearing their brightly colored jockey caps when the chief of staff returned. He laughed at the sight and the men cheered, flinging their caps in the air.

Rabin was escorted along the city line by Colonel Amitai, for whom this had become an almost daily exercise. The Jerusalem Brigade commander suggested that Hussein might move against

Government House at the opening of hostilities, since the international compound was the one piece of non-Jordanian territory in Jerusalem which he could seize easily. There were no troops in the demilitarized zone abutting it except for the five Israelis in the Lonely House. General Narkiss, who was also present, requested permission from Rabin to move troops into the Israeli side of the demilitarized zone and to have a bulldozer dig trenches there, even though this violation of the armistice agreement would be easily noted by the UN officers in Government House. With some reluctance Rabin agreed, and Narkiss passed on the order to Amitai. The Arab attack, however, was to come before the order was carried out.

Stopping off at the mortar position in the Valley of the Cross, Rabin—to the surprise of the Jerusalem artillery commander—asked to see the barrage plans which had been prepared to defend Mount Scopus against attacks from a number of possible directions. The shelling would have to be accurate and precisely timed, since a single three-minute barrage would consume close to a thousand shells and ammunition was severely limited. After carefully examining the plans, Rabin gave his approval.

Rabin and his party were luncheon guests at Jerusalem Brigade headquarters. The brigade operations officer, Lieutenant Colonel Amos, found himself sitting opposite the number three man on the General Staff, General Ezer Weizmann. Amos asked the dapper flyer, who had been the prime shaper of the Israel Air Force, how long it would take to destroy the Egyptian Air Force. "It will take us four to five hours," Weizmann said. "The Arabs are ready for us and we may lose half our planes, but we'll finish them in four to five hours."

At the meal's end, Rabin was the first to rise. As he reached the doorway, he stopped and turned. The room hummed with the conversation of a hundred officers. Raising his voice Rabin said, "Fellows," and a hush descended. "I fought here in forty-eight," he said. "I hope you will fight here in this war. I hope what we didn't finish, you will finish."

For two weeks the nation had been frozen in a tableau with its hand upraised. Now, with the Dayan appointment, there was little doubt that it would strike. Along the Jerusalem border a trickle of residents started leaving their homes, and authorities feared that the spontaneous pullbacks might generate panic. The Haga sector commander in Mamilla, a Yemenite school janitor named Zecharia Maimoni, patrolled his neighborhood at night and on several occasions stopped families as they slipped through the darkened streets with belongings on their backs. He assured them they were in no danger if they remained and warned of the effect on morale if they left. All the families turned back.

At Maimoni's request, the Haga commander of the central district, Dudu Cohen, addressed a gathering of local residents in the Mamilla Synagogue, about one hundred meters from the Old City wall, on Saturday night, June 3. Cohen, a portly and jovial public relations man, told the Yemenite, Kurdish, and Turkish immigrants who filled the synagogue that if the border residents pulled back, then the people who lived in the streets behind them would pull back too. "What would become the front line?" he asked.

"We're not accustomed to war," said one elder. "Surely God is watching over us and everything will be well, but what if the Arabs start shooting at us with machine guns?"

"If you put sandbags in your windows," said Cohen, "they will stop the bullets."

Another man stood up. "Israel has nothing to fear from her enemies but what if the Arabs start shelling us with cannon?"

Cohen assured him that the quarter was so close to the Arab positions on the wall they would not shell it for fear of hitting their own men.

"God will preserve us," said another man, "but what if their soldiers come out of the Old City and attack us?"

"In that case," replied Cohen, "you have nothing to worry about."

1. Uzi Narkiss.

Maj. Yussi, commander of the Jerusalem Reconnaissance Company.
ARON ZUCKERMANN

Dani Bachrach, first Israeli soldier to enter Jordanian territory.

Burnt-out Jordanian jeeps at Government House.

He saw the puzzled faces but waited until someone asked why. "Because if they attack," he said, "then we're going to attack, and we're going to take the Old City." The men broke into prolonged applause. "We know you're busy," said one elder, "and we don't want to keep you any longer." As Cohen left, the men gathered around him and assured him that everything would be well.

Despite the firm line taken at Mamilla, scores of families in more exposed areas did pull back, generally moving in with relatives or friends deeper in the city. In Yemin Moshe, separated from the Old City wall only by the two hundred-meter-wide Hinnom Valley, one-fifth of the residents left the area. Just below Yemin Moshe, in the valley itself, was the community of Shaama, inhabited by sixty largely illiterate families from Persia. Abrupt slopes cut it off from view of the rest of Jerusalem, and the community's vineyards and wandering goats placed it centuries away from the modern city above it. Its access road was completely open to view from the Old City wall, and it was plain that Shaama would be completely isolated once shooting started. By Saturday, all but three families had left.

Whereas Israeli Jerusalem was marked by both an apprehension of war and preparations to meet it, Jordanian Jerusalem saw mounting war frenzy unmatched by any steps to prepare the civilian population. The frenzy reached a peak with the arrival on Friday of Ahmed Shukeiry, who was lifted on the shoulders of the crowd when he visited El Aksa Mosque for noon prayers. In an impassioned speech the Palestine Liberation Organization leader promised that Israel was on the verge of destruction. Swept away by rhetoric, people in Jordanian Jerusalem believed that they would be in West Jerusalem a few hours after the shooting started and in Tel Aviv a few hours after that. Those who spoke Arabic in the Mount Scopus garrison could hear preachers exhorting over loudspeakers from nearby mosques to "slaughter and kill."

In quieter moments, however, less sanguine visions sometimes intruded upon the Arabs of Jerusalem, and a foreigner walking through the Old City bazaar this last weekend before the war could detect fear. There was a realization, among some residents at least, that the outcome of the battle was not certain and that virtually nothing had been done to prepare the civilian sector. There was no mass blood collection and no preparation of hospitals for war. A municipal official attending a meeting of top civil-defense officers discovered that civil-defense equipment consisted of little more than armbands. A suggestion that arms be distributed to the populace was quickly rejected on the grounds that the Palestinian nationalists would use them against the pro-Hussein establishment in the city. Some brushed aside disturbing thoughts by assuring themselves that with the Israeli part of the city ringed on three sides by Legionnaires on dominating heights, its fate was sealed.

Sunday, June 4, brought no special portent of war. General Dayan, in his first press conference as minister of defense, had said the day before that the time for spontaneous response to the closing of the Straits of Tiran had passed. A diplomatic solution, he said, would now be sought.

Despite this lulling note, preparations continued unabated. A group of Haga officers were sent from Jerusalem in the morning to an army base for a half-day course in gas warfare. The French expert who had installed the famed Chagall windows at Hadassah Hospital—twelve windows, each representing a tribe of Israel—flew in at the request of hospital officials and was driven up to Jerusalem. After approving the method proposed for removing the windows and storing them until the crisis had passed, he wished his hosts good luck and returned to Lod airport to catch the night plane back to Paris. In the border streets of Musrara, a beauty in miniskirt and high heels—one of the volunteers from the university's school of social work—started filling sandbags by herself and was soon joined by a swarm of neighborhood youngsters. A few hundred meters away, scores of yeshiva students from the Mea Shearim quarter worked late into the night filling sandbags to be stacked in the windows of the blockhouses overlooking Mandelbaum Gate.

On a slope in the northern part of the city where tourists were taken if they wished to plant a tree in the soil of Israel with their own hands, an infantry unit was this Sunday busily uprooting freshly planted saplings. They had been ordered to dig a trench line facing Shuafat on the Ramallah road. The men used air compressors lent by the local branch of a construction firm to cut through the rocky soil. (Most of the army's engineering equipment was in the south.) At night the unit put out ambush teams, the men forming a wheel as they lay facing out in the darkness, their boots touching at the hub. Not far away, sappers lay mines along the city's northern border. Other sapper teams silently crossed the border to probe the enemy minefields. In the south of the city a squad planted antitank mines alongside the blockaded road from Jewish Jerusalem to Bethlehem. Behind the lines, mortar crews stood by their weapons to cover the mine-laying teams if necessary.

On Sunday evening a somber mood enveloped the second-line unit near the university. Word had been received that it would move up to the line in the morning. The visiting relatives stayed on after dark, and Captain Guri invited some of the children to sing at the campfire. A private looked about him and sensed that the men were drawn closer together this evening than they had ever been.

On Mount Zion, the night was peaceful enough for the commander of the platoon posted there to challenge one of his men to a game of chess. There was little conversation as the pair concentrated on the board. Suddenly the officer looked up and said, "I have a feeling the war is going to start tomorrow."

Neither he nor Colonel Amitai nor anyone else in Jerusalem Brigade knew about any plans for war the next day, but by 7 P.M. on that Sunday night every private in Motta Gur's brigade knew it. The word had been passed to prepare equipment for a combat jump. "The play is about to begin," a company commander told his men. The paratroopers cleaned their weapons, filled magazines, and put grenades on their belts. They were transported to a kibbutz near an air force base, where they dug foxholes and waited for dawn. Some of the officers went to the air base, where they met the pilots who were to open the attack in the morning. The pilots, like the paratroop officers, were predominantly children of the kibbutzim, and many of the men in the two forces had grown up together.

Lieutenant Yoav Tsuri, the swimming champion from kibbutz Afikim, visited another camp nearby where his younger brother, Udi, was stationed. Udi, also a paratroop lieutenant, was doing his regular military service and had been posted at a logistical base rather than with a combat unit. The nineteen-year-old soldier had grown up obscured by the shadow of Yoav, a shadow which he saw still dogging him. "You've got it good again," said Udi. "You're going to war and I'm staying here." Yoav said he would gladly change places.

Returning to base, Yoav wrote his final letters home. They reflected both the desire to strike the blow that would finally end the tension and the awareness of what the face of war was really like. "The tension here has gone up since Dayan was made defense minister," he wrote his parents. "If all of us were pacifists before, now—after sitting and sitting—everybody wants to go out and finish whatever's possible. Naturally, they know that it's not training or child's play. At the same time, until they meet face to face that other reality—which is pretty miserable —they're willing to exchange [the present waiting] for it."

To his wife, Gali, and their infant he wrote, "Is this *the* letter before me? I don't know. In any case, this time we're ready and moving more than ever before. Have we thought of everything? . . . Am I afraid? Homesick? Repelled? I don't know. Everything is taken up in orders, organizing. . . . Gali, I have given my love to you two. Remember this. Everything is for you. And you are mine. . . ."

It was now after midnight. At the nearby airfield the planes were shrouded in darkness. Far to the south, the tank armies lay silent in the desert.

# 5 MONDAY

From the main lookout post on Abu Tor, which Private Gershon Mack mounted at dawn, sunrise over the Moab Mountains across the Jordan was like the opening scene in the drama of Creation. As the sun lifted above the mist clinging to the horizon, a ribbon of light glanced dully off the Dead Sea, lowest point on the surface of the earth, and the gaunt, white hills of the Judean Desert came into view. This rugged wasteland beginning at the very edge of the city had served as a refuge for the hunted and a retreat for the mystic at least since David fled there to escape King Saul's wrath. In the foreground the shadows parted from the Judean Hills, revealing the Arab villages south of Jerusalem, clusters of cubelike houses draped with infinite grace across the slopes. No unusual movement could be seen on the roads, and Gershon descended to say his morning prayers and eat breakfast.

On the roof of the Pagi blockhouse at the northern end of the city line, Corporal Salmi, a forward mortar observer, scanned Ammunition Hill with binoculars at dawn. During the night he had heard the sound of digging from the Jordanian positions and had made out the changing of the guard, six men moving along the line and dropping off in pairs. The sun was coming up behind the Arab Legion position now, and Salmi saw a Legionnaire looking through binoculars, his elbows spread at eye level. The Legionnaire was looking at him.

On the coastal plain where the men of Gur's brigade had spent the night, an officer from the Eighth Battalion had also risen at dawn, even though he had no duties at this hour. Like the Egyptians, he believed that when an air attack came it would be carried out at first light, and he looked toward the nearby airfield for the sight of planes lifting. But the sun rose in silence. The men were wakened at six, and the kibbutz orchards where the brigade had made camp were soon bustling.

The soldiers were in the middle of breakfast an hour later when a roar was heard from the direction of the air base. The sound grew in intensity, and planes began to rise above the tree line—dozens of them following each other into the sky like children playing tag. The aircraft, low-slung with bombs and rockets, wove themselves into formations of four and headed south at low altitude. At the airfield a young mechanic wept as the planes swept past him, wave after wave, glinting in the sky like a sword unsheathed. In the orchards the paratroopers watched the planes disappear in silence, awed by what they had seen and by what they knew must come. Then they drifted off to write final postcards home. "We're seeing the start of the war," wrote one. "We hope it's finished soon. We'll do what we can to finish it soon."

At Haga headquarters in Jerusalem, duty officer Yoram Hamizrachi, a barrel-chested ex-paratrooper, received a message at 7:55 to sound the sirens. Thinking someone must have erred, he contacted national Haga headquarters, which informed him that the order had come directly from the air force. (In Sinai and Egypt the Israeli planes had already risen from the desert floor, which they had hugged to avoid radar detection, and were bombing the enemy air bases.) Yoram ordered the alarm sounded and ran outside the building to listen. From every direction siren sounds began to climb, pursuing each other until they reached a high-pitched wail that filled the streets and froze people in their tracks. Yoram returned to the building in a daze.

The phone began ringing immediately. The police duty officer told Yoram that he had already radioed patrol cars that the sirens had gone off by mistake and that the public be so informed. "Idiot," replied Yoram. "It's war." Colonel Amitai also telephoned. He had called a routine meeting of his unit commanders at Schneller for 8 A.M. and wanted to know why the sirens were intruding on such a pleasant June morning. Yoram informed him. Amitai himself was to receive a call shortly from General Narkiss, at Central Command headquarters. "They've begun," said Narkiss. He suggested a champagne toast. The danger of political backtracking was past. The nation was committed, and the officers had every confidence about the outcome.

The alarm had caught children on the way to school, men on the way to work. After the initial shock, most concluded, like the policeman, that it was a test, a notion seemingly confirmed by the fact that by mistake the sirens were sounding the steady note of the all-clear instead of the warble meant to signal imminent attack. Within a quarter hour, however, the meaning of the siren was made clear on Kol Yisrael. At 8:10 A.M. six high-pitched beeps signaling a news bulletin interrupted the morning music program. The announcer reported that Egyptian armor and aircraft had begun moving toward the border and that bitter fighting had broken out. Men took a deep breath and experienced a tangible shifting of mental gears—a detached awareness that the talk was over, that soon, in minutes or hours, violence would be upon them.

The city hastened its preparations for Armaggedon. Barefoot shopgirls in downtown shop windows fixed strips of tape or gauze to plate-glass windows to prevent shattering. Men slapped blue paint over car headlights, leaving only a tiny gap in the center to serve as a blackout light.

At Bikur Cholim Hospital, closest of the city's three general hospitals to the front line, cots were set up in the corridors under the supervision of a short doctor, whose urgent demands for speed seemed overly dramatic to a visitor stepping in from the still-tranquil streets. A column of high school boys and girls arrived at the building breathing hard after a forced march from

81

their school. The youths, who had been assigned to fill sandbags and carry stretchers, sat down on the stone steps just inside the entrance and waited to be called. They would still be there twenty-four hours later, slumped over from exhaustion, their blue school uniforms covered with the blood of wounded men.

Officials at Hadassah Hospital were notified by the army at 9:10 to enter the emergency-room stage, setting up an eighty-bed facility in one of the lobbies to receive casualties from the south who would be brought by helicopter to the hospital landing pad. No fighting was expected in Jerusalem itself, and indeed the taping and blacking out of the hospital's two thousand windows, which had begun only two days before, was still far from complete.

At the Israel Museum, director Yohanan Boehm received a telephone call from army headquarters advising him to start removing exhibits to the shelter. Cases were unlocked, and the red-tabbed, top-priority items were handed to the office personnel and cleaning women who had been staging dry runs of the exercise during the past week. They had been taught to lift pottery from the bottom, not by the fragile handles, and to lay the pots down on their sides if there was any danger of their tipping over. The cleaning women, Boehm noted, cradled the exhibits with great tenderness. Sometimes a curator would carry a pet item down to the shelter himself.

The museum's greatest treasures, seven of the Dead Sea Scrolls, were housed in a separate building, the Shrine of the Book. The architects had taken the uneasy political situation in the Middle East into account in the design of the structure. For display purposes, they had mounted the scrolls on a raised cylinder in the center of the floor which could be lowered, like a submarine periscope, into a protective drum. But engineers who inspected the drum during the crisis period had decided that it would not protect the scrolls if a shell were to penetrate the roof and score a direct hit. Upon their advice, sandbags were now piled atop the drum after the cylinder was lowered into it.

The treasure the city was most concerned about was its 47,-000 schoolchildren. As long as the Jordanian front was silent, officials were determined that life continue as normally as possible and that children remain at school. One school near the railroad station, however, was located in an open field in view of the Arab Legion positions on the Old City wall, and the Haga commander in the area ordered its evacuation soon after the sirens went off. About 10 A.M. Colonel Bengal, the Haga commander in Jerusalem, received word from the army that the Jordanians might begin shelling within the hour. He ordered all children transferred from the eighteen schools without shelters to schools with shelters.

Radio news editor Arye Hauslich had been shaving when his wife called out that she heard an air-raid alarm. Turning down the radio, he heard a faint wail in the distance. The news broadcaster at 8 o'clock reported the sounding of the siren but gave no explanation. After the 8:10 war bulletin, the radio began playing military marches.

Hauslich drove to the studio and found that nobody knew anything beyond the threadbare bulletin issued by the army spokesman on the outbreak of fighting in the south. Hauslich was sure, however, that if the war spread to the Jordanian front, Kol Yisrael would be among the first to know. The main studio, on Queen Helena Street, was just three hundred yards from the border. The Arab Legion had had nineteen years to get the range, and in the first minutes of fighting in the city, Hauslich was certain, the studio would be leveled by shellfire. Auxiliary broadcasting facilities had been prepared for this eventuality elsewhere in Jerusalem and in Tel Aviv, but any sudden outbreak of fighting would catch the bulk of the radio staff at the main studio.

In one wing of the studio, the war was already in full swing. Unlike the other Kol Yisrael departments, the Arabic section did not depend for its items on handouts from the army spokesman.

83

Linked by direct line to army intelligence, with the first announcement of war it unleashed a propaganda campaign that was to be as effective in its way as the military campaign. "Today Nasser has carried out his threat," the Arabic announcer said after the 8:10 flash. "We said to you that if war comes it will be a bad war for you. Israel will bring the war to your territory. This time will not be like 1948 or 1956. This time the victory will be great. Rivers of blood will be shed but the responsibility is President Nasser's. We are fighting for our preservation."

By 9 A.M. the announcer was addressing himself directly to a score of Egyptian Air Force and Army commanders. "Colonel Jamal Ser Aly, commander of El Arish Airdrome: Where is your airport? Nothing has remained. We hope you have succeeded in fleeing. . . . Major, your son is only three months away from graduation. He would want to have his father there. . . . Colonel, your son is waiting for you in Cairo. It's a pity for you to be killed."

The writers for the Arabic section were Jews from Arab countries, like the network head, Yaacov Haazma, a genial Iraqi-born lawyer. Unlike Radio Cairo's Hebrew-language broadcasters, whose fractured Hebrew provided the only comedy relief available on the air, Kol Yisrael employed Arabs to speak Arabic, including an Egyptian who spoke to his people in native dialect. Warning against any attempt to bomb Israeli population centers, an announcer told the Arabs that for every bomb dropped on Tel Aviv, fifty would be dropped on Cairo. He reminded his listeners that it was harder to miss in Cairo, which had a population of 4 million compared to Tel Aviv's 500,000. Haazma's men also addressed themselves to the Jordanians but in conciliatory tones. "We have coexisted for nineteen years. Now Nasser wants you to fight us."

At 9:15 A.M. the section broadcast a report that, coming just an hour after the announcement of war, would have been incredible had its source not been the army itself. One hundred and twenty Egyptian planes, the bulletin said, had already been destroyed. This announcement was the only one made on any Kol Yisrael network during the day which referred to Israeli successes in the air or, for that matter, on the ground. The report was correct but its broadcast was a slipup. The dimensions of the Israeli victory were becoming apparent at General Staff headquarters, but it was important that it be kept cloaked for a while. If it were realized by the world at large, the Arabs and their friends would be certain to move for a swift cease-fire resolution in the United Nations.

This was the third war in which Israel was fighting against a deadline to be determined not by military considerations but by the action of diplomats at the United Nations on the other side of the world. Until the outcome of the vital opening battles had been decided conclusively, the Israelis would not talk about their victories—even if this meant keeping their own people in the dark as to whether or not the nation would survive. Meanwhile, the Egyptians could be relied upon to proclaim the triumph of their armies. Although one of the afternoon papers printed the report it had picked up from the 9:15 bulletin on the Arabic network, the unconfirmed claim remained a rumor.

Esther Zellinger had been getting her two children ready for school when the siren sounded. The children said they heard an alarm, but Esther dismissed it as a neighbor's teakettle and sent them on their way. Not until she left the house later in the morning and saw a column of soldiers move by in battle dress did she realize the war had begun.

A slightly built divorcee in her early thirties, Esther was the only female to hold the Ziyon Leshabach (Tsalash) medal for gallantry. She had won it during the Sinai campaign when she was an army nurse stationed at a Negev air base. A plane carrying ammunition had crashed, and Esther ran into the burning craft to drag out the pilot and navigator. The Italian-born woman had recently given up her job as a driver-nurse with Magen David Adom to take a tourist guide's course. During the crisis, however, she had volunteered to give first-aid courses in government offices.

Esther walked to her children's school and found them in the basement shelter. Assured that the teachers would remain with the children until the danger was over, she hitchhiked to Magen David Adom headquarters, where she collected the keys to an ambulance and two pillows which would allow her to sit high enough to see over the steering wheel.

While the soldiers along the line warily eyed the Jordanian positions from blockhouses and trenches, duty brought some civilian Jerusalemites into the open area along the border, sometimes forward of the Israeli lines. Jack Wurmband, foreman of the municipal sand-digging crew, found his men reluctant to move out to the quarry, since the approach was along a kilometer-long track that skirted the border. Wurmband told his men that every sack filled from the sand they dug could save a man's life. At this the crew rode out to resume its digging.

Just north of Mandelbaum Gate a jeep from the Solel Boneh construction company pulled up on the slope directly opposite the main Jordanian positions on this part of the line. Aboard was a compressor with which the workmen intended to dig a trench at the army's request. The burnt-out shell of the jeep was to be noticed later by the Israeli assault troops moving past this very point.

Perhaps the most conspicuous individual along the city line this morning was sixty-four-year-old Shimon Diskin. He was a member of a prominent Jerusalem family whose export-import firm had been one of the largest in the Middle East before the borders with the Arab states were sealed in 1948. He still maintained his office downtown, but, there being little business to warrant his visiting it frequently, he had recently taken a job as foreman with a government company redeveloping an old marketplace in the Hinnom Valley. The site was on the edge of no-man's-land directly beneath the wall of the Old City. The

86

area was so vulnerable to the Arab Legion positions on the wall that Diskin had told his workers on Friday not to come in for the next few days. Diskin himself, however, had left his house according to custom at 6 A.M. and walked down to the valley. He did not hear the sirens when they sounded, and there was no one was strolling through the Hinnom Valley this morning to tell him that the war had started.

At 8:30 A.M. General Odd Bull, commander of the UN Truce Supervision Organization, received a phone call from the Israeli Foreign Ministry at his Government House headquarters, requesting his presence. General Bull asked if 10:30 A.M. would be suitable, but the official on the line said the matter was extremely urgent. The UN officer arrived at the ministry at 9 A.M. He was handed a message to King Hussein and the Jordanian government, and asked to transmit it through his office in Amman immediately. The message declared that if Jordan refrained from intervening in the conflict which had broken out between Israel and Egypt, Israel would take no warlike steps against her. If Jordan did intervene, Israel would fight with all the means at its disposal.

General Bull hurried back to Government House. By 10:30 A.M. the message was in King Hussein's hands across the Jordan Valley.

Colonel Amitai's first act upon learning of the fighting in the south was to order the immediate mobilization of the two second-line battalions that he had released Thursday. At 10 A.M. an announcer on Kol Yisrael recited a list of code names, beginning with "Lovers of Zion." Around the city hundreds of men and women dropped what they were doing and headed for assembly points.

Nina Alkalai, a blond immigrant from Yugoslavia, heard her unit's code name in the shelter of the Geulim School, where she was a sixth-grade teacher. Her first concern was her clothing. She did not want to return home for her uniform, and her schoolteacher's dress did not seem suitable for a military campaign. Two girls from the eighth grade ran to their homes nearby and returned with a khaki blouse and khaki slacks. The girls' clothing fitted Nina perfectly. She boarded a bus, one of the few still running, and headed for Schneller.

Meyer Aranowsky, a lawyer in the Justice Ministry, had thumbed a lift downtown shortly before 10, buses in his neighborhood having disappeared completely this morning. Despite the sirens he intended to go to work, but he had taken the precaution of carrying a transistor radio with him. As he stepped into the ministry building, the radio at his ear, he heard his unit's code name. He pivoted back to the street and hitchhiked home for his kit bag. A religious man, Meyer added a prayer shawl and phylacteries to the socks, soap, and razor blades. His wife insisted on accompanying him partway to Allenby Barracks—his unit's assembly point—and the couple went out to the main road for a lift.

Arye Newman had arrived at his desk in the Jewish Agency at 7:30 feeling like a shirker. Although he was forty-three, an ordained rabbi (he had held a pulpit in his native England) and the father of a son serving in the army, Newman was still a member of the Jerusalem Brigade. His unit had been released Thursday, and he found himself now virtually the only male in his office. A secretary didn't help when she said, "Are you still here?" Neither one imagined that the diffident, bespectacled rabbi would be spending the night under a canopy of Jordanian machine-gun fire in a position forward of the main Israeli defense line. When he heard his code, he gratefully got into his car and drove to Allenby Barracks.

The news of the outbreak of war did not reach many of the soldiers manning the city line till well after the civilians knew about it. Private Kogut, a cheerful Brazilian immigrant who worked in the Foreign Ministry, had slept almost until 10. He had worked late the night before filling sandbags and dragging them up to his gun position on the roof of an apartment building overlooking Mandelbaum Gate. The soldier manning the post with him, an immigrant from France, went down to buy milk at the neighborhood grocery store in the morning. "I've got bad news," he said in this thick Gallic accent when he returned. "The war has started." Kogut knocked on one of the apartment doors and asked if he could listen to the radio. He heard the unit code names being read and began helping the residents down to the shelter.

Lieutenant Genzel, commander of the main blockhouse near Mandelbaum Gate, had gotten on his Vespa in the morning and driven to a hardware store to purchase nails. He wanted to build a machine-gun mount at one of the windows and knew it would be a lot simpler to buy the materials and build it himself, rather than putting in a request through channels. As he walked into the store, he heard the news bulletin. Without waiting for the nails, he climbed back on his Vespa and rode back to his men.

At the Pagi blockhouse opposite Ammunition Hill, one of the soldiers who had stepped outside got the word from a passing policeman. The march music the men heard when they switched on their radio confirmed the report. Corporal Salmi, the mortar observer, still thought it unlikely that anything would happen in Jerusalem. It was his turn to prepare the food that day, and he set about making a salad of tomatoes, cucumber, pepper, onion, and oil.

The northern half of the line, a two-kilometer stretch from Pagi to Notre Dame, was manned by a single company of first-line troops. The battalion of second-line troops that had been encamped near the university had been scheduled to relieve them this morning. The outbreak of war now lent the takeover a sudden urgency. About 10 A.M. the battalion boarded buses and moved up to the line.

Chaim Guri's company taking over at Pagi debarked on Shmuel Hanavi Street. Residents of the local *shikun* rushed to the men with buckets of hot coffee and loaf sugar. As soon as they had drunk their coffee, the troops moved swiftly across open ground and filed into the empty trenches alongside the Pagi blockhouse. Acting Gunnery Sergeant Mike Ronen made a quick tour of the trench with Guri and found it more suited for a mass grave than a defensive position. The trench was only about four feet high and had no bunkers or head cover. Worse still, it was situated for the most part behind the crest of the slope, offering the men little view of the enemy positions or the section of no-man's-land they were supposedly covering.

Ronen, a spade-bearded newspaperman who had served as an officer with the Australian Army, was annoyed to see that the men in the blockhouse had managed to put pinups on the walls, while no work had been done to improve the trench outside. If the Arabs attacked, Ronen reckoned, they would come out of the dead ground behind a knoll to the left. He set up a .30-caliber Browning at that end.

A mile to the south a platoon from another second-line company also found itself taking over an unprepared position when it moved into the two-story building at Mandelbaum Gate which served as a customs post. A police detail was still on duty when the soldiers arrived at 10:30.

The platoon commander immediately set his men to fortifying the upper story, which had been sealed off years before. A team was set to work reopening the internal staircase linking the two floors. Sandbags were filled in the back yard and stacked in window firing positions. One team smashed holes in the walls of the rooms to permit quick access from one end of the building to the other. Downstairs, in the tourist reception hall, glass windows were removed and furniture piled against the doors. Behind the building a detail began clearing debris and vegetation from the clogged communication trench leading to the rear.

The activity along the city line was not all on the Israeli side. Shortly after the sound of the sirens from Jewish Jerusalem drifted across no-man's-land, Jordanian police and Legionnaires began clearing people from the border areas. From the Musrara blockhouse Lieutenant Chesin had seen a minibus unload tourists the day before at a Jordanian hotel up the street. The tourists now hurried out of the hotel with their bags and drove off. At the American Colony Hotel on the Jordanian side of no-man's-land, a site which would figure in the coming battle, all twenty foreign guests checked out within two hours after hearing the Israeli sirens, most of them going to Amman. One of the first to leave town, after hastily checking out of the Ambassador Hotel, was Palestinian leader Ahmed Shukeiry, who for the past three days had been whipping the crowds into war hysteria.

From the Abu Tor lookout post, Gershon Mack saw buses filled with soldiers roll into the Arab half of the village just below him. Loudspeakers blared, and one of the men in the blockhouse who spoke Arabic translated the message as "The war has begun. Now we're going to finish the game." Across the valley at Azariya, sheep were being driven back in from the fields.

The deputy commander of the Jerusalem Brigade mounted the roof of the Notre Dame position for a look at the other side of the line. A Jordanian army car with a blaring loudspeaker appeared at Damascus Gate, the principal entry into the walled city. People began to scatter, vendors pushing their carts in front of them as they ran. In minutes the gateway was deserted. Legionnaires could be seen moving into positions facing the Israeli lines. They had replaced their cloth headdresses with helmets. In the distance a few shots were heard. The men on the Notre Dame roof put on their own helmets and picked up their weapons.

At the main blockhouse near Mandelbaum Gate, Lieutenant Genzel was preparing to turn over the position to the platoon of second-line troops waiting on the first floor when he glanced out an upstairs firing hole. His shout brought his men running to their posts. At the YMCA Building, the construction workers had begun to descend the scaffolding.

91

## 6   WAR

Shooting broke out about 10:15 A.M. from Jordanian positions at the southern end of the city line, a single rifle shot followed quickly by automatic fire. The sound did not carry far, and for an hour soldiers and civilians in the rest of the city went about their tasks unaware that the war had already come to Jerusalem.

At Mixed Armistice Commission headquarters near Mandelbaum Gate, Colonel Stanaway had summoned his forty truce observers by radio after learning of the fighting in the south of the country. The meeting had just started, Stanaway telling his men that war looked imminent on the Jordanian front, when a Bren gun opened up from an Arab Legion position fifty meters away. Stanaway looked at his watch. It was 11:22. The firing was coming from the same position which had fired at the Bait Yisrael trench a few days before. Stanaway got the Jordanian liaison officer on the phone and told him that the Bren gunner was at it again. The Jordanian said he'd see what he could do. Within moments, however, the sound of the Bren was lost in a clatter of light weaponry spreading all along the line. Stanaway ordered his men to the basement.

The second-line troops who had just arrived on the line and the first-line troops they had come to relieve were mixed together in the Israeli positions when the fire hit.

At the Pagi blockhouse Corporal Salmi had taken the mortar observer who was replacing him up to the roof to point out the Jordanian positions on Ammunition Hill when a bullet hit the sacks on the parapet directly between their heads, spraying them with sand. It seemed to be just a trigger-happy sniper, but the

93

two Israelis had no sooner descended than they heard machine guns open up. Salmi climbed back through the trapdoor to the roof, this time to open radio contact with the mortar battery. Before he could call in his first round, a recoilless rifle shell exploded against the parapet, sending him crashing through the trapdoor to the floor of the blockhouse, his arm almost torn from his shoulder.

Outside the building Mike Ronen had found some thick wooden boards and was dragging them over the trench to serve as headcover when a machine gun from Ammunition Hill opened up, sending him diving for cover. The men in the trench laughed at what they assumed to be the Jordanians' nervousness. Within minutes the laughter turned to terror as mortar shells began to scream down on the position. A shell from a recoilless rifle exploded in one of the angles of the trench which happened to be empty. The blockhouse, considered to be too vulnerable, was evacuated. Salmi was carried into the trench and laid on a blanket. The siting of the trench offered the Israelis virtually no opportunity to answer the enemy fire, which was cutting the grass about them. It was clear to Mike that if an attack came they would have to move out of the trench to meet it. He had only fifty bullets and put his submachine gun on single-shot.

At the opposite end of the line, the four soldiers manning the observation post at kibbutz Ramat Rachel likewise prepared to meet an enemy attack. As far as the corporal and three privates could tell, they were the only soldiers guarding the southern approach to Jerusalem. They had been on the roof of the kibbutz dining room when fire opened from the Jordanian bunkers buried in the hillside below Mar Elias Monastery opposite. The four descended into the weed-grown trench girding the kibbutz, a remnant of the battles during the War of Independence, when the kibbutz changed hands seven times. The trench dominated the wadi separating the kibbutz from the monastery, and the quartet felt that they could hold off a company.

In Notre Dame it had been quiet—until a girl soldier accompanying a supply officer on his rounds asked if she could have a look at the Old City wall across the road. The firing slits in the room were covered by metal flaps. Happy to oblige a pretty girl, a soldier began to slide a flap open when a bullet ricocheted off it. On the roof the commander of the Notre Dame position, a bearded yeshiva student, suggested to Colonel Amitai's deputy that they move back from the sandbagged position at the edge, from which they had been observing the Jordanians taking up positions. As soon as they had moved back, a shell slammed into the sandbags. All men on the exposed roof were ordered below.

At the Mandelbaum customs house an Italian television crew which had come down to do a film on war preparations found more news than it had bargained for. The Italians were standing at the entrance interviewing the platoon commander—a Jew of Italian heritage—whose men had just taken over the building, when machine-gun bullets kicked up dirt a few yards from them. They made it safely inside the building.

After some initial hesitation due to uncertainty at headquarters as to whether the Jordanians were serious, the order was passed to all positions to return fire. Some soldiers on the line, sufficiently convinced by the opening salvos that the Jordanians were serious enough, opened up without waiting for orders.

Commanding the downstairs floor at Notre Dame was Sergeant Shai, the newlywed who had stayed up two weeks before listening to his neighbors get their mobilization orders. The building's thick walls were shaking from the intense Jordanian fire. Shai picked up a bazooka and ran from firing hole to firing hole, putting shells into the Arab Legion positions atop the Old City wall. His shots sent stones flying off the top of New Gate, where the Legionnaires had set up a light machine gun. Shai was leaning against the wall for a moment when a Jordanian shell exploded on its exterior. The shell could not penetrate the stone, but the impact knocked Shai off the wooden firing platform onto the concrete floor.

In the neighboring blockhouse in Musrara, Lieutenant Chesin was told by headquarters that they could not understand him when he shouted into the phone. Forcing himself to speak slowly, Chesin repeated that the Jordanians were firing on his position. He was ordered to answer them. The lieutenant yelled at the men nearby to open fire. He repeated the cry at the top of his voice as he ran from room to room—"Fire, fire!" In a moment the building was filled with smoke and the crash of battle. Walls shook and Chesin felt the fear of death. A door next to him was suddenly blown outwards, and he thought the room behind it had received a direct hit. It was filled with smoke when he entered; three men ran out coughing. The smoke, however, was not from an enemy shell but from the backblast of an Israeli bazooka.

Unleashing the pent-up hostilities of two decades, the two sides hammered at each other with everything at hand, often at point-blank range. Two bazooka shells exploded inside the main Israeli blockhouse on Abu Tor, but miraculously no one was hurt. In a Mount Zion blockhouse a machine gunner poised behind his weapon as the firing slit in front of him was opened. Before he could fire, a Jordanian bullet came in through the hole and passed through his hand and shoulder. At the blockhouse near Mandelbaum Gate, Lieutenant Genzel went to the roof after hearing the first burst of firing and found one of his men wounded. Genzel had so few of his own men in the large blockhouse, half a dozen, that he picked up a bazooka himself and began firing. One of the soldiers, an artist, had his right elbow shattered by a bullet.

The Israelis were soon giving far better than they got. At Abu Tor, Mandelbaum Gate, and other points all along the line they unleashed a secret weapon in the opening moments of the battle. Bazooka shells and even artillery hardly chipped the stone walls of the Arab Legion blockhouses, but the new weapon, which contained a powerful charge, laid them waste with the force of an aerial blockbuster. The device had been developed by a remarkable sixty-two-year-old ordnance officer, Colonel

"L." A veteran of both the Russian Army and the British-led Jewish Legion, he had developed an arsenal of ingenious devices for the Israeli armed forces. (Later that night he would be wounded after activating another of his weapons on the front line.)

At the main Arab position on Abu Tor from which the Legionnaire had gestured to the Israeli soldier to throw an apple the week before, the Israelis now tossed Colonel L's blockhouse-buster, which completely obliterated the top story of the Jordanian post.

Although the new weapon cleared some of the strongest enemy positions, the bulk of the Arab Legion posts had to be dealt with by the soldiers manning the firing holes in the Israeli blockhouses, many of them men in their thirties. To return fire meant to expose themselves to the bullets and bazooka shells which the Jordanians aimed at the apertures.

A thin, bespectacled accountant, Alex Hadari, was the bazookist with a squad occupying a strongpoint on Mount Zion, eighty meters from the southwest corner of the Old City wall. Hearing the sound of firing coming along the city line like the sputter of a fast fuse, he raced up a ladder to the roof in order not to endanger the men in the main room below with his weapon's backblast.

Alex tore off the cloth covering a firing hole and heard the whine of bullets passing through it the wrong way. They were coming from the Arab Legion position at the corner of the wall. Dispensing with a number two man, he loaded his weapon himself and stepped into the opening. The backblast from his shot sent smoke whirling into the room below and echoed through the building. He heard someone shout, "They got Alex." Instinctively, he ran his hands over his body. Finding himself intact, he shouted down through the trapdoor, "Alex is fine." His first shot had missed. Three more times he moved into the opening and fired. Each of these shells exploded inside the Arab Legion position. The Jordanian fire ceased, and Alex decided to save his shells in case the Legionnaires remanned the post.

Perhaps the most enthusiastic warrior on the line was Arye Comay—the rotund, thirty-nine-year-old company philosopher who had insisted on remaining with his first-line unit. Unlike the Pagi trench farther north, the trench at Bait Yisrael where Comay was serving as a machine gunner was well sited for firing across no-man's-land. A pipe propped on two metal legs had been set up at one end of the trench. While the Jordanians concentrated their fire on it, Comay opened fire from the other end, the top of his body exposed. Even as he pulled the trigger he rejoiced at what he would be able to tell his children and grandchildren.

By 11:30 the Jordanians had brought artillery and mortars into play, destroying any chance that the firing might be confined to an exchange of light weapons. The shells reached past the front-line positions and struck targets within the city. One of the first barrages landed squarely on a mortar position behind the former Italian Hospital in Musrara, killing three men and wounding eight. The position was out of sight from the Jordanian sector, but its position was apparently known to Jordanian intelligence.

All military camps in the city were hard hit, particularly Allenby Barracks, the main staging area in the southern part of Jerusalem. The barrage coincided with the arrival there of hundreds of men who had heard their mobilization code on Kol Yisrael. The reservists, many of them still in civilian clothes, dove for cover as the mortar shells struck across the camp and slammed into supply huts. The supply clerks stayed at their suddenly hazardous posts distributing equipment to the men as they arrived.

Meyer Aranowsky, whose wife had hitchhiked partway with him, had taken shelter with two other reservists in a house on Keren Hayesod Street when the vehicle they were in was straddled by shells. The aristocratic-looking lady of the house, the

98

wife of a high government official, left the shelter to bring tea and crackers to her guests from her kitchen. Finishing the snack, Meyer continued on to Allenby on foot. He found the camp under constant fire. The clerk in the supply hut tossed him a uniform, boots, and equipment and said, "Grab it and run." Meyer had a giddy feeling. It was the first time he had ever gotten as much as a shoelace from the army without having to sign for it. He grabbed the pile and ran.

In the Israeli Army supply clerks distribute uniforms and boots with no regard to size, the soldiers swapping among themselves until they have a reasonable fit. But there was nobody around for Meyer to swap with. Crouching outside behind sand-filled barrels which offered protection against shrapnel, he stripped off his civilian clothing and wriggled into the tight-fitting uniform, ducking whenever a shell came close.

Rabbi Arye Newman was also putting on his uniform nearby when a man two meters from him was hit. Newman used his just-issued bandage on the wound and returned to the storeroom for another one. "Did you lose it already?" asked the clerk. "No," said Newman, "used it." The clerk tossed him another.

Lieutenant Colonel Bill, commander of the second-line battalion being mobilized at Allenby, was a veteran of the British Army and his demeanor showed it. While his men hugged the ground behind logs, rocks, and anything else which seemed to offer cover, the colonel strolled through the camp seemingly oblivious to the falling shells, a swagger stick under his arm. "I give him five minutes," said an officer to the man lying next to him. As they watched, shrapnel ripped into the colonel's midsection. He was carried away, bleeding profusely. An order was passed for all men to get out of the camp and take shelter in the stone buildings across the road.

Jerusalem Brigade headquarters was evacuated under heavy shelling to a preplanned site in a school basement deeper in the city. Nina Alkalai, the teacher from Geulim School mobilized two hours before, ran through the compound looking for her

99

unit, a communications company, as shells exploded around her. She reached the communications building and found it wrecked. Desperately seeking shelter, she dashed into a nearby store-house. The place was filled with gasoline drums, and a soldier told her to get out. She found her company preparing to pull out, and grabbing her helmet and Uzi submachine gun, she grate-fully joined the convoy forming up. On the main road past Mount Herzl shells knocked out the truck at the head of the column and two other vehicles.

The smoke beginning to rise from the city alarmed the troops out in the Jerusalem Corridor. Corporal Avneri, a brigade radio-man, saw the dark plumes from his post at Mevasseret Jerusa-lem, a village about four kilometers from the city. He had been sent there to provide communication between brigade head-quarters and the local defense force, composed of the villagers themselves. Shortly before noon a score of gray puffs blossomed on the hillside below Hadassah Hospital. Similar shell bursts were soon visible at Motza, Bait Zayit, and other corridor vil-lages, as the Arab Legion guns methodically zeroed in on targets. Avneri's observation was interrupted when four shells landed behind his building, sending him scrambling for shelter.

The shelling of Hadassah could also be seen from Mount Herzl on the western edge of the city where Private Yussi Goell's battalion was digging in. Goell's wife, Edie, was a nurse at the hospital but he was confident she could take care of herself. Other men in the unit, who lived in the adjacent neighborhood of Kiryat Yovel, watched apprehensively as shells fell among the houses there, few of which had shelters. The soldiers themselves were still not finished digging foxholes when Mount Herzl was hit. The deputy battalion commander standing near the top of the hill was wounded by the first shell. (The attrition rate among top officers of the brigade was to be remarkably high. In the first thirty hours one battalion commander was to be killed and two battalion commanders and a deputy battalion commander were

100

badly wounded.) The men hunched over in their shallow holes and continued to scrape away to make them deeper.

Dan Ben-Dor, a consulting architect to Hadassah, had arrived in the hospital courtyard at 8:30 A.M. to begin removing the twelve Chagall windows. Ben-Dor had served with the British Army in India during World War II, and his quaintness and distracted air were patently British. An amateur ironworker "blessed," as he put it, "with two right hands," he had taken it upon himself to carry out the delicate job of removing the windows. (He was also a sculptor, and in the living room of his home hung a mobile he had constructed entirely of willows. It was, he told visitors, the lightest mobile in the world.)

The putty holding the sections of the windows to the concrete frame had hardened to a rocklike consistency, and Ben-Dor employed a fifteen-pound rotating Carborundum saw normally used for cutting marble. The work was arduous, and when the shells began falling, three hours after his arrival, he had removed only half of one window.

The siren at the hospital sounded and the courtyard, which had been filled with people, instantly cleared. Ben-Dor and the two workmen who had been helping him went inside. After waiting half an hour, it occurred to him that it might be three or four days before the all-clear was sounded. If the windows were to be removed, he decided, it had better be now. He went back outside and found that several shells had hit nearby. Nine of the protective glass shields which had been put up around the Chagall windows were shattered. Six of the windows themselves had been hit. Of the hundreds of tiny glass fragments composing the windows, about thirty had been broken. His two assistants had not returned, so Ben-Dor resumed work by himself in the deserted courtyard.

Inside the hospital, patients were being removed to the safety underground corridors when the shells hit. Nurse Edie Goell, whose husband was watching the bombardment from his foxhole on Mount Herzl, was on the first floor when a shell exploded in an empty room next to her. She was terrified but unhurt. There had been little time to worry about her husband or their three children. She had told the kids—all of them of school age—that if war started she would remain at the hospital. Her only injunction had been for them to get to the nearest shelter and not to wander the streets.

The treasures at the Israel Museum barely escaped the fate of the Chagall windows. The last of the fourteen hundred items on exhibit had just been carried below when the first shell struck. It exploded against one of the window frames in the archaelogical pavillion, sending shrapnel ripping through empty exhibit cases.

The civilians caught along the front line when the firing broke out managed against all odds to get back to safety. Shimon Diskin, the elderly construction foreman, was pouring water on the newly laid cement steps leading down to the bottom of the Hinnom Valley when the Arab Legion guns on the Old City wall opened up. He didn't know whether to run toward Mamilla Road, one hundred meters to his left, or toward Yemin Moshe, twice the distance to his right. Either way he would be like a slow target in a shooting gallery to the Legionnaires above him. Diskin chose Yemin Moshe, perhaps because it was the way he normally went home. The Arabs were firing at the district with rifles and machine guns, but Diskin somehow made it safely to the community shelter.

At the quarry on the northwest edge of town the sand-digging crew found itself pinned down in a crossfire between Israeli and Jordanian positions. For two hours the men hugged the ground until a lull in the firing permitted them to cut across a field to the nearest houses. In Bait Yisrael the Solel Boneh jeep on the front line was hit and set aflame, but the crew managed to crawl up the slope to safety.

Behind the borders, however, civilians began to fall with the first shells. At a small plant near Pagi, a truck was being loaded with the last of the transportable storage tanks ordered by the city Water Department when a shell hit the back of the vehicle, killing one of the plant employees. In the western part of the city a mother running to get her child from school was fatally wounded.

Dr. Henry Schiffman, the chief anesthesiologist at Shaarei Zedek Hospital, had started his workday with a varicose-vein operation on a woman. As the operation was being completed, the surgical team heard explosions outside. The doctors looked at each other over their masks but continued to work. Seconds after the patient was wheeled out, a twenty-one-year-old girl was wheeled in, her right arm shattered. The girl was a secretary in the Foreign Ministry who had been in her home shelter when the phone rang with a summons to her office. As she was preparing to leave her apartment a shell crashed through the window. Her arm had to be amputated. For Dr. Schiffman, an escapee from a German concentration camp, it was to be the beginning of seventy-three continuous hours of operations.

Civilians still abroad were shooed off the streets by helmeted wardens, who had suddenly materialized. In a bank on Ben Yehuda Street the tellers put the money away in safes and came out from behind the counters to listen to transistors with the customers. Near Zion Square the sound of five hundred girls singing in the shelter of a vocational school could be heard clearly through the explosions.

It was still quiet near the Geulim School at 10:50 when Mrs. Ish-Shalom, the principal, received a call from the Education Department. "I have a message," a secretary there said. "Please take it down." An emergency situation would be declared in a few minutes. If there was enough space in the shelter, the children were to stay in school. If not, they were to be sent home in small groups. Mrs. Ish-Shalom had already decided that it was too risky to send the children out.

She was glad of her decision when heavy firing broke out

103

shortly. The school was adjacent to Allenby Barracks, and the firing was intense. Candy and chewing gum were distributed. Some of the younger girls began to weep, and the older girls and teachers took them on their laps. The boys, however, seemed to be glad something was finally happening. They debated whether the explosions were from artillery shells or aerial bombs. One twelve-year-old, an immigrant from Iran, stood against a wall with a prayer book. The boy had no father, and his three brothers were serving in the army. When someone asked if he was praying for his brothers, he said, "I'm praying for all the people."

The northwest corner of the Old City protruded into the heart of Jewish Jerusalem at Allenby Square. Here the Jordanians and Israelis were at such close quarters that echoes off the building walls made it impossible to tell from which direction the firing was coming. This writer, who was visiting the area, was invited to take shelter in a shoe store by the proprietor, a bearded man in a black suit. He was very much at ease despite the furor outside and said he was waiting for things to quiet down a bit before trying to get home to his wife and eleven children. He had been in the country for ten years. When I asked where he had been during World War II he replied Dachau. At the mention of the name his eyes reddened. "We must stop them now," he said, suddenly agitated. "The people want this war. We will fight to the last child."

On an adjacent border street an old woman was trapped on the top floor of a house, the only exit from her apartment being an outdoor stairway directly opposite the Old City wall. Her son, a burly man in his mid-forties, yelled encouragement from the rear of the building in Ladino, the native dialect of many Sephardic Jews. A teen-aged boy scaled a drainpipe to the apartment window with a length of rope the son had given him to lower the old lady out the rear window. But that scheme was wisely abandoned. The son disappeared up the street and returned with two short ladders which he tried to place one on top

Prewar view looking from Israeli Jerusalem toward Old City. Street at left is blocked by a fire wall to prevent pedestrians from being hit by snipers from western edge of Old City wall beyond. In center, slender turret of David's Tower can be seen. Square turret to left marks Jaffa Gate. The city wall ends at right on Israeli-held Mount Zion, dominated by massive bulk of Dormition Church and its bell tower. Hinnom Valley separates Old City from new. Wooded ridge in distance is Jebel Mukaber with its Government House compound. Trees on extreme right of ridge mark training farm.

Ancient Monastery of the Holy Cross in West Jerusalem. Sharing this peaceful vale with it during Six-Day War were batteries of heavy mortars, providing principal support for Israeli troops during battle.

ISRAEL GOVERNMENT PRESS OFF

Col. Motta Gur (bareheaded) confers with officers in Rockefeller Museum courtyard during lull in battle.

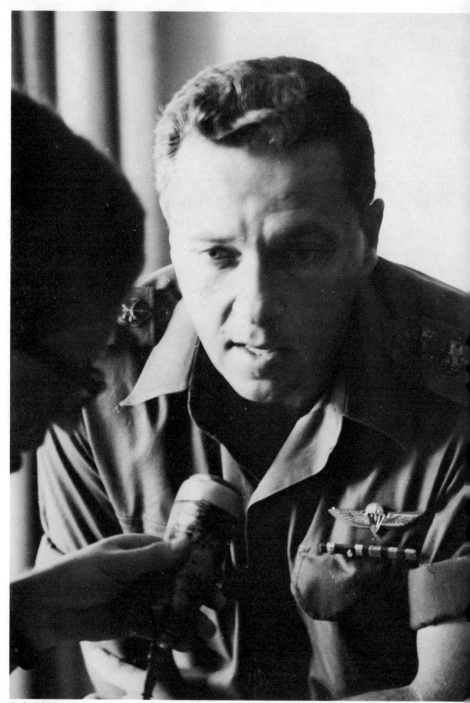

Col. Eliezer Amitai, commander of Jerusalem Brigade.
BAMAHANE

of the other. The trick might have been managed by a good circus team, but the son, despite patient effort, couldn't bring it off. A call was finally placed to Haga, who brought her down with a fire ladder.

A small park nearby was empty of people, but the singing of birds in the trees—gay and persistent—produced a strange counterpoint to the crash of shellfire. Taking shelter in a building facing onto the park, I discovered from a plaque on the wall that I was in City Hall. I asked a guard if Mayor Kollek was in the building and was led to the top floor. I had never met the mayor, but in a moment he appeared at the door to his office and beckoned me inside. Two pretty secretaries and a couple of aides sat in chairs or leaned against desk tops. Kollek seemed weary and wore the resigned look of someone who knew that events were now out of his hands. He spoke easily and with surprising candor. He said the army had informed him of an intercepted conversation between Hussein and Nasser earlier in the morning, in which Nasser asked the Jordanian leader to make a move against Israel to ease the pressure on Egypt. "We didn't know if Hussein would do it," said Kollek.

The phone rang and he spoke into it briefly. "Our first fatality," he said. "A woman. No other details yet. We've got about half a dozen wounded already." Only once did Kollek lapse into officialese: when asked if Jerusalem was prepared to withstand a siege similar to that during the War of Independence, he replied, "We're ready for any contingency."

The beeps of a transistor radio in the next room signaling a news bulletin reached through the partially opened doorway, and Kollek excused himself to lean across his desk and turn on a radio built into a penholder. The mayor was called away briefly, and when he returned he paused at the window. The view was spectacular. Across the breadth of Jerusalem, dirty plumes of shell smoke rose into the air and hung for a moment before disintegrating. Kollek's aides stood alongside and ticked off the places they could recognize being hit. "That one's by Terra

109

Sancta. . . . There's the Kings Hotel." From the great bank of smoke from burning scrub drifting over the Hinnom Valley, it seemed as if the Yemin Moshe quarter had been burned to the ground. The flags of the foreign consulates and embassies flew high through the haze, proclaiming neutrality, but the gesture was futile under the indiscriminate shelling. As Kollek watched, the Jordanian guns seemed to be methodically blowing his city apart. The mayor said he was going down.

Trailed by two aides and myself, Kollek took the lead. He moved close to the wall of City Hall until he reached Allenby Square at its rear. The streets were deserted, and the racket of automatic weapons echoed off the buildings. The Arab Legion positions were less than one hundred meters away, directly behind a former post office, now a tenement, across the square. Israeli troops were presumably stationed in the building, and it seemed likely that the residents were still there too. Kollek moved out at a jog, taking shelter behind some parked cars halfway across until the others had caught up with him, then moving on. Two soldiers were standing behind a concrete fire wall alongside the building. Down the street, past a similar wall, was the Old City's Jaffa Gate. A soldier, addressing Kollek as "Mister Teddy," drew two lines in the dirt with his toe and tapped the second, indicating his position. One hoped that the first line of defense was a bit more formidable.

Inside the building the residents had assembled on the ground floor. They seemed to be bearing up well, considering the circumstances, but were plainly relieved to see Kollek. "What's going to happen?" a woman asked. He assured her it would be all right. "Our fellows are fighting well in the south," he said.

When Kollek mounted to the second floor, a tall sergeant hustled over and warned the visitors to stay away from the windows. The sergeant, a government economist, said his men had just taken over the apartments directly facing the Arab Legion positions on the Old City wall. In one room a soldier with a bazooka stood on a bed, his boots sinking deeply into the once-white bedsheet. He gently nudged aside a window curtain. Forty yards away was a sandbagged position on the wall. As we were leaving the building the *whump* of the bazooka was heard and a gust propelled by the backblast pursued us down the corridor.

At Kol Yisrael the Arabic section addressed itself to Jordan in disappointed tones. "You began the war. We know your air force is mauled. Hussein relied on Nasser, and Nasser is in a very bad position." There was no indication yet, however, that Jordan was seeking anything more than an exchange of fire sufficient to satisfy Hussein's honor.

# 7 COUNTERATTACK

The Jerusalem Brigade Reconnaissance Company had trained until 3 A.M. Sunday night in trench fighting, and the men were still asleep when the sirens went off in the city five hours later. Their camp in the Jerusalem Corridor was too far out to hear them, but Major Yussi heard the sirens as he was driving into Jerusalem to attend the conference at Schneller. He continued on to brigade headquarters, where he telephoned his second in command, Captain Solomon, and ordered him to disperse the unit.

The men, who lay in sleeping bags on the rocky ground around their vehicles, were slow at first to grasp what Solomon was shouting at them. But within five minutes boots were laced, sleeping bags rolled, and the vehicles were moving toward the woods. Nearby, Major Aaron's tanks lumbered out of their shed and took shelter beneath the trees.

At 9:30 the reconnaissance company was ordered into Jerusalem. As the jeeps and half-tracks entered the city, it seemed to many like a restaging of the Independence Day parade of three weeks before—except for the presence in the column of armored vehicles and the virtual absence of men among the hundreds of persons cheering from balconies and sidewalks. Fruit and candy were thrown into the vehicles, and in Ein Kerem a taxi driver thrust a clenched fist forward in a gesture of "go."

Downtown Jerusalem was quiet when the column turned into the Street of the Prophets and entered the compound of the Hadassah School of Physiotherapy. Here, just five hundred yards from Mandelbaum Gate in the center of the city, the company would be in position to respond to any Jordanian thrust along the city line.

The site had been prepared as the unit's forward position during the previous two weeks. The female director of the school had left the key to the main building under a rock in the garden before going home each evening in case the unit had to move in during the night. But the doors were open when the men arrived. As they were lugging in their radios, a medical officer appeared and said that according to the plan he was to set up a field hospital in the building. He was told to use the corridors. The company had hardly settled in when the sound of shooting was heard outside. Within minutes a fifteen-year-old boy was carried into the field hospital with a stomach wound.

Yussi assembled his officers and broke out a map of the Judean Desert. He had received fresh orders at the Schneller conference that morning, he said. In the event war broke out with Jordan —and from the sounds outside it evidently had—he was to be prepared to send a unit across the lines at night to blow up a section of the Jericho road. The object was to delay the arrival in Jerusalem of the Patton tanks near Jericho. Yussi said he would lead the raid himself. They would make their way on foot to the bleak desert hills where the road climbs out of the Jordan Valley. Folding his map, the company commander lay down on the floor. He had gotten only two hours of sleep the night before, but the men were keyed up and their questions made sleep impossible.

Meanwhile, out in the Jerusalem Corridor, Major Aaron, who had been one of the few who believed the Jordanians would attack, had moved his tanks closer to the city. At 10 A.M., even before the firing had broken out, he had jeeped to Schneller and obtained Amitai's consent to an advance to Bait Zayit, about five kilometers from Jerusalem. At the base camp Aaron left behind a few tanks under his second in command, Captain Rafi, in case they were needed in the corridor.

At Bait Zayit Aaron's men spread camouflage netting over the

114

tanks and began digging foxholes. However, the site had been used by an army unit the week before and Jordanian intelligence had evidently marked it, for shells shortly started hitting fifty meters from the tanks. To Aaron the explosions were a signal that the years of waiting were over. He had received no orders from Schneller (radio silence was still being maintained), but he knew clearly what he was going to do. "On the tanks," he shouted. "Follow me."

The rumble of the column as it entered the city brought scores of people out of the shelters despite the shelling. They cheered, but to many the sight of the great clanking machines covered with yellow dust was more menacing than reassuring, hinting at terrible battles to come, very soon and very near. Downtown the column turned into the Russian compound and Aaron dismounted. From police headquarters he telephoned Colonel Amitai and informed him that most of the brigade's tanks were in the city awaiting orders.

At 10:30 A.M. Israeli monitors picked up a bulletin on Radio Cairo reporting the Jordanian capture of Jebel Mukaber in Jerusalem, the Arabic name for the hill on which Government House was located. The report was passed on to Amitai, who queried his battalion commander in the area. The officer, Lieutenant Colonel Asher, was on the neighboring hill of Abu Tor. He reported that he could see no unusual activity at Government House nor had he heard anything from his outposts. He felt the broadcast was probably alluding to the part of the hill the Jordanians had always held. But despite the apparent bogusness of the bulletin—also issued on Radio Amman—the fact that it had been made gave General Narkiss a feeling that the Jordanians might be presenting him with more than an artillery "salute." Something seemed about to happen on the ground.

The UN guard assigned to duty at the east (Jordanian) gate of the Government House compound had grown concerned

115

after hearing the sirens and was granted permission to return to his home in Jordanian Jerusalem to look after his family. At 10:30 his replacement arrived at the gate, a Burmese named U Than Aye. A cheerful bachelor who preferred to be called Charlie, the Burmese could hear the firing break out along the city line, and from his booth he saw the smoke drifting across the Hinnom Valley. Bullets began to hit near him as he sat down to make an entry in the gate log. Hearing the whistle of an incoming shell, he dove under the table. An explosion shattered the windows and covered him with dirt and pieces of wood. Other shells hit deeper within the UN compound. The phone on the table rang, and Charlie reached up for it. The caller was Colonel Johnson, a U.S. Marine serving as deputy to General Bull, the UN's chief representative. "I thought I lost one of my boys," said Johnson who had seen the explosion. The colonel asked Charlie if he had seen any troop movement. The Burmese said he hadn't.

Charlie had risen to his feet and was facing the main building as he talked. When he hung up he turned around and saw 150 armed Arabs coming toward him. They were walking straight up the road, moving very slowly as if after a hard climb. The soldiers gestured at the handful of Israeli planes wheeling overhead and smiled, apparently believing them to be Jordanian. Behind the Legionnaires came a group of unarmed teen-agers wearing white racing shoes and carrying boxes of ammunition.

The guard notified the duty room and stepped out to the red and white pole blocking the road. He confronted the officer at the head of the column and told him he had reached UN territory and could go no farther. The officer, who identified himself as Major Daoud, said that Jordan was at war with Israel. "We're only going to look around for a while," he said.

As Charlie attempted to argue, the Legionnaires flowed around the barrier and entered the compound. When the UN guard returned to the booth and picked up the phone, a Legionnaire entered and grabbed him by his blue scarf. Another soldier

116

pointed his weapon at him, but four Arab border policemen who manned the permanent Jordanian checkpoint opposite the UN booth intervened. The telephone line was cut and Charlie was left alone. It was 11 A.M. The sound of firing was getting louder, and Charlie got back under the table.

Every morning since arriving at the Lonely House on Jebel Mukaber thirteen days before, with his squad and bottle of cognac, Corporal Paz had slipped into his sandals upon rising. This morning, without knowing why, he had pulled on his boots. At 10 A.M. a metallic voice drifted across the valley to them from the loudspeakers in El Aksa Mosque inside the Old City. Such broadcasts by the mosque's preacher were a regular part of Friday services, but this was the first time the men had heard the loudspeakers on a weekday. Private Darzi, who spoke Arabic, went to the window and listened. "This is your day," the preacher was saying. "This is your chance to take back your country stolen by the Jews. Take up your weapons."

When fire broke out along the line Paz's men watched entranced from their windows, which offered the best view in Jerusalem of the war. Paz had orders not to open fire, and besides, there was nothing within range to fire at.

To understand the subsequent events at the Lonely House it is necessary to understand the design of the two-story building, which was built against the slope. The men were gathered on the bottom floor, whose windows faced only two directions— north toward the Old City and west toward Jewish Jerusalem. The Government House compound, just thirty meters to the east, was blocked from view. Only from the upper floor was there a window facing in that direction. There was also a doorway there facing south toward the road which linked Government House with the training farm on the Israeli side of the demilitarized zone. The fact that from the bottom floor they were blind on two sides didn't disturb the men—they were certain the Arabs would not attempt to come through the UN compound.

117

Nevertheless, at 12:15 Paz decided to go up to the second floor and look around. There was no staircase connecting the two floors. Exiting on the side hidden from the UN compound and walking up the hill, Paz entered the second-floor doorway, which was flush with the slope. Casually glancing out the east window, he saw a soldier setting up a machine gun at the edge of the woods inside the UN compound. It was a Legionnaire. Diving for a hole in the floor which provided the only direct link with the men below, Paz yelled down to Private Darzi to notify Schneller that Legionnaires were at Government House. The corporal asked for his Uzi to be handed up through the hole. He was going to get the machine gunner.

Rising from the floor with the weapon, he glanced out the door and halted in his tracks. On the road forty meters away a company of Legionnaires was walking—almost strolling—toward the training farm, guns on shoulders, some of them smoking cigarettes. Paz dove for the hole again. It wasn't a single Legionnaire, he yelled. It was a whole bloody company, and it was moving past them straight toward Jewish Jerusalem. Somewhat skeptical, Darzi decided to look for himself before reporting an invasion. The short, portly private—a motor scooter repairman in civilian life—went outside and looked around the corner of the building. He dashed back to the phone and raised Schneller. The officer on the other end listened to his excited report and told him to hang on.

In a moment another voice came on the line. "This is the Jerusalem commander. What do you see?"

Darzi realized he was speaking directly to Colonel Amitai. "There's a company of Arabs moving past us on the road to the training farm," he said.

The colonel asked his name. Sensing that Amitai was as doubtful as he himself had been, Darzi identified himself and asked if they had permission to leave the building. If there's a company of Legionnaires coming, Amitai said, you can leave.

On the top floor Paz scooped up his maps and weapon and

118

started toward the door, but stopped in the entranceway. Half a dozen Legionnaires had detached themselves from the main column and were coming down the path to the house. Paz ran to the window on the west side and leapt to the ground, ten feet below. One of the men who had exited from the ground floor was caught in the barbed wire near the building, and Paz stopped to free him. The Arabs on the road to their left rear opened fire as they ran, but Darzi, sure that he was a dead man, didn't even bother to duck. The five Israelis headed across the slopes of the demilitarized zone toward the wooden huts of North Talpiot, about a kilometer away. As they broke into the clear, Arab positions in the valley to their right rear opened up on them, and positions on Abu Tor to their right front joined in. Paz was certain the fire was coming from both Arab and Jewish positions on Abu Tor. After forty minutes of crawling through scrub and sprinting across open patches, they reached the huts. Somehow none of them had been hit.

The Legionnaires, meanwhile, had continued on to the training farm. General Narkiss's order on Saturday that troops be stationed at the farm even though it was in the demilitarized zone had not been passed on to Colonel Asher, commanding this section of the line. Upon learning of the outbreak of war at the morning meeting in Schneller, Asher had asked to move troops to the farm. Permission was granted, but by the time the men had gotten under way the road was cut off by fire. The only people at the farm as the Legionnaires approached were five terrified old men and a single resolute woman.

A contingent of foreign students at the university had come to the farm in the morning to help out, as they had for the past fortnight; but with the 8:10 A.M. war bulletin they returned to the campus. In midmorning the farm was visited by Mrs. Rachel Ben-Zvi, the elderly widow of Israel's first president. Mrs. Ben-Zvi had founded the farm in 1927 as an agricultural training school for girls. (It was converted in 1959 to a station for experimental hill farming.) She had come out to see that everything
119

was prepared for an emergency, and it was still quiet at 10:45, when the farm director, Shaul Kaufman, drove her back into the city.

Remaining behind was Kaufman's forty-year-old wife, Rachel, who lived at the farm with him. Their two children had gone off to school, and the only other persons there were five laborers, all over sixty.

Fifteen minutes after her husband left, Mrs. Kaufman heard an explosion. Then another. Stepping outside, she saw that the farm was being shelled and laced with machine-gun fire. She ran back to the office and dialed the emergency number the army had given them. She got a busy signal. Breaking out a cache of old Czech rifles and ammunition, she distributed them to the laborers. None of the five, who were immigrants from Arabic countries, had ever fired a weapon before. Mrs. Kaufman herself had not been in the army, but she had had a military course at a farming settlement during the War of Independence. She quickly showed the men how to load, hold, and fire the rifles. One of the laborers promptly fainted and was carried to the shelter. Mrs. Kaufman gave him first aid and hurried back upstairs. Another man was so frightened he could not hold the rifle. Mrs. Kaufman placed the remaining three at firing holes in two concrete pillboxes that had been built off the main corridor.

From the firing holes the men could see virtually nothing. A line of trees forming a windbreak ten meters in front of the building blocked their view. Even if there were no trees, however, they would have been unable to see the main entrance to the farm, which was to their extreme left. Mrs. Kaufman told one man to go up to the roof and keep an eye on the entrance but he declined. "I'm s-s-scared," he stammered. With no alternative, Mrs. Kaufman left the shelter of the building and scurried up the path to the edge of the windbreak for a look at the surrounding area. Bullets whined overhead and shells exploded within the compound. The flag atop the building was shredded by shrapnel.

120

With the evacuation of the Lonely House—which she knew nothing about—Mrs. Kaufman's irregulars were in front of the entire Israeli Army. The possibility of leaving, however, didn't even suggest itself. Her one crying wish was for the army to come, but until it did she had no intention of abandoning the farm. Mrs. Kaufman had stood up to adversity before. She had grown to be a teen-ager in a Nazi work camp, where she had worked twelve-hour days in an ammunition plant. Her sister died there, and the rest of her family was murdered in other camps. But Rachel held on for three years and she had survived. When Colonel Asher asked her later why she hadn't escaped from the farm when she had the chance, she replied, "For us there's no escaping."

For an hour and a half Mrs. Kaufman continued on her rounds, dialing the army number and getting a busy signal, tending the man in the shelter, encouraging the men at the firing holes, and going outside to scout, despite the enormous risk. At 12:30 she moved out to the windbreak and saw soldiers coming through the trees at the edge of the farm, one hundred meters away. They were Legionnaires. Beyond them others were running on the road from Government House. Mrs. Kaufman dropped to all fours and crawled back to the building. "Start shooting," she shouted. The workmen inside were in no position to see the Arabs, but she felt that their only hope was to let the Jordanians know there were armed men inside the building. Perhaps it would make them pause. As the men opened fire, she ran to the phone but didn't bother again trying the army number. Instead, she dialed 999, the police emergency number, and said, "This is the training farm. The Legionnaires are coming. If you don't get here, we're lost." Before the policeman could reply, an explosion rocked the building and the phone went dead.

Throwing the receiver down, Mrs. Kaufman ran back to the corridor just as five soldiers burst through the rear door. They leveled rifles at a laborer standing at the firing hold directly in front of them. "Are you Arabs or Jews?" one of the soldiers demanded. The soldiers were Israelis, but the man at the firing hole, an immigrant from Syria, was wearing an Arab *khefiya* (a cloth headdress) on his head. Flooded with relief, Mrs. Kaufman asked, "Do we look like Arabs?" The soldier glanced at her as if he had a garrulous woman on his hands and said, "No time for jokes." Stripping off their packs, the soldiers dashed out the door to the windbreak, and in a moment their machine gun was driving the Arabs back to cover.

The soldiers were from a company of academic reserves—Hebrew University students enrolled in an ROTC program—under Asher's command. More men from the company had cut their way through the fence at the rear of the farm and were crossing the courtyard behind the building when a shell exploded in their midst, killing one and wounding two, including a medic. Mrs. Kaufman went out to direct the evacuation of the casualties to the basement. She went down to nurse them, leaving the army to carry on the war.

The news of the Arab seizure of Government House galvanized the Israeli command. The attitude toward Jordan had been gradually shifting since the early hours of the war. The chief concern then had been to keep things as quiet as possible along the Jordanian frontier, while the bulk of the nation's strength was committed in the desert and skies of the south. By late morning, however, indications of amazing success were pouring into central headquarters—two hundred Egyptian aircraft already destroyed, armored forces cracking the forward Egyptian defenses. The need for restraint on the Central Front was being lifted just as the Jordanians opened fire the length of the border, not only at military targets but at population centers. Hussein had chosen to come into the game when the ultimate outcome could already be read in the columns of smoke rising over Egyptian airfields from Sinai to the pyramids.

Narkiss had been pressing the General Staff all morning—

122

futilely—for permission to attack at Latrun and Sheik Abdul Aziz in the Jerusalem Corridor. Now the Arab seizure of Government House pointed the way for the first response.

General Bull's headquarters contacted Israeli liaison officers by telephone and confirmed the Arab Legion takeover, but asked the Israelis to desist from any overt action while they themselves persuaded the Jordanians to leave. The Israelis agreed to Bull's request for a cease-fire, but the Jordanian shelling continued. Shortly after 1 P.M. Colonel Amitai received his orders from Central Front command—counterattack.

Colonel Asher's jeep and radio had been destroyed by shellfire at Abu Tor, so he did not learn of the events at Government House until he had made his way on foot to Allenby Barracks, a kilometer away. He immediately assumed control of the situation with a tenacity which was to earn him the country's highest military decoration, the Tsalash.

Allenby Barracks was situated on the western foot of Jebel Mukaber, but the UN compound and the training farm on the crest could not be seen from the camp. Spreading a map, Asher called down mortar fire on the crest road to clear it of Legionnaires. Then moving up on foot to survey the scene from the training farm, he shifted the fire back into the UN compound itself to hit the Legionnaires who could be seen digging in at the edge of the woods. The brigade commander raised him on the radio and asked what forces he had in hand. Asher said he had one company at the farm and a second on its way. He didn't ask for additional help, but Amitai told him he was getting some— the reconnaissance company and tanks. Asher was told to prepare to drive the Arabs from Government House.

The phone rang at police headquarters in the Russian compound, and the policeman who answered it went out to the tanks parked outside to summon Major Aaron. The caller was Colonel Amitai. He ordered Aaron to move to Allenby Barracks immedi-

123

ately and await further orders. Leaving a few tanks behind with Lieutenant Sassoon as a reserve, Aaron started south with eight. He decided to take the most direct route, moving straight down King David Street even though this meant crossing an open stretch past the King David Hotel in plain view of the Old City wall, five hundred meters away. When he reached the hotel, he halted and ordered all tanks to turn their guns left, where the Old City would appear when they cleared the cover of the building. If they were fired at, he said, they would answer in volleys.

The column moved into the open, and the fire from the wall stuttered—then died at the sudden apparition of the armor.

On reaching Allenby, Aaron saw Corporal Paz, a good friend in civilian life. The corporal and his men, still shaken, related their narrow escape. "Don't worry," said Aaron. "I'm here."

In the previous two weeks Major Yussi had led his men along the city line to study the four points where they were most likely to be called upon to launch counterattacks—the Police Training School, Mandelbaum Gate, Mount Zion, and Ramat Rachel. There was a fifth point where the Arab Legion might conceivably choose to attack—Government House. But since this area had been declared the responsibility of Asher's battalion, the recon men had not even looked it. It was thus with some surprise that Major Yussi heard his orders from a runner arriving from brigade headquarters. He must proceed to Allenby immediately and prepare to drive the Arabs from the UN compound.

Yussi led his column through back streets to avoid the area open to the Old City. At Allenby he conferred briefly with Aaron and discovered that neither had any idea of how they were supposed to carry out the attack. The two majors even asked each other which of them was supposed to command the operation. They had not been told that Colonel Asher and his men were involved.

The order came to move to the farm, and Aaron started his

124

tanks up the road toward the battle that waited at the top of the hill. "We're beginning to make history," he said on the intercom. A calm figure who grew calmer as the point of action neared, he told his men half jokingly that they could sing "Jerusalem of Gold" if they felt like it. As the column reached the high ground, Arab guns opened up from Abu Tor to the left. The tank cannon, already turned in their direction, spoke for the first time in anger, a thunderous volley that silenced the enemy for a few moments.

On the open road ahead a short figure suddenly appeared and flagged the column down. He ran to the rear of the Aaron's tank and picked up the telephone used by people on the ground to talk to the tank commander. "Tank, do you hear me?"

Aaron recognized Asher's voice. "What are you doing here?" asked Aaron.

"I'm commanding the operation," Asher replied.

The road was a magnet for enemy fire, and the battalion commander sheltered himself in the lee of the tank as he spoke. To the considerable annoyance of Aaron, who had been prepared to barrel straight up the road into the UN compound, Asher outlined his battle plan. Five tanks would remain at the farm to provide covering fire. The remaining three would break into the compound and sweep the area between the gate and the radio antenna mast rising from the highest point of the hill. Telling Aaron to pass on the orders to his tanks, Asher dashed back into the farm to flag down Major Yussi, who was just arriving.

The recon commander had brought his men in across the fields at the rear of the farm to avoid exposing the vulnerable jeeps on the fire-swept road. As he paused at the farm entrance to get his bearings, Asher rushed up shouting orders. Yussi found it difficult to grasp what the excited bantam-sized battalion commander was saying.

"Take it easy," said Yussi. "Let's take a minute and get the exact breakdown. Who's doing what?" Apparently thinking

125

Yussi was deliberately stalling, the battalion commander pointed his Uzi at him and said, "If you don't begin moving, I shoot." The flash of anger passed as quickly as it came (Asher was to apologize to Yussi later in the day), and the battalion commander outlined the plan in detail.

Two recon platoons would follow the tanks into the compound on half-tracks. One platoon would seize Government House itself. The second would proceed to the antenna, where it would stand by to descend into "The Sausage," a serpentine Jordanian trench position on the southern slope of the hill just outside the UN compound. Meanwhile, the company of academic reserves at the training farm would enter the compound to clear the woods on the northern side of Government House.

As all units prepared to roll, a terse order came from brigade: Stay where you are. The effect on Asher, Aaron, and Yussi—three aggressive commanders straining to move—was agonizing. The order indicated a hesitation somewhere in the chain of command, perhaps in the government itself, about taking the step that would irrevocably commit the army to all-out battle on the Jordanian front.

Asher ordered the tanks off the exposed road. In turning up the narrow tree-lined path into the training farm, Aaron found himself in a cul-de-sac in which it was impossible to turn the tanks. As he was trying to extricate himself, a new order was flashed from brigade to begin the attack. Aaron clambered out of his tank and climbed aboard his command half-track, which followed directly behind. The half-track cut off the path, knocking down and dragging a tree for one hundred meters before it regained the road. Fortunately, the three rear tanks had not yet turned into the path, and Aaron ordered them to break into the Government House compound. It was 3:15 P.M.

As they approached the entrance archway the commander of the lead tank reported with apparent alarm that the gate was closed. "Are you kidding?" shouted Aaron, who was following the tanks in his half-track. "Go through." The gate splintered as the tank plunged inside, its guns firing. As they drew near the

126

main building, Colonel Asher, riding in Aaron's half-track, spotted three Jordanian jeeps in a driveway. One of them was mounted with a recoilless rifle, a potent antitank weapon. The jeeps had been abandoned by their crews, apparently during the mortar bombardment, but Asher now saw several Legionnaires burst from cover and run toward the vehicles in an attempt to turn the recoilless rifle on the tanks.

The colonel grabbed the half-track's machine gun and set the three jeeps ablaze with one long burst. Unable to swing the weapon sufficiently to bear on the Jordanians, he picked up his Uzi, but before he could fire, a shell burst next to the half-track and shrapnel tore into his right forearm, severing an artery. Blood spurted onto the face of the man alongside him, and when Asher turned to avoid him, he splashed a man on the other side instead. Pinching his arm above the wound with his left hand, Asher stopped the flow, and a soldier applied a tourniquet. For the next ten hours the battalion commander was to stay in action with his arm bent across his chest.

The shell which had wounded him had come from one of several recoilless rifle jeeps on the eastern side of the compound. These were engaged by the tanks and destroyed in a brief exchange of fire. The Shermans continued out past the east gate of the compound and descended toward the Bethlehem–Old City road, one hundred meters beyond.

"Where are you going?" Asher asked Aaron.

"We're going to take the Old City, aren't we?" asked Aaron.

"Let's take this first," replied Asher.

The colonel dismounted from the half-track and ran to the antenna, where there was supposed to be a recon platoon ready to descend into The Sausage. But the area was deserted. Considerably agitated, Asher started back toward the main building to find some troops.

To the men of the reconnaissance company, all the years of training had suddenly become academic. Instead of the usual meticulous planning and map study, Yussi had barely had enough time to issue an improvised attack order on the radio, which some of the officers didn't even hear. Others, unfamiliar with the physical appearance of the target, were not sure what their orders meant. Lieutenant Muni heard Yussi order him to attack the UN building from the right side, but from the training farm, where they were, the building and its approaches could not be seen.

Muni, a student at the university, had walked along the city border from his boyhood and had seen the Old City from a distance in every season and time of day. Now, as his half-track burst into the UN compound, a new panorama opened up before him, stunning in its scope. Drifting shell smoke added to the dreamlike quality of the scene. The men fired over the sides of the vehicle at fleeing groups of Legionnaires, until Muni ordered the driver to join the other half-tracks in firing on Government House itself. The lieutenant assumed that Legionnaires had taken positions inside the building, but there was also an undisguised joy in being able to fire at the white building symbolizing the UN presence. For Muni, the UN represented an arrogant authority that advocated removal of even partial Jewish sovereignty over Jerusalem and turning it into an international city.

Meanwhile, in the main driveway of the building Major Yussi sat in his command half-track, somewhat disconcerted. He had led the way into the compound, planning to join whichever platoon encountered the stiffest resistance. However, instead of one platoon turning behind him into the driveway of the main building, all the half-tracks swept past toward the other end of the compound. Suddenly, a single half-track lumbered up the road behind him, and Yussi flagged it down. The vehicle had fallen behind when it accidentally went off the road approaching the main gate and had to extricate itself. Yussi told its commander, Sergeant Gershon Cohen, a trim former paratrooper, that they were going to take the main building.

The pair ran up the driveway, each followed by five men.

They found the main door locked. At Yussi's instruction, it was blown open. Furniture had been piled against the door, and the men had to climb over it before they reached the main corridor. Here the two squads began working their way in opposite directions, tossing grenades through the transoms of each room, kicking open the door after the explosion, and firing inside.

As Gershon neared the end of the corridor, a door in front of him opened and someone shouted in English, "Don't shoot." The sergeant cautiously glanced in and saw about thirty people sitting on the floor. There were women among them and crying children. Gershon yelled for Yussi. The company commander had had no idea there were UN personnel in the building. He asked the people in the room if there were any Legionnaires in the building. Some said there were no Arabs there. Others said they had been there and left. The Israelis assumed the UN had let the Arab Legion into the compound, and the ambiguous answers to Yussi's question didn't reassure him. Cautioning himself not to be too quick on the trigger, he mounted warily to the third floor, where he found General Bull and his senior staff gathered in General Bull's office.

One of the UN officers asked Yussi why his men had fired so heavily on the building when there were no Arabs inside. Yussi replied that as soldiers they should appreciate the use of firepower in attacking what is presumed to be an enemy-occupied position. Bull said he wanted to get in touch with his headquarters in New York and asked permission to use his radio. Yussi said he must first get instructions from brigade headquarters.

While thus engaged in high diplomacy, Yussi had glanced out the rear window and seen Legionnaires moving through the woods. He ordered Gershon to mount the machine guns from the half-tracks at an upper-story window. The furniture piled against the front door had been set afire by the demolition charge, and Gershon barely succeeded in passing around it as he left the building. By the time he returned with the gun, the fire had spread, blocking passage. Gershon, a physical education instructor in civilian life, clung to the bars on a first-floor window and handed the gun up to soldiers on the second floor. Then, grasping a rain pipe, he shinnied up to the top of the three-story building and swung his body over the projecting edge onto the roof.

From the top of Government House he was in view of hundreds of Israelis and Jordanians arrayed along the city line. The moment he lowered the UN flag, every Arab gun in the vicinity opened up on him. Gershon went flat and crawled to the edge of the roof, where he called down for an Israeli flag. There was none on hand, but Major Aaron volunteered his tank signal flag, which had horizontal white stripes separated by a horizontal blue stripe. It was passed up to Gershon, who raised it on the pole from a prone position.

With smoke spreading through the building from the fire at the door, Yussi returned to the UN personnel on the first floor and asked the ranking UN officer to detail men to put out the blaze. Surveying the assembled personnel again, Yussi saw several who were suspiciously swarthy. He beckoned one forward and addressed him in Arabic. The man replied in English that he was a Greek. Yussi mustered a jovial *"Kalimera* (Good day)."

Another man asked to step forward was Sri Ram, an Indian employee who had been praying to his family deity as the sound of grenades had come closer in the corridor. Ram had not been sure which side was attacking the building. Before noon he had seen an Arab officer and several Legionnaires enter and mount the stairs to the third floor. There had been the sound of angry voices, and a few minutes later the Arabs were being ushered out by Colonel Johnson. Ram was not sure if the soldiers standing in front of him now were Jordanians or Israelis. He had been in the Middle East just a short while and his knowledge of local languages was confined to two words: *"shukran"* and *"shalom,"* the Arabic and Hebrew words respectively for "thank you" and "hello." When the Israelis handed him back his identity card he chose the wrong word. His *"shukran"* visibly startled the

130

Israelis, and Ram edged back into the crowd under the dark stares of the soldiers.

When Yussi spoke to another man in Arabic, he drew a response in the same language. The major asked him to bring the other Arabs. Six Jordanians were soon assembled, all servants at Government House. When Yussi took their identity cards, General Bull approached and said, "These are my people." Yussi assured him they were safe. "Do you think I'm going to kill them?" Bull nevertheless made a point of going up to each of the Jordanians and shaking his hand. Yussi, who had been impressed earlier by Bull's calmness, was impressed still more by this display of loyalty to subordinates. He was less taken by Colonel Johnson, who addressed him as "Hey, Major," a summons Yussi chose to ignore. (Johnson was reported to have summed up Yussi afterwards as "a typical sabra," a designation generally meaning brash.)

At this point an order came through from brigade to evacuate all UN personnel immediately. Yussi told Bull that he and his people had to be out in ten minutes. They could take anything they could carry except material from the radio room. Bull declined Yussi's offer of his personal jeep and said that he would be the last to leave the building. The UN contingent piled into those of their vehicles not disabled by shrapnel and left in convoy for the President Hotel in Jewish Jerusalem.

Stepping onto a balcony at the rear of Government House, Yussi saw men from the Academic Reserves company moving through the woods in pursuit of Legionnaires pulling back. He called his runner, Corporal Zerach Epstein, and told him to go down and inform the commander of the unit where the recon men were deployed in order to avoid any accidental shooting.

With this order Yussi injected into the battle one of the most formidable soldiers to emerge from the Six-Day War. Along with Yussi and half a dozen others, Zerach had been with the company since it was formed twelve years before. He was from an old Jerusalem family, his grandfather having been principal

131

of a yeshiva in the Old City until forced to abandon it during the 1932 Arab riots. A school dropout with a natural gift for whatever he put his hand to—business, card-playing, even poetry—the brawny Zerach had become a successful electrical contractor, and he looked the part of a tough, savvy executive.

He approached war with the same thoroughness as he would a business deal, leaving as little as possible to chance. Although as a runner he was supposed to be issued an Uzi, he provided himself with a rifle instead, feeling that the automatic weapon used up its ammunition too quickly. In addition, he carried a privately owned pistol, a .9-mm. Browning with fourteen bullets. It was specially mounted in a hip holster for a fast draw. (He had forgotten the month before to renew his registration for the pistol and hunting rifles, and the police had come to his house and confiscated them. It was not until the day before the war started that Zerach managed to stop off at police headquarters while driving Yussi to Schneller. After hollering loud enough, he was given the weapons back. He dropped off the rifles at his sister's house but kept the pistol with him.) For ammunition he managed to acquire a supply of tracer bullets, which would permit him to see where his shots were going, and he swiped an extra grenade to supplement the single grenade which had been issued him. In addition to his special armament, he wore crepe-soled boots which would permit him to move silently. All these items were to serve Zerach well this day.

The commander of the Academic Reserves company and five of his men were lying on the ground exchanging fire with Legionnaires in the surrounding woods when Zerach reached him. "Let's go," said the corporal. His orders had been merely to pass on a message but he saw work to be done. The woods were alive with Legionnaires, some firing from cover, some running. The company commander had gotten far ahead of most of his troops, and he sent two men to hurry them forward. Zerach didn't wait. He started forward alone and looked back to see two of the students following. Fire was opened on him from a shallow pit

132

thirty yards ahead. Zerach shouted to the two students to open up with their automatic weapons and keep the Legionnaires' heads down. Swinging wide, Zerach dashed toward the pit from the side and flung in a grenade. When he reached the lip of the depression, he found five dead Legionnaires inside.

The turf suddenly kicked up around him, and he dove into the pit atop the bodies. Peering over the top, he saw that the fire was coming from a group of Legionnaires upslope and another group farther away downslope. He yelled at the covering team to pin down the nearest ones. There was no answer, and he looked back to see that the two had disappeared. He was alone except for the better part of an Arab Legion company in the woods around him. Till now Zerach had been proceeding with all the precautions of an old soldier, availing himself of all possible cover. His brother had been commander of an Irgun company in Jerusalem during the War of Independence and had always warned him of the fighting prowess of the Arab Legion. "They're not Egyptians," he had said. But Zerach sensed that the Jordanians on the hill around him were badly frightened. Most were running, and those who were shooting seemed so shaken they couldn't fire with any accuracy. A dozen weapons had already been fired at him and he had not been hit. He began to feel that he *couldn't* be hit.

Climbing out of the pit, he ran straight toward the nearest Legionnaires. At forty yards, three of them rose from prone positions and fired at the rushing figure. Zerach halted, raised his rifle to his shoulder, and knocked them down with three shots.

Jordanian mortars had begun to put smoke shells on the slope, apparently to permit their men to pull back. Zerach found himself wrapped in the drifting white smoke. Sometimes it parted for an instant to reveal running Legionnaires. Zerach moved across the slope, firing into holes and flinging in grenades taken from the bodies of the dead Legionnaires. From one of these holes a broad-shouldered Legionnaire slowly rose and

133

glanced with utter disdain at Zerach, standing ten meters away. The big soldier seemed to be crying. He bent down and lifted a wounded man onto his shoulders. Turning his back deliberately on Zerach, the Arab walked slowly away with his burden. Zerach let him go.

Continuing to the edge of the woods, the Israeli saw a group of Legionnaires emerge from a gap in the smoke a few meters away. They saw Zerach, too, but most seemed intent only on escape. One Legionnaire, however, turned and charged toward him. The soldier, like all Legionnaires, was wearing a dish-shaped British helmet. Most Israelis were equipped with round American-style helmets, but some, including the two students who had been covering him earlier, wore British-style helmets. Not until the Arab was two meters from him was Zerach certain that he was a Legionnaire. The Israeli fired first.

Leaving at least nine dead Legionnaires on the slope behind him, Zerach returned to Government House to rejoin Yussi. But his day had just begun.

Unable to find Yussi, Asher was singlehandedly collecting the forces roaming through the compound. His task was complicated by the fact that he and the recon men were strangers to each other. Near the antenna he stopped a half-track and asked if there was an officer aboard. Lieutenant Muni presented himself. Asher asked him to organize his men in a defense line facing the woods, where the sound of firing could be heard, and to take command of any soldiers he found on the road between the east gate and the main building. Muni posted a squad under Sergeant Sitton opposite the woods and continued up the road.

Sitton, a young lawyer, spotted Legionnaires moving through the trees toward him and ordered his men to open fire. Sitton himself used a two-inch mortar as a direct-fire weapon. One of its shells hit a tree as a Legionnaire passed beneath it. The soldier was decapitated and remained propped against the lower branches. The rest of the Arabs pulled back.

Asher's primary concern was to get troops quickly into The Sausage, south of the compound. The trench position was protected by a heavily mined wadi that would have made any head-on attack costly. The Israelis, however, now found themselves at the position's most vulnerable point: its uphill flank, which drifted off inconclusively near the UN compound. The security of this flank depended on the neutrality of the Government House area, a neutrality which the Jordanians themselves had now breached.

Asher spotted the recon jeep platoons which he had ordered to remain in reserve at the training farm. They had disregarded the order and come into the compound looking for action. Asher promptly steered them to it, ordering a platoon to descend into The Sausage.

The command of the operation fell to Lieutenant Danny Bachrach, an architecture student at the Technion. Danny was a familiar figure around Jerusalem astride his motor scooter, his bushy blond hair askew in the wind. With one of his men— Private Yussi Ochana, a Jerusalem discotheque owner and sometime film actor—Danny cut through the thick fence surrounding the UN compound with pliers. As tanks from the antenna and the training farm pounded the enemy position to keep their heads down, Danny and Ochana ducked through the fence and sprinted downhill to an open bunker. It was 3:30 P.M. They were the first Israelis to cross the Jordanian frontier.

The trenches had not been visible from the top of the hill, but from the open bunker Danny could see them winding down the hill to his left. Yelling to make himself heard against the strong wind, Danny pointed out the direction to a squad headed by Lieutenant Zvika, which had come through the wire upslope. Danny and Ochana cut across to the trenches and met the squad as it descended.

The position, they saw, consisted of two parallel trenches with spurs leading to bunkers. The men entered the main trench and began employing the tactics they had been practicing just twelve

135

hours before in the night training exercise in the Jerusalem Corridor. Two men, known as trackers, moved at the head of the line, the lead man firing his Uzi around the bends of the trench. When his magazine was emptied, he yelled, "Magazine" and pressed himself against the side of the trench to reload while the second man passed to the front. Danny moved behind these two point men ticking off soldiers into the spurs. Zvika started up one toward the bunker at its end, but dashed back in a moment to the main trench yelling, "Grenade." There was an explosion, and Danny leaned to his left into the spur opening to see a Legionnaire charging toward them a few meters away. Danny's rifle was on his right side, and in the instant it would take to shift it and aim the Arab would be upon them. He yelled, "Zvika," and the lieutenant, who was on the other side of the spur entrance, stepped out into the opening and brought the Legionnaire down with an Uzi burst as the Arab plunged through the smoke of his own grenade.

Uphill, Asher was feeding men into the trenches as fast as he could round them up. Lieutenant Tsubai had never seen Asher before and disregarded his instructions, saying he would take orders only from his company commander. It took the intervention of Captain Solomon to get Tsubai to descend into the secondary trench, which he swept clear of Legionnaires with his platoon. Solomon himself entered the main trench with a few men, clearing the bunkers Danny's men had passed by. In one bunker he came upon an Arab who had just pulled the pin on a grenade. The officer pinned the Jordanian's arms and wrested the grenade from his grip. He handed it to one of his men to use, their own supply being nearly exhausted. (The husky Solomon had once captured a Syrian infantryman during a retaliation raid in the same manner, pouncing on him with his bare hands.)

Three men exploring one of the spurs came up behind two Legionnaires staring across the wadi toward Jewish Jerusalem. Dropping grenades on them, the trio continued downslope and

136

found five more Legionnaires with their backs to the main trench looking toward Jewish Jerusalem. The Arabs had been close enough to hear the grenades that had just killed their two comrades, but they seemed to have paid no attention. The Israelis flung concussion grenades and rushed the trench, killing all five before they could fire.

Whether they were stunned by the suddenness of the attack or whether they were just poorly trained troops, the Legionnaires in The Sausage died without making any coordinated fight. Instead of forming a line across the hill to meet the descending Israelis, the two platoons in the position had remained in their separate bunkers facing the wrong way. The absence of leadership was notable. Only one officer was found, a major lying wounded at the bottom of the position. If there had been any others, they were among those who had managed to escape. When the fighting was over, thirty Legionnaires lay dead in the trenches. About as many had fled. The Israelis, who carried out most of the battle with eighteen men, suffered one wounded, no dead. Another forty Legionnaires had been killed in the UN compound.

Colonel Amitai's intention was not merely to defeat the Arab Legion but to destroy its reputation. He wanted immediate and decisive confrontations which would finally eliminate the sheen of invincibility that the legion had won against the fledgling Israeli Army in 1948. Beyond encouraging his own men, he felt, such victories might spur the High Command to pursue the battle against the legion to its final conclusion. He did not know that the decision had already been made. His request to advance on the village of Sur Bahir, one kilometer south of Government House, was quickly granted. The brigade commander had ordered the battalion at Mount Herzl to move to Ramat Rachel, directly opposite Sur Bahir, but when it was held up by fire he decided to utilize the force already at Government House.

*  *  *

Charlie, the Burmese UN guard, had remained beneath the table at the east gate booth since he had tried to stop the Arab Legion from entering. At 3 P.M. he looked out and saw a Jordanian armored vehicle and jeeps crashing through the barrier into the compound. Shortly afterwards he heard the sound of men running out the gate. He continued to make entries in his log in the belief that he might not survive to give a verbal report. Hearing the sound of many armored vehicles nearby, he stepped out and saw—to his astonishment—Israeli half-tracks. One stopped nearby, and a soldier motioned him aboard. "So you're the one who let the Arabs in," said one soldier in what Charlie hoped was good humor.

"You ought to thank me for letting them out," he said.

The Burmese was deposited at the main building. Finding all the UN personnel gone, he went down to the shelter to spend the night, the last symbol of the UN presence remaining at Government House.

Shells were falling nearby when Asher and Yussi sat down beneath a tree near the antenna to discuss the attack on Sur Bahir. Asher suggested moving to somewhere more sheltered, but Yussi glanced at the shells bursting across the length of the compound and asked, "Where?" In his prewar planning Asher had estimated that two companies would be needed in any attack on Sur Bahir, with a third company in reserve. Now he would have to send whatever recon men he could scrape together, about half a company. But by moving down the Jordanian road to Bethlehem they would be able to attack the fortified village from the rear.

One of the armored buses normally used on the Scopus convoy run entered the compound, after running a gantlet of fire on the open road with a much-needed supply of ammunition. At 6:30 P.M., a quarter hour before sunset, the attack force moved out. Three tanks rode in front, two more behind. At the first sharp turn in the road, the column was halted by a roadblock

138

—two cars drawn across the road. In a small cave on the right several Arabs were huddled, apparently the occupants of the vehicles requisitioned by the Arab Legion. In his command half-track Aaron waggled an admonishing finger at them and ordered his lead tank to roll over the cars.

The war, however, was still young and not everybody had yet adjusted to its brutalities. Crashing through a United Nations gate and rolling over gleaming new cars was something they had never been trained to do. The tank commander hesitated before plowing his Sherman into the cars to a sound of cracking eggs and the sudden whiff of gasoline. The second tank, meanwhile, had begun to swing left around the roadblock. The shoulder was narrow with an almost sheer drop of thirty meters beyond it. When Aaron saw the tank swinging wide, he shouted, "Don't!" But it was too late. The tank teetered at the edge and fell into the wadi, injuring all its crewmen, one of them fatally. With a vengeance, the rest of the column passed across the hulks of the automobiles.

It was dusk when the column approached Sur Bahir, all the vehicles' guns firing in a broadside which deafened the men in the half-tracks. The fortified position known as "The Bell" lay on the other side of the village, the side facing Ramat Rachel, whose fields came virtually up to the bunkers. Yussi knew that it consisted of a trench system and a main bunker whose high, pinched shape gave the position its name. But again there was no time for map study or for any plan except to move in fast. A half-track broke down, blocking the bulk of the column on a narrow village road. Unaware of the mishap, the two reconnaissance half-tracks up front—Yussi's and Muni's—and Aaron's command half-track continued forward behind the two lead tanks. Reaching the far edge of the village, one of the tanks bulled its way through a stone house and opened fire on the fortified position just beyond.

As at Government House, Yussi did not attempt to coordinate the company's movements. An officer, he felt, must first of

139

all prove himself to his men. Only after they had been fighting together for some time should he concern himself with coordination. As soon as the lead half-track halted, Yussi leapt out and ran to the nearest trench, yelling for the others to follow. He moved forward alone and soon found himself discarding the basic rules of trench fighting that he and his men had been training in for years. The practice of the point man's throwing out a steady stream of fire was based on the assumption that the fighting would be done at night, when such a tactic would eliminate any enemy waiting in the darkness ahead. As long as there was light, however, he could see what lay ahead. Random firing merely alerted the enemy and wasted ammunition.

Yussi's newly adopted tactic paid off as he moved silently around the very first bend. Two feet in front of him stood a Legionnaire staring in the direction of Ramat Rachel. Yussi pressed his Uzi against the Arab's back, grabbed his rifle, and said, "Hands up." Sending the prisoner back with one of his men, he continued on. When the maze of trenches seemed to be carrying him no closer to the central bunker, he climbed out and ran across the open ground to another trench, killing two Legionnaires inside before leaping in. A tank came up and hit the main bunker with a shell. Yussi and another soldier ran forward and dropped grenades through the bunker's firing holes.

The only men to have come up behind Yussi were those from his half-track and some from Lieutenant Muni's, the rest of the force still being stuck in the village. Darkness was closing in fast, and the major ordered Muni to clear the right side of the position. As the lieutenant and his men moved down the trench, a shout in Arabic came from one of the bunkers ahead: *"Min-hada* ? (Who's there?)."* After a grenade was tossed inside, Muni entered. Despite the darkness and the dust from the explosion, he could see that the bunker was L-shaped. There was nobody in his arm of the L. Holding his Uzi in one hand like a pistol, he leapt across to the bend and fired in an upward arc into the other arm. Something heavy fell to the ground. Muni reached

140

forward and touched the hot barrel of a rifle. A dead Legionnaire lay beside it.

The center and right side of the position had now been cleared, but Colonel Asher, who had remained aboard Aaron's command half-track at the edge of the fortified position, saw three Arabs moving in his direction down one of the two trenches on the left. He fired a burst at them from the vehicle's machine gun with his left hand (his right arm, wounded at Government House, was now in a sling). The battalion commander fed four men into the trench, running along the top as they moved below. Grenade fragments ripped into his one good hand, but he didn't pause to bandage it. The men below pursued and killed all three Arabs.

Meanwhile, Zerach Epstein and Private Steiff entered the other trench on the left, a heavily bunkered one which covered the position's southern flank. Zerach looked into the first bunker and saw that it had more than one room. He set down his rifle, too unwieldy for these close quarters, and drew his pistol. Entering silently on his crepe-soled boots, he turned the far corner and saw two Arabs firing through the firing slit. They had evidently heard the shooting outside and did not imagine that the enemy was behind them inside the position. Zerach shot them dead. At the next bunker he threw in a grenade and entered, to find three dead. It was his last grenade, and he took some from the dead Legionnaires. As he approached the third bunker, two Legionnaires started to come out the entranceway, apparently alerted by the grenade explosion. Zerach had a grenade in his right hand instead of his rifle, but Private Steiff pegged a shot that drove the Arabs back into the bunker. Zerach tossed in the grenade after them. Reaching the end of the trench, he found a bunker wall. Climbing over the top, he saw a low opening into which he rolled a grenade. Two fatally injured men crawled out. Looking through the firing hole, Zerach saw two more men lying motionless in the light of flames kindled by the grenade. Steiff, meanwhile, cleared another bunker Zerach had missed.

141

Looking south beyond the barbed wire of the position, the pair saw groups of Legionnaires downslope about 150 meters away, fleeing in the direction of the village. There were about thirty in all, and they had evidently slipped out of the position through a tunnel or a hole in the fence. The two Israelis fired at them as they went by in the dusk, but it was impossible to tell if they hit any. Although Zerach was in the habit of counting his shots in order to know how many bullets he had left in his magazine, he lost track in the hasty firing.

Starting back down the trench they had cleared, the pair almost bumped into two Legionnaire sergeants coming around a bend. There was no time to wonder where they had come from. Zerach squeezed off a shot and saw his tracer go between them. He squeezed the trigger again, and this time nothing happened. His magazine was empty. Steiff was behind him and could not fire without the danger of hitting Zerach. Dropping his rifle, Zerach drew his pistol and killed both Legionnaires before they could fire. They were the twelfth and thirteenth men he had killed in the trench. They were not to be his last victims. Before the day was done he was to have a hand in killing at least twenty-seven Legionnaires at Government House and Sur Bahir—about one-third the total killed in the two battles. For his exploits he was to be decorated with the Tsalash. (In addition to him and Asher, eight paratroopers were to win the award from the chief of staff in the Jerusalem battle. In all, fifty-one such Tsalashim would be awarded in the Six-Day War, twenty-one of them posthumously.)

Silence descended now on the position as the men began assembling near the main bunker. One of them reported to Yussi that he had seen an Israeli helmet lying in a trench outside a bunker. The soldier guided the company commander to the spot. A body blocked the bunker entrance and Yussi, risking a match, saw that it was one of his men, Sergeant Joshua Walzer. He was the company's first fatality. Opposite him lay a dead

142

...unteers, including yeshiva students, digging trenches in Jerusalem's rocky soil a few days before ... Trenches were to serve housing developments such as one in background, which had been built ...out shelters.

Apartment in West Jerusalem holed by shell. One thousand apartments on Israeli side of city w[ere] damaged by intensive Jordanian shellfire, three times as many as were damaged in Jordan[ian] Jerusalem by heavy fighting there.
BAMAHANE

school youngsters fill paper sacks with sand on eve of war.
SSAH HOSPITAL

Col. Uri Ben-Ari (left), commander of Harel Brigade, prepares to set off on reconnaissance in helicopter during battle.

Legionnaire. Yussi returned to the main bunker and sent two men to retrieve Walzer's body. (Walzer had been born into war in Belgium as the Germans were overrunning the country in 1940. After his father was seized by the Nazis, his mother placed Joshua, his eleven-year-old sister, and his nine-year-old brother with a Christian family. The children, who were never to see their parents again, hid for two years in a windowless basement. After the war they lived together as a family unit in their own apartment, the sister working to support them. In 1949 they decided to go to Israel. Joshua was persuaded to enter a youth village, where he proved to be an extremely able student. Just before the outbreak of the Six-Day War he had completed his studies for a masters degree in physics at Hebrew University. The degree would be awarded him posthumously.)

The officers and a few of the men stood on the slope of the bunker and stared into the darkness toward Ramat Rachel, two hundred yards away from where an infantry company was to open a way through the minefield and relieve them. By radio, the force at Ramat Rachel asked the men on The Bell to indicate their position with a light. Asher produced a pocket flashlight, and one of the men stood atop the bunker swinging it in slow circles.

Suddenly there was shooting near at hand from the direction in which the two men had gone to carry back Walzer's body. The outline of several soldiers could be made out in a shallow bowl about four meters from The Bell. Asher thought they were from the relief company and yelled, "Stop firing." In reply came a shout in Arabic: *"Alehum* (At them)," followed by a burst of fire. Asher was desperately trying to move his Uzi off safety with his freshly wounded left hand when he was hit and knocked backwards. The mortar observer standing at his left fell dead with a bullet in his head. Another soldier was fatally shot, and a tank officer who had come forward with Major Aaron was hit in the eye. The five Israelis remaining on their feet opened up on the Legionnaires lined up against them, the two rows of men

147

firing at each other at point-blank range. Zerach had been the first to react, emptying his rifle at the muzzle flashes below. Yussi joined in, and Aaron picked up Asher's weapon. When the shooting stopped, the Israelis descended into the bowl and found the bodies of five Legionnaires. Beyond them in the trench were the bodies of the two recon men who had gone to bring back Walzer's body.

Yussi had only ten soldiers left with him. They were out of grenades and virtually out of ammunition. Around them was a catacomb of unexplored caves, and it was likely that there were other Arabs at large. The two lead tanks were ordered forward to the center of the position, and the men formed a tight defensive perimeter around them, the wounded lying in the middle. When men from the rear of the column finally joined them, Yussi's force numbered thirty. They had three hours to wait before the minefield was breached and the company from Ramat Rachel crossed to relieve them.

It was close to midnight before Asher's small force started back to Jewish Jerusalem. In two sharp actions they had eliminated the enemy threat in the southern part of the city and demonstrated clearly that the Arab Legion could be defeated. But the men were dispirited rather than triumphant, for on the floor of the half-tracks lay the bodies of four of their comrades. Shortly after the recon company pulled up at the school in Rehavia where they were to bivouac for the night, wives and parents arrived to greet them.

Even though Government House and Ramat Rachel were little more than a mile apart, Colonel Amitai decided to keep a battalion of first-line troops at each location. From his experience with the Arab Legion in 1948 he anticipated a quick counterattack. He would be ready to meet it with decisive strength.

Asher returned to Government House and despite his three wounds organized his battalion in defensive positions. At 1 A.M. —ten hours after the artery in his arm had been cut—he permitted himself to be taken to Hadassah Hospital.

# 8 ARMORED ATTACK

All Monday afternoon Lieutenant Sassoon had sat glumly in the turret of his tank in the Russian compound, where he had been left behind by Major Aaron with a small reserve force. His frustration reached a peak when he heard Aaron on the radio maneuvering the other tanks into battle at Government House.

Sassoon, a lawyer in civilian life, was parked in front of the district court where he was a regular visitor. Early in the afternoon two women came out of the building gingerly carrying cups of tea to the men in the tanks. One of them was a lawyer Sassoon knew. He yelled, "Ruthie," but the woman did not recognize him in his helmet at first. When she did, she climbed on the tank and kissed him.

For four hours after the Jordanians had moved into Government House, news of the seizure was not broadcast by Kol Yisrael. Not until Sassoon's men heard on their tank sets that the Arab Legion had been driven out of the UN compound did their transistors pick up a bulletin on Kol Yisrael reporting the Arab takeover. The announcement made no mention of the successful Israeli counterattack. "Listen to that," said one of Sassoon's crewmen. "The Kol Yisrael studios are just a block away. Let me go over and tell them. What will people think?" Sassoon told the crewman to sit tight. He knew there were others worrying about what people would think.

The radio announcement did indeed cause alarm. At the Water Department, an aide rushed into the deputy manager's office and said, "We're supplying water to Government House. Let's shut it off." The official called army headquarters and asked if the flow should be discontinued. The officer told him

149

to wait a minute. "Don't worry about Government House," he said when he came back, "can you supply Sur Bahir?"

There was no such reassurance to those at the Geulim School, just a thousand yards from Government House. The report of the Arab advance and the heavy sounds of firing outside frightened the students and teachers in the shelter. But there was no panic. Late in the afternoon Nina Alkalai returned. She was the teacher who had gone to Schneller in the morning after hearing her unit code on the radio. Nina brought with her a report she had heard on the army communication net that two hundred enemy planes had been destroyed. The news was greeted with applause and cheers. The children crowded around Nina and demanded to know what it was like outside.

Her unit had come under shelling in the field near Ein Kerem to which it had driven after evacuating Schneller. Although she was in a valley far behind the lines, Nina took shelter under a tree on the principle, vaguely remembered from training, that one should find a place where the enemy can't see him. She sheepishly relinquished the tree when the men in the unit started laughing at her. She disliked wearing her heavy helmet and had been carrying it in her hand but her commander told her to put it on. Nina was the only one of the four girls in the unit to have reported for duty. After a few hours she was told to spend the night at home. She had walked back across the city, passing a building with shell holes directly above and below a friend's apartment.

During the lulls in the shelling, children across the city were being sent home in small groups from school shelters in the care of older students or parents. Their schoolbags dangling on their backs like knapsacks, the children nonchalantly searched the ground for shell fragments on the way and stopped to look at cars pockmarked by shrapnel.

The question of releasing patients from Hadassah Hospital had become for the deputy director, Jack Karpas, the most difficult decision of his career. It was essential to send home as many of the civilian patients as possible in order to make room for the military casualties who would be flowing in shortly. But to send them from the security of the hospital into a city under heavy shellfire could be tantamount to sentencing some of them to death. At 3:30 P.M. fire slackened, and Dr. Karpas decided he must risk it. Of the five hundred patients who had been in the hospital, three hundred had been termed fit enough to be sent home. These were loaded into buses. An hour later Karpas was notified that all had been delivered safely.

The lulls sometimes proved fatal as people were lured out of the shelters only to be trapped by a sudden barrage. Three shells all told were to fall on the isolated neighborhood of Givat Mordecai, but one of them hit just as two boys emerged from a shelter, killing them both. Ambulances were so busy picking up the scores of wounded during the day that they could not be spared to pick up people who died of natural causes. Two hundred fifty civilians were to be wounded by Arab fire in Jerusalem and twenty killed, almost all of them in the first twenty-four hours. When an old woman in the Yemin Moshe shelter died of a heart attack, Shimon Diskin phoned Magen David Adom and told them someone was seriously ill. An ambulance removed the body from the crowded shelter. Diskin, the elderly building foreman who had found refuge in Yemin Moshe in the morning, had continued on to his home in fashionable Rehavia but returned again to share the lot of the frightened immigrants in the front-line shelter.

The shelling touched off scores of fires and cut telephone lines. Less than an hour after the shelling began, the water main paralleling the main road—one of the two pipes bringing water to Jerusalem—was cut. The thirty-year-old pipe was made of cast iron, and, although buried underground, it shattered when a shell exploded above it at the very entrance to the city. The flow of water, which cascaded down onto the road, was shut off, but since the area of the break was

151

under direct observation from the Arab Legion observation post at Nebi Samuel, nothing could be done about repairing it before nightfall.

While the interior of the city was pounded by artillery throughout the day, most of the Israeli blockhouses along the line grew quiet after the first couple of hours, the Arab positions opposite them having been bludgeoned into silence. In the house Kollek had visited on Allenby Square, the sergeant in command reported late in the afternoon that his men heard a transistor playing Arabic music on the corner of the Old City wall facing them. The Legionnaires had come back to their damaged position, but they didn't appear eager for any more shooting. Sometimes it proved dangerous to leave the relatively tranquil front line for the rear. The machine gunner who had been wounded in the hand on Mount Zion was taken back through a tunnel crossing the Hinnom Valley. The 250-meter-long tunnel dated from the War of Independence. As he emerged from it, a mortar shell exploded nearby, wounding him again, this time in the stomach.

In the northern part of the line, where the Israelis fought from open trenches instead of blockhouses, the Jordanians dominated the field. The Israelis could not lift their heads without risking instant death from the Arab machine gunners in their bunkers across no-man's-land. The enemy fire was relentless, and men grew numb with fear. Exploding shells stung them with showers of hot pebbles and shredded their back packs on the lip of the trench. The sun was equally remorseless, and water was soon gone. Every inch of air seemed filled with flying metal. The men could only crouch in the shallow trenches and hope that nightfall would bring respite. Some men became physically sick. In the trench at Bait Yisrael a volunteer from the Hebrew University Economics Department, Dr. Robert Szereszewski, stood up to scan the enemy lines and was fatally shot in the head.

In the northernmost section of the Pagi trench another university faculty member, Shmaryahu Rivier, had taken shelter in one of the few bunkers on this part of the line. The twenty-nine-year-old corporal, one of the most admired lecturers in the Philosophy Department, had fought in the Sinai campaign as a young paratrooper. With him were three men from his squad, including Private Amitai Spitzer, a philosophy student.

For three hours the men huddled in the bunker as shells pounded the area without letup. Spitzer felt as if his mind were crumbling under the din. One of the men, a Moroccan immigrant, sat in a corner reading aloud from the Book of Psalms. Spitzer stared at him and then reached into his own pocket and pulled out a book. It seemed the only way to preserve his sanity. The book, produced by Spitzer's publisher father, was a collection of poems by a medieval Italian Jewish author. "How can you read?" asked Rivier.

At 2:15 the men heard a deeper kind of explosion outside—recoilless rifle fire. Spitzer could hear the shells getting closer as the Jordanian gunner methodically hit every bunker and trench angle along his stretch of line. With a recoilless rifle it was virtually impossible to miss. Atop the weapon, Spitzer well knew, was a device which fires a .50-caliber tracer bullet. When the gunner sees the tracer hit his target, he fires his main shell in the near-certainty that it will hit where the tracer hit.

The walls shook as a shell hit the adjoining bunker. It was their turn next. Spitzer shifted to another spot. Rivier was sitting by himself in the far corner. Just a few days before he had walked with Rivier from the battalion encampment to the university cafeteria for lunch. They had met a professor who had informed Rivier, studying for an advanced degree, that his recently submitted thesis had received the highest possible grade. Now Rivier seemed to be concentrating on something.

"What are you thinking?" Spitzer asked.

"If we get out of here," said Rivier, "I'll tell you."

A .50-caliber tracer came through the bunker firing hole and struck the rear wall. Rivier rose to move to the place Spitzer had just vacated. At that instant a tremendous explosion wracked the

153

confined space of the bunker. To Spitzer, the noise seemed to be forcing its way through his throat and face to his brain, numbing it. He was knocked back, and it was several moments before his head cleared. He realized his eyes were wide open but he could see nothing. He shut them and tapped his body but could find no wounds.

The philosophy student felt calm and logical. If I lost my sight and nothing else, he thought, it isn't so bad. After a few moments he opened his eyes and saw light and mist. He closed and opened his eyes again. This time he saw that the mist was dust kicked up by the explosion. Two of the men were running out the door, pointing to the rear of the bunker. Spitzer braced himself before turning around. He knew the fourth man was lying there. It was Rivier, lying on his face. Spitzer forced himself to go over. He tapped Rivier's body but could see no wounds. Then he saw the hole in the helmet. Rivier was dead.

Late in the afternoon the battalion which had been digging in on Mount Herzl was ordered to load into buses and move up to the front at Ramat Rachel. The last half mile of the route ran along the border. The column paused at the edge of the open area near the home of Nobel Prize novelist S. Y. Agnon. The soldiers crouched below window level, but the civilian drivers had no choice but to sit upright. They stomped the gas pedals to the floor and hurtled across the open space safely. Upon reaching the kibbutz, the men tumbled out of the buses and sought shelter behind rocks and buildings until they could figure out where the fire being leveled at them was coming from.

Their arrival was witnessed by the four soldiers who had taken to the kibbutz trench in the morning expecting to hold off the Arab Legion by themselves. One of the quartet, the Canadian-born Private Grover, saw a bus move up too far and come under fire from the bunkers below Mar Elias Monastery. Before the last man was out of the bus, others already had reached the trench and had a machine gun working. They moved so deftly that Grover assumed they were young draftees on regular service. He was surprised to learn later that they were reservists like himself.

No soldier on the line was as isolated as Private Kogut in the apartment building overlooking Mandelbaum Gate. There had been no time to lay telephone wire to the building, and ever since his partner had been called away in the morning Kogut had been alone. He was not bored, however. He had opened up on the blockhouse opposite with his bazooka from a sandbagged parapet on the roof. When the position became untenable, Kogut descended to the floors below. Moving from apartment to apartment, he would crawl across the floor to a window and shove it open. If the movement drew no fire, he raised up and fired his bazooka at the blockhouses opposite, dropping quickly to avoid the inevitable fusillade that followed. Before leaving, he would always remember to reach up and close the window.

In the afternoon an officer arrived. Kogut, choking and squinting from the bazooka smoke which filled the building, asked how the war was going. The officer said more than one hundred enemy planes were down. "We're fighting on their territory," he said. The lieutenant began to weep and Kogut, who had begun to think he was fighting the war alone, found himself crying too. The report was the first indication that the war was being won on the decisive Southern Front. Neither had any idea that powerful forces were already moving up from the coastal plain with orders to drive the Jordanians off the crest of the Judean Hills and relieve Jerusalem.

Ever since the start of the Jordanian shelling, General Narkiss had been pressing for permission to attack at Latrun and Sheikh Abdul Aziz, but Rabin held him firmly in check. The chief of staff was still hoping that Hussein would consider his honor satisfied with an artillery barrage and that the Jordanian front might be kept from boiling over. At 12:15, however, Private Darzi's report of the Arab takeover at Government House had

155

come. Half an hour later Radio Amman announced that Scopus had been captured. The enclave had been under heavy fire all morning from the trenches at Augusta Victoria and French Hill, but there had been no assault by ground troops. However, the Scopus claim seemed a clear indication of Jordanian intent, coming as it did after the earlier announcement of the capture of Jebel Mukaber (Government House), which had turned out to be accurate if premature. At General Staff headquarters, the decision was taken to start the Harel Brigade moving toward Jerusalem.

Colonel Ben-Ari got the word from Narkiss at 1 P.M. A few hours before, with the outbreak of the fighting, he had summoned his officers and broken out a bottle of cognac. They had toasted "*Lechayim* (To life)," and the colonel settled down to follow the progress of the battles in the south on the military radio, battles he might have been directing had he remained in the regular army. Now, completely unexpectedly, his remote front had come alive, and he was being given the most dramatic assignment an Israeli officer could receive—to move on Jerusalem. It had been eleven years since he had led an armored brigade into action, and once again his mind raced with the myriad calculations involved. So defense-oriented had thinking been on the Jordanian front that he had drawn up no plans for the job Narkiss was now giving him. Colonel Zvika, whose tanks would have to play a major role in the attack, had in the past two weeks scouted the Latrun area and along the country's narrow waist, but he had not made a single reconnaissance of the Judean Hills into which he was now about to plunge.

The brigade radio net had remained dormant since mobilization, to prevent signals from being picked up by the Jordanians. Ben-Ari now ordered it activated. Meanwhile, he started drawing up an attack plan. In fifteen minutes the radio net was completed and so was the plan. Ben-Ari ordered his battalion commanders to start rolling. Instead of broadcasting their route in the clear, he said, "Move through the two towns in the

156

direction of the capital." The officers knew he meant the road passing through Lod and Ramle. Ben-Ari said he would catch up with them on the way to give them their attack orders.

Out under the trees, where the men had been waiting beside their vehicles since 8 A.M., a single word was shouted from tank to tank: "Move." The forest thundered as engines came alive and Shermans and half-tracks rolled down the wooded slopes into the open parade field in the center of the encampment. Under clouds of dust they formed company columns and moved out to the main road. To the surprise of the crews who had been reconnoitering to the north since mobilization, the column turned southwest toward Jerusalem.

Ben-Ari's original order had been to get his brigade into the hills and await further instructions before attempting to break through enemy lines. He pressed, however, for permission to cross the border as soon as his forces reached the target area, without losing momentum by halting. Narkiss passed the proposal on to Dayan, who said that if Scopus was in danger Ben-Ari could keep going. The defense minister suggested that the brigade thrust straight toward Scopus through the wadi between Ammunition Hill and Mivtar Hill. Narkiss, however, pushed for a more roundabout route. The wadi was thickly sown with mines and dominated by the Jordanian positions on the two hills. He proposed breaking through the enemy line out in the Jerusalem Corridor, then swinging around to the north of the city. Dayan acceded to Narkiss's request. Narkiss's insistence on the roundabout route for the Harel Brigade was one of the key decisions in the battle of Jerusalem, and one of the most controversial. To Narkiss, the long way was the surer and faster. After the war there were some who would challenge this concept. Passage through the wadi, they would claim, might have been costly but not as costly as the final price proved to be in what they believed was an unnecessarily prolonged battle. (Ben-Ari would believe a still easier breakthrough could have been achieved by armor inside the city at the American Colony, a route to be taken by

157

the paratroopers.) All this, however, was in retrospect. As his brigade started up the road to Jerusalem, Ben-Ari set about executing his order unquestioningly.

His plan was to send his three battalions at the enemy line in three prongs. If one succeeded in breaking through, the other battalions would be pulled back and fed through the hole. But stopping by Narkiss's headquarters before going to intercept his battalion commanders on the road, Ben-Ari noticed a new route across the corridor border marked on a map. It was a goat path, he was told, but it had been checked out by a foot patrol which had crossed the border at night some months before and determined that it could be navigated by tanks. About one-and-a-half kilometers west of the city, it was closer to Ben-Ari's prime target—the Jerusalem-Ramallah road—than any of his three prongs, and he decided on the spot to make this his fourth and major line of attack.

He was waiting in the Paz gas station in Ramle when Zvika arrived with his tanks. (The spot was a familiar one for Zvika, an executive with the Paz Petroleum Company.) "Everything we've talked about till now is canceled," said Ben-Ari, spreading a map on the hood of a jeep. "We've got a new plan." He showed the battalion commander the goat path and told him it would be his route. "You have to reach and take a position controlling the Jerusalem-Ramallah road and be ready to conquer Jerusalem. You'll have to get there before first light." The Jordanian tanks, if they did not reach the city in a few hours, could be expected to wait until dawn before attacking Scopus. Ben-Ari was determined to be there waiting for them.

Zvika, who until now had not even considered the possibility of fighting in Jerusalem, did not pause to wonder how he was going to get his tanks up a goat path and reach the Ramallah road deep in the hills in fourteen hours. He had served under Ben-Ari since he was a young lieutenant and had implicit faith in him. If Ben-Ari said it was possible, then it would be done. The brigade commander told him enemy Pattons might be racing the Shermans for the road.

"Whoever gets there first will take it," Ben-Ari said. "You're going to have to get there first."

The briefing was over in five minutes. Zvika collected his company commanders and sped up to Jerusalem in jeeps for a reconnaissance, while his tanks followed behind up the main road. (The two other battalions climbed the hills on secondary roads.) Despite shelling, people emerged from shelters in settlements along the road to cheer. A radioman in a command half-track saw a helmeted warden herd three people from the roadside. A moment later a shell exploded where they had been standing. Farther up the road a man made a V sign with his fingers, and the radioman could hear him over the noise of the engine as the vehicle came abreast. The man was shouting, "Save Jerusalem."

Minutes after the radio announcement of war, Motta Gur's three battalion commanders assembled their officers to outline their mission. In twelve hours, shortly after darkness fell, the brigade would be parachuted into the desert outside El Arish on the northern Sinai coast. It would fight its way into the town and prepare to destroy the enemy armor, which would have to funnel through El Arish to and from the battlefronts of the Gaza Strip, thirty miles along the coast. After the officers had had a chance to study the attack plan, the battalion commanders assembled the soldiers and addressed them briefly. "We've waited for two weeks," said Colonel Yussi, commander of the veteran Eighth. "Now the time has come to do the job. I know you're good." The men responded with an Israeli version of three cheers: a soldier shouting *"Kifach"* and the others responding with a resounding "Hey." While the battalion was assembled, a knapsack belonging to an officer inexplicably caught fire on the ground where it had been left. (The incident was to be remembered when the officer was shot to death inside the Old City, the last member of the brigade to be killed in action.)

The men packed their gear in jump bags for parachuting and dispersed in the shade of olive trees to be briefed by their

159

company officers on the night mission. Jumpmasters arrived at the camp and told the units which troop carriers they would fly in.

The paratroopers could see the fighter-bombers returning to the adjacent airfield from their first missions over Egypt, the craft waggling their wings in triumph, some of them looping. Formations with gaps in them made one level pass before landing, a salute to their comrades who had not come back.

Two pilots jeeped over to the paratrooper encampment while their planes were being refueled to talk to a company commander who belonged to the same kibbutz as one of them. The Egyptian Air Force, they reported, was a smoking ruin. For the senior brigade officers, the news was a mixed blessing. The success of the air force, accompanied by indications of solid gains by the armored division of General Tal hammering at the Gaza Strip, was beginning to raise doubts about whether the paratroopers would be needed at El Arish. More portents were soon to come.

Sunday a small unit had been detached from the brigade and dispatched to the coast to join a seaborne assault force scheduled to strike behind enemy lines Monday night. Corporal Stolar, the kibbutznik who had taken a copy of *The White Nile* with him when mobilized, found his choice of reading material prophetic; he was going to war in a boat. His platoon passed the night comfortably on the sand in the midst of the assembled task force. In the morning Stolar and his buddies, enjoying a late breakfast, could hear tank engines warming up nearby. While they were drinking coffee, however, an officer stopped by to announce that the expedition was canceled. General Tal's division would overrun the target area before the seaborne force could arrive. With the sea assault called off so early, a night drop seemed more remote than ever.

At 12:30 P.M. two of the paratroop battalion commanders, Uzi and Joseph, were summoned to Gur's headquarters. The General Staff had requested one paratroop battalion to be dispatched to Jerusalem. The mission seemed most likely defensive. Whoever went would miss out on the night jump—if there was one. Jotting their names on separate slips, Gur turned up the loser: Joseph. (Yussi's battalion enjoyed sufficient seniority to be spared the lottery.) Uzi's gratification was short-lived. At 1 P.M. Gur was notified to shift a second battalion to Jerusalem.

With most of his force now assigned to the city, Gur was obliged to go there too. Before he left camp a call summoned him to the Central Front command post. He drove there with a few officers to find Narkiss highly excited. Word had just been received that the third battalion was to be diverted to Jerusalem, too. But the paratroopers were not going up to hold defensive positions. Theirs would be the historic task, General Narkiss declared, of breaking through the enemy lines north of the Old City walls and linking up with the Scopus garrison. Narkiss added that he hoped to be able to give the order later for the capture of the Old City itself.

All Narkiss's calculations for relieving Scopus had rested on the ability of the Harel Brigade to reach the Ramallah road by dawn Tuesday in sufficient strength to neutralize the enemy Pattons bound to come up from Jericho—an admittedly long shot. Narkiss had not expected to have a crack paratroop brigade placed at his disposal. He gave Gur the boundaries of his attack area. Breakthrough would be on the kilometer-long stretch between Mandelbaum Gate and Ammunition Hill. Zero hour would be midnight.

Gur and his aides piled into the mobilized civilian car assigned to them and started toward Jerusalem. Before them lay a task which even in the fast-moving Israeli Army requires at least forty-eight hours—drawing up a detailed battle plan from scratch and moving a brigade into position to carry it out. Following the major retaliatory raid at Kalkilye in 1956, where the attacking unit suffered heavy casualties, General Dayan had been sharply criticized for the speed with which the action was launched. It was begun just twenty-one hours after the paratroop

161

brigade commander involved was given his assignment. Now Gur had less than ten hours to prepare for a far more formidable target. He and Arik were thankful for the reconnaissance of the city line they had carried out the week before.

As their car labored up the hills—the driver pulling over periodically to pour water into the steaming radiator—Gur began to draw up the attack plan. He would have liked to have four breakthrough points, increasing the chances of at least one being successful, but there was neither time nor equipment for that. He settled for two thrusts, one near Ammunition Hill, one in the Mandelbaum Gate area.

Meanwhile, the three battalion commanders, each accompanied by his own company commanders, had already started separately up to Jerusalem on the main road, leaving the troops to be loaded into buses and brought up in convoys. Colonel Joseph and his officers, who had a half-hour start on the others, drew machine-gun fire from the Latrun area as they turned into Shaar Hagai (Gate of the Valley), the defile through which the road passes as it leaves the plain and begins climbing into the Judean Hills. The shots, which presumably came from the Egyptian commando unit known to have taken position at Latrun, missed the two jeeps and kicked off the stone wall of an old Turkish inn. Instead of risking the last open stretch of highway before Jerusalem, the jeeps turned off at the suburb of Bait Zayit and entered the city from the rear.

Uzi and his officers went all the way up the main road into the city. They were prepared for a grim scene, but the first thing they saw as they entered were four boys about ten years old, enthusiastically splashing through water pouring out of the broken water main. "Hasn't there been any shelling?" called out Captain Bikel, the young commander of Uzi's weapons company.

"Yes," one of the boys said. "It just stopped."

"Then why aren't you inside?"

"As soon as it starts, we'll go inside again."

The three battalion commanders met each other at Schneller. Neither Amitai nor Gur were on hand, but the Jerusalem Brigade operations officer supplied a quick briefing. He told them the city had been heavily shelled since morning and that the Jerusalem Brigade had taken Government House after the Arab Legion had moved in. By nightfall Sur Bahir should have fallen and the Southern Front would be secure. The Harel Brigade, whose tanks the paratroopers had passed on the way up to the city, would begin their attack to the north before dark. It would be the paratroopers' task to punch through in the middle and link up with Scopus. The officer gave the paratroopers a map and lent them an intelligence sergeant as a guide.

Gur arrived and led his officers to nearby Zefania Street, which ran along the crest of the hill sloping toward the border. Looking around the corner, the paratroopers could see straight down Bar Ilan Street to a white rectangular building across no-man's-land, a thousand meters away. Painted in black across the top of the two-story structure was UNITED NATIONS RELIEF AND WORKS AGENCY. To its left was Ammunition Hill.

Despite the shells falling randomly in the area, Gur spread a map on the sidewalk, and the officers crowded around him. Near them a car with the blue license plate of a cabinet minister sat forlornly with its windows blown out.

The brigade commander outlined the plan he had formulated in the car driving up to the city. Joseph's battalion, the Sixth, would undertake the northern breakthrough, taking the Police Training School and Ammunition Hill, then moving on to clear the Sheikh Jarrah residential quarter at the foot of Mount Scopus. Uzi's battalion, the Seventh, would break through the Mandelbaum Gate area and clear Wadi Joz, the central gulley separating Sheikh Jarrah on the north from the American Colony on the south. The American Colony itself, plus areas contiguous to the Old City, would

163

be the target of Yussi's Eighth. Gur's briefing concluded, the battalion commanders dispersed to reconnoiter their target areas in the two hours of daylight remaining and prepare their attack plans.

After spending half an hour packing his gear in jump bags at the paratroopers' camp following his return from the coast, Corporal Stolar was told to unpack. He would be traveling neither by boat nor plane. The brigade was going to Jerusalem in Egged buses. Stolar didn't mind the effort of repacking or the humble means of transportation. He had been looking with dread toward the prospect of lugging the 110 to 130 pounds of equipment he carried as a mortarman through the desert sands around El Arish. The reaction of the other soldiers was mixed; some were disappointed at what they expected would be a static defensive assignment, others sensing that they were about to touch history. "The Jews conquered Jerusalem three times," said Sergeant Pheda of the Eighth to a buddy. "We're going to do it the fourth time." He was referring to the conquest of the city by David, the Maccabees, and Bar Kochba. The religious soldiers were especially excited by their new mission. "Better to fight for Jerusalem than the Sinai Desert," said one when a friend asked what he thought about the change.

The buses the men boarded still had their regular city route numbers above the windshield. Private Hananel Mack found that his bus was a number 18, which served his neighborhood in Jerusalem. He even recognized the driver as a regular on the route. The soldiers started calling out destinations, and one, playing bus conductor, marched down the aisle with an imaginary ticket punch demanding tickets from the passengers. The aisles were quickly filled with gear, and the men stuck their helmets into the overhead racks as the buses started rolling.

Passing a farm settlement a soldier in an engineering unit yelled, "There's my house. There are my cows." One of the men in the company, a carpenter, had been out of work during the country's recent economic slowdown, and the farmer told him to come to his settlement when the fighting was over. "We've got a couple of weeks' work for you," he said. (The farmer, however, was to be dead before Tuesday's sun rose.)

The buses left the main road at the foot of the hills and started up a dirt track in separate battalion convoys. Periodically the buses halted while a tractor widened bottlenecks or leveled irregularities. Planes circling overhead provided constant cover. The soldiers settled back to look at the brown, rocky hills swelling round them. Some slept. In one bus a young private who studied at the Rabbi Kook Yeshiva in Jerusalem recited psalms aloud.

All day long Kol Yisrael had been playing martial music and songs of the south—of the Negev and Eilat—where the nation's attention was focused. But as the buses climbed deeper into the hills, the radio suddenly switched to songs of Jerusalem. The effect was electrifying. Cut off from the world on this dirt track, they had been winding through empty hills toward an unseen city and an unknown mission. Now the unexpected burst of triumphant music seemed to make it all real, heralding their coming and revealing in its passion the magnitude of what awaited them. The men began singing with the radio: *"Veyehuda l'olam tayshave, veyerushalayim l'dor v'dor* (Egypt shall be a desolation and Edom a desolate wilderness, but Judah shall dwell forever and Jerusalem from generation to generation)." The biblical refrain could be heard coming from other buses, repeated over and over, and men could be seen weeping.

The sound of cannonading underscored the singing. The outskirts of the city came into view, and Captain Meyer, a staff officer of the Eighth, saw shells hitting Bait Zayit, where he lived. Before being mobilized, he had dug a shelter in his yard, decking it with wood and sand. His wife and children were there now, somewhere beneath the bursts of smoke to his left, and he prayed that he had built strongly. It was nearly dusk when the buses halted at Bait Hakerem, a neighborhood about two kilometers from the front, and the men took shelter inside the houses.

Through binoculars Lieutenant Colonel Zvika studied the goat path his tanks were to take from the suburb of Mevasseret Jerusalem and from the Romema quarter at the northwest edge of Jerusalem itself. From neither side did it look feasible. At 4:30 he turned back down the main road; at Motza, four kilometers from the city, he met his tanks coming up. The column veered off the road and headed for the border. Unlike the paratroopers, the mechanized brigade had been ordered to begin its attack in daylight.

Zvika had distributed two of his four Sherman companies to the brigade's half-track battalions. He in turn had been given two companies of half-track-borne infantry. He also commanded twelve Centurion tanks, which had arrived virtually straight from the port the day before. The Centurions, far superior to his Shermans, were placed at the head of the column so they could confront the Pattons when they emerged on the Ramallah road.

The column followed a dirt track through a fruit orchard. After two kilometers the trees thinned and the track disappeared. The tanks were at the foot of Khirbet Talila, a barren hill covered with boulders, some of them the height of a man. Running up the slope was the goat path. It was perhaps half a meter wide, hardly the width of a single tank tread. Shells began exploding around the column as soon as it emerged from the orchard and began lumbering up the slope. At 5:30 P.M., four-and-a-half hours after Ben-Ari had received his orders on the coastal plain, his tanks had penetrated two kilometers into the hills forty kilometers from their starting point and were crossing the border in attack formation. (The Harel Brigade attack was launched two hours after the Jerusalem Brigade counterattack at Government House and eight-and-a-half hours before the paratroop assault was to get under way.)

166

The Centurions ran into trouble almost immediately. Some became hung up on boulders, their treads raised off the ground and thrashing futilely. Motors broke down under strain. Those Centurions still mobile drifted to the left where the grade was less steep, but their movement was carrying them away from the crest. The Centurions evidently were not going to make it. The more experienced Centurion tankmen were in the south and these drivers, new to the battalion, were incapable of handling their tanks in this terrain. Darkness was approaching and Zvika feared that the Centurions could block the rest of the column. He ordered them to halt in place and told the Sherman commanders to pass them. If anyone could make it over these slopes, it would be his own veteran drivers.

Major Uri, commander of the first Sherman company, was riding the lead tank. Visibility was perhaps one hundred meters by twilight when he barked, "My tanks—after me." He ordered his driver to cut left beyond the stalled Centurions. During the reconnaissance earlier in the day he had studied the slope from the Israeli side and said to himself, Here, tanks don't go. He had been a tankman for fifteen years, active and reserve, and had never seen tanks ascend a kilometer-long slope of ten to twenty degrees, let alone one covered with such formidable rocks. His tank soon waddled onto a boulder and resisted all efforts to dislodge it. Uri shifted his command to the tank behind, directing it around the abandoned vehicle. Darkness was virtually complete now, and he strained to see the outcroppings ahead.

At the same time that Zvika's prong crossed the border, a second armored prong was moving out from Mevasseret Jerusalem, four kilometers to the west. Sappers had advanced to remove the mines—Israeli and Jordanian—which lay between Mevasseret and the Jordanian bunkers at Sheikh Abdul Aziz, four hundred meters opposite, but heavy mortar fire drove them back. Major Natan, whose tank company spearheaded the force, decided he could not wait any longer for a path to be cleared. Leading the way in his command tank, he steered for the outcropping of rocks glistening white in the late afternoon sunlight, which would be safe from mines. But it was impossible to bypass broad patches of earth sown with explosives. A tread blew off Natan's tank, and he leapt into the tank behind.

Explosions racked the column as it worked its way through the minefield and up the far slope. Sometimes a track was knocked loose, but the tank would struggle on until disabled by a second explosion. Infantry dismounted from the half-tracks and advanced in the tracks of the tanks. When Natan reached the Arab Legion positions atop the ridge he found them deserted. Behind him on the slope seven of his eleven tanks lay immobilized.

Between the Mevasseret force and Zvika's force on the right wing was Ben-Ari's third prong—the brigade reconnaissance company moving on the fortified village of Bait Iksa. As the jeeps and half-tracks crossed the slopes a half-track tipped over, but the column pressed on.

The brigade's left prong, seven kilometers west of Mevasseret, faced awesome defenses. The force's objective was the Radar (named after the radar station the British had built there during World War II when Rommel had begun moving toward Suez): three hills—Radar 1, Radar 2, and Radar 3—straddled a dirt road leading from the Israeli border kibbutz of Maale Hahamisha to the Jordanian village of Bidu, three kilometers away. Steep slopes on either side constricted vehicular traffic to the narrow road, which was thickly sown with mines for three hundred meters. Mines had grown wild along this stretch of the border. After almost twenty years of planting, neither side could chart its own minefields. Any attempt to clear a path would be suicidal as long as the enemy held Radars 1 and 2, which dominated the road. The two hills, set back three hundred meters and seven hundred meters respectively from the border, were heavily fortified with bunkers and covered trenches; their perimeter was ringed with minefields.

The commander of the force, Lieutenant Colonel Yigal, had summoned his company commanders to his half-track to formulate the attack plan as they were climbing up from the coastal plain. Radars 1 and 2 would have to be overrun by infantry before sappers could attempt to clear the road. The riflemen were likely to take high casualties as they crossed the open slopes, but there was no alternative. Reaching the kibbutz, Yigal halted his half-track in front of the guest house, which normally accommodated vacationers. He watched the branches of a tree overhead being chewed by machine-gun bullets.

As soon as the tanks came up, Yigal ordered them to silence the enemy bunkers. They systematically began pounding the firing slits. While 81-mm. mortars opened on Radar 1, 120 -mm. mortars hit Radar 2, the main defense position. The first round on Radar 2 hit dead center, touching off a fire which was to illuminate the hill well into the night. Two planes joined in the attack, strafing Radar 2.

The sun was beginning to set when two infantry companies moved out on foot toward the hilltops, through gaps in the enemy minefields reported by intelligence. Radar 1, on the left side of the road, was reached first. Cutting past barbed wire, the men leapt into trenches—only to find them deserted. The barrels of the machine guns in the bunkers were still hot.

The second assault force, meanwhile, was closing in on Radar 2, whose fire had already wounded four men on Radar 1. When they reached the barbed wire, it was discovered that no one had brought pliers. A lieutenant parted the strands with a burst from his Uzi. Swarming into the enemy position, the Israelis found it too abandoned. The bombardment had pried the defenders out of the bunkers, and incredibly, both powerful positions had been taken without a fatality.

The sappers were now free to remove the mines from the Israeli side of the border. As soon as a path was cleared, a tank started up the road, pushing aside Israeli antitank barriers as it crossed the border. Antipersonnel mines exploded harmlessly beneath the treads. Yigal followed in his own half-track, which lurched to a sudden halt under a deafening roar. The tank had rolled by an antitank mine, but the half-track had set it off. The battalion commander called the sappers forward. The most arduous job was just beginning.

On his cattle ranch in northern Israel, Meier Harzion had been putting up a fence Monday morning when his wife called from the house with news of the onset of war. Advising his Arab helper to return to his village nearby, Harzion dropped off a borrowed trailer at a neighboring kibbutz and headed south.

Harzion was the most famous soldier in Israel. Moshe Dayan, a man not given to overstatement, had termed him the greatest warrior the Jewish people had known since Bar Kochba (the first-century guerrilla leader who had led an uprising against the Romans). As a commander of many of the retaliatory raids before the Sinai campaign, Harzion's scouting ability and fighting prowess had become a legend. He was credited with the instincts of an animal in the field, an unfailing sense of direction guiding him through trackless territory in the dark. His regular military service had ended eleven years earlier when he was severely ripped by a machine-gun burst during a raid. He was saved by a doctor operating in the field with a penknife. Ever since, he had had only partial use of his left arm, and his voice still rasped from his throat wounds.

After his disability, he had left his kibbutz and started his ranch on a lonely plateau called by the Arabs "Wind of the Stars." Some said he had struck off on his own to avoid the communal embrace of the kibbutz, which he may have feared would cater to him as a cripple. His house, which he built on the very edge of the plateau, offered one of the most breathtaking views in Israel, looking across the Jordan Valley to the heights of Syria. He named it Shoshana's Ranch, after his murdered sister.

Shoshana, whose adventurous spirit matched her brother's, had slipped across the border more than a decade before with her boyfriend in an attempt to cut through Arab territory to the ancient Israeli fortress of Masada on the Dead Sea. They were caught by bedouins in the hills near Hebron and killed. When the news reached Harzion, he crossed the border with a few friends and made his way to the same area. Seizing a group of Arabs, Harzion's party killed them all except for one, whom they released so that he could tell what had happened. When the raiding party returned to Israel, they were arrested for illegally crossing the border but released after a couple of weeks.

Now, free of any military obligations because of his wounds, Harzion could pick any unit he wished to attach himself to. He chose a paratroop reconnaissance company commanded by Major Kapusta, who had once served under him. Kapusta himself was a famed scout who before the Sinai campaign had prowled the Sinai Desert at night to reconnoiter the camps of Arab raiders. His unit, all of whose members he had picked, was part of another paratroop brigade which, like Gur's, had seen its original target overrun during the day by the swift-moving armored forces. The men had become restless as it became increasingly evident that there would be no need for them.

Kapusta was determined that his unit would not remain in camp following the war's progress on the radio. He had heard of the shelling along the Jordanian front and decided that even if it was too late to get at the Egyptians, there was a fair chance of having a go at the Jordanians. Individual companies, even handpicked reconnaissance companies, are no more independent in the Israeli Army than any other, but Kapusta somehow got road clearance for his unit from Southern Command and, an hour before sunset, set out for Jerusalem. Kapusta knew little of what was happening there and nothing of what was planned. But like a "hired gun" riding into a strange town, he was ready to offer his men's services to whoever would have them. He knew that Gur's brigade and the Harel were on their way up to Jerusalem. If neither of them could use him, he thought, perhaps the Jerusalem Brigade could. Even if the city itself was quiet, someone might be needed to force the Latrun bottleneck.

As darkness came, Kapusta's men, rushing across the coastal plain in their jeeps, could see flashes in the hills and hear a distant rumbling as if, despite the dry season, a violent thunderstorm were raging over Jerusalem.

## 9 TWILIGHT

The sun drops quickly behind the hills west of Jerusalem but the stone buildings continue to reflect light for perhaps a quarter hour, glowing golden and unreal against the darkening eastern sky. Twilight in Jerusalem is a holy hour, and never had the city seemed more serene than on this evening. Firing had completely ceased along the line, as if both sides had turned to watch the light slide from the hills. There was no sound of traffic to intrude on the silence, no footsteps in the streets. There was only the distant barking of dogs, a chilling of the air, and the tapering silhouettes of cypress trees.

In Mea Shearim the sound of singing and handclapping could be heard coming from a yeshiva. The students had finished their evening prayers, and through a window scores of figures could dimly be made out dancing in a circle in almost total darkness. A young man with the broadbrimmed hat of the Chassidim emerged, flushed and exultant. "We'll be all right," he said, wiping his brow with a handkerchief. "God is with us."

With the failing light, rescue workers began to evacuate people from the more exposed of the front-line houses. One of the university volunteers in Musrara found an old man sitting in a forward shelter. "Come, grandfather," she said, taking him by the arm. As they started toward the rear, the old man raised his voice in the empty street and began to sing. In Talpiot, Haga officials touring the battered border found a sick man sitting alone in his darkened house, water dripping through the ceiling from a burst pipe.

The rescue operation was short-lived. Places had been pre-

173

pared for twenty thousand refugees, but only two thousand had been removed before the shelling resumed at dark. As for the thousands of others who remained along the border, they would have to endure a long, stormy night. In the Bukharan quarter, one hundred people were shifted to another shelter under fire when the one they had been in began to flood with water from a burst pipe. An old woman alone in her room nearby was killed by a shell.

Before the war the immigrants from North Africa and Asia, who had never experienced war, seemed relatively calm about the prospect of one, while those who had lived through World War II in Europe were tense. Once the shooting started, however, Haga workers found these attitudes reversed. The Orientals had grown far more alarmed, while the European reaction was, "It's not as bad as we expected."

The commander of the central Haga district, Dudu Cohen, found the well-to-do people from Rehavia more taxing than the slum-dwellers along the border. One Rehavia caller, who would only speak to the district commander, told Dudu that a shell had come in through his window and lodged unexploded in the middle of the living room couch like a brass ashtray. The man refused to be satisfied with the assurance that a sapper team would be dispatched immediately. "What if a bullet comes in through the window now and sets off the shell?" he demanded.

With nightfall, the Water Department learned that the worst had happened. Of the two mains bringing water into the city, the northern one paralleling the main road had been broken during the day. Now the southern one had ceased pumping. Somewhere out in the Jerusalem Corridor the electric cable supplying power to the pumping station had been knocked out. As if in a bad dream, the city was completely cut off from its water sources, just as it had been during the siege of 1948.

With darkness, a work crew set out to repair the break in the northern line. Here at the entrance to the city the houses gave way to reveal a panorama of Jordanian-held hills to the north. The hills were now streaked with tracers, as half-tracks and tanks of the Harel Brigade pushed across the deep wadis toward the Arab Legion positions on the crests. The continuous shelling made it too dangerous for the crew to remain outside. While most of them descended into a shelter, a bulldozer guided by a single man with a flashlight opened a trench above the broken pipe. By midnight the enemy positions opposite had been over-run, and the shelling in the area had stopped. The rest of the crew emerged to begin replacing the pipe.

Other municipal employees were also venturing out into the dangerous streets. Joseph Stark, the sixty-six-year-old head of the city street-lighting section, led a crew consisting entirely of men over forty-five to the border areas to extinguish streetlamps that were breaking the blackout. Fuses in subcenters for all the city's streetlamps had been disconnected during the day, but on some streets electric utility lines knocked down by shellfire had fallen across the wires feeding the lamps, activating them. Mea Shearim Street, just behind the front line in Musrara, was incongruously lit up. On border streets where it was too risky to drive, the men made their way between buildings, ladders on their backs, tools in their belts. Electricity company employees went out three times to repair downed lines feeding a warehouse in Romema containing most of Jerusalem's meat supply in deep-freeze units. Without refrigeration the meat would go bad in twenty-four hours.

Touring the dormitories in Hebrew University where the three hundred remaining foreign students were concentrated, Professor Talmon found an uneasy situation. He could see that a number of girls had been crying. Other students were wandering outside with a dangerous foolhardiness. Several buildings on campus had already been hit. Talmon ordered that all the students be assembled in a shelter at 9:30 P.M. so that he could address them. He first passed on the news of the two hundred

Egyptian planes being destroyed, which he had picked up on the army radio net, a report that exercised an immediate calming effect. Two Israeli girl students attached as liaison to the foreign students struck Talmon as competent types, and he announced that they were now "military commanders" of the dormitory— They were to see that no one left the campus without permission. Talmon recognized students from his own classes in the shelter, but at first they did not recognize him in his uniform. At the sound of his voice, they came forward and stared at their scholarly Bible professor lecturing them now in crisp military tones.

The resumption of shelling after dark meant that the three thousand children not yet evacuated from the city schools would have to spend the night there. At Geulim, where two hundred of the five hundred children remained, the shelter took on a warm, family atmosphere as blankets were spread on the floor and candles lit. Older girls and teachers held the smaller children on their laps, and boys even detached themselves from their friends to sit with their sisters. The small children managed to sleep, but the others were to remain up all night listening to the transistors.

Although most of the teachers had young children of their own at home, all of them had stayed with their classes in the school shelter. Mrs. Ish-Shalom, the principal, had made no special arrangements for her children, but she knew neighbors would look after them.

At Haga headquarters an urgent call was received shortly after dark from a home for mentally retarded children in Talpiot which had received several shells. Yoram Hamizrachi, the Haga officer who had sounded the air-raid alarm in the morning, volunteered to drive out and see what could be done. Utility lines were strewn over the streets and shells exploded nearby as he drove. Arriving at the institution, he found a Dantesque scene. Squealing children crawled around the floors while staff members sat among them exhausted and hollow-eyed. There

176

Conical roof of Dormition Church morning after its sheathing was melted following hit by Jordanian shell. Two Israeli soldiers observing activity inside Old City from gallery beneath roof escaped safely. Smoke can be seen issuing from Arab Legion positions atop city wall to left. In no-man's-land between church and wall is Armenian Cemetery.

Harel Brigade tanks speeding from coastal plain toward Jerusalem early on afternoon of June 5. Gen. Narkiss relied on these outdated Shermans to save Mount Scopus from Jordanian Pattons approaching from Jericho.

Infantry and half-tracks from Harel Brigade move out across terraced slopes toward enemy position fronting Jerusalem Corridor.

Smoke drifts from former Police Training School, now local UNRWA headquarters, hit by Israeli guns prior to night paratrooper attack. Trench and bunkers in front of building dominated crossing point. Fire also came from building itself. Ammunition Hill is out of sight to left.

was no water or electricity, and a stench permeated the building. "Don't wake the children," a staff member whispered. Looking around, Yoram saw that all the children were pitifully awake.

"How good you came," said a woman. "Now please take the children home." Yoram replied that they could not be taken home since there was no way of knowing their parents would be there. The woman, who seemed to be on the verge of collapse, began weeping. "Please do something," she pleaded.

The phone was still working and Yoram called headquarters. An officer said a truck would transport the children to an evacuation center.

When it arrived an hour later, the driver, who had run a gantlet of fire, began shouting at Yoram, who went out to meet him. "Are you crazy calling for a driver out here? Where's the shelter?" When he entered the building and saw the children he calmed down. Blankets were spread on the back of the truck, normally used to carry asphalt, and Yoram went to the shelter of a nearby apartment building to recruit people to load the frantic children aboard. It was difficult to count the children because they kept leaping from one side of the truck to the other, but it was finally discovered that one was missing. He was found inside under a bed, a boy about six with the sidecurls of the ultra-Orthodox. When carried outside, he started to shriek in endless gusts of terror.

The truck and two cars traveled with blackout lights to the railroad station. Beyond lay the open stretch to the King David Hotel which the Jerusalem Reconnaissance Company had avoided in the morning on its way to Allenby Barracks. Yoram, in the lead car, shouted back to the other two drivers to turn off their lights to avoid being seen from the Old City wall. They were halfway across the open area when a vehicle came at them from the direction of the hotel with its lights full on, illuminating the convoy. Yelling to switch on lights, Yoram stepped on the accelerator. The convoy made it safely across.

*      *      *

Despite the constant pounding of the Arab guns and the seemingly ominous reluctance on the part of Kol Yisrael to claim any Israeli successes, there was little fear among the population that the gates were about to burst. Occasionally, however, restraint gave way. In Katamon a psychological first-aid team had to be dispatched to a shelter to quiet a hysterical woman who kept shouting that the Arabs were coming. In Mea Shearim there was also hysteria among the women crowded into the shelter presided over by Rabbi Amram Blau, the anti-Zionist leader. (Women and men were assigned to separate parts of the shelter.) Shrill Arabic exhortations piped by loudspeakers from El Aksa Mosque inside the Old City could be heard at the foot of Jabotinsky Street in Talbiya, six hundred meters from the city wall. Drifting through the noise of explosions, the sound was chilling. An unnerved civil defense warden ran into a shelter yelling, "Everybody out, they're coming over the walls." The people in the shelter calmed him down.

Those who understood Arabic and were tuned in to Radio Cairo were occasionally convinced by the vivid descriptions of Arab armies approaching a burning Tel Aviv. An official from the Water Department searching for a missing employee found him at home. When the official reminded him that municipal employees had been mobilized and had the same obligations as soldiers to attend to their duties, the employee admitted that he had been simply too frightened to go out. He had been watching Cairo on his television set, and the pictures of the Egyptian Army moving into the desert had persuaded him that the end was near.

In the German Colony an American woman immigrant had taken shelter with Arab neighbors who lived on the ground floor. The neighbors, among the one thousand Israeli Arabs who lived in the city, were listening to Radio Cairo. As they translated the news items, the American grew increasingly frightened. Although she liked her neighbors and believed that if it came to it they would try to save her and her family, she detected an

182

unmistakable note of satisfaction in their narrative of Egyptian victories. Not until she heard tanks roll by outside, the soldiers aboard them singing—in Hebrew—did she relax.

The first encouraging news from an official source was buried in a nighttime broadcast from the Knesset, where Eshkol reported for the first time that the fighting in the south was on enemy territory. He also indicated that the Egyptian Air Force had taken a beating, but he gave no details. It was not until 1:15 A.M. that the nation received its first clear indication of what had been happening through a report on Kol Yisrael by Chief of Staff Rabin and Air Force Chief Hod. Despite the hour, there was hardly anybody in the country over the age of ten who was not awake and listening. Except for Eshkol's oblique remarks, there had been nothing to indicate how the bitter battle reported in the initial war bulletin seventeen hours earlier had developed; whether the two sides were still engaged along the Gaza Strip border, whether any Israeli settlements had been overrun, whether the Israeli and Arab air forces had neutralized each other or, indeed, whether disaster was imminent.

Speaking clearly and with immense calm, Rabin reported that Israeli troops were deep in enemy territory and had reached El Arish. He announced that Jenin, on the west bank of the Jordan, had fallen, indicating for the first time penetration of the Arab Legion front to the north. Then Hod came on to describe in a dry voice the destruction of the Arab air forces, letting fall the incredible figure of four hundred enemy planes knocked out. In case any listeners thought they had heard wrong, he proceeded to give a detailed breakdown of losses by each of the Arab countries like a careful housewife going over a grocery list. (Three hundred Egyptian planes destroyed, twenty of them in the air.) Israeli losses were given as nineteen planes.

At the main Kol Yisrael studios, broadcasting had continued most of the day, despite shells and bullets which struck within the compound. Bulletins were carried at a run across an open courtyard from the newsroom to an announcer in the broadcasting studio. Only for a two-hour period of heavy firing was it found necessary to switch Hebrew broadcasting to the standby studios in Tel Aviv. In this interval Arye Hauslich and his English-language section transferred to one of the standby broadcasting facilities in Jerusalem, about a kilometer and a half away, to reduce congestion at the main studio, where the battle din was so loud one had to shout to be heard. Two women had already fainted from fright.

In the Arabic-language wing, broadcasting continued without a break. Like a rolling artillery barrage, the section directed announcements at specific targets in front of the advancing Israeli Army. Arab field commanders from Gaza to El Arish, addressed by name, were called upon to put up white flags and surrender. In case the commanders didn't realize the extremity of their position, the broadcast informed them of the number of tanks and positions they had already lost. Residents of towns in the path of the advancing army were advised to hang white flags outside their homes, to stay indoors, and to close windows (so that no sniper could fire out without revealing himself). The instructions to the Arab civilians were delivered with the same detail and matter-of-factness that had marked the civil-defense instructions Kol Yisrael had given to Israeli civilians in the previous two weeks.

In addition to providing this close support to the front-line troops, Haazma's men also engaged their opposite numbers in the Egyptian propaganda services directly. The Egyptians had been asserting that British and American planes were joining the Israelis in the attack. You claim to have shot down eighty planes, retorted Kol Yisrael. Surely there must be some British or Americans among the pilots. Why not put them on television? The Israelis reminded the Egyptians that Nasser himself had a few days before said Russia would not intervene if America didn't. "Well, Russia hasn't intervened." Nasser probably had more air time on Kol Yisrael that day than on Radio Cairo. His speech of May 22 in which the Egyptian president told Israel, "Welcome to war" was rebroadcast. This is your leader, said Kol Yisrael. Now you know how he lied.

Although physically remote from the Egyptian front with which it was principally concerned at the moment, the Arabic section was receiving some pointed communications from the neighboring Jordanians. A light in a downstairs room which filtered through a blackout curtain drew two bursts of machine-gun fire. Another bullet put a neat hole through the window of the political commentator's office. He was not at his desk, but if he had been the bullet would have caught him squarely between the shoulder blades.

The editors of the English-language *Jerusalem Post*, the only daily published in the capital, were old hands at getting out a newspaper under adverse conditions. The plant was blown up by a terrorist bomb in 1948, but the next edition had come out on schedule in mimeographed form. Now, although many of the regular staff members had been mobilized, those remaining managed to meet the regular deadline. During the crisis period the paper had published instructions on sandbagging windows in rooms where people would be assembled, but nobody had bothered to sandbag the numerous windows in the newsroom on the second floor, where editors and reporters were concentrated throughout the day's shelling. In the evening Mayor Kolleck came up to dictate a message to the citizens of Jerusalem for the morning edition. During the day he had been touring the city in his car, and near the Ramat Rachel observation post it had collected some bullet holes. Kollek stayed for a while in the newsroom, his hands in his pockets, chatting with the staff. He had changed the white short-sleeved shirt he had worn during the day for a dark gray one to thwart snipers during his tour of the border areas. About 1 A.M., an hour after the staff had left and the presses in the basement had begun to thunder with the morning edition, a shell crashed through the roof, two stories above the newsroom.

On the streets, darkness was almost total. The last sliver of the dying moon would not rise until 2:35a.m.. Until then there was only pale starlight and a dull red glow clinging to the horizon in the direction of the Police Training School, where Israeli artillery had set a storehouse ablaze. The few people abroad felt their way by touching the sides of buildings and tapping with their toes to find the curb.

Stumbling by accident into Haga's northern district headquarters, I was led down a staircase to the basement in utter darkness. A curtain was suddenly pulled away, revealing a large, brightly lit room that looked the way one imagined a British fighter command headquarters looked during the Battle of Britain. Smart-looking girls sat at long tables answering telephones and typing reports. There were maps on the walls, radio sets, and, at the far end, a command room from which men in uniform emerged every few moments. In one corner children climbed on a gymnasium vaulting horse. A Haga officer explained that they were among a score of schoolchildren who had taken shelter at the headquarters when shelling had broken out while they were on their way home from school.

As the officer was escorting me back up to the street, the darkness was broken by a white shaft of light from a projector on the roof of the nearby Histadrut Building. The area to which the projector was directed could not be seen from the street, but the light was evidently pointing at something beyond the border in northern Jerusalem. To the Haga officer, familiar with Israeli Army tactics, the beam was as clear a signal of intent as a trumpet call. "We're going to attack," he said.

## 10  ZERO HOUR

All day long the projector crew had waited apprehensively in the Histadrut Building for nightfall, when they would go into action. In lighting up targets for the artillery observers, the men knew, they themselves would become the principal target in Jewish Jerusalem. Dennis Silk, the poet, had always believed that in peacetime a searchlight unit was a suitable assignment for an "artiste" like himself, but that in war the job carried exceptional hazards. He had worked as a proofreader at the *Jerusalem Post* and vividly recalled a story he had once handled describing a retaliation raid against a Syrian position. The Syrians had thrown on a projector which was eliminated by Israeli fire in twenty seconds. Dennis had already been assigned to a searchlight unit at the time, and he had read the story with a pang of empathy for the Syrian crew. Now it was his turn.

At 7:45 P.M., just after total darkness had settled, the crew was ordered into action. The projectors were hauled out of their enclosures and trundled into the open. Dennis felt an unexpected exhilaration in the physical effort of pushing his projector up a ramp and into battle. Jerusalem was spread out below him in the throes of apocalypse. Every quarter in the Jewish part of the city was being pounded by shellfire. Tracers reached toward each other across no-man's-land, and flares hung suspended on the horizon. An officer on the roof shouted, "Light" and ducked behind the parapet. Like a man pulling the switch of an electric chair in which he himself is sitting, Dennis reached up and yanked the projector handle.

*　　　*　　　*

Mike Ronen in the Pagi trench saw the light suddenly flick on, illuminating the Arab positions at the Police Training School opposite him. Far to the rear there was the sound of guns firing, and seconds later the area in the spotlight erupted in smoke and flying debris. The light switched off, but before the eyes had grown accustomed to the night again the projector was holding another position in its glare. For the men in the trench, who had endured an unremitting pounding from the Jordanians since morning, the sight was euphoric. It was as if someone were putting a giant finger on their tormentors and crushing them. A massive barrage hit Shuafat to the north, where Jordanian twenty-five-pounders had been firing. The enemy shelling became even more frenzied; shells hit just behind the Pagi trench, making an ugly clanking sound before exploding. The shells were red hot and coming in so low that Mike could read his watch in their glow. The men had become almost indifferent by now to the fire which had enveloped them since morning. When a supply vehicle came up, Professor Don Patinkin—American-born chairman of the Hebrew University Economics Department and a volunteer in the unit—climbed out of the trench to help unload it.

The Israeli counterbarrage—delivered with only a portion of the guns available—was largely confined to the northern edge of the city and failed to revive weary troops along other parts of the line. Shells had snapped communication lines, and some of the troops knew nothing more than what they could hear and see. What they could hear was Jordanian shelling all around them, and what they could see was a small but steadily growing number of casualties. Officers, hoarse from shouting above the noise of firing all day, found it difficult to talk. Many of the troops had had nothing to eat.

In the trench at Bait Yisrael, where the men had been cut off under direct fire and shelling all day, a supply detail guided by an intelligence officer reached them after darkness. The officer found the men in the trench dispirited. Their ammunition was almost exhausted, and casualties lay at the bottom of the trench awaiting evacuation. The commander of the position summoned his men in a weary voice to distribute the ammunition. The intelligence officer passed on the report that two hundred Egyptian planes were down. "You're kidding!" someone said happily. When the officer assured them it was true, he could hear the figure being passed along the trench. As the supply party headed for the rear, they could hear the firing from the trench pick up.

With the coming of darkness the Jordanians had begun putting heavy fire on the Mandelbaum Gate crossing, the only direct road connection between the two halves of the city. Their evident concern that an attack might be launched from this direction was warranted, since the paratroopers had indeed contemplated such a move. Inside the Mandelbaum customs post the men could feel the walls shake from mortar explosions, and a door on the first floor was blown in. Shells crashed through the roof of the "pope's shed," the large hangarlike construction put up outside the building at the time of the pontiff's visit. The Jordanians nervously sent up flares over the crossing every few moments, and the men at the windows twisted back into the shadows until the light had died. Except for the passing flare-light it was black inside the building, and men had to feel their way along the walls. When a soldier at an upstairs firing hole was killed, his body was passed down the reopened staircase to the first floor only with considerable difficulty. Near midnight movement was spotted on the Jordanian side of the crossing. Captain Nitzan, the cool young Jerusalemite commanding the sector, called for shelling to break up a possible attack. Headquarters asked for a fire to be lit in the field on the edge of no-man's-land, to serve as a marker for the artillery spotter. The assignment was extremely hazardous. Not only would the men carrying it out be exposed to the steady mortar fire, but in lighting the beacon they would expose themselves to the Jordanian front-line positions. Two young unmarried soldiers were chosen, one of them having volunteered. The volunteer, a Moroccan-born youth named Dadon, took off his boots to make less noise as he crossed within hearing of the Jordanian positions. Two high school girls from a neighboring house, who had taken shelter in the building earlier in the day, told Dadon and his companion that they would pray for them. The two soldiers slipped out of the building and sprinted across to the field and started a fire in the stubble. They returned safely to the building only to look back and see that the fire had died. They ventured out again. This time when they returned to the building the sky was red behind them.

Along the city line other men left the security of blockhouses to man forward listening posts which offered little or no cover. At the principal blockhouse near Mandelbaum Gate, Lieutenant Genzel made use of the hidden door shown him by the neighborhood children to place two men on the far side of the fire wall facing no-man's-land. It may be recalled that the fire wall and the blockhouse—and the apartment building between them—were on one side of a narrow street facing the Arab Legion positions on the other, twenty meters away. On the far side of the fire wall the Israeli lookouts could see up and down the street, which constituted no-man's-land, and warn against any attempt by Arab sappers to place charges against the apartment building (where the basement shelter was filled with residents) or against the blockhouse itself. Except for the darkness, however, the pair were naked to the enemy positions, and when they were spotted and fired on during the night they were obliged to pull back.

At Notre Dame a few men slipped out of the main building and set up an advanced listening post in a small structure closer to Damascus Gate.

Perhaps the most exposed outpost in Jerusalem was on Abu Tor. The position was just below the observation post to which tourists were taken for a distant view of the golden Dome of the Rock inside the Old City. The Arab Legion strongpoints were

190

just down the slope, beyond a tangle of barbed wire. Three soldiers manned the outpost, among them Arye Newman, the English-born rabbi who had gone to work at the Jewish Agency in the morning feeling like a shirker. Two of the Israelis lay in a bunker, which provided adequate shelter from the steady machine-gun fire beating about them. The field of vision from inside, however, was limited, and the third man had to be posted outside to ensure that there was no movement on the flanks. Their orders were to report enemy activity but not to fire unless attacked.

In the middle of the night Newman's turn to serve as outside man came. Bullets struck the other side of the meter-high stone wall he lay behind or skimmed just overhead. Periodically he would inch his head over the wall, but he could see no movement except shadows scudding away from falling flares. To the left the Hinnom Valley was lit by a fire burning through the enormous conical roof of the Dormition Church, atop Mount Zion. The night was cold and Newman covered himself with a blanket from a bedroll. The chances of getting hit by a bullet were not too remote, but there was certainly no sense freezing to death.

The fire in the Dormition Church had been started in the afternoon by an Arab shell and by dark it was eating through the lead plates covering the roof. The molten metal ran down the drainpipes or hung from the roof's edge like tallow. A unit of second-line troops arrived on the hill after nightfall to relieve the first-line unit which had been engaging the Arab positions all day. The relief force came through the tunnel which crossed the Hinnom Valley from Yemin Moshe, but for some reason the first-line unit left the hill on the open road. The men walked gingerly, almost tiptoeing, as they passed beneath the Old City wall and crossed the valley to rejoin the rest of their battalion.

Two kilometers behind the city line, in the Valley of the Cross, the men of the 120-mm. mortar battalion had been

191

waiting beside their silent weapons since morning with growing frustration. They had rolled back the camouflage netting at the sound of the sirens, but except for a few ranging shots they had not begun firing until dusk—and then only sporadically.

Night had just settled when the valley was suddenly lit by powerful projectors. Under Mayor Kollek's beautification program, landmarks, including the Monastery of the Holy Cross, were illuminated by floodlights which came on automatically after dark. No one had remembered to turn these off. Seizing the opportunity for direct action, the mortarmen grabbed rifles and Uzis and opened up on the projectors until they were shattered and the valley was again wrapped in darkness.

About twenty shells had landed in the valley during the day without causing damage, although one had exploded only six meters from an ammunition dump. The mortarmen could not understand why their batteries, the principal artillery support for the Israeli forces in Jerusalem, had been so lightly treated. Their position, easily viewed from heavily traveled Ruppin Road during the past two weeks, could hardly have been a secret to the Arabs, especially since a Russian diplomat was known to have seen it. If the Jordanians had put a couple of hundred shells into the small valley, instead of pounding the surrounding residential neighborhoods all day, the batteries would have been badly hurt, if not eliminated.

The handling of the Jordanian guns was indeed one of the most puzzling factors in the battle for Jerusalem. Their artillery units seemed to have divided Jewish Jerusalem among themselves, each battery hitting its sector without any attempt to coordinate the fire. About six thousand shells were to fall on the city, the bulk of them in the first twenty-four hours. Of these, five hundred were duds, indicating something radically amiss in the Jordanian armories. One thousand apartments were hit by shells.

On the roof of the Histadrut Building, it seemed to Dennis Silk—still alive, to his amazement—that the Jordanian shelling pattern reflected hysteria. It was almost as if frustrated Arab Legion gunners were indulging a grudge and trying to inflict as much damage on Jewish Jerusalem as they could after waiting nineteen years for the opportunity. There seemed little military purpose to the shells exploding across the city. His own projector, the only visible object in the entire Jerusalem area and an obvious military target, had been almost totally ignored.

Just once during the night did the men on the roof think they might be a target. A shell crashed in front of the building and a second one behind it. Thus bracketed, the light was instantly switched off, but the third shell failed to come. At the beginning of the evening, the light was kept on only for ten to twelve seconds but as the night wore on and the enemy counterfire failed to materialize, the projector would brazenly grip a target for ten minutes or longer.

The difference in the shelling pattern, Dennis felt, reflected the intellectual difference between the opponents. The Arabs were venting their passions without any apparent plan. Out in the darkness, the Jewish gunners were waiting silently under fire to deliver their blow at the telling moment.

On the roof nearby, Colonel Amitai was also thinking about the Jordanian artillery. The paratroopers would attack in the next few hours and there were no armored half-tracks available to carry them across no-man's-land. For decisive minutes Gur's men would be strung out between the lines as they charged across. If the enemy could concentrate his artillery and mortars at this juncture, Amitai felt, it was highly questionable if the attack could succeed.

To units of the Jerusalem Brigade deployed along the edges of the Jerusalem Corridor, the shelling of Jerusalem seemed more intense than it did to those in the city. In their foxholes at Mevo Betar, ten kilometers from Jerusalem, the men of a second-line infantry unit could clearly hear the distant crash of artillery. From the persistent reddish glow in the eastern sky it

193

seemed as if the whole city lay in flames. Somewhere in that holocaust were their wives and children. "We've got to do something," an officer said helplessly. Near midnight the unit's radioman picked up a report that the Arab Legion's Radar position had been taken by an armored force. It was the first sign that an offensive had begun.

Several hours had passed since Radars 1 and 2 had been taken, but Lieutenant Colonel Yigal's task force remained immobile at the edge of kibbutz Maale Hahamisha, while sappers cleared the road past the enemy position. Normally this job called for tank flails—heavy chains on a rotating drum which thrash the ground to detonate mines. But all flails had been sent to the south. The sappers had instead to probe with bayonets, gently removing the topsoil when they touched a mine. In darkness, under mortar fire, the job was a nightmare. At intervals a popping sound would be followed by a scream and a sapper would be rushed to the rear, a limb blown off. (Fifteen sappers were to be wounded at Radar, another dozen at Sheikh Abdul Aziz.)

At one point an anguished scream froze the sappers in their tracks, and they appeared gripped by mass shock. Yigal ordered his engineer officer to blast the road with bangalore torpedos (pipes filled with explosives). Although no bangalores for anti-tank mines were available (most had been consigned to the south), there were some light bangalores at hand which could set off antipersonnel mines. Their detonation revived spirits, and when Yigal dismounted from his command half-track and started up the road, the sappers moved forward again.

A broad-shouldered officer trailed by two men suddenly appeared, his face smeared with blood. Lieutenant Colonel Peikes, of the Jerusalem Brigade, commanded a battalion stationed in the Jerusalem Corridor. For the past two weeks he had trained his men for the assault on the hills now being overrun by the Harel. Unwilling to be elbowed out of the war, he had marched his force to Maale Hahamisha. Accompanied only by two radiomen, he had continued down the hazardous Radar road. Along the way a sapper stepped on a mine nearby, and shrapnel cut Peikes above one eye. Now, as blood trickled across his chin, he confronted Yigal and requested a role in the attack.

Ben-Ari, raised by radio at his command post below Kastel, proved obliging. Radar 3, according to Yigal, had not yet been taken, though no hostile fire was evident from that direction. Let him take it, Ben-Ari said. Peikes dispatched a company across the slopes and the men found abandoned emplacements. Colonel Peikes was to get his fight—but not until the following day

The tankmen stalled at Maale Hahamisha knew little of events forward. At one point the company commander saw a file of sappers moving to the rear, and, presuming the way cleared, he started his tank forward—directly onto a stack of mines by the roadside. The officer, who had been standing in the turret, lost an eye in the explosion and was carried to the rear. When the sappers reached the edge of the minefield several hours later, it was only to find themselves confronted by a yawning antitank ditch two-and-one-half meters deep. Beyond it were concrete tank barriers. Yigal ordered the ditch filled. The battalion commander joined his men as they began pitching in rocks.

Across an eleven-kilometer front, Ben-Ari's tanks and half-tracks were crawling forward in darkness behind determined commanders. None of these motorized units could move as fast as a man could walk. At Sheikh Abdul Aziz, in the brigade center, Major Natan's four remaining tanks had started toward Bidu. The track they followed was little wider than a donkey trail, and Natan led the way on foot, a flashlight in one hand and a pistol in the other. At times the tanks had to swivel back and forth to knock loose the trailside embankments in order to open rough passage.

On the brigade's right wing Major Uri was still inching his Shermans up Khirbet Talila at the head of Lieutenant Colonel Zvika's task force. Mines were no concern here, since the Jordanians had judged that nature rendered the slopes sufficiently

195

impassable. Under a moonless sky the only visibility was provided by the Arab Legion. Shells from twenty-five-pounders exploded regularly around the column and by the intermittent flashes Uri could sight the terrain immediately ahead. More helpful were the flares the legion sent up periodically, which lit the slope for a full thirty seconds. The driver could see nothing out the periscope, and Uri, upright in the turret, directed him. The goat path had long since been lost, and he steered for the dark outline of the ridge visible against the sky. The topheavy tank tended to nose downward toward the contour of the slope, but Uri kept turning it back toward the crest. Whenever the motor appeared to labor or the tilt seemed too reckless, he ordered the driver to halt, backtrack, and veer off. Once it took thirty minutes to clear a single outcropping. Uri could discern one or two tanks trailing and shone his pocket flashlight to the rear as a beacon. Periodically a tank behind reported its tread snapped or its motor broken down. Some of the Shermans were hung up on boulders. Uri began to wonder if any of the others would make it to the top. He was determined that he would.

In some of the vehicles men clambered out and walked ahead to guide. One of them fastened a white undershirt to the back of his belt for his driver to follow.

Slouched in the cab of a half-track, one Jerusalemite who was vaguely familiar with the terrain concluded that it was a stroke of brilliance to be advancing along ground the enemy considered tankproof. The driver next to him was not so certain the Jordanians were mistaken.

All day Monday two platoons of Jerusalem Brigade tanks had sat immobile in the Jerusalem Corridor, where they had been left by Major Aaron when he had taken the main elements of the tank company into the city that morning. The detachment —under Captain Rafi, the company's second in command— had been intended as a reserve force in the corridor, but the arrival of the Harel Brigade had made this mission superfluous.

At 5 P.M. Rafi—a calm, bespectacled lawyer—telephoned Schneller and pressed for an assignment. An hour later the tanks were ordered into Jerusalem. In the city Rafi linked forces with the small tank detachment under Lieutenant Sassoon left behind by Aaron at the Russian compound. Rafi now had more than half the company under his command. With Aaron fighting alongside the reconnaissance company in the southern part of the city and the Harel Brigade launching its attack in the Jerusalem Corridor, Rafi's collection of leftover tanks was the only armored force available to assist the paratroopers.

The tank officers were summoned to the basement of the Evalina de Rothschild School, a school for religious girls in Rehavia, to which Jerusalem Brigade headquarters had been shifted from Schneller. Passing through an outer room equipped with a battery of telephones, they entered the brigade war room.

General Narkiss was telling a joke when they walked in, but nobody seemed to laugh. A girl soldier served coffee to staff officers from the Jerusalem and paratroop brigades who sat around the table. In contrast to Narkiss's jauntiness, Gur looked solemn. Rafi introduced himself to the paratroop commander, who briefly outlined the general plan of attack. One of the tank officers asked Gur when the battle would begin and he said, "Perhaps close to eleven." It was then about 7 P.M. Rafi and his men left with one of the paratroopers for a close look at the northern breakthrough point, where the bulk of the tanks would be concentrated.

In the war room, staff officers of the two brigades remained to work out the complex details of coordination. In addition to the tanks, the Jerusalem Brigade would be providing the paratroopers with vital artillery support. When the paratroopers were ready to make their thrust, Jerusalem Brigade positions along the rest of the line would open fire to create a diversion.

In addition, the Jerusalem Brigade would have to supply the paratroopers with the equipment and ammunition they needed to make the attack. In preparing for the jump into Sinai, the paratroopers had stripped themselves to bare essentials. More grenades, in particular, would be required for the house-to-house fighting which lay ahead. Mortar shells were needed and bangalores to blast the barbed-wire fences in front of the Arab lines. The Jerusalem Brigade supply officer, a fatherly looking soldier who had been wounded while fighting in the Russian Army twenty-five years before, wrote down the paratroopers' requests on a sheet of paper, holding his eyeglasses like a magnifying glass in one hand, the lenses reversed. (Unknown to him, his eldest son, a paratrooper serving in the south, had been killed a few hours before.)

There was much to be done, and it began to appear increasingly unlikely that the attack could get under way at midnight, as Narkiss had requested earlier in the day. Even such a basic prerequisite as a communication net enabling the paratroop units to talk to each other by radio would not be completed before midnight. Gur told Narkiss he would need another hour or two.

Time was pressing even more urgently at battalion level, where the commanders of the three units were devising the tactics upon which the success of the operation and the lives of their men would hang. After the initial briefing by Gur on Zefania Street in the late afternoon, the battalion commanders had split up to survey their separate target areas. Accompanied by their company commanders, they had climbed onto rooftops offering a view of no-man's-land and beyond. The officers kept a discreet distance away from the border as long as there was daylight, to avoid tipping off the Jordanians to their interest in the sector.

As Colonel Uzi and his officers tried to get their bearings in the deserted streets of Bait Yisrael, two Chassidic boys with sidecurls came up and guided them to the building they were seeking. The boys would not leave the paratroopers and finally had to be shooed away. Uzi's assignment was to make the southern breakthrough, but the precise point of attack was his to choose. As they checked the view from the rooftop against their maps, the battalion's second in command, Captain Dan—a tough, taciturn kibbutznik from the Galilee—suggested that they force Mandelbaum Gate behind a phalanx of tanks. (When the possibility was mentioned later to Gur, he ruled it out on the basis of intelligence reports citing the strong Jordanian defenses behind the Mandelbaum crossing.)

Uzi preferred attacking from the Bait Yisrael area, about five hundred meters north of Mandelbaum. At points the gap between the Israeli and Jordanian fences was fifty meters or more, but opposite Bait Yisrael they almost touched, virtually eliminating the danger of mines, which the paratroopers feared had been laid between the fences.

At twilight Uzi's group ventured down to the border for a closer look at the breakthrough area. The dim light shielded them from enemy observation if they stayed close to the building but was sufficient to reveal the shape of no-man's-land, which opened out in a broad sweep to right and left.

The ground formed an uneven bowl, falling away steeply from the houses on the Israeli side to the fences in the bottomland and rising gently from there to Nablus Road, which paralleled the border on the Jordanian side. It was three hundred meters from one lip of the bowl to the other. The paratroopers' main concern was safely negotiating the slope on the Israeli side, which was devoid of structures and completely exposed. The Jordanian half of the bowl was largely filled with a warren of low houses and stone walls which would provide the paratroopers with ample cover once they were through the wire. The Arab Legion had some small firing positions just behind the wire, but their main defense line was a complex of bunkers and blockhouses along Nablus Road, which ran along their lip of the bowl 150 meters behind the crossing point.

In the northern breakthrough area Colonel Joseph and his commanders waited until darkness before approaching the border. Accompanied by Rafi and the tank officers, they entered a

199

*shikun* building directly opposite the Police Training School, 150 meters away. An old man praying in a corridor offered to guide them upstairs, but an officer said, "No, father. Just go downstairs to the shelter." The intelligence sergeant from the Jerusalem Brigade took out a set of keys and opened a door on the top floor.

Joseph, who had to pick a breakthrough point, looked out from the darkened apartment at a discouraging scene. Streams of tracers spewed from dozens of bunkers running the length of the enemy line. The ground sloped gently upwards from the Israeli side, rising abruptly beneath the enemy positions in a steep five-meter-high bank. His men would be moving up a slope straight into fire from the concrete bunkers. North of the Police Training School, no-man's-land was dominated by the massed bunkers of Ammunition Hill, whose fire could devastate any attacking force. South of the Police Training School there was the added physical obstacle of the fire wall built atop the earthen bank by the Jordanians during the previous two weeks. Behind this on a slight rise was an entrenched position dubbed "Yellow Blanket." (One day a yellow blanket had been seen hanging out the window of a fortified house in the center of the trench complex.)

Joseph decided to aim the attack at the southern corner of the Police Training School itself. Here they would be shielded by the width of the school from Ammunition Hill to the north, while the fire wall to the south would not be a hindrance since it stopped just short of the building. By attacking at this point, the men of the Sixth would have to contend only with a score of bunkers dominating the crossing point and random hazards like mines and artillery fire.

Artillery, indeed, might be the decisive factor. At some moment the battalion would have to commit itself and move into the open across no-man's-land. If the Jordanian guns caught them, the battalion could be shredded in minutes. But the paratroopers hoped that the Israeli bombardment just prior to

200

the assault—by artillery, mortars, and Rafi's tanks—would stun the Legionnaires in the bunkers sufficiently to permit the troops to close on the enemy trenches.

As for the mines, at least fifty meters separated the two enemy fences, but it would take too long to attempt to blow a way through this probable minefield with bangalores. The Israeli Army had adopted a straightforward tactic for such situations— the assault force would run through the field in single file. If the lead man stepped on a mine, the men behind would keep moving. In any event, the bulk of the force would make it across.

Where the other two battalion commanders had approached the breakthrough areas as closely as they could, Colonel Yussi of the Eighth remained on the roof of the Histadrut Building, eight hundred meters from the line. His would be the only battalion not making a breakthrough, passing instead through the hole in the line made by Uzi's battalion. On the Histadrut roof, Colonel Amitai pointed out to him Rockefeller Museum and other landmarks just outside the Old City walls which would be Yussi's targets. When night fell, Yussi and his officers descended and drove to Bait Hakerem to meet their men.

As was befitting in a new, middle-class neighborhood, the most distinguishing landmark in Bait Hakerem was the supermarket facing Denmark Square. The brigade had split up here after its arrival at dusk, each battalion spreading out along a different street, funneling into the square. Some of the men lay in building corridors and tried to sleep. Many were invited into apartments by residents who plied them with food and coffee. They sat on the floor chatting and sometimes singing, then growing silent to hear a news bulletin. Housewives put fresh sheets on beds and invited the soldiers to rest, even with their boots on. Although many of the residents had been too frightened all day to leave the shelters to go to their apartments, women now went out into the streets with trays of food and drink for those soldiers who had not come inside.

Some of the paratroopers descended to the shelters out of curiosity. They had been vaguely aware that the cities might be targets in the war but they were taken aback by the sight of women, children, and elderly men huddled in the light of candles and listening to the thump of shells. A trembling old man in one shelter asked a soldier whose guns were firing. The soldier had no idea, but he patted the man on the shoulder and assured him that they were Jewish guns.

Not all the soldiers appearing in the shelters were strangers. In a crowded Bait Hakerem basement Aviva Goren, a stunning, dark-haired beauty, was sitting with her two young children when a helmeted soldier entered in full battle gear, grenades dangling from his belt. It was her husband, a staff officer of the Eighth Battalion. The children and neighbors ran to him, but Aviva could not move. They had only a moment to look at each other across the room before he turned and hurried back to his headquarters. (Several hours later he would be lying in a street a few miles away, blinded in one eye.)

Private Inbar of the Sixth also lived in Bait Hakerem, but he didn't attempt to visit home for fear his unit might move out while he was gone. When some civil-defense personnel came by, he recognized his sister, Mina, under a helmet. He asked her to go home and bring some hot coffee for him and his buddies and a sweater against the cool Jerusalem night.

Most of the soldiers took advantage of the telephones made available to them by the Bait Hakerem residents. Lieutenant Raviv of the Seventh, a Jerusalemite who had been mobilized immediately upon his return from a European honeymoon two weeks earlier, telephoned his wife on the other side of town. When she told him Jerusalem was being heavily shelled he said, "Really?" in as surprised a tone as he could muster. He declined to tell her where he was, but from the clear connection she guessed that he was not very far away.

Many got no answer when they phoned home, their families being below in shelters. Nir, an officer who was to prove a major

202

figure in the coming battle on Ammunition Hill, was fortunate enough to call just as his wife was returning to their house near Tel Aviv from the neighborhood shelter. He told her the men were angry because they had not been given a chance to fight but that they might have something to do the next day. When she asked where he was, he said, "In a good place." A dentist on Herzl Boulevard invited dozens of men into his house to use the phone. Some men, protesting that his phone bill would run into hundreds of pounds, tried to pay him. Not satisfied with making his phone available, the dentist called out to the men on the darkened street, asking if anyone was having trouble with his teeth. At least one soldier was seen submitting himself to an examination by flashlight.

A private visited a couple in the neighborhood who were old friends of his parents. The wife tearfully kissed the soldier whom she had known as a young boy. The husband soberly shook the paratrooper's hand and asked where they would be attacking, and when. At this point neither the private nor any of his comrades had any idea.

The three battalion staffs had set up temporary headquarters in apartments made available to them by people in the shelters. Risking the wrath of civil-defense wardens, who had been enforcing a strict blackout, the officers covered the windows with blankets and switched on the lights. Maps were spread over the tables, and the women of the house, including those from neighboring apartments, served hot drinks and food.

At 10 Bait Hakerem Street, the staff of the Seventh had taken over the apartment of lawyer Jacob Cohen. While Uzi and his deputy drew up the attack plan on the kitchen table, the rest of the battalion staff and company commanders waited in the living room, spilling over from the couches onto the floor. The officers smoked and drank coffee and filled the room with buoyant, confident tones. Sometimes

203

there was a gust of laughter. Several officers asked Mrs. Cohen if it would be all right to go down to the shelter to look at the children sleeping.

One of Uzi's officers, Captain Zamush, was the only religious company commander in the brigade. Upon learning that they were going to Jerusalem, he had asked that his company be the first to fight in the Old City. Uzi said he would ask Gur about it. Now, in the apartment, Zamush asked Mrs. Cohen for a flag. When she produced one, Zamush told her he would fly it from the Western Wall.

He could hardly have chosen a more humble banner to proclaim the return of the Jewish nation to the site of the Temple. The flag had been purchased by Mrs. Cohen's mother in 1947, just prior to the formation of the State of Israel, and was not of regulation proportions. In addition, the Star of David and horizontal blue stripes had been applied only on one side, and their color was faded at that. Although popular legend was later to describe the flag as having been flown by the Cohens in the Old City prior to their expulsion from the Jewish quarter, the Cohens had in fact never lived in the Old City and had only flown the flag from their Bait Hakerem window on Independence Day each year.

After an hour Uzi emerged from the kitchen. He hung a map from a bookshelf in the living room and outlined the plan to his commanders.

Colonel Joseph, whose battalion had drawn the most difficult assignment, did not finish his plan until 11:30. He had first assigned the fence-busting operation to the company led by Captain Dodik—a kibbutznik from Gonen in the Galilee— which was to have performed a similar job in the canceled drop at El Arish. After Dodik had already passed word to his officers to prepare bangalores, the plan was changed. Respected by his fellow officers as an especially forceful leader, Dodik would instead get first crack at the enemy trenches. His men would cross no-man's-land after another company, Captain Giora's, had blown a path through the fences. Intelligence had given the paratroopers no information on the depth or width of the Jordanian trenches, an omission that was to be felt when Dodik's troops tried to move through the narrow trenches without having taken off their bulky backpacks.

Ammunition Hill was assigned to Captain Dedi, a young officer who would be getting the toughest position in Jerusalem in his first crack at combat. Joseph told Dodik his company might have to be used on the hill as well if Dedi's men needed help.

Unlike the other two battalion commanders, Colonel Yussi of the Eighth found himself confronted with what looked like a fairly easy mission. Not only would he be spared the necessity of making his own breakthrough, but according to intelligence he should reach his principal target—Rockefeller Museum—virtually without a fight, once he had brought his men across no-man's-land. It was the probable second stage of the battle, it seemed, which held the danger and the glory. By ordering the Eighth to take the museum directly across from the Old City wall, Gur was placing Yussi in position to assault the Old City itself. He told Yussi to be prepared for an order to break in through Herod's Gate, two hundred meters from the museum. Such an order would have to await decision at the highest political level.

Herod's Gate was one of three in the city's north wall. It was where the last successful storming of Jerusalem's walls had taken place nine centuries earlier, during the Crusades. The north wall, indeed, had been the only one successfully stormed by a conquering army since David's capture of the city three millennia before. On east, south, and west, the city is bounded by deep wadis which leave any would-be attacker completely exposed to fire from defenders atop the wall. North of the city, however, the approach is flat, and attackers can approach the wall on more even terms. The prophets had warned that "danger comes from the north," and the city's conquerers, from the

Babylonians to the British, had approached from that direction. (The Turks evacuated the city in 1917 before the British reached it.)

Yussi was asked by one of his company commanders if they were to enter all houses on their route or just those from which fire came. Yussi told them what Gur had said—to move as quickly as possible and enter only those houses from which they were fired at.

While it was seniority that had won Yussi's battalion the coveted position at the gates of ancient Jerusalem (a position which the tide of battle would subsequently ignore), the unit was treated like a poor relation by the brigade when it came to distribution of the vital aerial photographs of the target area. The photos—taken by the light planes which had cruised over the city during the previous two weeks—were the basic material on which the commanders would have to rely in their planning and in finding their way during the battle itself. Jordanian bunker and trench positions invisible to the naked eye were drawn on the photos by intelligence. Street names and other landmarks were also indicated, so that the officers could orient themselves when they pushed into the heart of the enemy half of the city. But after photos had been distributed to Uzi and Joseph's breakthrough battalions, there were only two left for all of Yussi's battalion. His officers crowded around them trying to memorize the area they would be fighting in. It was a hopeless task, and the Eighth would pay for its unfamiliarity with the target area.

The other battalions were not much better off. While they had more photos to go around, there simply was not enough time to study them. Platoon commanders would be leading men into night battle against complicated trench and bunker positions that they had studied on the photostats for little more than a minute or two.

After the battalion commanders had outlined their plans, the company commanders dispersed into the dark streets to find their units and brief their officers. Dodik gathered his lieutenants and outlined the company's mission on a photostat illuminated by flashlight. Each platoon commander was given his specific task. Lieutenant Lanier, a kibbutznik from the Beisan Valley, drew the point assignment—his men would be the first into the trenches. The company commander noticed Lieutenant Yoav Tsuri's face in the lamplight. The former swimming champion would be in the center of the line, following Lanier's men and the light machine-gun section. Dodik told the deputy company commander, Nir, to study the trench pattern on Ammunition Hill if he had a couple of minutes because there was a chance that the company might have to fight there too. But Nir, who had the photostat just seven minutes before having to pass it on to another company, needed all that time for studying the company's primary target area. In a few hours he was to bitterly regret his unfamiliarity with Ammunition Hill.

Dedi assembled his officers beside a bus and in the faint illumination from the door light showed them an aerial photo of Ammunition Hill. "Fellows, we have to take this," he said. Of the five officers gathered around him, three would be dead within a few hours and the other two wounded. One of the platoon commanders had a minute with the photostat and made a quick pencil sketch of the enemy trenches.

After briefing their officers, the company commanders addressed the troops. In the portico of an apartment building Dodik explained to his men what lay ahead in a clear, calm briefing that made the mission seem almost matter-of-fact. They would be passing through a minefield, he said. Nobody was to stop to pick up wounded. If the man in front of you falls, he said, step on him and keep moving.

Captain Giora, whose company would have the vital breakthrough assignment, found his men already inside the two buses that would carry them to the front. His deputy told the drivers to shut off the motors as Giora mounted each vehicle to address the men. "Our job is the breakthrough," he said. "It's a difficult one but we will break the fences at all costs."

On Bait Hakerem Street, Captain Zamush of the Seventh told his men of his request that they be the first to fight for the Temple Mount. Touching the flag, which he had stuck in the webbing of his equipment, he said, "We might be raising this flag tonight or tomorrow on the Western Wall."

For the soldiers the most important briefing came from the platoon commanders at whose side they would go into battle. The lieutenants, who often had only a sketchy knowledge of the target area, described it as best they could.

A red-haired young platoon commander from the Seventh, Lieutenant David, took his platoon, half at a time, to the front of a bus where a light above the driver's seat permitted them to scan a photostat. In the brief time they had, few could understand what they were looking at. David reminded the young soldiers to pass on any orders they heard in the darkness and to respond immediately to his commands. If the bazookist or automatic rifleman heard him call, they were to move directly to his side.

Lietuenant Yoram, one of the officers from Dedi's company, held an aerial photograph of Ammunition Hill against a street billboard while his men gathered to look at it by flashlight. The photo was too small and too dark for them to see anything. "Perhaps there will be Arabs on the hill, perhaps not," Yoram said. This left some of his men thinking they might take it without a fight, but aboard the bus Yoram told his bazookist they were in for a hard battle.

Some of the officers attempted jokes. "The legion has orders to fight to the last man," a lieutenant told his men. "Our orders are the same—to fight to the last Legionnaire."

Supply officers, meanwhile, had been bringing up equipment and ammunition obtained from the Jerusalem Brigade armories. Extra grenades were tucked into pouches or hung from belts.

bunker taken on Ammunition Hill. Bunker's side wall and roof which had covered trench at
ɔoint were blown in by explosives placed by paratroopers. Side wall at far end of bunker has
partially shifted into trench by force of explosion. Entranceway was on near side of bunker.
ɾe, taken two years after war, shows new housing development of Ramat Eshkol rising across
had been no-man's-land.

ᴎER BRAUN

Lt. Yoav Tsuri.

Shell-battered tower of Rockefeller Museum, from which Israeli troops exchanged fire with Jordanians on Old City parapets. Makeshift flag was devised by a soldier out of a sheet and ink found in nearby house.

HANE

Tanks and paratroopers take shelter behind stone walls at rear of museum, prior to aborted assault on Mount of Olives in background.

The northern breakthrough force found itself short of bangalores. Taking a flashlight, Doron, the deputy battalion commander of the Sixth, poked his head into supply trucks parked along Herzl Boulevard for half an hour until he found one containing the explosives.

Lieutenant Colonel Stempel, the brigade's second in command, spread a map on the hood of a truck and showed Dr. Jack the two prongs of the attack. The brigade medical officer picked the streets where he would set up aid stations in support of each thrust. "*Nu*, Stempel," said a passing officer, "we're going to take Jerusalem." Stempel, a squat professional soldier, responded not with banter but with a challenge. "That depends on you."

Major Kapusta found Gur in the headquarters the latter had set up in a small apartment building at the corner of Zefania and Bar Ilan Streets. The pair were old comrades, but Gur had to tell the recon commander he could not help him. The plans were already complete, and there was nowhere Kapusta's force could be inserted. Nevertheless, the recon commander clung hopefully to headquarters, peering over Gur's shoulder at the maps as a succession of officers from the three battalions came in to report on their plans. Whenever Kapusta heard them mention some point likely to be tough, he hopefully interjected, "Well, use us there." But his efforts were in vain.

Late in the evening Gur visited the roof of the Histadrut Building, where he found Narkiss. The general, who had originally set the attack for midnight, now passed on to Gur a new alternative offered by the General Staff—the paratroopers could either attack as planned that night or wait till morning, when they could have air support. Gur, who personally preferred a night attack, nevertheless decided to consult with his battalion commanders.

It was close to midnight when Uzi, Joseph, and Yussi, each

accompanied by his second in command, met with Gur at the Zefania Street headquarters for a final war conference. The choice of all six officers was immediate and decisive—a night attack. They were trained in night fighting and preferred it, while the Arabs, experience had shown, were weakest at it. The officers also felt that any delay might give the enemy time to bring up his tanks from Jericho. They did not believe that planes could attack the front-line Jordanian positions, which were only one hundred meters from the Israeli apartment houses. The most important consideration was that darkness would afford them cover as they crossed the open expanse of no-man's-land. A 2 A.M. starting time was fixed. (It would later be advanced to 2:20).

There was little more the brigade staff could do now. At 12:15 Gur lay down to nap for forty-five minutes in a large storeroom off the portico serving as his command post. A woman and three children who had taken shelter in the storeroom watched impassively as the colonel slept. On the lantern-lit portico, the brigade intelligence officer, Arik, spoke in hushed tones with officers coming up to make final arrangements.

The dark hulks of Rafi's tanks were drawn up on the street outside. Lieutenant Sassoon had dismounted from his tank and, propping himself up on two motor scooters, had dozed off. A teen-age boy approached one of the tank commanders and related a shoemaker's prophecy which had been spreading through the country the past week. The elderly shoemaker—from Ramat Gan, near Tel Aviv—had died earlier in the year. Some said he was one of the Thirty-six Righteous Men who, according to Jewish tradition, exist anonymously in every generation and upon whose sanctity the world rests. He had left a will to be opened on the holiday of Lag ba'Omer, which this year had fallen on May 28, just a week before. The will foresaw three weeks of terrible tension, followed by three days of difficult battle. The conclusion, however, would be a victory unlike any enjoyed by the Jewish people since the time of Moses.

While in the city the paratroopers prepared to assault, out in the corridor Ben-Ari's right wing, under Lieutenant Colonel Zvika, had managed to push a force of Shermans and half-tracks to the top of Khirbet Talila. The commander of the lead company, Major Uri, had crested the ridge at 11 P.M. It had taken four hours for his tank to climb the last five hundred meters. Six tanks soon joined him—this was all that remained of the fourteen which had started. The second Sherman company in the column had been diverted to another prong, so no more tanks would be joining them. The seven Shermans descended the rear slope of the hill onto a dirt road, which they followed to a junction at Nebi Samuel. Ben-Ari radioed Zvika to take up a defensive position and wait for more of his forces to come over the hill. But as the hours went by, Zvika's force did not grow much larger. A few half-tracks with infantry struggled over the crest, and the brigade reconnaissance company linked up after having taken the village of Bait Iksa without a fight. But there were no more tanks. Finally, at 2 A.M. Ben-Ari radioed to begin moving with what he had toward Shuafat intersection on the Ramallah–Jerusalem road. Not much farther off to the east a convoy of forty-four Jordanian Pattons was already moving up through Judean Desert toward the same intersection.

In Jerusalem, the hour of attack approached. Gur shifted his command post to the roof of a yeshiva on Yael Street overlooking both the northern and southern prongs. Three bus convoys moved out from Bait Hakerem for the front, each carrying a paratroop battalion. Along the city line Jerusalem Brigade soldiers manning the blockhouses were ordered to open diversionary fire at 2 A.M. The trench positions north of Mandelbaum Gate, however, would hold their fire, to avoid hitting the paratroopers who would be moving across their front.

The artillery officer coordinating all Jerusalem Brigade artillery and heavy mortars paced the roof of the Histadrut Building like a restless conductor as he checked his batteries. One reported that it was not quite ready. "The whole State of Israel," said the officer, "is waiting for you."

In the Valley of the Cross, the mortarmen rose to their guns.

# 11   AMMUNITION HILL

The convoys carrying the troops to the border moved through streets illuminated only by the distant flash of exploding shells. A sergeant riding in an open jeep found the silence and the darkness of his native city awesome. Inside some of the buses overhead lights had been switched on to permit final checks of weapons and equipment. On one street a civil defense warden shouted, "Douse those lights" at the passing vehicles. The men had never felt so drawn together as they did now moving up to battle. They discussed the small details of the soldier's trade—such as whether it was better to hook grenades to belts or to keep them in belt pouches. A noncom was surprised to see bottles of oil, normally hoarded like good cognac, being offered around as the men cleaned their weapons. A squad leader advised his men to drink water now, since there might not be a chance later.

The buses carrying the Sixth were to park on Eli Hacohen Street, about a kilometer from the border. After debarking the men were to march to the rear for a hundred meters in order to reach Bar Ilan Street, which would take them down to the barbed wire. The battalion had therefore been loaded onto the buses in Bait Hakerem in reverse order, the spearhead company in the rear bus. The plan foundered, however, when a line of tanks on Zefania Street blocked the convoy short of its goal. When the men debarked, they found that they now had to march forward to reach Bar Ilan Street. The commanders were forced to reshuffle the entire battalion in a dark, narrow street half filled with buses. The street rang with the shouts of officers trying to assemble companies and pass them around each other.

The men were burdened like housewives coming home from market—extra packs of explosives or bangalores tucked under their arms or lashed down to already bulging packs.

Abie, a lieutenant from a religious kibbutz in the Beit Shean Valley, freed himself from the press of bodies and made his way quickly down Bar Ilan to the Shmuel Hanavi *shikun*. As commander of the heavy machine platoon, he had to choose a position in one of the apartment buildings overlooking no-man's-land from which he could give effective covering fire during the assault. He selected the northernmost building in the block, the only one whose field of fire included both the break-through point at the southern corner of the Police Training School and Ammunition Hill, north of the school. Looking out an upstairs apartment he saw the Arab positions opposite, dark and silent.

Returning to Zefania Street, he extricated his platoon and an ammunition truck, guiding them down to the rear of the building. While the men assembled the weapons in the portico, Abie took the squad leaders upstairs to the third floor and showed them their positions. The six machine guns were distributed among five apartments, the two weapons in the center sharing adjoining rooms of a single apartment. Three of the apartments were empty and their doors open. The other two, whose occupants were in the shelter below, were locked, and the soldiers had to break in the doors.

Abie told the men in the inhabited apartments to pile furniture beneath the chest-high windowsills to serve as firing platforms for the guns. A soldier protested that the furniture would be ruined. Abie said, "If you have a better way, do it." Nobody had a better way, and the soldiers dragged beds and desks to the windows. In the empty apartments, however, there was nothing on which to prop the guns. Abie told two men in each crew to grasp the gun by its front legs and to let the barrel of the heavy weapon rest on their shoulders. (At dawn Abie was to break open the door to the roof to get a better view of the battlefield and

218

find the roof lined with concrete firing positions far more secure than the apartments below. Nobody had told the paratroopers about them.)

The Jordanian positions had by this time come alive, alerted by the sounds of the Israeli tanks approaching. Ignoring for the moment the line of muzzle flashes etching Ammunition Hill, Abie told his men to open fire on the trench in front of the Police Training School and on two machine guns firing from the upper floor of the school itself, since these positions dominated the breakthrough point.

When one of the guns in the center apartment jammed, the squad commander, Sergeant Mevorach, told his men to set it down on the floor and strip it. While they worked, he stood at the window and took up the fire with his own automatic rifle. In the adjoining room Abie himself had taken over from a slow-moving gunner and was raking the enemy trench, when an explosion threw him against the wall, his machine gun clattering to the floor. Smoke filled the apartment, and it became difficult to breath.

The explosion had been in Mevorach's room. Abie found the three men who had been stripping the gun lying injured on the floor but able to get up. The squad leader, however, lay near the window murmuring incoherently. Abie reached down to pull him out of the room and found that his hands had been blown off at the wrists. The Jordanians, apparently attracted by the muzzle fire of Mevorach's automatic rifle—faster than that of the machine guns in the other windows—had fired a recoilless rifle shell which hit him in the hands. Nearby his gun lay twisted. Moshe Mevorach, a farmer from Tsur Moshe, was the first paratrooper to be fatally injured in the battle for Jerusalem.

Rafi had ordered his tanks to roll down Bar Ilan to the border with motors off to avoid being heard by the Arabs. But the squeal of their treads drifted across no-man's-land, and mortar shells began to hit around them before they reached the bottom of the street. Four tanks rode over a small stand of olive trees to the left of Abie's building and opened fire on the Police Training School even before they stopped rolling. Three tanks took position among the *shikun* buildings and opened up on the Yellow Blanket position. The remaining three tanks moved eight hundred meters south to assist the breakthrough of the Seventh Battalion.

The Histadrut projector illuminated the Police Training School, and Lieutenant Sassoon found his gunner drawn to the brightly lit target. The officer told him to shift his fire to the trench below. After a few moments the enemy position was obscured by smoke, and the tank gunners concentrated on the gun muzzles sparkling in the haze. (The one-hundred-meter stretch of trench in front of the Police Training School was to receive a heavier concentration of fire per square meter than any other Arab position on any front.) Antennas atop the Shermans were ripped by shrapnel and machine-gun fire, and the men's personal kit bags tied down atop the hills were shredded. When the roll of camouflage netting on one tank caught fire, crew members ventured out safely to pull it off. But a crew member in Rafi's tanks was wounded when he put his head out a hatch.

The Jordanian fire reached back to the battalion's mortar positions near the Sanhedria tombs. A shell hit in the middle of a battery, wounding three men—one of them fatally. There had been no time to dig foxholes, and the mortar commander ordered his men to leave the guns and find shelter. Some of them took cover next to one of the nearby apartment buildings. But a shell exploded against the building's stone facing and sent a spray of shrapnel below, killing five of the mortarmen and wounding seven. The battalion now had seven dead and twelve wounded—and the attack had not yet begun.

At 2:20 A.M. the Israeli guns opened up. Twenty-five-pounders slammed into Ammunition Hill, and 160-mm. mortar shells struck across the Police Training School compound, setting a

220

large storehouse afire. In the Valley of the Cross, the mortarmen began feverishly pumping 120-mm. shells at French Hill to the north. From the trench opposite Ammunition Hill, where he had crouched helplessly all day beneath the Jordanian fire, Mike Ronen watched in fascination as artillery, tanks, and heavy machine guns simultaneously poured fire into the enemy positions.

In the portico of the apartment building, usually alive with the sound of children, lines of paratroopers waited in silence for the barrage to lift. The photostats supplied by intelligence indicated that they would have to pass through two Jordanian barbed-wire fences. The fences were not visible on the print but had been hand-drawn midway between the opposing lines. Since the paratroop officers had not seen no-man's-land for themselves in daylight, they could not know the photostat was in error. Captain Giora, whose company was assigned the breakthrough mission, organized three bangalore teams. Two of them carried a pipe ten meters long composed of ten separate bangalores which had been screwed together. A reserve team under Micha, the deputy company commander, carried nine separate bangalore sections to deal with any unexpected development.

The Israeli barrage lifted after half an hour, and Colonel Yussi led Giora to a gap between the apartment buildings and pointed to the southern corner of the Police Training School, directly opposite. The first bangalore team swung out from the shelter of the portico behind Lieutenant Blum and started toward no-man's-land. Ten meters in front of the building the men at the head of the column ran into barbed wire. Although it was an Israeli fence, it had not been indicated on the photostat. The strands were trampled down, and the men moved through into the dry scrub beyond. The bangalore team charged toward the first Jordanian fence fifty meters ahead, carrying the length of pipe on their shoulders like a coolie gang. Fire-support teams ran right and left, threw themselves flat, and opened up on the Jordanian line with bazookas and automatic weapons.

The men with the bangalores reached the fence—a tangle of

221

concertinas five meters deep—and thrust the pipe into the wire, the rear men pushing forward. The Jordanians, alerted by the Israeli barrage, opened fire along the line. They evidently did not realize where the breakthrough was taking place, but their tracers laced no-man's-land indiscriminately. The rear man on the bangalore team suddenly pitched backwards, a bullet in his chest. The weight of his falling body caused the rear bangalore section—the one containing the detonator—to uncouple. In the darkness, however, the break was not seen. When the detonator was activated, only the rear section exploded—leaving the fence virtually intact.

The commander of the second bangalore team, Lieutenant Buki, was waiting with his men in a sheltered swale when Lieutenant Blum came back and led him up to the wire. Buki could make out a small section of severed wire backed by a huge mound of concertinas. He assumed the severed wire was the first Jordanian fence and the remaining concertinas the second fence. His men pushed their bangalore into the wire and detonated it. This time the barrier parted.

Dodik's company lay in single file just inside in no-man's-land waiting for the cry of "Exploded" which would signal that the second fence had been cut. Nir, the deputy commander, lay behind the first platoon. He heard no shout but recognized for the second time the distinctive explosion of the bangalore. Yelling "Exploded," he started forward. Dodik had told Nir to stay behind the lead platoon, but he dashed to the head of the column as it passed through the breach in the fence and entered the minefield.

Out on Shmuel Hanavi Street a Jerusalem Brigade intelligence officer returning from one of his forward posts stopped to listen to a strange, keening roar suddenly audible through the explosions. It was a moment before he recognized it with a chill as the full-throated shout of men charging into battle. The paratroopers were going in.

*      *      *

Distant flares faintly lit the area as the men raced behind Nir toward the enemy trench. Tracer bullets left a phosphorous glow as they glanced off rocks on either side of them. Rafi's tanks were still firing to keep down the Jordanians' heads, and Giora's covering force threw a mantle of tracers over the assault team. The Arab Legion bunkers in the trench atop the embankment dominated no-man's-land. As Nir closed on the enemy line, he could see muzzle flashes to his left from the bunkers in front of the Police Training School and to his right from the newly completed fire wall in front of the Yellow Blanket position. Reaching the foot of the embankment, Nir was protected by his very proximity, since the enemy guns could not be depressed sufficiently to reach him. He scrambled up the short, steep slope, bracing himself for the drop into the enemy trench. To his dismay, he found a barbed-wire fence on the lip of the embankment barring his way. This was the second Jordanian fence, which had been mistakenly drawn on the photostat halfway across no-man's-land and which the bangalore teams thought they had already disposed of.

Its sudden appearance portended disaster. The battalion was committed now, strung out in the open behind Nir as it ran toward a breach that wasn't there. If it was spotted by a single Legionnaire in radio contact with his mortars, the battalion could be crippled in minutes. For a moment Nir thought of running left until he found an opening in this unexpected obstacle. But he reasoned that this would put his men into the minefield in the worst possible way: broadside instead of in line. He considered throwing himself atop the wire and having the troops pass over him. But he had run so far ahead of his men that he feared they wouldn't see him if he suddenly went flat. Instead, he shouted, "Another fence."

Men threw themselves flat as the shout was passed down the line. Lieutenant Eli, commander of the MAG (light machine gun) section, following the spearhead platoon, ignored the danger of mines and told his men to leave the line and take shelter

223

from the enemy machine guns along the foot of the embankment.

Micha, commander of the reserve bangalore team, was waiting by the first Jordanian fence when Nir's message reached him. The religious kibbutznik (from Tirat Zvi in the Beisan Valley) snatched a bangalore from one of his men and sprinted forward. Throwing himself against the embankment, he thrust the bangalore into the barbed wire and attached one of the spare detonators he carried in his shirt pocket. As he worked, he noticed the firing hole of a bunker one meter from his face. Nobody showed himself on the other side, but a grenade came out of the trench beyond and exploded a few meters away, cutting the face of a lieutenant lying nearby and bouncing a stone off Micha. He activated the detonator and ran back.

With the explosion, Dodik's men scrambled up the slope and reached the trench. Placing their hands on its lip, they swung themselves down. Nir and squad leader Ilan Angel, the first men in, fired to their left and moved in that direction, immediately stepping on two bodies. Ilan noticed two dead Legionnaires wearing gas masks. (A small mortar had been lobbing smokeshells from the *shikun* to shield the breakthrough point.)

The trench was so deep that the men inside could not see over its edge, and so narrow they could not pass each other. With the bulging packs on their backs, it was difficult for even one man to move freely. Lieutenant Lanier, near the head of the first platoon, saw the men ahead suddenly bunch up. He pounded their backpacks and yelled, "Move," but nothing happened. Thinking they were afraid to advance, Lanier swung up out of the trench, glancing apprehensively at the Police Training School looming above him. "Platoon, after me," he shouted.

Reentering the trench past the bottleneck, he discovered that the jam was caused by the second man in line vainly trying to pass the first man, whose magazine was empty. Because of their packs, it was impossible to get by. Lanier shouted to his men that from now on the point man would lie down after he emptied his magazine and let the others run over him.

224

Bunkers opened off the trench to the left every ten meters. Arabs emerged from a few of them, only to fall dead under the steady automatic fire the point men threw out ahead of themselves as they pounded down the trench. The paratroopers flipped grenades into the bunkers from which fire came but did not pause to enter them. Private Yehuda Kandel saw a blur of figures ahead and fired a burst, but he saw only one fall, the rest seeming to disappear. When he drew abreast, he found three dead Legionnaires stacked one on the other. Kandel told a wounded comrade who blocked his way to lie down so that he could run over him. Once Nir took the point and got so far ahead of the rest of the men that he had to stop and yell back, "Nir ahead—don't shoot."

North of the Police Training School the trench angled to the right, running along the edge of a large asphalted parking lot which separated the building from Ammunition Hill. Dodik, advancing with the lead platoon, ordered Lieutenant Eli on the walkie-talkie to put two of his MAGs out of the trench and have them fire across the parking lot toward the hill. Eli himself continued with the main force and at the foot of the hill ordered his third MAG section out to screen the right flank. One member of the gun crew was Private Naphtali Cohen, the Yemenite youth who had gone from the folk-dancing session at Even Yehuda straight into the mobilization bus two weeks before. He had been gripped by a trancelike feeling as he crossed no-man's-land. Stepping on a body in the trench, he had recoiled for a moment, then suddenly grew calm. He knew where he was and what he was supposed to do.

Climbing out of the trench at the foot of the hill, Naphtali saw three buildings to the right. They were Arab Legion officers' quarters. To a figure running near one of them Naphtali yelled, "Password." There was no answer. Naphtali fired his rifle and the figure fell. The gunner on the team, Israel Tsuriel, set fire to the gas tank of a tender with a burst of the MAG. In the light of the burning vehicle he

225

saw a soldier topple from the low roof of an adjacent building and arc over the flames, apparently hit by the MAGs firing across the parking lot.

In the trench Dodik's main force continued to a trench junction at the southwestern corner of the hill, which had been designated "Iron 4" in the attack plan. Here Dodik's company was to halt and wait in reserve while Dedi's company swept in from the parking lot to the right and attacked the hill from the south.

Dodik had written the code words "Iron 4" in ink on his palm as a reminder, and now he spoke them into the radio. In a moment distant guns opened up for a final shelling, four minutes of "iron" designed to break up the expected Arab Legion counterattack. The men took shelter in the legion bunkers as shells hit as close as ten meters away. They had completed their assigned mission—clearing the trench dominating the crossing point.

To the rest of the battalion the crossing seemed more like a training exercise than war. A strip of white tape guided them through the holes in the fences and the minefield just as on maneuvers, and the signalers were kneeling as usual by the fences to guide them to the tape. The noise of explosions and the tracers overhead were likewise familiar training background. For one of the soldiers the only jarring note was the sight of the UNRWA sign on the Police Training School. It seemed they were about to attack a United Nations force and he wondered why. A signaler at the first fence noticed a slight widening of the eyes as the man moved past him. One of his friends recognized him and casually asked, "What's new?" In the light of a flare Major Doron, the deputy battalion commander, saw an appalling sight: scores of bodies scattered motionless across no-man's-land. He looked again and realized it was Giora's breakthrough company taking over.

Company A under Captain Gabi had followed Dodik's company across. Its mission was to take the Police Training School.

226

Leaping across the trench, Gabi unexpectedly ran into a chain-link fence ten meters beyond and cut the top links with pliers. The bearded company commander hurdled over and smashed open the main entranceway on the south side of the building with his foot. His men raced inside to the second floor, using flashlights in the dark corridors. The plan was to conquer the second floor first, before the defenders could organize at the head of the stairs. The building was U-shaped, and Gabi positioned himself at a second-floor window at the bottom of the U overlooking both wings. The courtyard below opened out toward Ammunition Hill. Gabi could hear the tramp of boots as his men raced down the empty corridors on either side of him. From the far ends of the wings came shouts of "Clear." As he watched, five Arabs, the last in the building, ran into the courtyard from the first floor and disappeared north across the parking lot in the direction of the hill thirty meters away. The two MAGs which had been firing across the lot were silent, their crews lying wounded next to the weapons.

The Yellow Blanket position south of the Police Training School had worried battalion command. Although not as strong as Ammunition Hill, it dominated the breakthrough point. Two platoons from Heavy Weapons Company were assigned to clear it. Crossing behind Gabi's men, they entered the trench and turned right instead of left, as Dodik had done. Tree limbs which had been cut in the mortar bombardment covered the ground. In the light of a burning kerosene can Private Dani Biegelman saw a grenade roll out of a bunker into the trench in front of him. There was enough light to make out that it was a British Mills grenade. He picked it up and flipped it back into the bunker, where it exploded. An Israeli grenade set fire to a recoilless rifle jeep.

The fight was quickly over. A middle-aged Jordanian sergeant had been taken prisoner, perhaps the same one who had been seen from the Histadrut Building the previous week directing construction of the fire wall. His face was black with battle soot and his clothes were torn, but he seemed calm. One of the paratroopers thought he looked just like an English sergeant would look if taken prisoner. All told, however, there were hardly half a dozen Legionnaires in the position. As at the Police Training School, the enemy had fled to the deep trenches of Ammunition Hill.

Dedi's company, the last to cross no-man's-land, ran beneath the walls of the Police Training School toward Ammunition Hill. They could hear grenades exploding inside the building and bursts of automatic fire as Gabi's men moved through the first floor. Fires burned in some of the rooms. Rounding the corner of the building, the men moved across the parking lot to a barbed-wire fence at the foot of the hill. The acrid smell of cordite from the shelling made the bottom of their throats dry. Although water pulsed from a mobile water tank punctured by shrapnel, there was no chance to drink. The bombardment called down by Dodik at Iron 4 was hitting the hill just beyond the fence. The sights and sounds of war were all about, but for the moment nobody was shooting at them and the men felt strangely uninvolved. A kibbutznik pointed to a bright red plant and said to the man next to him, "Look at that bougainvillea." Dedi was uneasy about keeping his men waiting in an exposed position and requested that the shelling be lifted so his company could get onto the hill.

Radio contact with the force at Yellow Blanket had been broken, and Colonel Joseph, who had reached the parking lot, had no idea of what was happening there. Changing the attack plan, he ordered Dedi to stay where he was and asked Dodik if he could mount the attack on Ammunition Hill. From the parking area between the hill and the Police Training School, Dedi would be in a position either to swing behind the school and attack the Yellow Blanket position from the rear, to attack the school itself from the rear if Gabi needed help, or to move onto the hill if Dodik needed help.

228

Dodik asked for a moment to move a fresh platoon to the front of the line. In the narrow, winding trench he had not been able to see more than a few meters behind him. Now, as he called for the second platoon to come forward, he discovered that most of his company were missing. They had gone astray when a soldier had been wounded in no-man's-land and the man behind stopped to tend him, forgetting Dodik's instructions to leave the wounded during the attack. The rest of the troops had piled up behind. When they finally moved forward to the trench, the front of the company had disappeared. The necessarily sketchy briefing before the attack left the soldiers in ignorance of where they were supposed to go. Some waited until Gabi's company came up and followed it to the Police Training School. Others began feeling their way down the trench. Dodik, meanwhile, radioed Joseph that he did not have enough men to press the attack and that Dedi had better continue onto the hill as in the original plan.

Dedi's men moved through a gap in the barbed-wire fence blasted open by a mortar shell. On the other side was a long stone wall, half of it backed by storerooms. The men moved through an opening into a courtyard lit by the tender set afire by Tsuriel's MAG. An Arab was lying next to the vehicle with his clothes on fire. Some of the paratroopers tried to beat the flames out. It was plainly hopeless, and one of the Israelis shot the Legionnaire in the head. It was the last act of mercy on Ammunition Hill.

On the uphill side of the courtyard were the three officers' barracks. A bazookist fired a shell at one of them. He was too close to the stone wall of the storehouse, however, and the weapon's fiery backblast was deflected back at him. Scorched, he rolled on the ground and cried, "I'm dying. Help me!" Private Yaac Haimovitch, one of four men who would win the nation's highest award on Ammunition Hill, pondered for a moment whether to go to him. He decided he must move ahead. A moment later an order came back down the line from the platoon commander, Lieutenant Yoram, to retrieve the bazooka and Yaac went back for it.

No fire came from the officers' quarters, and Yoram led his men past them to the open slope beyond. He ordered a four-man section to lead the way up the hill. It was the first probe at the heart of the Arab Legion defenses, and the Israelis quickly learned what they were up against when fire ripped into the section, killing three men and wounding the fourth. The shooting came from a trench near the southern crest of the hill, about fifty meters upslope. This crest trench, which contained three bunkers, dominated the entire left side of the slope and clearly made any movement across it suicidal. Yoram turned right, leading his men into a trench which ran alongside a road running up the center of the hill.

Dedi's second platoon, under Lieutenant Yochanan, moved toward the right side of the hill through a stand of broken pine trees, halting behind a two-meter-high stone wall. About one hundred meters beyond, a building with a TV antenna showed on the skyline. Yochanan saw a light flicker inside and ordered his bazookist, Itamar, to fire. Itamar could hear glass tinkle as his second shell slammed into the narrow window over the entrance. The building, just outside the barbed-wire perimeter, was the residence of the chief judge of the appellate court in Jordanian Jerusalem, but all its occupants had left in the morning. The platoon began moving uphill, feeling its way in the blackness. The third man in line, Private Menahem, saw what at first appeared to be a hole one meter to his right. "Trench," he shouted. Yochanan told him to get into it, and the rest of the men followed.

The chest-high trench ran alongside the perimeter fence. As he moved forward, Menahem began to hear bullets hitting near him and suddenly saw three helmeted figures around a bend five meters ahead, illuminated by their own tracers as they fired. Yochanan flung a grenade forward and jumped out of the trench. Fully exposed, he placed the stock of his Uzi to his

230

shoulder and fired. The Legionnaires ducked into the trench, and Yochanan threw a second grenade. Menahem saw the lieutenant's eyes glistening with excitement as he reentered the trench. Moving forward, the men passed three Arabs killed by the grenade. One of them was a medic wearing an armband with a red crescent. A few meters beyond, shooting began again from up ahead. Yochanan threw a phosphorous grenade, which set dry reeds afire outside the trench. By the flames, two Arabs could be seen slumped half out of the trench. When the Israelis came up, they found a third Legionnaire dead on the trench floor.

Fire from the front grew stronger as the men moved deeper into the enemy position. Grenades were being rolled down the slope from the left, and one soldier saw two Legionnaires on the roof of the judge's house to the right also flinging grenades. Yochanan asked Dedi, who was following behind the platoon, to check the position of the other platoons on the walkie-talkie to be sure that the fire was not coming from their own men. The trench had fallen off to knee height, and Yochanan ordered his men to lie down. When Dedi reported no Israelis ahead, Yochanan started the platoon forward again. He ordered three men with automatic rifles to lie outside the trench to the left and fire to the front. One of them was promptly wounded, so they were ordered back into the trench. Casualties mounted steadily. A paratrooper was hit in the eye, and the platoon medic was shot dead as he knelt over him.

Just past the judge's house Yochanan climbed out again to the right with a few men to see better where the fire was coming from. A grenade exploded nearby and one of the soldiers next to him yelled, "My arm is crushed." Yochanan calmed him. "We'll get you out," he said. The lieutenant's trousers snagged on the barbed wire and as he tried to extricate himself another grenade exploded, driving shrapnel into his arms and leg. Reentering the trench, he moved forward until he began to black out from loss of blood. Yochanan turned and staggered back up the trench to ask Dedi to call for help on this side of the hill.

231

With the wounding of the platoon commander, Itamar, the bazookist, found himself at the head of the line. He had placed his weapon on the lip of the trench, and when he picked it up to fire at Jordanian helmets visible above a wall upslope he found it punctured by grenade fragments and inoperable. He swung forward the Uzi which had been slung on his back and opened fire. Magazines from the wounded were passed up to him, and he emptied them uphill. Itamar lost track of time, but with only a dozen rounds left he looked around to find himself alone. He ran back over the bodies of the dead until he found the remnant of his platoon with the wounded at the far end of the trench. "Why are you sitting here?" he shouted. "The Arabs are up front. Isn't there a commander here?" There wasn't. Lieutenant Yochanan and all the platoon's noncommissioned officers had been hit. Only seven soldiers, all privates, remained of the eighteen-man platoon. They were out of grenades and almost out of ammunition. Not knowing what to do, they sat with the wounded and waited. Movement on the right flank had been stopped.

At the Iron 4 trench junction Dodik picked up a call on the walkie-talkie from Dedi, who was reporting that he had lost radio contact with his other platoons. It was unclear if they still existed as fighting units. Nir, who had been wounded in the hand by shrapnel, heard Dodik's end of the conversation as he was being bandaged.

"What's happening?" he asked.

"Dedi's asking for help," said Dodik.

Nir said, "Let's go," but Dodik said he was moving a fresh platoon to the front. He ordered Nir not to take the point.

Looking up the left side of the slope where one of Dedi's platoons (Yoram's) was supposed to be, Dodik could see nothing but enemy fire. Dedi was evidently fighting on the right side of the hill. From the Iron 4 junction, at the lower left corner of the slope, a deep trench ran uphill along the left to form part of the main trench line. A shallow communications trench forked off from the junction along the southern foot of the hill toward the right side of the slope. At Dodik's order, Lieutenant Yoav Tsuri passed Lieutenant Lanier's spearhead platoon and started moving down the southern trench with the second platoon. He soon reported that fire from the crest trench above made it impossible to move. Dodik told him to return to the junction and take the left fork instead. As Yoav came back Lieutenant Lanier heard him shout, "What fire, what fire!"

Half of Yoav's men were still missing, and to beef up the point force Dodik yelled, "Uzis to the front." Lieutenant Eli, who was carrying an Uzi, handed his walkie-talkie to one of his men and ran after Yoav. They moved up the deep trench with Yoav in the lead firing. When his magazines were emptied, Private Tsuriel passed him and took the point with his MAG. Belts of ammunition were draped over his shoulders, but after about thirty rounds the belt broke and his gun went silent. Moving into the lead, Lieutenant Eli saw two helmets up the trench. Yoav yelled, "Throw a grenade." Eli tossed one and the helmets disappeared. "Beautiful," said Yoav, "you got them." Reaching a sharp bend in the trench, Eli paused and looked around the corner. Bullets were beating steadily against the floor of the trench and the near wall. Until now the trench had zigzagged in short stretches, but the section ahead ran up the slope in a straight line, and Legionnaires at the top of the trench were raking the entire length. Eli heard Dodik yell somewhere behind him, "Why are you stopping? Don't stop." Dodik could not see the shape of the trench from where he was, but Eli decided not to go back and explain that it was impossible to continue. He thought if he could get across the bend to the far wall of the trench he might have some cover. The lieutenant jumped into the open and immediately felt a powerful blow on his left shoulder. He managed to get back to cover. Blood from his wound soaking his uniform, he made his way to the rear.

A moment later Nir, back at the fork, heard Yoav shout, "I

can't go forward." He turned to Dodik and asked if he should move up to the point. Wordlessly Dodik slapped him hard on the shoulder, and Nir ran up the left trench in time to see Yoav and a few other men running across the open slope. Nir clambered out of the main trench and jumped into a shallow pit to the right shouting, "Yoav, to me." Yoav, who may have been planning to outflank the Legionnaires in the main trench, was instead being driven back down the slope by a storm of fire from the crest trench. "No one backward," Nir yelled. "Everyone shoot to the bunkers." In the din, however, his shouts went unheard, and Yoav was swallowed up in the darkness.

Blocked on the left, Dodik determined to push once more toward Dedi on the right. He yelled, "Lanier, take the front again." As Lanier moved forward, into the southern trench, he encountered such a crashing sound of fire that he was certain Israeli artillery was again pounding the slope. Dodik checked and said no guns were being fired. Crouching in the shallow trench at the head of his men, Lanier saw helmets silhouetted upslope and thought they might be Dedi's men. He yelled, "Password," and when there was no answer he began singing at the top of his voice. "The Song of the Palmach," the anthem of the Haganah shock troops in Israel's War of Independence, had been designated as a recognition signal. Lanier's men joined in, crouching in line and shouting the song up the slope as loudly as they could in order to be heard above the noise of the battle: "We are, we are the Palmach." The bizarre battlefield scene ended with a burst of machine-gun fire which cut Lanier's throat open in midverse and ripped through half a dozen men behind him. The lieutenant fell to the bottom of the trench, blood pulsing from his wound. Breathing hoarsely, he lay with his head on a rock abstractedly watching bullets shred the branches of a tree above his head.

The platoon medic, Didier Guttel, bleeding badly from a wound in the arm, asked the soldier in front of him to apply a tourniquet. The soldier had hardly finished the job when he was fatally shot. Guttel—a religious, red-bearded immigrant from France—was in great pain and took out a morphine syringe from his medic's kit. Igal Arad, the company medic, crawled up and told Guttel he had lost too much blood to receive morphine. Guttel, who was to lose his arm, gave the syringe to Arad to use on someone else and lay back hoping to lose consciousness.

The trench was too low for effective counterfire, and Dodik ordered Sergeant Harlem to take some men and open fire from behind a rock a few meters upslope. When Harlem said none of the other men in his platoon had reached the hill, Dodik told him to take anybody he could find. Harlem called to four men lying nearby and scrambled up to the rock. The company first sergeant bounded up the slope behind them, and Harlem heard two shots from upslope. The first sergeant rolled back into the trench, wounded. Two attempts to pass through the southern trench had failed, and now Dodik mustered the remnants of Lanier's platoon for another try. Taking the lead himself, he began crawling over the bodies of the wounded as the men behind the rock gave covering fire.

The paratroopers had been stopped on both the left and right flanks, but the center column—consisting of the bulk of Dedi's company—continued to move up the shallow trench paralleling the road leading to the top. Lieutenant Yoram at the head was doing virtually all the fighting himself as his men passed up magazines and grenades to him. He moved as methodically as on maneuvers, carefully looking in all directions and periodically sending men with automatic rifles out to the side. Several times Yoram brought down individual Legionnaires who suddenly appeared ahead of him, but he met no effective pockets of resistance. Behind his platoon came Lieutenant Dani's platoon and the MAG section under Lieutenant Zvika. The Legionnaires, buttoned up in their bunkers, called down mortar fire on the hill, hoping to sweep the Israelis off. The paratroopers dove for cover, but several were hit.

The crest trench whose fire had proved so murderous on the

235

left slope did not reach all the way to the center of the hill, and Yoram probably did not realize that he had passed it as he continued to push toward the top of the hill. Silhouetted there were two round-roofed barracks. As Yoram left the trench with two men to approach the buildings, a grenade or bazooka shell blew the head off the man next to him. Yoram pulled back to the trench for a moment. He told Yaac Haimovitch to cover him from the road with his bazooka. The lieutenant rose up and charged the nearest barracks. He flung a grenade into a side window and entered the front door firing. Two rows of beds lined the walls, their sheets neatly folded back, foot lockers aligned precisely at their feet. But the men who slept here were outside in the dark trenches fighting for their lives.

One of Yoram's squad leaders, Corporal Eylan, was ordered to clear out a smaller noncom's barracks down the slope to the right. The corporal found the building empty. But continuing down the slope, he heard voices in Arabic coming from a low opening. It was an entrance to the Arab Legion command bunker, a large cave set back from the main trench line and fitted out with ventilators. Eylan flung in a grenade and heard a scream inside. (The cave contained Jewish tombs from the Second Temple period.)

Yoram's platoon had penetrated so deeply into the position that Legionnaires began to appear at its rear. Yaac looked back from the barracks entrance and saw a dish-helmeted figure crossing the road where he had just lain with the bazooka. The Israeli swung forward his rifle, which was slung on his shoulder, and sunk a tracer into the running Legionnaire. Two badly wounded Israelis were lying at the side of the barracks when a wounded Jordanian fell next to them. The Legionnaire hoarsely asked, "Are you Arab?" One of the Israelis replied yes in Arabic; then, straining for his gun, he shot the Arab dead.

The seven men still unwounded in Yoram's platoon entered a communication trench beyond the barracks and started down the rear slope toward the northern trench. Partway down Yoram turned a bend and was caught by a burst of fire from below. The officer who had led the column so ably was carried into a bunker, mortally wounded.

Yaac Haimovitch now found himself at the head of the column. The private, an engineering student at the Haifa Technion, had no idea of shape of the trenches or where the other platoons on the hill were supposed to be. He knew only that the Arabs who had just killed Yoram were still there waiting for the next man to round the bend. Yaac stood still for a few moments. Then he laid his bazooka on the trench floor, unslung his rifle, and started forward. With movement on both flanks stalled, the Israeli assault on the main Arab Legion position in Jerusalem had come down to a single frightened private moving forward in a black maze, certain that he would be dead before he had taken five steps.

Turning the bend Yaac saw the outline of a recoilless rifle jeep twenty meters below. Several figures stood alongside it. He pegged a shot at them and the figures disappeared. The ground steadied beneath Yaac's feet, and he began moving slowly, as he had seen Yoram do, carefully scanning each side. Tracers skimmed the hill and trenches opened to right and left, but he could not tell where they went.

Suddenly the recoilless rifle jeep burst into flame. Lieutenant Zvika, the commander of the MAGs, who had been following at the rear of the column, had been called forward when Yoram was hit. He had found Yaac's bazooka and put one of its shells into the jeep. Yaac reached the northern trench and turned left, away from the burning vehicle. A Legionnaire lay on the bottom of the trench ten meters ahead, waiting for him. The Arab fired three times, each bullet hitting the trench wall closer to Haimovitch's head. Pieces of stone and metal struck the Israeli in the face. Covered with blood, he began to black out, but as he reeled back he squeezed off a shot which caught the Legionnaire. Recovering, Yaac stepped over the Arab's body and continued for-

237

ward. Behind him the sky was beginning to show an edge of gray.

Gabi and Giora had assembled their companies in the UNRWA parking lot and prepared to move up the road leading past Ammunition Hill to the Sheikh Jarrah quarter. Fire was coming from the left of the road, and Gabi sent his deputy, Lieutenant Ami Yaacobi, and a platoon under Lieutenant Ophir Fenegar to root out the snipers.

The platoon took a short cut across the southeastern corner of Ammunition Hill to the stone wall where Itamar had earlier fired his bazooka at the house with the TV antenna. Ami saw two Legionnaires moving near the house just outside the barbed wire surrounding the hill and brought them down with his Uzi. As he prepared to hurdle the wall and sweep the area flanking the road to Sheikh Jarrah, he heard someone call from the hill above him. It was Dedi in a trench twenty meters away. "I don't have any ammunition," the company commander shouted, "and I've got a lot of wounded and dead." Ami, a husky but gentle ex-kibbutznik, debated for a moment whether to continue on his assigned mission. But he could see no Legionnaires beyond the wall, and Dedi plainly needed help. (Just moments before Dedi's deputy, Lieutenant Eshkol, had been shot dead a few meters away as he returned from upslope.) Ami asked which trench he should enter. Dedi, who was still out of contact with his platoons, seemed to hesitate, and Ami led Lieutenant Ophir's men toward the survivors of Yochanan's platoon, whom he could see clustered around their wounded in the right trench. He asked them if there were paratroopers up ahead, and they replied that anybody to the front was Arab. Ami had just moved about twenty meters when a grenade thrown from outside the perimeter fence exploded five meters from him.

Abreast of the judge's house, Ami noticed that the fence had been pried up at the bottom, evidently by Arabs escaping from the hill. He rounded a bend into the northern trench (fifty meters from where Yaac would enter a few moments later) and saw two soldiers in khaki three meters away walking toward him. Ami was also wearing khaki, and for a moment he thought they might be paratroopers who, like himself, had not received their camouflage uniforms. But when one of the pair shouted in Arabic, "*Yahud?* (Jew?)" Ami answered with a burst from his Uzi that caught both Legionnaires in the chest.

A few meters ahead Ami came upon a young Legionnaire neatly placing his helmet and rifle atop a bunker. The soldier was fair-haired and looked as if he might be one of Ami's own troopers. Before the Israeli could react, the Jordanian bolted down toward the wadi. Ami squeezed his trigger, but his magazine was empty. The Legionnaire seemed to be running atop the barbed-wire concertinas as he disappeared, Lieutenant Ophir firing after him. Up ahead Ami saw the recoilless rifle jeep. As he prepared to throw a grenade, Lieutenant Zvika's bazooka shell slammed into it from uphill. Ammunition began to explode, and Ami carefully worked his way out of the trench around the burning vehicle, Ophir and his men following. (It is probable that the three Legionnaires Ami had encountered were the ones spotted moments earlier by Yaac near the jeep, the same ones who had killed Yoram.) Beyond the jeep Ami turned down a short spur leading to a bunker and threw a grenade inside. When it failed to explode, he put his head in. Three Arabs stared back at him. From the corner of his eye he saw one of them swinging his rifle up. Jerking his head back and flattening himself against the outside wall of the bunker, Ami fired a burst into the entranceway to discourage the Legionnaires from coming out and yelled to Ophir in the main trench to fling him a grenade. Ami caught it in one hand, pulled the pin, and tossed it through the opening. This time the grenade exploded.

Ophir and the rest of the platoon moved past him down the main trench. As Ami started after them, two bullets caught him in the right arm. The shots had come from the Jordanian positions of Mivtar Hill to the north. But the war wasn't over yet for Ami. After a corporal bandaged his wounds, he shifted his Uzi to his left arm and again started after Ophir. Two Jordanians descending a communication trench were shot dead by Ami and the corporal. Suddenly bullets hit the trench wall next to the officer. A badly wounded Legionnaire in the middle of the trench—perhaps the one who had lain in ambush for Yaac—had struggled to his knees and opened fire as the two Israelis approached. The Legionnaire, however, was falling forward even as he fired. Ami made sure he would not rise again.

From the turret of his tank Rafi stared unbelievingly at the paratrooper running ahead of him across no-man's-land shouting, "This way, this way." The engineers had cleared a path for the tanks, but the field was still thickly sown with antipersonnel mines, which popped harmlessly beneath the tank like firecrackers. Rafi could not understand how the paratrooper could avoid stepping on one.

To clear the path just north of the Police Training School the engineers had crawled under the fire of Ammunition Hill, pushing bangalores out ahead of them. Antitank mines were probed for with metal spikes and set off by explosive charges. One soldier was hit by a bullet before he could get clear. After activating a detonator, he fell beside the mine and was killed in the explosion.

As Rafi's tank started to nose over the trench in front of the school, he heard a voice below cry, "There are wounded in here." He ordered reverse and took the tank across the trench farther down, dragging a trail of barbed wire after him. He turned in his turret to look back at Jewish Jerusalem emerging faintly in the light of the new day. It had been two decades since he had seen it from this side. Someone shouted up at him over the roar of the engines to take his tanks to the Ambassador Hotel. Rafi could hear no sounds at all from Ammunition Hill as he passed it.

*　　　　　*　　　　　*

To the battalion staff in the parking lot, it was unclear what was happening on the hill. Questions on the radio to the commander there drew only terse replies. At one point Dodik and Dedi could be heard talking to each other on the walkie-talkie. One said, "I'm by the house with the arches. Where are you?" The other replied, "I don't know where that is. I'm by the brown house." Major Doron thought the two of them might be on opposite sides of the same house. (They weren't.) Colonel Joseph told him to find out what was going on. As Doron started up the hill he passed two paratroopers in shock. Bodies were strewn over the slope. It was apparent that something brutal was happening. He heard the sounds of the tanks passing below and ran back to Joseph to ask for some armor on the hill.

It seemed to Nir that he and the four men with him were the last paratroopers alive on Ammunition Hill. He was still in the pit into which he had jumped when Lieutenant Yoav Tsuri disappeared. The firing on the hill seemed to have died down, and he could see no movement anywhere. He shouted, "Dodik" and "Dedi," but there was no response. It was as if both companies had been swallowed up. He told his men to fill their magazines with spare bullets from their packs. Nir had no thought of pulling back. He had a personal account to settle with the Arabs. A decade before his brother had been among a group of five youths who had crossed the border and attempted to make their way to the ancient Nabatean cliff city of Petra, carved out of the living rocks in southern Jordan. The bodies of the five were returned by the Jordanians several days later. All had been shot to death.

As dawn dimly lit the battlefield, Nir began to grasp the topography of the hill for the first time. If he moved to the right in the direction Dodik had taken, he saw, there would be no one to stop the Legionnaires from moving down the main trench on the left and cutting off the forces on the hill—if there were any left besides his own small group. Naphtali Cohen, in fact, reported seeing helmets moving down the left trench, and Nir sent him up the slope to block them. Naphtali, who had given up any thought of staying alive, ran along the lip of the trench and came upon three Arabs moving below. He shot two; the third escaped back up the hill.

The men remaining with Nir looked at him expectantly. Mustering as confident a tone as he could, he ordered them to take a position in the nearest bunker in the left trench. They had hardly reached it when they heard an ominous and unmistakable clanking that chilled the blood. "Prepare for tanks," said Nir. "With what?" somebody asked. Nir asked if there was a smoke grenade. Somebody had one. There were also four other grenades among them. Under cover of the smoke, Nir said, they would leap aboard the tanks when they got close and drop grenades inside. In a moment, the tanks lumbered into view, two Shermans with Israeli markings moving up the center of the hill.

Halfway between Nir and the tanks Sergeant Harlem and his four men lay behind the rock above the southern trench. They had stopped firing to conserve ammunition. From time to time they could hear Nir calling the company commanders, but they didn't know why he was shouting and did not signal to him. Behind them in the trench was Lieutenant Yoav Tsuri. He had ended up there after being driven down the slope by the Arab Legion fire. Harlem's men had not seen him in the darkness and had no idea of his state of mind.

Twice already Yoav had failed to carry out his assigned mission. There had been sound reasons why he had been unable to. Lieutenant Lanier and the other wounded in the southern trench were testimony enough to the crippling fire from the crest trench which had stopped Yoav's first move. And passage up the left trench had been impossible. as demonstrated by Lieutenant Eli. Nevertheless, Yoav had not succeeded. His platoon had disappeared, he was taking no part in the fighting, and he was still unwounded. Now, in the light of dawn, Yoav made his decision to charge the crest trench. It seemed suicidal now to assault head on a bunkered position which had proved so deadly. But Yoav's determination was tempered by sound military instincts. Sergeant Harlem saw the lieutenant rise when the tanks came into view and run toward them. In a few moments he came running back and called to the men behind the rock. "Enough lying down. The tank is covering us. We're moving forward." The men rose unhesitatingly and began moving up the slope toward the enemy trench. They sprinted from tree to tree and rock to rock, periodically throwing themselves flat to fire. To one of the men, Yoav seemed wild-eyed and disoriented. To Sergeant Harlem, however, Yoav appeared cool and unbelievably courageous. One man was to remember him as zigzagging up the slope, another as moving in a straight line toward the trench. All agreed that he alone remained continuously upright, moving steadily up the slope and signaling "Forward" with his left arm.

In the left trench, Nir was dismayed to see Yoav's men emerge into the open. "Yoav, to me," he shouted. "I'll cover." But again his shouts went unheard. He ordered the men with him to begin moving up the left trench parallel to Yoav's movement. They turned into the straight section of the trench where Yoav and Eli had been stopped in the darkness, but Naphtali's sweep along the lip of the trench had cleared it. While Nir moved up to the left of Yoav, one of the tanks took position to the right of the crest trench and raked it with machine-gun fire, as Yoav had requested. Yoav's men hurled grenades and swept forward in a final rush. One paratrooper fell dead one meter from the trench but the rest hurdled it safely, emptying their Uzis into the Legionnaires below.

Naphtali Cohen had been halfway up the slope, near the point where he had stopped the flanking movement, when he heard Yoav shout to the men behind the rock, "Move out and charge." The Yemenite waited until the attack came abreast of

243

him and joined it, leaping the crest trench beside Yoav. Instead of halting, the lieutenant slanted toward the upper part of the left trench, which was swarming with some thirty Legionnaires. After walking to the lip of the trench firing, Yoav came back a few paces and asked Naphtali for a grenade. Naphtali didn't have one, but another soldier near him threw one. Yoav got down on one knee until the grenade exploded, sending a helmet flying out of the trench. He cried, "Bullseye!" and started to move forward again toward the trench. Suddenly he whirled, clutching his chest. "I caught it," he said. "I caught it. I caught it."

Naphtali reached out for him, but he saw three Legionnaires looking over the top of the trench and had to let the lieutenant slide to the ground. The private shot two of the Jordanians in the head before his rifle went empty. Turning his back to the trench, he went down on one knee to insert a new magazine. Something struck his back, and he thought Nir had thrown a stone to catch his attention. But when he turned there was no one there. The private rose and began firing again, but the rifle quickly grew heavy in his right hand. He asked the paratrooper who had thrown the grenade if he could see anything on his back. "There's a bullet hole there," the soldier replied. Naphtali started back to find a medic. A few yards away, a religious soldier —Tsuriel, the MAG gunner—smote the ground with one hand and gestured toward the sky, crying, "Yoav has fallen."

Out on the open slope, Igal Arad, the only unwounded medic in the area, worked his way among the fallen. Arad, a mechanic, had arrived from Russia seven years before, and the sabras in the unit good-naturedly called him "Refugee." He was the most exposed man on the hill as he lay propped on his elbow next to the wounded, cutting their clothing away from wounds and lifting their bodies in order to wrap bandages around them. Running out of supplies, he restocked from the kit of the wounded Guttel. He dragged wounded from the bullet-swept slope to the trenches, and at one point picked up two boxes of MAG ammunition dropped by one of the wounded and brought them to Tsuriel, whose ammunition was running low. Nir saw bullets kick up around Arad and yelled for him to get into the trench. The medic, who was to win a Tsalash, shouted back, "It's all right. I'll manage."

The harrowing night had taken its toll. Most of the officers on the hill were dead or wounded, and dozens of their men lay beside them on the slopes. A soldier stumbled across the hillside in shock. Central control of the battle had disintegrated, but in the muddy dawn, obscured by smoke, half a dozen groups of paratroopers moved independently toward the upper left corner of the hill, where the bulk of the Arab Legion garrison was now pressed. Some of the groups were decimated platoons still led by their original commanders. Others were remnants of different platoons assembled by individual officers. Also stalking the trenches independently were four or five soldiers who had become detached from their units and continued forward, each man on his own.

Yoav's charge had cleared the way for the final thrust. When Nir reached the intersection of the left and crest trenches, he called the survivors of the charge to him. This gave him eight men—enough with which to begin driving up the main trench. He ordered squad leader Avremele Edut to take the point. Edut had emptied his magazine in the charge and paused to refill it with bullets from his pack before starting forward. Just past the intersection, the trench bent to the left and was roofed over for a short stretch where it passed through a bunker. Edut put his head around the bend, and a Legionnaire waiting there shot off the tip of the paratrooper's nose.

The blow sent Edut reeling back, blinded by the blood covering his face. His sudden turn knocked down several men behind him. With their heavy packs they found it difficult to untangle themselves in the narrow trench. Nir, who was pressed beneath

245

two soldiers, feared that the Arabs would come around the bend and finish them off as they lay helpless. He saw the blood smeared across Edut's face.

"Turn and kill them," shouted Nir.

"I can't see," replied Edut.

Nir shouted back, "You can do it. Turn."

Edut righted himself and flung the grenade he still held. With the explosion, he turned the corner and emptied his Uzi into the Arab on the bunker floor. The men behind him regained their feet and Sergeant Harlem, a kibbutznik from the Upper Galilee, took the point. Some grenades had been thrown into the trench ahead by paratroopers near the barracks at the top of the hill, and Harlem saw a Legionnaire's severed head, still wearing its helmet, fly up out of the trench after an explosion.

The trench ahead was obscured by dust from the grenade explosions, and Harlem glanced left into the bunker Edut had knocked out. Suddenly, the dirt kicked up at his feet. Looking forward again, he saw two Legionnaires running out of the dust toward him, firing as they came. He opened up with his Uzi, but as he shifted weight his leg gave way. A bullet had passed through his foot without his feeling it. His finger still on the trigger, he emptied his Uzi at the sky as he fell backwards. The other soldiers moved over him and the drive continued. Harlem found it amusing that the men all said "Pardon" as they stepped on him. With ammunition nearly exhausted, they took his magazines, leaving him just one for his own Uzi. He had been holding a live grenade when he fell, and he gingerly handed it to Nir.

As the others disappeared up the trench, it dawned on Harlem that he was steadily rising and falling. He turned his head and saw that he was lying atop a wounded Legionnaire. The trench floor was covered with Arabs, their weapons at their sides, and Harlem kept very still, not wishing to announce his presence with groans. Arad came up and tied Harlem's legs together with slings from Jordanian rifles. Some men arrived from the rear

246

Aaron, commander of Jerusalem tanks.

Lt. Ophir Fenegar.

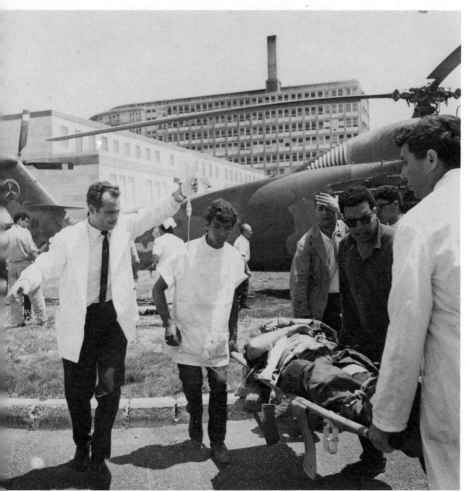

nded soldier brought by helicopter unloaded at Hadassah Hospital landing pad.

Shell hole in outer wall of Shaarei Zedek Hospital.

SHAAREI ZEDEK HOSI

with a stretcher, but as they were placing Harlem on it, a wounded Arab emerged from a bunker five meters behind them. Shouting in Arabic, the Legionnaire shot one of the men in the back. Arad swung his Uzi up and finished the Legionnaire. The paratroopers left Harlem for a few moments and went through the bunkers shooting at anything that moved.

Nir ordered new men into the lead whenever the point man was hit or his magazine exhausted. Once when a soldier hesitated Nir shouted, "Forward." The man started moving slowly, then suddenly raced ahead, firing furiously. When Nir caught up with him, the soldier apologized for his slow start explaining that he had had to take a deep breath. Afraid that Arabs running along the top of the deep trench could trap his force from above, Nir ordered two men out of the trench to the right to stop any such movement. Private Eytan Nava ran parallel to the point man in the trench. Nir could see the top half of Nava's body as the husky farm boy from the Jezreel Valley ran above him firing his automatic rifle from the hip. Eytan, who was to earn a Tsalash, pulled magazine after magazine from his belt and slammed them into his weapon, which emitted a seemingly continuous burst. Periodically Nir shouted up at him to drop back a bit, since he was getting ahead of the men in the trench. Nava's effective fire interdicted any attempt by the Legionnaires to move forward in the trench when the point men were hit and the drive faltered. He killed four Arabs lying outside the trench on the left side and three more on the perimeter fence. Suddenly, the sound of Eytan's weapon ceased and someone shouted, "They got him."

While the grinding battle was going on in the left trench, other paratroopers were swarming over the top of the hill, fighting their way through the secondary trenches and bunkers around the barracks. Looking out a bunker firing hole, Lieutenant Dani—commanding Dedi's third platoon—saw an Arab bazookist in the left trench twenty meters below aiming at him.

251

For a fraction of a second he debated whether to raise his Uzi and fire, but decided there wasn't time. He shouted, "Bazooka," and the men with him dropped to the bunker floor just as the bazooka shell knocked the roof ajar. Dani told his sergeant, Pink, to descend one of the communication trenches and deal with the bazookist. As he started down with Private Gartner, Pink saw an officer moving down a parallel trench. It was Lieutenant Zvika, who had earlier fired the bazooka at the recoilless rifle jeep.

After reaching the northern trench, the three swung into the top half of the left trench. All the Legionnaires still fighting on the hill were now squeezed between them and Nir's men, fighting up the left trench from the southern end. The trio passed the short spur leading to the open bazooka position, but the bazookist who fired at Dani had apparently ducked into a side bunker because the Israelis didn't see him. They continued on a few meters toward a dark roofed-over section of the trench which, unknown to them, protected the entrance to a heavy machine-gun bunker with specially thickened walls. A shot from the shadows ahead wounded Pink in the arm, and he ran back to an empty bunker to bandage his wound. Looking out the entrance he saw that Zvika and Gartner had come back a few paces in the trench. The private was crouching at the corner of the bazooka spur holding his Uzi in one hand like a pistol. He had evidently heard something, for he suddenly thrust his weapon around the corner and fired up the spur. Zvika was standing just behind him in the main trench when grenades came hurtling out of the roofed-over section of the trench at their rear and exploded beside them. When the dust settled Pink saw Zvika and Gartner lying motionless on the trench floor. A soldier from Dodik's company, Avraham Katan, joined Pink in the bunker. He was part of the force Dodik has brought safely through the southern trench to the center of the hill, but Katan had become separated and continued forward on his own. He had been wounded during the breakthrough and had ignored

252

Nir's order to go to the rear. During the fighting on the hill he had been wounded again. Now he ducked out of the bunker entrance and ran toward the two bodies. Grenades exploded near him, and he returned, hobbling from his third wound.

Returning upslope to report on the fire coming from the roofed trench section, Pink saw Dodik in Lieutenant Dani's bunker. He found the company commander's strong presence reassuring. In Pink's own company Dani was the only officer, except for Dedi himself, who was still on his feet. After listening to Pink's report, Dodik told the sergeant to sit down and rest. Dani told Dodik that resistance was stiff. His men were rolling grenades into the trench below, but the Arabs were throwing them back. Less than half his platoon were still in action. When Pink returned wounded, the lieutenant told Dodik he was going down into the main trench himself. Following Pink's route, Dani had reached the bazooka spur when something exploded near him. His face grew hot and he reached up to touch it. When he pulled his hands away they were covered with blood. Dani made his way back to find a medic. Every one of the platoon commanders from Dodik's and Dedi's companies was now a casualty.

For the commanders of the two tanks on Ammunition Hill, the most difficult problem was avoiding the wounded and dead covering the slopes. In his turret Sergeant Ben-Gigi saw a wounded paratrooper flexing his fingers in what seemed a wave. Ben-Gigi waved back before realizing that the man's gestures were uncontrollable. Major Doron rode atop the tank, bullets passing under his arm and glancing off the metal hull as he hung on. The Arab Legion positions of Mivtar Hill to the north were now shooting at anything that moved on Ammunition Hill, and Doron told Ben-Gigi to respond. The tank gunner put his head out the hatch to see what was happening and had his shirt nicked by a bullet. Ben-Gigi took position on the reverse slope, just his turret and gun showing, and opened up on Mivtar.

253

The other tank, under Sergeant Ariel, had given the vital flank support in Yoav's charge, but Ariel found it impossible to depress his gun sufficiently to bear on the bunkers in the main trench. The paratroop sergeant major, Yoash, rode atop the tank, directing its movement and firing the 50-caliber machine gun on the turret. Near the barracks a bazooka shell exploded against a stone wall in front of the tank. Ariel told the driver to engage the reverse gear and prepare to hit the gas. Ariel waited a moment, then gave the order. The tank shot backwards as a shell crashed into the wall where it had been standing.

Yaac Haimovitch had entered a bunker in the northern trench to look for grenades. The need for grenades had become almost compulsive after people had seen their effectiveness in this sort of fighting. Breaking open a box, the private cut his hand but found no grenades. There was firing outside, and a wounded man stumbled in from the trench. Yaac gave him water from his canteen. Wrapping a handkerchief around his cut, he slung a bandolier of ammunition over his shoulder and hefted the 30-caliber machine gun mounted in the bunker, thinking he might put it to use out on the hill. But when he attempted to test-fire the weapon out the firing hole, he discovered that it would not work. He picked up his own rifle and stepped outside.

Two more wounded paratroopers passed him. Up ahead a soldier was shooting to the front. The soldier had also been wounded and had a bandage around his arm. (It was probably Pink.) Yaac moved forward, and in a moment there was nobody in front of him except the two dead paratroopers on the trench floor. He ran past the bodies and entered the first opening on his right, the spur leading to the open bazooka pit. Kneeling in it was the Arab bazookist. He had apparently been wounded in the stomach by Private Gartner. Yaac shot him in the head. Looking back out into the main trench, he saw a dark opening about five meters ahead of him obscured by dust. He fired into

254

it, and a grenade came flying out. Yaac thought the men on the other side might be Israelis coming up from the southern end of the trench and yelled the password. The only reply was more grenades, at least a dozen. Fragments from one caught Lieutenant Dani as he came abreast of Yaac.

Yaac waited until the grenades stopped exploding. When he looked out again the dust had settled, and he could see into the dark opening. Dimly, on the right side, he could make out a bunker entrance. He realized that while he and the other paratroopers had been firing futilely up the trench, the Arabs had been shooting back from the sheltered entrance on the side. Yaac yelled in English, "Hands up." When nothing happened he tried the only Arabic he knew, *"Ruch minhon* (Go from here)"—with the same result.

From the bunker uphill, whose roof was knocked ajar, a single soldier started uncertainly across the slope toward the main trench. Yaac didn't know his name but recognized him as a soldier from Dani's platoon. "Arabs to your left," he shouted. "Enter here." The soldier, Private David Shalom, jumped into the spur. Yaac was glad to see that he carried an Uzi, far more suited to trench fighting than his own rifle, but was disappointed to find that Shalom had no grenades.

There was the sound of footsteps outside, and a short, unshaven soldier covered with dust entered from the main trench. Yaac had never seen him before. The new arrival was Private Yehuda Kandel, who was with Dodik's force. A taciturn loner from a religious kibbutz, Kandel had little taste for discipline and had put in some guardhouse time for minor infractions. But on the hill he had shown himself fearless. He had been at the front of the line for much of his platoon's operation on the hill, emptying more than a dozen magazines. When he became separated from the rest of his men, he had continued forward alone, stumbling into Haimovitch and Shalom. Kandel asked what they were doing, and Yaac explained that fire from the adjacent bunker was blocking all movement. Kandel said he would crawl across the slope to the top of the bunker and drop in a grenade. Yaac told him it would be suicide. The slope was open to fire from all directions, particularly from the Mivtar. Ignoring the warning, Kandel climbed out of the bazooka position and crawled to the top of the machine-gun bunker. Pulling the pin on a phosphorous grenade, he leaned into the trench and swung it down inside the bunker entrance. With the explosion, he dropped into the trench and continued matter-of-factly on his way.

Smoke from the grenade swirled out into the trench. Yaac pushed through it and told Shalom behind him to clear the bunker. Shalom fired into the smoke and followed. Yaac had gone just a short distance when he thought of the grenades the Arabs had been throwing so lavishly from the bunker. He turned back to see if there were more, but something told him to enter carefully. A wounded man capable of shooting might still be inside. Entering the bunker, he could see light from the firing slit to the front where the machine gun was mounted. Out of the corner of his eye he noticed an opening into a side room. Standing erect in the entrance was a Legionnaire. Yaac twisted and gun flashes lit the room as he and the Arab fired almost at the same instant. The Legionnaire fired across Yaac's chest, and the shot struck the wall. Yaac's muzzle was touching the Legionnaire's stomach when he fired. As the Arab fell, Yaac could see movement in the room behind him. He jumped back out into the trench.

Catching his breath in the bazooka pit he had vacated just a few moments earlier, Yaac realized that Kandel's grenade had had little effect. The bunker consisted of two rooms, the main chamber being L-shaped. Persons at the bottom of the L were sheltered from any explosion at the entrance. Likewise, anybody in the side room would probably be unharmed. Yaac shouted to Shalom, who was still on the opposite side of the bunker, not to pass the entrance. Beyond Shalom, Yaac could see the helmets of Nir's men moving up the trench from the south. Yaac

256

shouted to the men in Dani's bunker upslope, who were acting like theater prompters for the drama being played out below them. He told them to tell the southern force that two paratroopers were just beyond the Arabs they were pursuing and that beyond them was a bunker with more Arabs. There were now two sandwiches, but it was difficult to tell who was in the middle.

Kandel had been moving down the trench alone when he saw five to ten Arabs flushed out by Nir's men running toward him. Ducking into a bunker entrance, he leaned out into the trench and opened fire. The Arabs halted and took positions facing both ways in the trench. Kandel dueled with them, leaning out the entrance and firing until his magazine went empty. He grabbed his spare magazines, but they were empty too. The private scrambled out the bunker and raced as fast as he could back up the trench. Rounding a bend, he passed Shalom, who yelled at him to stop. Kandel, however, was in full stride and could not brake. He leapt past the entrance to the machine-gun bunker, a burst of fire from the startled Arabs inside chipping the trench wall behind him as he flew by. Reaching the bodies of the two dead paratroopers, he stripped them of their ammunition and took their canteens to slake a burning thirst.

The platoon from Gabi's company under Ophir Fenegar came around the bend from the northern trench, and Ophir joined Yaac and Kandel in the side spur. Ophir's bazookist fired two rounds at the bunker with no visible effect. Ophir said he was going to crawl out on the slope and put a grenade into the entrance. Yaac told him it had already been tried. Like all the commanders, Ophir had taken off his insignia before the battle so as not to draw enemy fire, and Yaac did not realize that he was an officer. Seeing the pack on his back, Yaac asked if he had explosives. As with all of Dedi's men, who knew they would be fighting in the trenches, Yaac had taken his pack off before the attack. But the men of the other companies were still wearing theirs. Ophir had a sack of TNT in his, as did Kandel. Ophir

257

sent one of his men up the trench to find more. Yaac hailed Shalom on the other side of the bunker. He still didn't know Shalom's name and addressed him "Company C," the unit to which they both belonged. He told him they would try to blow up the bunker.

As soldiers from three companies—Dodik's, Dedi's, and Gabi's—deployed around the last bunker, a soldier from the battalion's fourth infantry company—Giora's—was on his way to participate in the final bloody rite on Ammunition Hill.

The soldier, Private Yoav Nardi, had been helping wounded across no-man's-land. Near the Police Training School he met a friend walking slightly stooped. There was a hole in his chest. "Help me a little," his friend said. Nardi took him to the aid station set up in the *shikun*. (The soldier later died in the hospital.) It was light when Nardi returned to the breakthrough area. He could see a headless paratrooper lying in the field. At the side of the Police Training School, he met Major Doron and asked where to find Giora's company. Doron told him to go help out on Ammunition Hill instead. Nardi followed the trail of bodies in the main trench. In some sections there were so many it was impossible to step on the ground. Near the top of the trench he found a few paratroopers with an officer he didn't know. It was Nir. Nir asked the private if he had grenades and full magazines. When Nardi said he did, Nir told him to take the point. Where the trench ahead dropped off, Nir could see Israeli helmets to the front. "We've reached our people," he told his men jubilantly. He recognized Lieutenant Ophir Fenegar ahead and shouted, "Ophir, we meet. At last." Ophir put a finger to his lips and motioned with his palms downward. Nir told his men to lie down.

Yaac flung the sacks of TNT past the bunker entrance to Shalom on the other side. Shalom threw the first sack opposite the entrance but Yaac shouted to him to place the rest against the bunker wall. He explained that the room in which the

Legionnaires were probably taking shelter was on the other side of the wall. Having seen the almost total lack of effect the bazooka shells had had, Yaac thought thirty kilos of explosives would be needed; he kept asking Ophir for more sacks. The lieutenant, seeing that the private seemed to know what he was doing, obligingly sent his men up the trench looking for more explosives. Finally, twenty-one kilos were assembled and thrown across to Shalom, along with a detonator from Kandel's pack. Activating the detonator, Shalom—who was also to be awarded the Tsalash—yelled, "Explosion," and the men scattered for cover. In the bazooka pit where he had taken shelter, Yaac was knocked back by the force of the explosion and the glass popped from his wristwatch.

Recovering, he ran quickly to the bunker to take advantage of the blast's effect on the Arabs inside. He had expected to find a small hole in the wall, but the result was awesome. The roof over the trench had almost completely disappeared and the wall was blown in, enabling Yaac to see the entire side room. A Legionnaire was kneeling inside, and the paratrooper shot him. The south wall of the bunker had been dislodged into the trench, stopping Nir's men who had come running forward after the explosion. Yaac, still without grenades, yelled across to Nardi in the lead to throw a grenade into the bunker. The concussion grenade exploded inside, and, to Yaac's amazement, a weapon was fired inside the bunker. Nardi threw a fragmentation grenade. From the depths of the shattered bunker came a cry in Arabic. The dust was too thick to see inside, but Nardi emptied three magazines into it, sweeping methodically from left to right. Yaac entered and found two bodies torn apart. Three other men lay on the floor. He thought he detected movement and fired until the bodies were still. It was over.

## 12  BREAKTHROUGH

For the Seventh Battalion at 1:30 A.M. it had not yet begun. The men sat against the houses on Shmuel Hanavi Street, watching tracers skim over the rooftops and the flashes of explosions deeper in the city. The noise was much louder than anything they had ever experienced in training. A young lieutenant asked his veteran sergeant who had fought in the Mitla Pass battle during the Sinai campaign if the fire there had been as heavy. The sergeant said no. The racket frightened a private who knew that he would shortly be leaving the shelter of the buildings and entering "that hell." He was reassured only by the memory of his feelings before his first parachute jump. He had been far more frightened then, and it had turned out all right.

Lieutenant Reuven, the deputy commander of D Company, saw a figure smoking a cigarette in a doorway. To his surprise, it was a civilian. The paratrooper asked for a cigarette. "May God look after you," said the man, handing him his pack. Reuven lay down on the sidewalk and slipped off into broken patches of sleep in which he dreamed of his wife and two sons and of Dafna, his kibbutz in the Upper Galilee. Once he was snapped awake by the image of Syrians descending on the kibbutz from the neighboring hills. Whenever he wakened he had a sinking awareness of where he was and what still lay ahead. His main concern was how he would prove himself to his men. They had never been in combat together, and his conduct in the next few hours, he knew, would either vindicate or make a mockery of his leadership.

The street shuddered as a tank rolled by, its commander

visible in the turret. Above the roar of the engine a paratrooper on the sidewalk, buoyed by the sight of the powerful machine, yelled up at him, "We're going in. . . . We'll take them."

Half a mile away, at the bottom of Mea Shearim Street, a truck pulled quietly to a stop and eight men climbed off carrying some odd-looking pieces of equipment. They made their way across an intersection to a short street dead-ending in a concrete wall. On the other side lay no-man's-land, here just twenty meters wide. Leading the group was Col. L, the sixty-two-year-old armaments expert whose blockhouse-buster had been used so effectively against the Jordanian front-line positions in the morning. The equipment he and his men were lugging was another of his inventions—two catapult devices designed to sling a heavy explosive over a short distance with measured accuracy. Their object was to launch the explosives precisely at zero hour at a gas station on Nablus Road, two hundred meters away. The explosion and hoped-for fire was intended to serve as a diversion from the main attack a few hundred meters to the north.

At 2:20 A.M. the team launched their missiles and raced back toward the truck. Two loud explosions and a flare of flames behind them told them that they had been on target. Almost immediately the Jordanian line erupted with machine-gun fire. As the men reached the intersection, mortar shells whistled down. A captain dove against the side of a building, and shrapnel tore gashes in a metal store shutter inches above his head. A few meters away someone shouted, "I'm hit." Col. L was standing in the middle of the shell-laced intersection, blood soaking through the back of his shirt. The captain ran to him, lifted him onto his back fireman's fashion, and carried him through the shellfire to the former Italian hospital on the southwest corner of the intersection. The building, now housing government offices, had been taken over by an army unit, and a medic was found to treat the colonel's wounds. Outside, the racket of gun and shellfire had become general.

262

Captain Dan, the deputy battalion commander who was in overall charge of the breakthrough operation, summoned a lieutenant and a sergeant from Heavy Weapons Company and led them down a wide alley running off Shmuel Hanavi. They emerged on top of the slope that led down to no-man's-land. Dan wanted to show the pair where to place their guns in order to cover the breakthrough force. But on an impulse he decided to make his way down and pick the exact point for the breakthrough.

The three paratroopers gingerly picked their way in the dark through the tin cans and other debris accumulated on the slope during two decades. After two hundred meters Dan reached a bristling metal object. He was at the wire.

He had been especially concerned about two bunkers shown on the photostat just twenty-five meters beyond the fences. If they could put the breakthrough point under fire, they would wreak havoc as the battalion tried to get through the narrow opening one man at a time. From one point, however, Dan saw that both bunkers were masked by a stone house close to the wire. He had found his breakthrough point. The spot was bracketed by three small trees on the Israeli side and a tall one on the Jordanian side. Dan told the machine-gun commanders to take a bearing on the trees to avoid any accidental shooting on the breakthrough area itself.

The Jordanians were not shooting at the wire but straight across the front-line bowl at the high ground on the Israeli side. Watching the Arab Legion's tracers far overhead, it occurred to Dan that if he had come this far without being fired at, perhaps the whole battalion could. He told the machine gunners that they were not to shoot during the attack unless they got a direct order from him on the radio. The battalion would attempt to get through the wire without firing a shot to betray its presence.

That determination, however, did not preclude shelling. Captain Bikel, the commander of the Seventh's Heavy Weapons Company—which included the battalion mortars—had been given command of the Eighth Battalion mortars as well for the preliminary bombardment. At twenty-three, Bikel was the youngest company commander in the brigade. A quiet, studious-looking soldier, he had become a company commander at twenty-one during his regular army service. He had been asked to stay on in the small permanent army but chose instead to join his father and brother on the family rose-growing farm.

The mortars had been set up a kilometer away in an open area adjacent to the Sanhedria tombs, where members of the supreme court of the Second Temple period are reputed to be buried. As Bikel stood on the bluff above the breakthrough area and began to range the mortars in on their targets, radio contact suddenly ceased.

Bikel told the three men with him they would have to break into the building behind them and attempt to reestablish communication from an upper story, where there would be less radio interference. They put their shoulders to the door and broke it open, to find two frightened boys about six years old just inside the entrance. "Children, what are you doing here?" Bikel asked. The boys said that the house had suddenly become dark and everyone had disappeared. The border-wise children had decided to stay together in the corridor away from any windows. Since there was no time to look after them, Bikel told them to go down to the basement.

The paratroopers raced up to the top floor and broke into an apartment. The radio worked perfectly from the balcony. Bikel's mortars ranged their shells just behind the breakthrough area to serve in direct support of the attack. The Eighth Battalion mortars sought out the enemy mortar battery in Wadi Joz, about a kilometer behind their line.

As he stood on the balcony Bikel suddenly sensed that he himself had become a target. Mortar shells had begun to hit around the building as if the Jordanians knew he was there. He couldn't be seen in the darkness, but it seemed that the Arabs had marked the spot as a likely mortar observation point and had

264

opened up on it when they felt ranging shots come down on their positions. With his guns on target, Bikel descended with his men. Just as they were leaving the building a shell hit the upper story, and the balcony on which they had been standing crashed to the ground.

The mortar platoons themselves had come under fire even before they debarked in Sanhedria, the Jordanians apparently having spotted the taillights of the buses. Lieutenant Raviv, commander of the Seventh Battalion mortars, yelled at his men to get out fast. One soldier was hit by shrapnel as he leaped from the door. As the lieutenant bent over him, the soldier grabbed Raviv's hand and called his name. Raviv told him he would be all right. The platoon's two radiomen had dashed for cover, leaving their radios in their vehicle. Without radio directions the mortars would be useless. Raviv ran after the men, hit one on the helmet with his Uzi, and kicked the other until they recovered themselves and started back for their radios.

The officer found himself in an open area pocked with meter-high mounds of dirt, apparently dumped by builders. He ordered the mortars set up between the mounds, which offered the men natural shelter from the incoming shells. There was no time to dig mortar pits. The weapons were set up on the ground, and aiming stakes with tiny lights were put to the front. Bikel's order to begin ranging came quickly. Whenever Raviv heard the whistle of incoming shells he would yell and the platoon would dive for cover. One shell exploded just five meters from him, but he was shielded by a mound. After each explosion, the men rose and resumed pumping shells the other way.

On Shmuel Hanavi, meanwhile, the whole attack was on the verge of collapse. Half of Company B had been organized to carry out the fence-busting operation, but the bus containing this force had disappeared. It had been the last one in the column leaving Bait Hakerem but had not arrived at the debarkation point on Ezekiel Street. A new breakthrough team could be organized, but most of the battalion radios were on the missing bus and there were no replacements for these. To send units into a complicated night attack without radio contact was to invite disaster. Colonel Uzi said there would be no attack if the radios didn't turn up. With dawn coming before 4 A.M., the attack could not be postponed beyond the fixed deadline without grave risk that part of the attack force would be hung up in no-man's-land when daylight revealed them to the enemy.

Nevertheless, Captain Eilat, the commander of Company B, began organizing a new breakthrough force with the remnant of his company. Sending men up the street to collect bangalores from the other companies, he assembled five skeleton teams composed of three men each—a commander, a sapper, and a man with an automatic rifle to cover them. With all his officers but one on the lost bus, he designated corporals as commanders of the bangalore teams. Most of the heavy machine guns were also lost, but he mustered a scratch force to provide covering fire if needed. Although prepared now to tackle the job if attack even without radio communications was decided on, Eilat prayed that his second in command, Lieutenant Menahem, who was in charge of the missing bus, would somehow materialize out of the darkness within the next hour.

Parked at the rear of the column in Bait Hakerem, Lieutenant Menahem saw the buses in front of him start to pull away into the darkness and ordered his driver to follow. The driver, a middle-aged civilian, said he wasn't driving without lights and threw them on. Menahem reached over and switched them off, again ordering the driver to start.

After a kilometer and a half, Menahem, straining to see ahead, could make out only a single bus in front of him. Actually, there were two: the buses containing the mortars of the Seventh and Eighth Battalions. But they had left the main column for Sanhedria, a kilometer north of where the rest of the battalion

266

was headed. With a flashlight Menahem signaled through the windshield for the bus in front to stop. He told one of his men to run forward and find out where they were. As the soldier moved out a shell exploded one hundred meters away. A moment later another hit fifty meters away. Menahem ordered the driver to reverse immediately before the next shell hit. As his bus started backwards, he could see the bus in front darting forward. The soldier who had been sent out was swallowed up in the darkness, but there was no time to stop for him.

The men in the bus had fallen silent, and Menahem could feel them watching him. A sturdy farmer from the center of the country, he was not familiar with Jerusalem and had no idea of where he was. What was worse, he had no idea of exactly where he was supposed to be. He knew what to do once he got to the breakthrough area, but he did not know exactly where that area was. He only knew that if he didn't get there immediately, the attack wouldn't start. In a very real sense the fate of the battle for Jerusalem was in his hands—and he was completely lost.

He ordered the driver to head for Schneller. There should be somebody there who knew where the Seventh was. When the driver, shaken by the close explosions, protested against continuing, Menahem told him to drive or be thrown off. When the bus pulled up outside the Schneller compound, the lieutenant raced inside to a building pointed out by the sentry at the gate. Officers were sitting around a large table. Next to Lieutenant Colonel Amos, Menaham thought he recognized Colonel Amitai. (Actually, it was Colonel Amitai's deputy.) Running up to him, Menaham placed his hand on the officer's shoulder and said, "I'm looking for Motta [Gur]. I'm alone with a bus and I don't know where to go." The deputy commander told a major, "Take this man to Shmuel Hanavi."

Following the major's vehicle, the bus began moving into the narrow border streets. With immense relief Menahem could make out paratroopers near the sides of the buildings. He halted the bus and, taking two lieutenants, began running through the

267

street asking soldiers, "Where's Motta?" A short figure called to him, "Come here, soldier." It was General Narkiss. When Menahem identified himself, Narkiss indicated he knew about him and his missing force. He said Gur was four hundred meters straight ahead.

Menahem found the paratroop commander standing next to the tanks on Zefania Street and sent one of his lieutenants back to the bus to bring the troops up on foot. But Menahem's tribulations were not yet over. Instead of waiting for the men to arrive, Gur led Menahem to the observation post on Yael Street, a few blocks away, where he summoned the brigade operations officer and told him to take the breakthrough force to the front. Menahem now dispatched his second lieutenant back to the spot where he first met Gur to collect the men brought up from the bus and bring them on to Yael Street.

The force had hardly arrived at the observation post when shells began to hit the area; everyone scattered for cover. One of Menahem's lieutenants had been given command of his platoon just two days earlier and didn't know the names of all his soldiers. He made sure he stuck with the bangalore men, since they were vital to the breakthrough operation and he was afraid of losing them.

When the shelling stopped, Menahem went to the middle of the street and yelled, "All belonging to Menahem, come." Of the sixty men in his force, only forty appeared. Fortunately, they were the most essential ones—the bangalore and radio men. There was no time to round up the rest. They set off quickly for Shmuel Hanavi Street, where, lined up on the side of the street, were the soldiers of the Seventh. At the head of the column Menahem found Dan and Eilat. They embraced, but there was no time for conversation. It was a few minutes before H-hour.

Eilat, who had just finished organizing the new breakthrough teams, instantly reorganized, feverishly sorting out the men in the darkness and giving those who had come with Menahem their original assignments. With the attack imminent, Dan ordered a flare sent over no-man's-land. There was nothing to be seen but shadows scattering before the falling light.

Bikel's reestablishment of radio contact with the mortars and the appearance of Menahem's force occurred almost simultaneously. Bikel had just heard the balcony on which he had been standing collapse when he saw Eilat's men moving down the alley from Shmuel Hanavi toward no-man's-land. Out on the street he found Colonel Uzi and reported that the mortars were ready. Uzi told him to commence firing. Bikel spoke a code word into his radio, and in a moment shells began to strike beyond the wire. The ground heaved and dust boiled up as shells blanketed the area between the fences and Nablus Road. Till now all the fire had been coming from the other side. Dan and Bikel watched with satisfaction as the Arab Legion positions grew silent under the pounding, the lines of tracers they had been spitting now snuffed out.

Bikel had planned to call off the fire after five minutes. They had brought less than two hundred shells up to Jerusalem with them, and he wanted to save some for emergencies. After three minutes he asked Raviv how many shells he had left. "Eight or nine hundred more," was the answer. When Bikel asked him to repeat, Raviv said that the battalion supply officer had driven up with a load of shells from the Jerusalem Brigade armory just as they were about to start firing.

Bikel told Uzi about their windfall, and the battalion commander ordered him to make use of the extra shells now. In the next quarter hour the mortars lobbed five hundred shells into the breakthrough area. (Abandoned weapons and ammunition later found in enemy bunkers just beyond the wire were probably left by Legionnaires who had fled the bombardment.) After hitting the forward positions, Bikel moved the fire back one hundred meters to Nablus Road.

The shells were still hitting just beyond the wire when Dan and Eilat reached it at the head of the breakthrough force. Eilat

269

was not quite sure how many fences his men would have to cut through. Two fences had been drawn on the photostat, but he didn't know if they were actual or merely symbolic. Things had been moving so fast that there had been no time for a briefing by anybody from the Jerusalem Brigade on this point. Some officers thought that there were two fences altogether. Eilat had been in Jerusalem a year before on a company commander's course and remembered being told about one Israeli fence and two Jordanian fences. In any case, five bangalore teams should be enough to meet any unlikely contingency. (Unlike the Sixth breakthrough force, Eilat's bangalore teams carried only separate bangalores, not several screwed together.)

Eilat cut through the Israeli barbed-wire fence with clippers, revealing a two-meter stretch to the first Jordanian fence. Dan told him to have a bangalore placed on the ground between the fences to set off any mines that might be there. A bangalore was laid, then the men ran back and threw themselves flat. Half a minute passed without an explosion. Dan and Eilat raised their heads from the ground and looked at each other. The bangalore was a dud. There was no more time to spare on precautions, and Dan said to move forward.

Eilat called for a second sapper team and ran through the gap to the first Jordanian fence. A bangalore was thrust diagonally into the wire, and the men ran back. This time the device exploded. Eilat was the first to run through the narrow opening blown in the fence. The company commander believed that the area between the two Jordanian fences was mined. But they could not afford to worry about it. Eilat—a short, well-built officer who played soccer on his kibbutz team—charged across the fifteen-meter gap toward the second Jordanian fence, followed by the third bangalore team. They found themselves confronted by a great heap of concertina fences which the Jordanians had piled on each other. A bangalore was inserted and detonated, but when Eilat ran back to the fence he saw that the explosion had had hardly any effect. He called for another bangalore. It went off, but the way was still impassable. Following each of the last two explosions, there was a cry of "Break-through," and the entire battalion surged forward—only to fold up like an accordian when the way was still found to be blocked. In running back up the slope in the darkness, units became mixed and some men lost their units altogether.

Eilat called for his last bangalore team. With each successive explosion he had been cutting farther back on the required thirty-meter safety distance he was supposed to put between himself and the bangalore. When the fifth one went off, he was lying only five meters away, and pebbles rattled sharply off his helmet.

Springing to his feet, he ran back to the wire and found it held together now only by a few strands. He cut these with his clippers. He passed through the gap and ran to the house just beyond, his hands taut on his Uzi. There was no sign of enemy presence. Eilat shouted, "Breakthrough." The way to Jerusalem was open.

Company C was first through the gap, its lead platoon under Lieutenant Rofeh moving straight ahead to clear the way for the rest of the battalion and secure a foothold on Nablus Road, one hundred meters ahead. Its movement was stopped almost immediately, not by enemy fire but by a window screen. A phosphorous grenade thrown by Rofeh at the window of a building bounced off the screen, which he could not see in the darkness, and exploded next to him, covering him with flames. The lieutenant cried out, but as his second in command, Corporal Amos, was beating the fire out with his hands Rofeh said, "Leave me, I'm all right."

The platoon was stunned. In their first moment of battle they had seen their leader wrapped in flames. The young soldiers bunched up, and when Amos yelled at them to move forward he got no response. He took the men bodily and placed them around the building. Amos broke windowpanes with his Uzi muzzle and yelled at the men to fire inside. When their shots drew no response, Amos ran to a small storehouse next to the

271

building. Kicking open the door, he sprayed the inside with his Uzi. From behind him he heard one of the men cry, "Nice, Amos, nice." The men, realizing they had a leader, had snapped out of their shock. Amos started them moving toward the road.

The Arab positions along Nablus Road had come back to life. Sergeant Shattner could see their tracers from his recoilless rifle jeep on Shmuel Hanavi. Like cannon of the Napoleonic era, the three recoilless rifles had been wheeled out into an open stretch of the street directly opposite the main enemy positions. Shattner aimed at a Jordanian machine gun firing in the direction of the Police Training School. The Legionnaire gunner had apparently seen the Sixth Battalion attacking to the north, but was unaware of the troops advancing across the bottom of the bowl right below him. Shattner pushed the firing knob and saw his shell hit home. An instant later the gun on the jeep next to him roared. The jeeps were now revealed to the enemy, and mortar and machine-gun fire swept the street. The men leapt off the vehicles and took shelter behind a foot-high wall along the sidewalk. A shell hit near the third jeep and wounded two men before they could fire.

When the firing subsided Shattner crawled back to the jeep with one of his men. The breech of the gun extended over the rear of the vehicle, and Shattner's companion reached up and rammed a shell into it. From a crouching position Shattner swung the gun in the general direction of an enemy machine gun. To aim precisely, however, he would have to climb into the exposed gunner's seat atop the jeep and make use of the sight. Taking a deep breath, he vaulted into the gunner's seat, aimed, and fired. An instant later he leapt for the shelter of the wall as enemy fire again swung toward him.

A platoon from Eilat's breakthrough company under Lieutenant Oded took up positions just beyond the fence facing to the right to respond to any fire from the main enemy bunkers. The Jordanians, however, were oblivious to the breakthrough, and their tracers continued to arc overhead toward Jewish Jerusalem. The bottommost strand in the fence had not been cut, and Oded saw men tripping over it. He cautioned the men as they filed through the wire. When soldiers who had become separated from their units came up, Oded directed them. Some of the young soldiers, he found, had become so confused they could not remember what company they were in or the name of its commander.

Passing through the wire with his staff, Colonel Uzi noted strong machine-gun fire from the upper story of a building on Nablus Road, one hundred meters to the right front. The building was outside the battalion's designated area. Nevertheless, Uzi turned to Captain Bikel and told him to take some men and knock out the guns, whose fire could sweep the breakthrough area.

Taking four men from the battalion staff, including Lieutenant Zeev, the operations officer, and Lieutenant Barry, the intelligence officer, Bikel climbed the three-meters-high fire wall shielding Nablus Road and looked over. Smoke from the mortar barrage he had called down was still drifting, but the street was silent and deserted. The roof of a two-story building (residence of the brother of former Jordanian Defense Minister Anwhar-el-Nusseibeh) had a gaping hole and was still smoldering. It was from this building that the machine-gun fire had come.

Bikel dropped into the street, followed by the rest of the patrol. They were the first Israelis to reach Nablus Road. The group made its way to the rear of the Nusseibeh house, which overlooked no-man's-land, but the guns on the second floor had stopped firing. The men moved around to the front of the building. Lieutenant Barry was in the lead now. He continued past the Nusseibeh house for about twenty meters and peered around the corner of the next house.

Although he couldn't see it in the dark, the principle Arab Legion positions covering no-man's-land in this area were just

273

behind a stone wall in front of him. He could make out a Legionnaire two meters away. Barry was holding his Uzi in his right hand and a live grenade in the left. He squeezed the trigger of the Uzi, but nothing happened. With little choice, he shoveled the grenade at the Jordanian and pushed the men behind him to the rear. The Legionnaire had been standing on a mound of dirt, and the grenade rolled back into the street, where it exploded. The blast killed the Jordanian, but Bikel was wounded by fragments and had to be carried back.

Meanwhile Corporal Amos had found a narrow opening in the fire wall and led his spearhead platoon out onto Nablus Road. He found that his battalion commander was there ahead of him, having hurdled the wall to the right. Bikel was being carried past to the aid station, and Colonel Uzi told Amos to take his platoon to the building with the burnt roof, where, he said, there was opposition.

The platoon moved in two lines, one on each side of the street. Passing a mosque on the left side, Private Youngman heard firing close behind him. He looked back and saw an officer down the street motioning toward the mosque. At its corner was a concrete pillbox. It had been silent when Youngman had first passed it, but fire was coming from it now. With one other soldier he ran beneath the firing slit and tossed grenades inside. Amos reached the Nusseibeh house, but finding it silent led the men across the street into the courtyard of the American Colony Hotel.

The Jordanian hotel staff had taken shelter in an annex overlooking the courtyard. Several of them had taken bottles from the hotel bar and had drunk themselves into a pleasant fog in order to soften the din of the battle. A kitchen worker looking out a window saw the paratroopers below and called jubilantly, "Iraqi soldiers." The desk clerk looked out and swiftly pulled the curtain shut. "Stay away from the window," he said, suddenly cold sober. Soon after, a grenade exploded in the courtyard, wounding Amos and two others. The corporal bandaged his own wounds and deployed his men in defensive positions.

With the way to Nablus Road open, Companies A and D moved up from the wire, guided by the shouts of Captain Meirke, the commander of Company C, who had posted himself at the gap in the fire wall through which Amos had passed. The two companies, keeping a slight distance between them, were to strike east for a kilometer along a road running above Wadi Joz, then take positions opposite the fortified heights of Augusta Victoria. As they crossed Nablus Road, one platoon from Company D detached itself and descended into the wadi to take out the Arab Legion mortar battery. A light machine-gun section took position on a rooftop overlooking the wadi to cover the platoon.

As the main column continued up the street, an Arab Legion ammunition truck rounded a curve ahead of it. The driver braked when he saw the advancing paratroopers and started to turn, but the truck was hit by a rifle grenade and the ammunition started to explode. The machine gunners on the roof, who had been facing north into the wadi, instantly pivoted and directed their fire eastward toward the truck. Their quick response proved fatal.

The roof on which the machine guns were posted was level with the street, the house being built partway down the wadi slope. It constituted the apex of a shallow triangle formed by the bulk of Company D moving up the street to the east and Company A coming up behind from the west. The machine-gun position was between the two companies and slightly off the street to their left.

When the machine-gun section opened fire on the truck, Company A mistook them for a force of Legionnaires coming out of the wadi and taking Company D under fire from the rear. A squad leader from Company A ran into the open toward the machine guns, firing his Uzi from his hip, while a soldier with an automatic rifle opened up from behind a kilometer marker to cover him. Men from Company D up ahead also joined in the crossfire.

Lieutenant Reuven, who had been near the head of the column, came running down the street yelling, "Stop, you fools." He had to grab the weapon from one overwrought soldier who was unable to stop shooting. When the firing had died, the commander of the machine guns, Lieutenant Arnon, rose white-faced from behind a low wall on the roof which alone had saved his men from total disaster. The Uzi hanging from Arnon's neck had stopped a bullet that would have caught him in the chest. He called for an ambulance.

It was still dark when the lone platoon from Company D descended into Wadi Joz to stalk the Arab mortar position. The platoon commander, Lieutenant Arie Dvir, had drawn a sketch of the area in Bait Hakerem for the men, and even in the darkness they felt they were on familiar ground. A first-year medical student at Hebrew University, Dvir had a dark complexion which earned him the nickname Kushi (Blackie), which his men called him.

The platoon had advanced a few hundred meters when Kushi pointed forward and said, "They're over there." The mortars were still not visible, but the men formed a skirmish line and advanced. At thirty meters they saw the guns. Their barrels were pointed toward Jewish Jerusalem and shells prepared for firing lay alongside them, but the position had been abandoned.

Kushi sent Corporal Kreutzmann, a squad leader, and two other men up the slope of the wadi to the left to guard that flank while the rest of the platoon remained with the guns below. It was dawning now, and the men could make out large caves in the side of the slope. The sound of voices came from one of them. The lieutenant thought the Jordanian mortarmen might be hiding inside, but hearing women and children, he told his men to hold their fire. Accompanied by an Iraqi-born private who spoke Arabic, he approached the cave mouth.

A wall had been built across it, so only a narrow entrance on the left side was visible. The two Israelis stood below it, and the private called on the people inside to come out, promising that they would not be harmed. The answer was a single shot, the bullet tearing into Kushi's throat and lodging against his spinal column. His men crawled up and dragged him away. (Kushi survived, but lost the use of his arms or legs, the only Israeli quadriplegic casualty of the war.)

Corporal Kreutzmann was summoned down from the hilltop. The platoon sergeant had been wounded earlier, and the only commanders left were Kreutzmann and two other squad leaders. Kreutzmann, a second-year physics student at the university, assumed informal command of the platoon. Placing men on both sides of the cave opening, he had the private shout again in Arabic for those inside to come out. A bazookist, meanwhile, crawled up the slope directly below the cave. At Kreutzmann's signal, the men on the sides opened fire to keep anyone from looking out the cave entrance. The wall across the cave mouth reached only two-thirds of the way to the high ceiling and the bazookist sent a shell through the gap. The explosion inside the cave had hardly faded when another shot came from inside. The men opened fire again, and the bazookist sent another shell over the wall.

This time there was no answering shot, but it seemed to Kreutzmann that whoever was inside the cave was still alive. Instead of ordering his men to go in, he ran up the path to the cave entrance himself. Flinging a grenade inside, he pressed himself against the outside wall, waiting for the explosion. As he did so, he noticed an entrance in a rock face running at right angles to the main entrance. He leapt through this side opening. It was black inside and the air was thick with dust kicked up by the bazooka shells and grenade. He fired a burst from his Uzi to the side of the entranceway to clear a place for him to stand, and from there he fired in an arc around the room.

As his eyes adjusted to the darkness he could see that the cave was L-shaped and divided by low stone walls into four chambers.

277

His room constituted the short leg of the L. In the next chamber he could make out the dim shapes of people huddled at the far end. From them came the weeping of women and the wailing of babies and children. Kreutzmann was holding a grenade in his hand. To move on to the other chambers he would have to clear the next one first or he would be inviting a shot in the back. Somewhere in the cave the man who shot Kushi was probably still alive. There might well be other Legionnaires too—perhaps the whole mortar platoon. If he didn't throw the grenade and fire into the next room he couldn't proceed.

A second squad leader entered the cave and Kreutzmann mentioned the dilemma to him, but the soldier had no advice to offer. Kreutzmann thought about it for a moment, then yelled outside to the platoon to give him covering fire. He replaced the grenade and with the other corporal slipped out of the cave. He left two men outside to cover the entrance, and he and the rest of the platoon rejoined the company.

A somewhat similar situation was facing Kreutzmann's deputy company commander, Lieutenant Reuven, at about the same time. With a single platoon, he had turned down a side street, clearing houses from which they drew fire. He sent some men to check a building, but they saw women and children when they opened the door and came back out. As Reuven continued past the house, there was firing from its windows. The man next to him turned toward the sound and a burst caught him in the chest. Taking shelter behind a low stone wall, Reuven calculated that there were four men inside firing. He signaled to soldiers on the other side of the house to break in. After kicking in the door and flinging in grenades, they entered with their Uzis firing. Reuven moved on without looking inside.

Captain Dan had started back toward Shmuel Hanavi as soon as the last man was through the wire. A counterattack from Augusta Victoria could be expected, and he was anxious to get the recoilless rifles forward in case the Jordanians used tanks in

278

the assault. Dan told Eilat's men, who were guarding the wire, to widen the opening for the jeeps.

Heavy shelling was in progress when he reached the street. The Eighth Battalion was waiting there impatiently, and Dan told its commander, Colonel Yussi, that the Seventh was across. He asked him to wait until the jeeps had crossed over before moving down to the wire.

The Eighth, however, was being mauled by the shelling, and Dan found them already moving when he passed them with the jeeps. Crossing through the wire, he searched for a way to get the vehicles out onto Nablus Road, the opening in the fire wall through which the troops had passed being too narrow. To the right Dan saw stacks of cinder blocks, marking the site of an open-air block workshop. He reasoned that there must be a way for trucks to get in for pickups, and he ordered the jeeps in that direction.

As they approached he saw paratroopers sheltering behind the blocks and exchanging fire with a machine gun in a pillbox at the corner of an adjacent building. Two officers from Heavy Weapons Company lay dead. Dan's jeep was about twenty meters from the pillbox but slightly below it, and the Jordanian machine gunner could not depress his weapon sufficiently to reach it.

The first shot from the recoilless rifle was high and Dan informed the gunner in uncomplicated terms that the army had wasted an enormous amount of money trying to train him. The second shot was lower but not low enough. The third shot hit home and the pillbox was silenced.

As Dan suspected, there was an opening in the fire wall here. The jeeps passed through and sped to the position Company A had taken across Wadi Joz from Augusta Victoria. When Zamush, the company commander, reported movement on the slope, Dan thought the enemy might be forming for a counterattack. He contacted Colonel Uzi on the radio and requested artillery fire. In a few moments, shells exploded on the Mount of Olives.

In the attack plan, no job had been assigned to Eilat's company after the breakthrough, since its losses in this operation were expected to be heavy. The breakthrough, however, had been carried out without a single casualty, and Eilat obtained Uzi's permission to move his company up behind Zamush's defense line. The area was alive with snipers; Eilat could even hear Jordanian machine guns on roofs firing at Israeli planes. A private atop a garage roof spotted three Legionnaires firing from the minaret of a mosque. They were too far for him to reach with his Uzi, so he summoned a soldier with a rifle. As the latter was about to fire, a mortar shell exploded at his side. Accurate mortar fire, possibly from the Old City, began to cover the area, and Eilat ordered his men to take cover inside the stone houses.

Sergeant Shattner lay with a group of wounded on Shmuel Hanavi Street. Hit by a mortar fragment, he was unable to move his legs and one hand. Shells were falling continuously, and the wounded men were completely vulnerable to them. In a group they crawled into a yard, knocking down a fence with the collective weight of their bodies. Two of the men were in shock, wide-eyed and robotlike in their movements but physically uninjured. Shattner told one of them to break the shutters of the house they were lying next to and carry the men inside. The soldier placed the muzzle of his weapon between the slats and pulled the shutter out, leaping through the opening into the room. Shattner yelled at him, and he dutifully came back out to carry the rest of the men inside.

They found themselves in the home of a man who was obviously religious. The bookcases were filled with copies of the Talmud and similar volumes. A white shirt was found and torn into strips for use as bandages, since the men did not have enough for all their wounds. After two hours, medics came to take them to the hospital. As he was being carried out, Shattner

280

noticed shell holes in the yard precisely where they had been lying.

When Captain Bikel had led his patrol to the Nusseibeh house just after the breakthrough, one of the men he took with him was Private Yaacov Hai, the colonel's runner. When, as the commander's runner, he stood holding the flag at the head of the battalion during parades, his dark brown skin stood out plainly against the sea of largely Caucasian faces behind him. The handsome twenty-one-year-old youth was one of the seven thousand Jews who had immigrated to Israel from Cochin, in the southern part of India. He had been ten when he came. In the year since finishing his regular military service, he had been working as a youth leader at the Kadoori Agricultural School. He was to have been married this spring to a pretty blond girl he had met in the army, but the crisis had intervened.

After Bikel was wounded, Hai and another soldier carried him back to a Jordanian house just beyond the breakthrough point which was to serve as a collection station for the wounded. Bikel was the first casualty to be brought in. As Hai left the building he heard someone shout, "There are people in here." From a nearby house paratroopers were leading a limping old man and a seventeen-year-old youth wearing a red *khefiya*. Hai suspected that the youth might be a soldier and told the paratroopers to search him.

Hai himself began to search the old man and discovered that he had a wooden leg. The other paratroopers, having made a quick search of the youth and finding nothing, left him. Hai turned his head just as the youth was reaching toward his shoe. The runner saw a glint of metal and fired before a knife could be pulled. The youth fell back dead. Hai lifted the old man on his back and carried him to the casualty collection station. On the way he could hear him muttering. It was a moment before the soldier understood what the old man was saying. The youth was his son. Trying to comfort him, Hai told him the boy was just wounded.

Setting out to find Colonel Uzi, Hai saw that fire had resumed from the Nusseibeh house. Since no officer was in sight, he asked two soldiers nearby, one of them armed with a grenade launcher, to join him. The fire was coming from the rear of the second floor, and on Hai's instructions the soldier with the launcher sent a grenade into a side window on the same floor. Slinging their Uzis around their necks, Hai and the other soldier scaled the outside wall of the building below this window, making use of the small handholds provided by the unevenly projecting stones at the corner.

At the second-floor level they swung onto a balcony and cautiously entered. Glass shattered by the grenade was scattered over the floor. They picked their way through it to avoid making any noise and passed into a corridor. There were two doors to their right. They quietly opened the first and found the room empty. Hai placed himself next to the second door. The other soldier stood against the corridor wall opposite and pulled the pin on a phosphorous grenade. The soldier braced himself, then charged forward. The door flew open under his violent kick, and he flipped the grenade inside. The explosion sent a cloud of smoke out into the corridor. Hai swung into the room, but the choking fumes drove him back out. When the smoke subsided he entered again, firing. Two dead Legionnaires lay next to the windows. Next to each was a .50-caliber machine gun. Belts of ammunition ready for feeding were neatly folded, British-Army style, atop a crate beside each gun.

Returning to the collection station to get some cuts treated, Hai heard someone shout, "Sniper." He ran into the building and found men dragging themselves away from the windows. Some of the less seriously wounded were returning the sniper's fire. Hai ran up the steps to the second floor; a bullet entered the window on the landing just as he passed it. The sniper had evidently seen him enter the building and was waiting for him to go up the stairs.

He continued up to the roof, and as soon as he stepped through the door a bullet cut through his boot, grazing his heel. He fell forward onto the open roof. A slight incline shielded him from the sniper, who was almost level with him in a building about seventy-five meters away. Hai crawled to the edge of the roof and put his Uzi on single-shot. If he fired bursts and used up his ammunition, he would have to change magazines; he was afraid he would fatally expose his body even in that simple maneuver. The sniper could apparently see the top of his helmet and was putting bullets close to his head. Periodically Hai would squeeze off a shot. At one point he raised his head and saw the Legionnaire's gun barrel drawing back inside the window. He figured that the Arab was either leaving the building or shifting his position to the next window.

The paratrooper put his Uzi on automatic and pointed it at the second window. Seeing a curtain move, he fired a burst and sprang to his feet. Hai ran down the stairs almost fainting from the sustained tension and loss of blood. Dan was just coming back from the forwardmost positions when Hai bolted out the door. The runner explained what had happened, and Dan sent three men into the building housing the sniper. In a few moments they returned with a rifle. They said they found a dead Jordanian at a window with three bullets in his chest.

Hours after the battalion's most advanced elements had reached their assigned positions below Augusta Victoria, the trouble-plagued company which had been first through the wire —Company C—was still involved in battle far to the rear. While its first platoon under Lieutenant Rofeh and Corporal Amos had plunged straight ahead to Nablus Road, the second and third platoons had turned left immediately after passing through the fence. Their mission was to clear the Jordanian half of the front-line bowl—the area between the barbed wire and Nablus Road—north of the breakthrough area. Except for a broad clearing immediately behind the wire, the area was covered by a warren of single-story dwellings, most of them slum

283

hovels. One platoon, under Lieutenant David, was to tackle an Arab Legion trench position at the edge of the clearing. The other platoon, under Lieutenant Gideon, was to sweep through the built-up area.

David had been taken aback when his target was shown to him on a photostat in Bait Hakerem the night before. Although no trench could be made out on the dark picture, one had been drawn in by intelligence. David's company commander, Captain Meirke, told him that there were reportedly up to sixteen bunkers spaced along it. David, a temperamental redhead, asked how he was supposed to tackle a position like that with less than twenty men. "That's how many men you have," answered Meirke, "and that's the job you have."

The problem, however, was not that the trench was too formidable a target but that there was no trench at all, at least not where it was indicated on the photostat. Gideon was the first to reach the area where it was supposed to be. Although not his to engage, he had to locate it in order to take a proper bearing in the darkness on his own target. Unable to find the trench, he led his puzzled men—who did not know what he was searching for—in a complete circle in the dark, through alleys and over stone walls.

David, meanwhile, pausing at the edge of the clearing to form his assault line, looked back to see that he had only half the platoon behind him. The rest had become lost in the battalion's back-and-forth surgings behind the bangalore teams. Even more disconcerting, he could not find the trench. He was sure he had come far enough to hit it. It was supposed to be fifteen meters in front of the houses, and he ran back and forth hoping at least to fall into it; but this maneuver was no more successful than Gideon's circle.

David continued north for one hundred meters to a long stone wall. As the men moved single file, Private Jonathan at the rear heard someone behind him say, in Arabic, "*Minhada?* (Who's there?)." Instinctively, he turned sideways and reached out with

284

Exhibits at Israel Museum removed from display cases just before first shells hit.

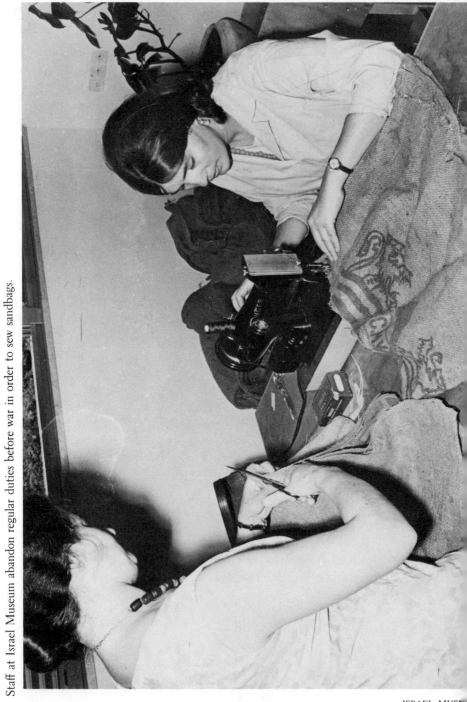

Staff at Israel Museum abandon regular duties before war in order to sew sandbags.

Gallery at Israel Museum after being struck by shell. All exhibits had already been removed from cases.

Before outbreak of fighting in Jerusalem, Dan Ben-Dor (right) shows Carborundum saw, with which he proposes to remove priceless Chagall windows at Hadassah Hospital, to French expert who had installed them. Behind them are exteriors of three windows. Packing case is designated Simon, one of the twelve tribes depicted in the Chagall work. Shrapnel was to rip windows before Ben-Dor could complete removal operation, but damage was repaired after war.

HADASSAH HOSPITAL

his left hand, touching a Legionnaire on the shoulder. The pair fired at the same time. The Legionnaire fell dead. His burst missed Jonathan but killed the man in front of him. David's small force returned to the casualty collection station near the breakthrough point carrying the body. Two more men were wounded on the way.

In the darkness Gideon and David passed each other without knowing it, the former heading toward the stone wall on the north of the clearing as David returned from it. Behind the wall were several substantial villas, each surrounded by stone fences and heavily foliaged gardens. Dawn had begun as Gideon led his men along the wall, which formed the southern boundary of the villa complex. At its western corner was an abandoned bunker. The lieutenant started moving along the western perimeter of the compound when a shot killed the bazookist at his side. The bulk of the platoon, strung out along the south wall, ducked behind it for cover but a burst of automatic fire cut through a metal door in the wall and killed a paratrooper who had taken shelter behind it. A soldier raised his head over the wall to fire and was immediately shot dead. Two more men were wounded when a grenade sailed over the wall. It was impossible to tell if the fire was coming from the villa windows, from among the trees, or from behind the stone walls separating the villas. Corporal Pach-Pach, a heavyset squad leader, was trying to feel the pulse of the man who had been shot through the door when Gideon came around the bend. "He's dead," said the lieutenant. "We're going back."

Events had disoriented the young lieutenant. His inability to find the nonexistent trench had left him confused and unsure of his location. Now, with stunning suddenness, unseen ambushers had cut down one-third of his platoon. He led his men back fifty meters to the slum warren. They sat down in the shelter of an alley while Gideon pondered what to do next.

To Pach-Pach, the pullback was a mistake. He suggested to Gideon that they try to enter the villa complex from another direction, but the lieutenant said no. Although Pach-Pach was only one of three squad leaders and subordinate both to Gideon and the platoon sergeant, he took it upon himself to go back for help. "I'm going to get Meirke [the company commander]," he said. Gideon said no, but Pach-Pach went anyway.

The missing half of David's platoon came upon Captain Meirke at the opening in the fire wall, where he had been directing the rest of the battalion toward Nablus Road. Upon seeing them, Meirke realized with alarm that David had gone to tackle the "trench position" with only a handful of men. He led the late arrivals toward the target area at a run. As soon as he stepped into the clearing, he was shot in the arm. A medic standing next to him was wounded, and the pair were taken into the adjoining casualty collection station. It was there that Pach-Pach found the company commander.

As the rest of the men Meirke had been leading waited in line outside, a soldier dragged a dead paratrooper by the feet into the yard of the collection station and dropped him next to three dead Israelis already lying in a row. Private Bower, David's grenadier, looking upon death in battle for the first time, found no nobility in it. The faces of the men lying in the yard were hideously caked red and brown, a mixture of blood and dust. The dragging of the corpse shocked him. Bower saw a radioman, a friend he had gone to school with, move by in the wake of the battalion commander, bending beneath the heavy set on his back. Although well built, he bore a posture of total fatigue that Bower had never seen before. As with all the paratroopers, his face had become blackened—particularly about the lips—with the dust and gunpowder drifting across the battlefield. Through the sweat upon it, Bower read an expression like despair.

Troops from the Eighth Battalion who had just crossed no-man's-land swarmed past the casualty station toward Nablus Road. One soldier, his eyes widened with excitement or fear, almost rammed Bower with his bayonet as he ran by, the grenadier slapping the rifle away just in time.

David arrived with his casualties at the collection station to find Meirke wounded. Pach-Pach had reported the predicament of Gideon's platoon, and the company commander told David, "Take care of the boys." Still bewildered over his inability to locate the trench, David found himself entrusted with leading the bulk of the company in another go at the villa complex.

Pach-Pach led David to Gideon's platoon in the alley. Looking around the corner of a house, David had his first view of the villas in the light. He didn't like what he saw. Somewhere in that maze of fences, windows, and foliage, the enemy was waiting for them to expose themselves again. At least the alleged trench and eighteen bunkers were to have been assaulted under cover of darkness. "I see they really want me to commit suicide," muttered David.

Both halves of his platoon were now together and in addition to Gideon's men, the company's light machine-gun section had also joined them. Except for the platoon under Amos, he had the entire company under his command. David ordered the machine guns to shoot at the villa windows. Under the covering fire, he and Gideon led their men in a dash to the southern wall of the villa compound. From behind the wall they opened fire, providing cover for the machine-gun section which bounded forward to join them. One of the men in the section was fatally shot in the head as he reached the wall.

David was now precisely where Gideon had been earlier, pinned down behind a stone wall by a phantom enemy who remained invisible and whose short bursts of automatic fire proved deadly. At this point a tall, thin officer appeared, walking upright among the crouched men along the south wall and directing their fire. He was Lieutenant Zeev, the twenty-three-year-old battalion operations officer. Sensing that Company C was in trouble, he had come to see what was happening. Now he took command of the fight.

Entering the compound, he mounted by himself the curving outdoor staircase of the southernmost villa. He tossed a grenade

291

inside and fired a burst with his Uzi. As he moved toward the next building, a soldier yelled that a Legionnaire had just run up the staircase Zeev had descended. Taking two soldiers, he went back up and searched all the rooms but found no one. As they were leaving, a burst of fire from the northernmost villa caught the two soldiers with Zeev. One of them, David Giladi, was mortally wounded. Zeev hurdled past the pair sprawled on the staircase and made his way with some men to the north villa. They found only a family gathered in one room and some Arab Legion backpacks.

On this inconclusive note the battle of the villa compound ended. The handful of Legionnaires who had made their stand there had fought tenaciously and well. They had killed four Israelis and wounded at least as many. At the final moment, when they were about to be overwhelmed by numbers, they made good their escape—at least for a while. Some of them may have been among the snipers subsequently killed by the Sixth in Sheikh Jarrah. They left behind only one casualty, a dead Legionnaire lying beneath a sweet-smelling fig tree. Private Bower noticed that, unlike the faces of the paratroopers, the Jordanian's was clean.

The sight of Giladi bleeding from a head wound shocked David. In the two weeks Giladi had been in the unit, the religious young soldier had made a deep impression on his comrades, and David in particular had come to love him like a brother. (When the men in the platoon had been assembled for the first time two weeks before to get their weapon assignments, David had asked who wanted the automatic rifle. The weapon, a platoon's most potent instrument of firepower, is generally avoided by soldiers because of its weight and complexity, not to mention its tendency to draw the heaviest enemy fire. Giladi, the new man in the unit, spoke up to ask for it. Well, David had said, somebody here wants the automatic rifle.)

With three other men, David placed Giladi on a door which had been blown off its hinges and rushed him to the collection station. To his despair, David found no doctor or medic inside. Feeling there was still a chance to save his friend, he started back with two soldiers through the break in the fence to find the battalion medical staff on Shmuel Hanavi Street. He did not know that the staff—as well as a company and a half of line troops—had been unable to cross because of the heavy fire which at dawn the enemy had begun to train on the very area he now proposed to cross.

Machine-gun bullets beating at their heels, the three soldiers sprinted across one at a time. When they reached the safety of Shmuel Hanavi Street, their faces had turned white beneath the grime. One of the men with David spotted a soldier from his kibbutz and greeted him, but the soldier could not recognize the worn and pallid face.

On the street David found Captain Dan. The deputy battalion commander had crawled and run back across no-man's-land a bit earlier on the same mission. He had found two half-tracks on the streets which had somehow been conjured up by the battalion supply officer, the same enterprising individual who had found the extra shells for the preliminary bombardment. Dan loaded the medical staff aboard the armored vehicles and started them moving toward the wire.

When the vehicles reached the gap in the fence, they found their way blocked by the small trees Dan had noticed when he first picked the breakthrough point. The half-tracks were placed as a shield between the trees and the enemy positions, and David, who had hitched a ride in one of the vehicles, hopped off with an ax he had found aboard. A farm boy—from Moshav Bizaron, near Ashdod—he neatly felled the obstruction. The vehicles passed through the breach and deposited the medical staff at the casualty station. They were too late for David Giladi.

It was now five hours since the breakthrough, and fire from Arab Legion positions to the south of the break was still continuing. Dan told David to take some men and put an end to it. The redheaded lieutenant began assembling everybody roaming through the breakthrough area. In addition to his and Gideon's platoons and the light machine-gun section, there was also a platoon of sappers from Heavy Weapons Company whose officer had been killed, strays from Company B, and even some men from the Sixth Battalion who had somehow landed there. There was more than a company of men behind him when he set out toward the buildings beyond the cinder-block workshop that seemed to be the source of the fire.

Lieutenant Zeev again joined David's force. He had not been happy about the battle at the villa complex. But as the force deployed against the southern buildings, it quickly became apparent to him that they had all learned something about house-to-house fighting in that frustrating skirmish. Moving with the smoothness of soldiers in a training film, the men with the heavier weapons opened sustained fire on the windows of the houses to discourage any sniping while the bulk of the force swiftly advanced. Private Bower, the grenadier, found himself lying next to an automatic rifleman. "You're firing bursts all the time," said Bower. "I've got only single shots. Let's switch." The pair traded and Bower, a slightly built bank clerk, found his borrowed weapon therapeutic. Some of the depression which had weighed upon him since seeing the dead bodies now lifted as he squeezed off long bursts at the windows.

Built against the corner of the building nearest the cinder-block workshop was the pillbox which Dan's recoilless rifle had knocked out earlier. The building itself, however, had not been entered. Now a door was blasted open, and Lieutenant Zeev entered at the head of a platoon. He found himself in a long corridor off which three rooms opened to the left. A Legionnaire faced him when he entered the first room, but Zeev fired first. Continuing down the corridor, he beat two Legionnaires to the trigger in the second room and killed a fourth in the last room. A paratrooper following behind killed a Legionnaire who had been hiding under a bed in the first room. The platoon started to mount the steps to the upper story, but smoke was rising from the entranceway where the explosives had been set off and the paratroopers left before they were trapped by fire.

The force moved on to three other nearby houses but found them all empty. Resistance at the breakthrough point was finally at an end.

David was at the head of the column when it emerged onto Nablus Road. He had been in constant action for almost eight hours now and had no idea where the rest of the battalion was. On the street he met a patrol from the Sixth Battalion making a sweep from Sheikh Jarrah to the Rockefeller Museum to eliminate remaining pockets of resistance. The patrol's radioman was a neighbor from David's village. He looked at the long column of men behind the lieutenant and asked, "Are you commanding a battalion now?" David casually gestured at the soldiers from the Sixth who had fallen in wth him and said, "Yes, and I've got some of your people too."

In the predawn darkness two teen-age girls in the religious neighborhood of Bait Yisrael, hearing a murmur of voices outside their house, opened the door and saw helmeted figures lining the street. "May God look after you and bless you," they called out.

The soldiers, startled by the apparition of girls wearing the long-sleeved dresses of the ultra-Orthodox, were from the Eighth Battalion. For more than an hour they had been waiting on the streets behind the border for the Seventh to signal that the breakthrough was completed. It now was 3:40, and the men were beginning to glance anxiously at their watches. Unless they began moving immediately they would have to cross a dawn-lit no-man's-land exposed to enemy machine guns. A platoon commander urged Colonel Yussi, who was standing nearby, to start the battalion moving, but Yussi replied that the Seventh was not yet across.

Company A, which was to spearhead the attack, waited on Shmuel Hanavi Street, the main road paralleling the border. The three other companies snaked back in line through narrow side streets. Captain Goren, the battalion operations officer who a few hours earlier had visited his family in their shelter in Bait Hakerem, waited on Ozer Street at the corner of Shmuel Hanavi, with the battalion medical staff. Behind them on Ozer were the lead elements of Company D, slated to follow Company A in the attack. The rear of Company D wound around the next corner.

The sound of shellfire was constant, but the border area had largely been spared. Suddenly a single shell landed on Ozer and the cry of "Wounded" went up. The injured men had hardly been taken away when, with appalling accuracy, a barrage struck the length of the street. Thrown by an explosion, Captain Goren found himself blinded in one eye and wounded in a leg. He yelled for a medic but there was no response. Turning his head, he saw that all ten battalion medics behind him were sprawled wounded on the street.

The battalion doctor lay bleeding in the gutter murmuring, "Morphine, morphine."

A medic next to him tried futilely to reach for a morphine syringe and said, "I can't move my arm."

One man had received a direct hit; his limbs were scattered over the street. Another who had responded to the cry of "Medic" in the midst of the shelling lay dead across a wounded man he had been tending.

One of the few people on the street still on his feet was Captain Chagai, commander of Company D. Among the wounded near him were his second in command, his first sergeant, and one of his platoon commanders. He directed the rear half of the company as it came running up and began evacuating the wounded. No sooner had they passed around the corner to Bait Yisrael Street than it, too, was struck squarely by a barrage. Stretcher-bearers were hit, and the wounded they were carrying tumbled to the ground. Men who lay on stretchers with helmets removed were now wounded in the head. Chagai could see half his company bleeding in the street.

Out on Shmuel Hanavi Street, Company A had escaped the worst of the bombardment, though a scattering of shells caused a few casualties. One was the champion marathon runner of Israel, David Simchoni, cut in the leg by shrapnel. Both his war and his running careers were over. A messenger dashed up to Colonel Yussi with Captain Goren's blood-soaked maps and a report that the operations officer was out of action. Just moments before, the battalion deputy commander, Gedalia, had been wounded as he ran toward the explosions on Ozer Street.

298

From Captain Chagai now came word of Company D's losses. All together the battalion had suffered sixty wounded and four dead in the brief shelling.

At precisely this point, with the battalion staggering, Captain Dan of the Seventh came up from the wire and told Yussi that the breakthrough had been completed. Dan asked for a brief delay until he collected the Seventh's recoilless rifle jeeps and brought them across. But Yussi ordered Company A to start forward immediately, rather than risk the battalion's further shredding by shellfire. He told Chagai on the radio to stay behind, evacuate his wounded, and reorganize his battered company. The two rear companies were ordered to move up quickly behind A.

Captain Alex, commander of Company C, found that Chagai's company in front of him had evaporated. He started his men forward at Yussi's radioed command, not quite certain of finding Company A. At the rear came Heavy Weapons Company under Kotcha. When the shelling had started, one of his officers, Captain Amnon, ordered the men to take shelter off the street. Those who did so were unscathed, but one squad which did not hear the order and remained on the sidewalk was badly cut up. Now Amnon, running forward, shouted for them not to stop in no-man's-land to pick up the wounded.

Esther Zellinger stood outside Magen David Adom headquarters looking toward the flickering lights and the sounds of explosions to the east. Since nightfall civilians were keeping off the streets, and there had been no call for ambulances for several hours. Suddenly, out of the darkness a solitary runner approached, breathing hard. "We need an ambulance," the soldier said.

Esther motioned toward her vehicle and said, "Let's go." The soldier seemed momentarily surprised at the idea of a woman driver but he got in. He sat tense and silent as they started rolling.

299

"How's it going?" asked Esther.

"There are a lot of wounded," he said.

The soldier guided her to the Tirat Zvi Yeshiva on Shmuel Hanavi, whose courtyard Dr. Jack had chosen for the brigade aid station serving the southern prong.

As soldiers loaded wounded aboard her ambulance, Esther walked through the yard. Dozens of severely wounded men lay there, but she could hear no groan or cry. The only sound was the murmur of doctor's voices. One medical team moved about, selecting patients in most urgent need of treatment. Esther knelt beside a soldier whose stretcher was covered with blood. Gently raising him, she saw a gaping hole in his back.

Dr. Jack came by and reported the ambulance loaded.

"I'm staying," said Esther. "You need more help and you can't do it by yourself."

Shells were falling near the open yard, and the doctor insisted she would have to leave. Esther ignored the order. She asked a nearby medic for morphine and gave an injection to the wounded soldier. Jack watched as she deftly applied a bandage to his wound. "Put on a helmet," he said.

From the lip of the front-line bowl, Colonel Yussi could see the battlefield spread out below him sparkling with muzzle flashes. A cold wind swept across the open space and knifed through the men's field jackets. Tracers from the Arab positions were still high when Colonel Yussi led his three remaining companies down toward the breakthrough point. But the sky was graying to the east, and as the light increased the tracers began to drop. Suddenly, bullets kicked up at the heels of a running paratrooper. The breakthrough had been spotted.

Most of the battalion had by this time passed through the gap in the fence. Elements of the Seventh were still mopping up in the area, and Yussi ordered his men meanwhile to take cover just beyond the barbed wire. One young soldier spotted the battalion commander for the first time in the growing light and found the

300

familiar figure a comforting sight as he moved upright among the prone men telling them not to bunch up.

The order to move came, and Company A passed through the gap in the fire wall onto Nablus Road. Sergeant Sagi of the lead platoon sniffed the still-pungent odor of cordite that lingered on the street from the mortaring. "We smell war," he said. A few meters to their right, the soldiers could see an Arabic sign over a gas station, the only reminder that they were in enemy territory. Utility lines lay tangled on the ground, but the loudest sound in the immediate area was the twittering of wakening birds. Dawn was brightening with the promise of a lovely spring day, and a rifleman found himself thinking of his regular early morning Sabbath stroll at his kibbutz.

A few men from the Seventh were still on the street. One of them, Lieutenant Zeev from kibbutz Kinneret, saw an officer from the Eighth coming through the fire wall with his helmet perched precariously atop a bandaged forehead. Zeev wondered how the officer expected to fight in that condition. Not until he drew close did he recognize Lieutenant Nachshon from his neighboring kibbutz, Dergania Bet. Nachshon, a platoon commander in Company A, had been wounded in the face by mortar fragments but remained with his troops.

To the north lay Sheikh Jarrah, where the Sixth Battalion was engaged. The target of the Eighth lay in the opposite direction. There, Nablus Road ran parallel to the border for a kilometer, until it reached Damascus Gate, the principal entrance to the Old City. The street ran along the rear of the Arab Legion positions facing no-man's-land, but a line of houses separated the roadway from the bunkers for most of its length.

The plan called for the Eighth to proceed along Nablus only for one hundred meters to its intersection with Saladin Street, which slanted off to the left at a 45-degree angle. By turning up Saladin the battalion would avoid brushing the border strongpoints. Small units would be dropped off at all intersections along the way, overturning cars and taking positions at windows.

301

The bulk of the battalion would continue on to Rockefeller Museum and attack it from the rear. (The museum, a fortress-like complex, is located directly opposite the northeast corner of the Old City wall. Situated at a major intersection, the museum could serve in blocking the expected Jordanian counterattack or become a springboard for an attack on the Old City.) The two companies of Legionnaires in the border positions behind Nablus Road would probably flee into the Old City when they realized that they had been outflanked. If they didn't, they would be rooted out after the museum was secured. According to intelligence, there should be virtually no opposition on Saladin.

The plan ran aground almost immediately.

Halfway to the intersection with Saladin, Lieutenant Ilan, commander of the point platoon, reached the Nusseibeh house with its smoldering roof. Beyond the adjacent house was a long stone wall, in front of which sprawled the Legionnaire killed by Lieutenant Barry's grenade, the same grenade which had wounded Captain Bikel. Set back about ten meters in a yard behind the wall was a two-story blockhouse. The building, whose rear overlooked no-man's-land, was the principal Arab Legion strongpoint on this part of the line. Ilan's platoon, taking heavy fire, ducked behind the wall. At Sergeant Sagi's direction, a grenadier hit the firing hole of a sandbagged position on the second floor, and the bags heaved from the explosion.

The gate into the yard was blown open, and two paratroopers dashed through. Splitting right and left, they sprayed the yard with fire, killing three Legionnaires. The yard was cut by trenches leading to bunkers which dominated no-man's-land, but with speed essential there was no time to clear them or enter the building. When the paratroopers left the yard, Legionnaires emerged and fired at soldiers passing the open gate. Private Amos, a chemist at the Weizmann Institute, was hit in the leg. The man behind, not knowing where the shots had come from, attempted to drag him into the yard and was himself hit. Lieu-

302

tenant Nachshon, coming up with his platoon, dragged them away from the entrance and swept the yard again with fire.

Meanwhile, Lieutenant Ilan and a few men had continued up the street to the end of the stone wall and looked into the yard from the far side. A Legionnaire burst from the blockhouse, either attempting to flee or to outflank the Israelis on the street. Ilan moved into the open toward the Arab, who veered toward the officer when he saw him. The pair ran toward each other until Ilan fired when they were fifteen meters apart, cutting the Legionnaire down. Ilan's duel had carried him up Nablus Road about fifteen meters past the turnoff into Saladin. Following behind him, the deputy company commander, Lieutenant Morty, paused at the intersection. Unlike Jewish Jerusalem, where the streets were well marked, there was no street sign here, and Morty could not be sure that the street angling off to the left was Saladin.

He turned to the company commander, Captain Avidan, coming up rapidly. "Here or here?" he called, gesturing up the two streets.

Without hesitation, Avidan pointed straight ahead up Nablus and said, "Here."

A century earlier, during the Crimean War, a British officer had made a similar gesture to a cavalry force in similar circumstances. The cavalrymen were supposed to move up an empty valley paralleling a valley in which Russian forces were drawn up in strength. There too the enemy was expected to pull back once he realized he was outflanked. But the officer had gestured toward the wrong valley, sending the Light Brigade charging into the teeth of the Russian guns. Avidan's gesture was to send the Eighth Battalion brushing against the length of the Arab Legion line along Nablus Road.

The gesture had not been whimsical. Avidan had only had a few minutes the night before to study the area on a murky photostat. He remembered—correctly—that Saladin was a wide street turning left off a narrower one, Nablus. But these propor-

303

tions happened to be reversed at the intersection, where Saladin was atypically narrow. The doubt that this created in Avidan's mind about the street to the left being Saladin was reinforced by the sight of a third street about thirty meters straight ahead, angling off Nablus to the right. This street was narrow, and Nablus bore the same relation to it as Avidan remembered Saladin's bearing to Nablus—that is, a wide street running left off a narrower street. He had the photostat in his breast pocket, but with Arabs shooting out the windows around him there was no opportunity to consult it. (He was to find later the folded photostat had stopped a ricocheting bullet.) There was another reason why he was disposed to move straight ahead—Ilan and his men were up the street engaging the enemy, and Avidan's instincts led him toward the fire. It soon became thicker.

Realizing that an Israeli force was behind them, the Arab Legion units facing no-man's-land had shifted 180 degrees and taken positions flanking Yussi's men. Buttoned up safely inside buildings, the Jordanians called down accurate mortar fire on the street, wounding a number of paratroopers. Lieutenant Gabbay, commander of Company A's third platoon, was badly hit—his leg ripped up to the crotch. When his first sergeant, Lazer, ran up, he found Gabbay's mind still functioning calmly. The officer told him to take command of the platoon, move fast, and not waste too much time on any one building.

Avidan, who had expected swift and virtually unopposed movement, found himself mired in a cruel street battle. By the time the company had gone one hundred meters, he had four dead and eight wounded. On the radio he asked Yussi if he was to clear all houses from which fire came or to move fast. The answer came back: clear the houses *and* move fast.

A Jordanian jeep rolled down Saladin but braked at the intersection when its driver saw the Israeli force. A score of guns opened up, killing the two riders.

Avidan's men moved close to the sides of the houses on both sides of the street, each column scanning the windows opposite.

A soldier at the point peered through a hole in a tin fence and saw a Legionnaire crouched in the yard on the other side. Sergeant Sagi boosted up the paratrooper, who fired a burst into the Legionnaire below. Lieutenant Ilan and two men entered a yard and killed a Legionnaire in a pillbox. The sun was up now, and the men in the lead took a brief rest in the yard of a gravestone workshop, where they removed field jackets and reloaded magazines. A paratrooper looked about him and noticed for the first time that some of the men who had started out with him were no longer there. Others had moved up to take their place.

Suddenly, the sound of heavy engines and the squeal of tank treads were heard. The men had been told to expect a possible Jordanian counterattack with armor but they had not expected to face it strung out in the naked street with concealed riflemen all about them. A soldier bandaging a wounded man on the sidewalk suddenly found himself alone as the sounds of the tanks grew louder.

"Come help, you bastards," he yelled.

Taking cover in doorways and behind walls, the men readied grenades and waited. As the tanks came into view, the paratroopers saw with relief the painted white stripes on Israeli Shermans.

Rafi had been waiting with his tanks at the Ambassador Hotel for half an hour when a runner came up with an order to move toward Saladin. As the tanks descended from Sheikh Jarrah, their commanders could see wounded paratroopers lying on the sides of the street. One of the wounded yelled up that the fighting was straight ahead. "It's tough," he said. Approaching the Saladin intersection, the tank officers could see Arabs firing from upper stories.

Rafi ordered each commander to pick his own target. The guns, swinging slowly, steadied on a target and spoke. Their blast was deafening in the confined space of the street and powerful enough to knock an unwary man off balance.

305

The tank commanders rode with the top of their bodies out of the turret, standard Israeli armored corps practice aimed at providing an unimpaired view of the enemy and the terrain. Hazardous enough in the open field, the open turret position in narrow streets filled with snipers was brazen.

Finding the heavy machine gun atop his tank awkward to maneuver, Lieutenant Sassoon began firing his Uzi at the upper-story windows. Dead and wounded paratroopers were strewn over the street. The unwounded dragged the fallen to one side and kept moving forward. A paratrooper approached the tank and yelled something. Sassoon took off his helmet and bent down to hear, but a bullet struck the soldier and he fell back into the gutter, blood on his chest. Another man fell nearby and dragged himself to the side. He lay back on his upturned helmet as if waiting indifferently for death or a medic, whichever came first.

Another tank commander, Sergeant Shlain, had seen the paratroopers charging across no-man's-land just before dawn and, judging from their unbroken pace, had presumed them to be young soldiers from the regular army. Now in gathering light he was surprised to see that many of them were in their late twenties or early thirties. A mortar shell exploded near some men behind a stone wall, wounding one. The rest merely shifted a few feet away, dragging the wounded man with them as if evading a troublesome water sprinkler.

Sassoon watched the paratroopers moving relentlessly forward and wondered if he would be able to do the same if he were on the ground. Actually, there were no better targets on Nablus Road than the tank commanders themselves, and the Legionnaires quickly put them under fire. One commander slumped dead in the turret, his head split by a bullet from a heavy machine gun. The crew, unnerved, dropped out of battle. A commander in another tank was shot in the cheek and leapt out to find medical aid. A private, long considered the unit misfit by his platoon commander, rose in the turret. He was to keep the tank in action for the next two days.

Practically every tank commander was cut by shrapnel. Lieutenant Mordecai wondered how he was still alive as bullets chipped the paint off the tank all around him. In the command tank at the head of the column, Rafi found the .50-caliber machine gun at his elbow knocked out by the fire. The light projector directly in front of him was shattered, along with the periscope. He himself was cut by shrapnel in the arm and eyebrow. But the roar of the tank drowned out the sound of firing, and he concentrated on giving commands to the other tanks in the line and to his own crew in his cool lawyer's voice.

Lieutenant Gabbay, the wounded platoon leader from Company A, heard the tanks approach as he sat against a wall, propped in the same position in which he had slid to the ground when hit. He had seen Legionnaires reappearing in the windows of the main blockhouse in the yard across the street and as a tank drew alongside, he motioned toward the building. But the tank commander, misunderstanding, waved back at the wounded man encouragingly. The commander of the tank behind picked up the signal and began pounding the building at point-blank range.

Fire came from the YMCA Building on the right side of Nablus Road as Company A drew abreast. The large building was set back from the street, and Avidan decided it would take too long to clear it. Rifle grenades were also being fired from the area of the basketball court across the street from the Y. One passed between Avidan and two other men before exploding harmlessly.

Just ahead, abutting the Y, was a two-story villa housing the American Consulate. The building sat on a triangular plot formed by the intersection of Nablus Road and a street angling in sharply from Mandelbaum Gate on the right rear. Beyond the intersection on the right side of Nablus lay an open field laced with bunkers and trenches. These were the fortifications guarding the Mandelbaum Gate approach, fortifications considered formidable enough to rule out Captain Dan's proposal that the

Seventh Battalion make the breakthrough here. Now Company A of the Eighth and a handful of tanks moved out to engage it.

The lead tank started into the intersection, but pulled back to the shelter of the consulate wall when bazooka shells exploded around it. The paratroopers, who had been expecting the tanks to blast the way open, were disconcerted to discover their presumed protectors so vulnerable. They reacted, however, with professional dispatch. Sergeant Pheda, a doctoral candidate in mathematics at the university and a squad leader in Ilan's point platoon, tied a half-kilo brick of explosives to the side gate leading into the consulate garden and blew it open. None of the men realized it was a consulate, but in the circumstances it would have made no difference if they had. The platoon opened fire from behind the garden wall on the Jordanian bunkers.

At the same time, Lieutenant Morty, who had been paralleling Ilan's movements on the opposite side of the street, shot the lock off the gate leading to the basketball court there. Taking four men, including an MAG team (the commander of the MAG section had been killed), he climbed over an adjacent wall into the courtyard of an Armenian tile workshop. The yard was crowded with sheep, chickens, and dogs. Their barnyard chorus was the first sound of life the paratroopers had heard since crossing the line. Hurdling a wall at the far end, they dashed across an open space to a fire-blackened filling station at the intersection. Heavy fire from the fortified area was beating about them, but they could not see precisely where it was coming from. Morty's men opened intense fire, and after a few moments they could hear the enemy shots receding, as if the Legionnaires were pulling back. (The filling station was the one hit by Colonel L's catapult device.)

Acting independently, the two fire teams—Ilan's and Morty's —had succeeded between them in pushing the bulk of the defenders away from the intersection and giving the tanks room to maneuver. Rafi told his driver to start forward again, this time at top speed. As the tank darted across the intersection, a bazooka shell exploded behind. The tank commander following Rafi saw the shot come from a pillbox built into the sidewalk on the road from Mandelbaum, just a firing slit showing above ground. He drove his tank onto it and crushed the pillbox before the bazookist could fire again. The Shermans opened fire on the bunkers in the field.

As soon as the tanks moved out Lieutenant Ilan's men hurdled the consulate garden wall and charged across the field toward a pillbox located at the rear of the first building beyond the intersection—a mosque. Ilan threw a grenade at the entrance. A moment later a grenade exploded next to him, wounding him badly in the leg. Sergeant Pheda ran up, but Ilan told him to clear the pillbox. Pheda and Sergeant Lazer flung in grenades and entered the bunker firing.

Private Hermeling, a husky young kibbutznik, lifted Ilan onto his back and started toward the rear. They passed a soldier who stared in dismay at the wounded officer who had led the fight up Nablus Road. Still exercising command, Ilan told him to move forward and keep fighting. As Hermeling moved slowly across the intersection under his burden, the asphalt kicked up between his legs, but it didn't register that these were bullets aimed at him. In the shelter of the consulate wall he laid Ilan down on the sidewalk. Taking the lieutenant's helmet off, Hermeling washed Ilan's face with water from a canteen. He was frightened at how pale the lieutenant had turned. Ilan who had touched his wound as he rode piggyback, said that his foot was about gone, hanging only by a piece of skin. Hermeling ventured up the street to find a medic. On the way he saw an Arab rifleman in a second-story window and paused to send a rifle grenade through the window.

One platoon—Lieutenant Nachshon's—had strayed from the rest of the battalion and inadvertantly wound up on the right street: Saladin. They proceeded for two blocks, losing a man to a sniper on the way. But finding themselves alone, they returned to Nablus. When they reached the consulate, Nachshon found

Ilan lying next to the wall alongside some corpses. The shooting seemed to have receded. "It's almost over now," said Ilan. It was, however, a long way from over.

Sergeant Pheda was prowling behind the mosque when he heard Sergeant Lazer call from the street, "Come quick, I see them."

He found Lazer and another soldier firing into an alley from the corner of a building. Pheda did not see any Jordanians, but he opened fire on the windows overlooking the passageway. He was changing magazines when a grenade exploded two yards away, felling him and the two others. Morty and his men dashed across from the filling station opposite and found that Pheda's throat had been cut by shrapnel. He was alive but could barely speak. (He would recover after being treated in the hospital by his father, former head of the Army Medical Service.) The second soldier was also badly wounded. Although there was no mark visible on Lazer's body, the sergeant was dead.

Avidan and Nachshon were near the mosque when Morty came running back. "We did good work," he reported, "but I lost Lazer." The two were old friends.

Nachshon saw Rafi's tanks approaching and said he would get them to rake the alley. Morty, however, returned impatiently to his five men near the mouth of the alley and said, "Start moving."

The first man, who carried a light machine gun, leaned out into the alley and fired a long burst at the windows until his gun jammed. He stepped back, and Morty said to the other men, "Why are you standing there? Let's move." The next soldier also leaned out partway and emptied his Uzi.

Morty now moved forward. The first two soldiers had not leaned out far enough to see the end of the alley, but Morty stepped boldly out into the alley mouth and fired up its length. Then, seeing something, he reached for a grenade. As he pulled the pin a burst of automatic fire caught him in the chest and

310

he fell forward. The grenade spilled from his grasp and exploded beside him. Morty lay dead a few feet from where his friend had fallen.

A string of roofless bunkers lined the street leading back from the intersection toward Mandelbaum Gate. A soldier climbing to the minaret of the mosque shouted down that he could see two Legionnaires crouching in one of the bunkers. A pair of prisoners had been taken in the pillbox behind the mosque, and Corporal Mualem now ordered one to coax his comrades out of the bunkers. An irrepressible jokester in camp, the Iraqi-born Mualem was terrifying on the battlefield, a missing earlobe—shot off in the Sinai campaign—adding to his fierce countenance. He walked close to a wall, keeping his gun on the prisoner moving down the center of the street toward the bunkers.

Mualem presumed that the near bunker was empty, but seeing something move as he passed, he fired and threw in a grenade. He found two dead Legionnaires inside. The prisoner had halted, and Mualem motioned him to continue. As they reached the second bunker he asked the prisoner to call the men out. The prisoner called, but when there was no response Mualem threw in a grenade, killing two more Legionnaires.

His one-man war ended here. The company was heading south on Nablus, and Mualem's walk was taking him away to the northwest. Sergeant Sagi came running up and told him to rejoin the unit.

Colonel Yussi followed the bloody train of Company A along Nablus, the waving antennas of his radiomen periodically drawing sniper fire. Fire came from the window of a building near the YMCA. With no other paratroopers nearby, Yussi ordered his two radiomen and his deputy to clear the building. When the dust raised by their grenades had settled, they found two dead Legionnaires.

Periodically Gur asked Yussi his position and urged him to move faster. At one point Gur asked how the Jordanians were

311

fighting. "They're fighting well in small groups of three or four," Yussi reported, "but they seem incapable of executing company or even platoon movements."

Company A had by now lost seven dead and thirty wounded, close to half its strength. Its deputy commander and MAG commander were dead, and two of the three platoon commanders were badly wounded. Yussi ordered Company C to pass through and take the point. The exhausted remnants of Avidan's company entered the walled-in compound of Saint Stephen's Monastery, across from the American Consulate, to rest. It had taken them three hours to cover six hundred meters.

Company C had been relatively unbloodied as it followed Avidan's men at a distance down Nablus Road. Sometimes the company commander, Captain Alex, could see the last man of Company A ahead of him. More often he could not. But the wounded and dead on the street and the sound of gunfire ahead clearly indicated the grueling nature of the fight. At the Saladin intersection, a mortar fragment wounded Alex in the leg, but he had it bandaged and kept moving.

Company C went into action at the YMCA. Enemy snipers, apparently four of them, were maintaining a steady fire from upper-story windows, and Colonel Yussi told Alex to put a stop to it. A squad pursued the Legionnaires, but was stopped at the staircase leading to the roof. The stairway was L-shaped, and the Arabs at the top checked the Israelis with fire every time they tried to turn the bend.

On the street below Lieutenant Sassoon's tank was coming abreast of the YMCA when he saw the silhouette of a soldier in an upper-story window and swung his gun high. The shadow materialized into a paratrooper who leaned out the window and gestured toward the roof. With his right hand, Sassoon swung the gun away from the window and with his left he reached down and grabbed the gunner by his collar and yanked him clear of the firing pedal. He fired a round at the roof, but when the

312

paratroopers rushed it they found that the Arabs had fled, apparently down the scaffolding at the rear of the building.

When Captain Alex reached the intersection, fire seemed to be coming from every direction, including the rear. One bullet grazed his neck. To many of the men, shots seemed to be coming from the upper story of the American Consulate. A tank commander at the intersection, who thought he detected fire from a consulate window, put a shell into it.

Alex conferred briefly with Avidan inside the monastery compound. Lieutenant Nachshon, the only officer remaining to Avidan, was troubled by the heavy casualties. He advised Alex to move slowly and in coordination with the tanks.

Meanwhile, however, a lieutenant and four men from Alex's company had entered the alley where Morty and Lazer had been killed. They fired bursts at the windows and roofs as they moved forward, although they could see no sign of the enemy. Suddenly, automatic fire chattered from the end of the alley, and three of the men fell. Two of them had been hit fatally.

The lieutenant, who managed to escape, took two men and ran south on Nablus Road looking for a way to flank the enemy position. Near the corner the road bent to the left, revealing a high, serrated wall three hundred meters farther on. Fire coming from the wall killed the two enlisted men.

Rafi's tank was now approaching the scene. He saw four paratroopers fall one after the other as they ran down the street. Fifteen to twenty wounded were scattered over the street and sidewalks. Pressed against a wall at the corner of the alley, Alex was gesturing at the alley opening. The tank commander ordered his gun turned right and a shell placed in the breech. The Sherman screeched to a halt at the alley entrance. From his high perch in the turret Rafi saw three Arabs running from behind a concrete wall at the far end. "Fire," he barked. The three disappeared in the explosion. A rifle grenade sailed over Rafi's head but did not explode.

Fire was still sweeping the street, some of it apparently from the monastery tower. (Two snipers were reportedly seen there.) Soldiers mounting the roof of a building found a still-warm blanket on which a sniper had apparently lain. Alex decided to abandon the open street and work his way to the Rockefeller Museum through back alleys and yards.

The company doubled back to the monastery and made its way through a door in the compound's southern wall to an alley. A sign indicated that a door in the opposite wall of the alley led to the Garden Tomb, where, according to a Protestant tradition, Jesus had been buried. To the Israelis, the grotto beyond the door was merely a dead end. At the end of the alley a car was parked beneath a metal canopy supported by four poles. They pulled out the two rear supports and the canopy tilted down, forming a ramp. Everybody except a platoon under Lieutenant Chanoch clambered up the ramp and over the alley wall.

Captain Alex had ordered Chanoch to pass through the mouth of the alley and secure the buildings at the end of the street. Like everybody else, Alex assumed that the street was Saladin. By posting men at its terminus, he thought he would be establishing a position opposite Herod's Gate, the likely breakthrough point into the Old City.

Chanoch and his platoon sergeant, Natan, took the lead, moving swiftly down the right side of the street. The platoon followed fifty meters behind on the left. Their view was impeded by the serrated wall at the end of the street. Sergeant Oren, with the platoon's rear detachment, thought it part of some monastery. None of the men realized it was the wall of the Old City they were approaching.

The Arabs atop the wall were evidently taken by surprise at the sight of soldiers running straight toward them in the open. Not until Chanoch and Natan were about thirty meters from the end of the street did bullets begin to hit the pavement around them. The pair dashed into the entrance of the Columbia Hotel, just one building up from the corner on the right side of the street. The rear section of the platoon sprinted into

314

a courtyard on their left. They took cover near the entrance and yelled across to Chanoch and Natan in the hotel entrance down the street asking whether they should try to continue forward. It was difficult to hear, and one man tried to get closer. He was shot dead from the wall. Sergeant Oren now looked more closely at the building behind him. On the roof was a sandbagged gun position, apparently unoccupied. The crosses carved into the stone facing of the building were what led Oren to think it was a monastery. Actually, it was the Schmidt School, a fashionable church-run school for daughters of wealthy Arab families, many of them from abroad.

Oren entered with two men. On the second floor they found an Arab civilian, who said no one else was in the building. As Oren started to mount a staircase, he saw movement above and quickly dropped back down. He asked the civilian again if there were soldiers there. This time the man said there were some young soldiers who had just arrived. "They're very frightened," he said. Oren instructed him to go up and tell them to surrender. The man mounted the steps, and the paratroopers heard urgent whispering. The civilian descended and said the soldiers were afraid that the paratroopers would kill them and wanted a promise that they would be allowed to leave if they came down. Oren ordered him to go up again and tell them they had ten minutes to come down. If they didn't, the paratroopers would come up after them. When the ten minutes had elapsed the paratroopers rushed the stairs—only to find the corridor empty. At its far end was an open door leading to another staircase, down which the Legionnaires had apparently escaped.

Entering one of the rooms, the three Israelis glanced out the window and found themselves looking down at the wall of the Old City and the domed rooftops beyond. Below and to the right was an elaborate gateway. Captain Alex's order for the platoon to reach a position controlling the entrance to the Old City had been carried out—but it was the wrong entrance. Since the battalion had mistakenly been following Nablus Road instead of Saladin, the platoon was now opposite Damascus Gate rather than the planned breakthrough point, Herod's Gate. From the side window facing Nablus, Oren talked with Chanoch and Natan on the third floor of the hotel directly across the street. As they spoke, Oren saw Legionnaires moving out of an alley near the hotel. He and his two men opened fire, cutting down three Legionnaires a few meters short of the hotel entrance.

All Rafi could see behind him on Nablus Road were his tanks, and he didn't like it. The paratroopers had vanished, leaving his Shermans alone in a built-up area. Besides being unprotected, he was low on ammunition and almost out of fuel. With his tank drawn up underneath a building, he was musing on the Hungarian Revolution and the Molotov cocktails flung from windows at the Russian tanks when he heard a window over his head open. He picked up his Uzi and saw a bazooka emerge. Right behind it came the helmeted head of a paratrooper with a transistor radio clamped against his ear. The soldier casually passed along the latest count of enemy aircraft destroyed and pulled his head back in.

Unable to raise Gur on the radio, Rafi moved his column forward to the end of Nablus Road and engaged the Arab Legion positions above Damascus Gate. It was a strange duel between tanks and an enemy firing from arrow slits. Rafi's gunner saw a bazooka being aimed through one of the slits and put a shell into it before the Jordanian could fire.

Sergeant Shlain was scanning the wall through binoculars when a machine gun blinked in another of the arrow slits. Bullet fragments tore into his right arm. He slid out of the turret and had his wound bandaged. Exchanging positions with the driver, he continued to direct the tank fire, using a periscope to sight on targets.

Meanwhile, Colonel Yussi and the blunted spearhead of the battalion were trying to find their way to Rockefeller Museum.

316

After climbing out of the alley alongside the Garden Tomb, the colonel had moved to the head of the line but a sergeant said, "Yussi, don't be a show-off," and replaced him at the point.

The paratroopers found themselves in a Moslem cemetery across the street from the Old City wall. Almost immediately they came under fire, and one man was killed. Pinned down behind the tombstones, the officers pulled out their maps and tried to find out precisely where they were. Locating the position of the cemetery, they realized for the first time that they had been battling the past few bloody hours up the wrong street. They were supposed to have taken the Rockefeller before sunup, but it was hours since the sun had risen, and they were still a quarter mile away. Just a few hours before Yussi had walked through the streets of Jewish Jerusalem at the head of a strike force of several hundred veteran paratroopers. All that were left to him now were twenty men pinned down in a graveyard. Company D had been put out of action by the shelling in Bait Yisrael. Company A—what was left of it—was back in the monastery compound. All Yussi had with him was Company C, minus the casualties it had left behind on Nablus Road, and Chanoch's platoon.

His fourth company, detailed to the rear as a reserve force, had simply disappeared. Yussi had not heard a word from Heavy Weapons Company since the battle on Nablus Road had begun.

Light had begun to reveal the features of no-man's-land as Kotcha led Heavy Weapons Company down toward the breach in the wire. He met Yussi just beyond the fence, and the battalion commander told him his job as company commander was over—he would replace the wounded Gedalia as deputy battalion commander. Kotcha called over his own deputy, Captain Michael, and told him the company was now his.

Michael took stock of his new command and found that he had only half the company with him. Machine-gun fire sweeping no-man's-land in the increasing light had stopped the men at the rear from crossing. Michael raised them on his walkie-talkie and ordered them to join up. They radioed back that it was impossible until the enemy positions had been silenced. Michael told them to follow as soon as possible and moved off with the men he had.

Twenty minutes after the rest of the battalion had passed out of view, the lead half of Heavy Weapons Company emerged onto Nablus Road looking for the war. The radio linking the company with Colonel Yussi was cut off with the rear contingent, so Michael was without either visual or radio contact with the battalion. He did not even have a photostat of the area. Some wounded men lying on the sidewalk gestured up the street when he asked where the battalion was.

Michael had not been happy with the attack plan when he heard it the night before. A scholarly kibbutznik studying at Haifa University to become a teacher in his kibbutz school, he had his own ideas about how fighting should be carried out in

319

a built-up area. It had seemed to him that by moving along open streets the battalion was exposing itself unnecessarily to Legionnaires firing from windows. It was even more true now that they had been overtaken by daylight. He felt that the approach to the Rockefeller Museum should have been through back yards and alleys.

From a glimpse of the photostat the night before, he remembered a left fork off Nablus as the battalion turning point. Opposite the Nusseibeh house he saw an opening to the left and turned into it. He had taken only three steps when he realized he was not on Saladin Street but in a wide alley. He did not, however, turn back. Accident had led him here, but without breaking stride he determined to keep going down the alley and find the back-yard route he had thought about the night before. Heavy Weapons Company was supposed to follow as a reserve while the other companies attacked and captured the museum. But now that he was cut off from the rest of the battalion through no fault of his own, Michael proposed to act as an independent command, an opportunity he was frankly delighted with. They would head straight for the museum through the back yards and take it themselves.

The alley, adjoining the American Colony Hotel, had already been vacated by Corporal Wohl of the Seventh and his breakthrough platoon. At the far end was a green door, which Michael's men passed through. The sloping ground beyond carried them down to the street paralleling Wadi Joz. An Arab civilian unwisely afoot was asked where the Rockefeller was. When he said he didn't know he was slapped, but he still insisted he didn't know. The paratroopers decided he wasn't a museum-goer and left him. Captain Meyer, the battalion personnel officer who had attached himself to the unit, vaguely remembered from his childhood that the museum was to the southeast. After about five hundred meters the top of an octagonal tower appeared to the right, and several men cried, "There it is!"

They scrambled up a grassy slope and lay in line near its crest,

320

Smoke billows from Jordanian trench position near Augusta Victoria after pass by Israeli plane on morning of June 7.

MAHANE

Tanks ascend Mount of Olives as smoke still drifts from air attack. View is from Histadrut Building in West Jerusalem. Building at lower left with vertical windows is YMCA in Jordanian Jerusalem. Conical roof abutting it on right belongs to American Consulate. Buildings in foreground are in Musrara quarter of Israeli Jerusalem.

Col. Michael Peikes (drinking) surrounded by his company commanders in Ein Kerem morning of June 6. Tension is visible in their faces as they plan attack on Abu Tor. Second from left is Capt. Eli. To his right (with hand to his mouth as he studies map) is Lt. Johnnie Hyman, who in a few hours would be engaged in hand-to-hand fighting. Wearing helmet on right is battalion medical officer, who would be decorated for going out to tend wounded under shellfire.

JOSEPH BEN-OR

Mandelbaum Gate before war. Building on left housed police and served as customhouse. Consular vehicle passes through to Jordanian Jerusalem. Shed was put up on occasion of pope's visit to Holy Land.

Mandelbaum crossing on June 7. Customhouse had been taken over as military position. Roof of "pope's shed" has been holed by shells.

surveying the scene as they caught their breath. A traffic circle with a street lamp in the middle separated them from the narrow side wall of the Rockefeller. To the wall's left was a gate leading to the museum's front yard. To the wall's right a gate led to a larger rear yard. No Legionnaires could be seen.

Michael had only twenty men. The other twenty who had started out with him on Nablus were coming up slowly, burdened by heavy machine guns and ammunition boxes. Michael and Captain Amnon, one of the veteran platoon commanders, glanced at each other wordlessly across the front yard of a house separating them. Amnon, who was closer to the museum, rose and dashed across the traffic circle followed by four men. Michael and four others came after them. The remainder stayed on the slope as a covering force. The silence was abruptly shattered as shots rang out from a building across the traffic circle. One of the men with Michael was slightly wounded but made it through the front gate with the others. Michael cut left to sweep the museum yard. Amnon crashed through the shrubbery along the museum wall, his men following his every turn like children playing follow-the-leader.

Reaching the front steps, the wiry platoon leader hurled himself at the massive metal doors and bounced off. They were shut tight. Before the dash across the traffic circle the men had taken off their packs, which contained explosives that could have been used to blow the door open. Amnon continued around the outside of the building until he came to a gate held by a chain. Opening fire at the links, the men suddenly came under fire themselves from the rear.

Turning, they saw the Old City wall just twenty-five meters away. The museum was built on a rocky outcropping, and the paratroopers were almost level with the top of the city wall, on which Legionnaires could be seen firing. The only way to reach cover was to run toward the gunfire for five meters and take shelter behind a low stone wall enclosing the museum yard.

The two sides were now separated only by the width of Suleiman Street, which ran fifteen meters below. From a crouching position Amnon reared back and threw a grenade atop the city wall. His men followed suit. The Legionnaires threw several, but all fell harmlessly into the street below.

Seeing no future here, Amnon led his men back to the gate and resumed firing at the chain in full view of the Legionnaires. The Israelis could feel bullets coming from behind and contributing to their fusillade. The chain gave way and the men dashed through. Passing through a side entrance into the building, they came upon five museum guards in uniform. They struck Amnon as pleasant-looking men. Reassuring them as he relieved them of the museum keys, he consigned the guards to the basement in the care of two soldiers. He posted another soldier at the entrance and with the one remaining man ran up to the tower to lower the Jordanian flag. Heavy Weapons Company had taken its objective without a fatality. It was a little before 6 A.M.

Sergeant Earon sat on a low stone wall one hundred meters from the museum absently watching the flag in the tower come down. The communications sergeant, assigned to Colonel Yussi, had become lost crossing no-man's-land and ended up with Michael's men. They had been running too fast for him, however, and he had paused to catch his breath. When he failed to see an Israeli flag being run up the museum flagpole, Earon entered the house behind him and searched the closets until he found a sheet. He spread it on the kitchen table and, with ink and a shaving brush, produced a rough facsimile of an Israeli flag. Making his way to the museum tower, he crouched beneath the chin-high parapet and ran his flag up the pole as the Jordanians on the city wall saluted with a withering fire over his head.

The covering force which had remained on the slope at the rear of the museum had meanwhile been busy. Hearing a shout down a side street, Captain Meyer saw several Legionnaires standing on a porch with their hands raised. As he approached

327

with three paratroopers, the Jordanians threw themselves flat and two armed Legionnaires crouched behind them opened fire, killing two Israelis. A tank was just coming up, and Meyer ran back to ask its commander to shell the front of the building. Taking several men, he made his way through rear yards and reached the back of the building to confront four Arabs running down the rear staircase. The Israelis opened fire at point-blank range, and the Legionnaires tumbled to the bottom of the steps, lifeless.

A lieutenant crossing the traffic circle to join the men in the Rockefeller was almost hit by a burst of fire from the museum's rear yard. On the slope Sergeant Ishai yelled to some men nearby to follow and sprinted into the yard. Large pieces of statuary from archaeological digs lay near the entrance. Leaping from stone to stone, Ishai and his men exchanged fire with the Legionnaires pulling back through the olive trees. When the Israelis reached the wall bordering Suleiman Street, they found a trench with a single Legionnaire inside. The others had disappeared. Fire had suddenly become so heavy that Ishai found it impossible to raise his head. The Arab rose and for half a minute there was silence. Then a single bullet fired from the city wall struck the Legionnaire in the side of the head and he fell dead. Under covering fire from the museum tower, Ishai and his men slipped out of the yard.

Up in the tower, Amnon found himself with a commanding view of the city wall and the intersection below. About two hundred and fifty meters to his right, Legionnaires were fleeing into the walled city through Herod's Gate. He fired into the gate's shadowed recesses and raked the positions atop the wall with his automatic weapon. After an hour with no sign of the rest of the battalion, he began to be concerned. If they had been stopped, it meant that the small force at the museum was isolated. He still had only his four men with him in the building. Looking out a window in the tower, he saw Michael and his group pinned down in the front yard. The men below heard the window squeak as Amnon opened it and yelled that he would give them covering fire. They broke for the building as he and the soldier with him sprayed the wall to keep the Arabs' heads down.

One of the men with Michael was Lieutenant Harris, the company's new sapper officer. The Detroit-born kibbutznik found the main entrance fastened from the inside by two large locks. He had once opened a locked army duffle bag by inserting a gun barrel in the lock and twisting. He did the same thing now, and the locks snapped free. Harris pulled open the doors, and Ishai and his men came trotting in.

Three hours after the men from Heavy Weapons reached the museum, an artillery forward observer arrived. Michael asked him to relay a message on his radio to Colonel Yussi that Heavy Weapons Company was at the Rockefeller.

In the cemetery, Yussi was on the point of informing brigade that he could not reach his objective and suggesting that the museum be taken instead by the Seventh when his radioman said he heard something on the artillery radio net about Michael's being in the Rockefeller. The radioman had no idea where the report had originated. Almost simultaneously Captain Chagai called in from the breakthrough area. He had reorganized the remnants of Company D and was prepared to bring them across. Yussi told him to move directly along the Wadi Joz road and capture the museum. He urged caution, however, since Michael's men might be inside.

It was four hours after the breakthrough when Captain Chagai began to cross no-man's-land. Enemy machine guns were still active. With Chagai was the rear half of Heavy Weapons Company, which he had found on Shmuel Hanavi. The half-track with Captain Dan of the Seventh was attempting to get through the wire as Chagai's force descended. Zigzagging three at a time, the men made it safely through the wire.

329

Chagai reached the slope behind the museum and halted, just as Michael had done. It was unnaturally quiet. No soldiers could be seen, and Chagai's shouts of "Michael" and "*chevra* (fellows)" drew no response. An Israeli flag was flying from the museum tower, but it was obviously a makeshift and might be a ruse. As if to confirm Chagai's suspicions, six Legionnaires dashed out of the rear yard as his men started across the traffic circle. Two Arabs were killed in a point-blank exchange, and the others ran into a nearby building, where they were hunted down. Chagai entered the front yard and proceeded cautiously along the museum wall. Peering around the far corner he saw the museum's front doors open. Framed in the entranceway was an unshaven paratrooper.

In the cemetery Yussi ordered a squad to make its way to Saladin Street and secure a tall building. The men crawled from tombstone to tombstone until they reached a staircase leading down to the street. They entered the adjacent Rivoli Hotel and took up firing positions on the roof. Under their cover, the rest of the men made their way out of the cemetery, where they had been pinned down an hour and a half, and reached the more amenable surroundings of the hotel.

The sounds of battle had long receded from the Nablus-Saladin intersection where Lieutenant Gabbay of Company A sat wounded. Around him lay three other wounded and four dead. The battalion medics had been under orders to follow the troops and collect casualties, but the medics had been the first to be wounded by the shelling in Bait Yisrael.

Gabbay, growing steadily weaker from loss of blood, lifted his head at the sound of approaching footsteps. He could make out Arab civilians and strained for his Uzi. When they drew nearer, he saw they were children accompanied by a weeping woman. He told her in Arabic to enter a house and wait until the battle was over before coming out. Two-and-a-half hours after he had been wounded, a Jordanian jeep approached. With a final effort he raised the Uzi. The jeep stopped next to him and two Israeli paratroopers, dismounting, lifted him gently and placed him in the vehicle.

With the arrival of Chagai's force at the museum, enough men were on hand to begin organizing a proper defense. Despite its fortresslike shape, the building proved to be a poor position. It was set far back in an elevated compound, and the streets below could be covered only from the front yard. Although the yard lay exposed to fire from the city wall, it was decided to risk posting a squad there. The men sprinted to the edge of the yard and took up prone positions behind its low outer wall. To see into the street below it was necessary to lift one's head. The squad commander tried it and was struck in the head by a bullet, becoming the first Israeli fatality at the museum.

Captain Chagai crawled out to survey the situation. Hoisting his helmet up on his Uzi, he promptly got a bullet through it. The yard was clearly untenable, and he ordered the men back into the building.

For the paratroopers inside the museum the war had come to an abrupt halt. They wandered through the galleries with the keen interest of archaeology amateurs, which most of them were. Lieutenant Harris, searching the building for the Dead Sea Scrolls which the Jordanians were known to possess, came upon an exhibit case with a label describing them; the case was empty. (Almost all the scroll fragments in Jordanian hands were found afterwards in the museum basement by Israeli authorities.)

To orient themselves and determine fields of fire, the officers consulted a scale model of the museum in the lobby intended for the guidance of paying visitors. Those who had been to the galleries as children found the displays virtually unchanged. To Captain Michael it all seemed an unlikely dream as he wandered through corridors confronted with sights he had thought as immutably lost as one's youth.

Dr. Avraham Biran, director of Israel's Department of Antiquities, had slept in his upstairs apartment in Jerusalem's Talbiya quarter Monday night, although most of his neighbors prudently spent the night in the building shelter. Early Tuesday morning he was notified by an army officer that the way to the Rockefeller might be open in a few hours.

It had been two decades since access to the Rockefeller had been denied to Israeli archaeologists. Biran's office in the new and widely acclaimed Israel Museum was just three kilometers from the Rockefeller, but the once-familiar old museum was more inaccessible than Nepal for all these years.

Collecting two colleagues, Biran drove to Gur's command post on Yael Street and presented himself to the brigade commander. At 10 A.M. the archaeologists climbed into a half-track with Gur and his staff. The vehicle crossed no-man's-land at the Police Training School and turned south toward the museum. Feeling his way along the Wadi Joz road, the driver turned a corner and the passengers suddenly found themselves underneath the Old City wall. The driver hastily backtracked and brought the vehicle to the rear of the museum.

Bullets whined through jagged windowpanes as the archaeologists started through the galleries. Exhibit cases had been smashed by ricocheting bullets, and the floor was littered with glass. Exhausted soldiers sat or sprawled in the corridors. A dozing paratrooper opened an eye as the group approached and fixed it on Biran. "Hey, fellows," he yelled, "now we can get an explanation."

A score of bone-weary soldiers picked themselves off the floor and followed the archaeologists on one of the most unusual museum lecture tours ever given. Shots echoed through the galleries and glass display cases periodically shattered as Biran explained what they were looking at.

The archaeologist confirmed that hardly anything had changed since he had last been there. Items marked REMOVED FOR REPAIRS on cards dated 1947 still had not been returned to the display cases. One of the few changes was the plastering over of Hebrew gallery signs chiseled into the walls; the equivalent signs in Arabic and English remained. Biran had hoped to make arrangements to protect the exhibits, but it was obvious that with a war going on around the museum this was impossible. He asked the soldiers to keep an eye on things and make sure nothing disappeared. Then with his two companions Biran returned to Jewish Jerusalem.

While the museum below was filling with soldiers, Captain Amnon kept up his duel from the tower with the Arab positions on the wall, sometimes assisted by one or two men. With the raising of the flag, the enemy fire became furious as they tried to dislodge it. Machine-gun bullets poured into the tall arched windows and bazooka shells beat a tattoo against the walls outside. If any of those shells entered a window, it would be all over for the men inside.

Amnon's legs and cheeks were bleeding from shrapnel. He sat on the floor firing through alternate windows, sometimes placing his helmet on a chair and shoving it with his foot in front of one window while he fired out the other. The young soldier with him —from kibbutz Gat—had a flask of cognac, and periodically they would pause for a nip. Machine guns, ammunition boxes, and sandbags were passed along up the winding steps, and the tower began to take on a cozy look.

Early in the morning Amnon descended briefly with the keys he had taken from the guards in order to make sure no one was hiding in the basement rooms. He came across a strongroom containing the museum's coin collection and remembered seeing it on exhibit when he was a boy.

Every time Amnon descended from the tower there seemed to be more soldiers in the museum, many of whom he didn't recognize. Late in the morning he was returning upstairs with a bottle of oil for the machine guns when a soldier guarding some Arab prisoners stopped him. Amnon was dressed in an old khaki uniform that looked more like the Arab Legion uniform than like camouflage fatigues which the paratroopers were wearing. It was a moment before he realized that the paratrooper mistook him for a Legionnaire and was trying to take the bottle away. Amnon yelled, "Idiot," and the soldier sheepishly let him go.

On the main floor most of the men dozed off on the stone floors, disregarding the whine of bullets and explosions. At one point the chandelier near the main entrance fell with a tremendous clatter. The men lying under smaller chandeliers in other rooms moved aside and resumed their naps.

At noon Colonel Yussi made his way from the Rivoli Hotel to the museum, where he met Gur. The brigade commander commiserated with Yussi on the number of casualties he had suffered but ordered him to take his men back now and clear the Nablus Road area. Yussi informed him that the area had already been cleared by mistake.

"Mistake or no mistake," said Gur, "we took it."

## 15  LINK-UP

The Nebi Samuel Ridge north of the city was still in darkness when Lieutenant Colonel Zvika's force—the Harel Brigade's right wing—moved through Bait Hanina, the last settlement before the Shuafat intersection. Of the seven tanks which had climbed the goat path, one had broken down at Nebi Samuel and one had run off the narrow road. Zvika sent his recon commander to scout ahead in his jeep and find a suitable firing position overlooking the Ramallah road. The officer soon returned and led the five Shermans onto a small hill where Zvika distributed them in a wide arc just below the crest.

In five minutes the horizon to the front began to show the edge of dawn and Zvika made out a warming sight eight hundred meters ahead—a broad ribbon of asphalt. He raised Ben-Ari on the radio. "I'm on Khirbet Zuresh and controlling the Ramallah road." He had reached it before first light.

Ben-Ari seemed incredulous. "Give me some landmarks," he demanded. Zvika saw a half-finished building atop a high hill on the other side of the road. He had seen it before from Jewish Jerusalem and recognized it as the summer residence being built by King Hussein on the same hill where the first king of Israel, Saul, had built his palace. "We're opposite Hussein's palace on Tel-el-Foul," he reported.

Ben-Ari said he was coming up with the rest of the brigade. Until they arrived, Zvika's small force would have to hold the intersection against anything the Jordanians might throw at them. "Hang on," said Ben-Ari.

Eight kilometers to the west, Lieutenant Dov in his tank

turret scanned a deserted village square. It was light enough now to make out the signs above the shuttered shops; they were all in Arabic. For the first time since the platoon commander had crossed from Maale Hahamisha with Yigal's task force on the brigade's left wing he had the feeling he was really inside Jordan.

Yigal's engineers had filled in the antitank ditch at the Radar and cleared the concrete obstacles beyond it at 2 A.M., thus opening the road through the position eight-and-a-half hours after the attack had begun. The force had moved on Bidu, a company of infantry dismounting from their half-tracks and attacking a fortified hill next to the village. Here the Legionnaires stood and fought. Twenty Legionnaires and one Israeli were killed in the trenches.

Dov had been ordered to enter Bidu itself to eliminate the source of fire coming from the village's edge. As his tank moved down the winding road, he swung his projector beam in an arc one hundred meters in front. He told his gunner to follow the beam with his cannon and fire on target without waiting for orders. At the last bend before the village the projector picked up a recoilless rifle jeep waiting in ambush thirty meters off the road. A fraction of a second later the jeep exploded as a tank shell ripped into it. When Dov entered the village, he found its defenders gone.

Shortly after Yigal's force rolled into Bidu, four dust-covered tanks entered from another end of the village. They were all that was left of the company with which Major Natan had broken through at Sheikh Abdul Aziz in the brigade center. The remnants of a third mine-decimated Sherman company under Major Eytan soon joined them. After reorganizing, the combined tank force, followed by the half-tracks, started moving toward Zvika at the vital Shuafat crossroads.

Halfway between the two forces, a small rear guard left behind by Zvika near the Nebi Samuel mosque drew fire at first light. The tank which had broken down here after climbing Khirbet Talila could still fire, and its commander tried to knock

336

down the minaret from which the shots seemed to come. The minaret—the most conspicuous landmark in the Jerusalem area —took a few shells without buckling, so the tank commander decided to save his ammunition.

On the still-silent hill overlooking the Ramallah road, Zvika's officers found it difficult to believe they could have penetrated this deeply into Jordan without a single shot being fired at them. They had been shelled climbing Khirbet Talila, but no enemy soldier had appeared. The Jordanians, in fact, still didn't know that Jerusalem was cut off from the north. They found out when two trucks loaded with troops started down toward the city shortly after dawn. A volley of tank shells set them ablaze. There was a scurrying in an Arab Legion camp at Neve Yaacov, a former Jewish settlement two kilometers up the road, and machine-gun bullets were soon peppering the hill. The Israelis silenced the fire.

At 6 A.M., two hours after Zvika's force had taken position, the recon officer squinted into the rising sun and called to Major Uri in his tank turret, "See there, three Pattons."

He was pointing to the lower slope of Tel-el-Foul. Twelve hundred meters away was the spearhead of an approaching Jordanian tank battalion. The five Shermans opened fire, but Uri saw their shells glance off the enemy tanks like rubber balls. The company commander had been taught that Shermans could not penetrate Patton armor beyond one thousand meters and now he had visual confirmation of this. Patton shells, however, could penetrate Shermans at fifteen hundred meters, and Zvika ordered his tanks to pull farther back behind the crest to reduce their silhouette.

A shell hit the corner of one Sherman and wounded its commander. Shrapnel from the blast killed one of the recon men as he tracked the enemy tanks through binoculars. It was Zvika's first fatality. The tank pulled back from the crest, and the crew scrambled clear. The guns on two other tanks—including Uri's

337

—broke down, leaving only two tanks in action. The pair kept shifting their positions and firing even though their shots had more psychological than material value. Uri kept his tank at the crest directing fire. When the company commander saw shell bursts advancing closer to one of the tanks, he ordered it to pull back completely behind the crest. The hill was so small that not all the half-tracks could find shelter on the reverse slope. One abandoned half-track was hit by a shell and set afire. The Pattons turned their attention from the Shermans and began hitting the half-tracks, setting fire to three more. Apparently satisfied by the smoke, the Jordanians pulled back behind Tel-el-Foul. Zvika made a quick casualty count and found he had twelve wounded. Taking advantage of the lull, Uri increased his effective force to three by calming down the men who had abandoned their tank and persuading them to bring it back to the crest. The three outgunned Shermans were the only force between the advancing Pattons and Jerusalem.

In a few minutes Pattons reappeared on Tel-el-Foul. This time there were six. Instead of facing the Israelis head on, as before, the tanks turned broadside and moved south across the slope, apparently heading toward Jerusalem. Zvika could make out gasoline drums on their rear and ordered his tanks to aim at them. The three Shermans opened fire, but their shells still glanced off the sides of the Pattons. Uri saw the commander of the other tank, whose cannon was not functioning, open fire with the heavy machine gun mounted on his turret. It seemed a quixotic gesture as the bursts crept steadily closer to the rear of a tank. Suddenly the Patton burst into flame as bullets touched off a gasoline drum. The crew of a second Patton leapt out, and the rest of the enemy tanks disappeared from view. Some headed back down the road to Jericho, intercepting the rest of the oncoming Patton battalion and sweeping them up in the retreat. Israeli jets rocketed them as they descended. (Several Pattons did not retreat. They were to be spotted later near French Hill moving toward Mount Scopus.)

It was more than an hour before Ben-Ari arrived with the rest of the brigade. He ordered a battalion to cross the road and take Tel-el-Foul. Major Natan's tanks pushed to the top of the hill and engaged in a fire fight with a rear guard of Pattons retreating down the opposite slope. Two more Pattons were knocked out, but not before two Israeli armored cars were destroyed and several men killed.

Natan was ordered to take his four tanks down the road to the Mivtar cutting, just north of Jerusalem. The cutting was a narrow pass where the main road between Ramallah and Jerusalem cut through the edge of Mivtar Hill. If there was opposition, Natan was told, he was to suppress it with machine-gun fire but not cannon for fear of accidentally hitting Scopus. He was not told, however, that Israeli forces had already broken into Jordanian Jerusalem and were directly in front of him.

Natan reached the cutting without incident but did not halt behind the crest. He brought his tanks about fifty meters down the opposite slope, which dropped sharply toward Jewish Jerusalem, and halted them in line, two on the road, the other two, including his own, off the road to the left. Jerusalem lay before him, with the golden Dome of the Rock in the distance. Natan did not have long to take in the view.

The two Jerusalem Brigade tanks which had fought on Ammunition Hill had descended after the battle and taken positions off the Ramallah road where it entered Jerusalem, five hundred meters south of the Mivtar. With the rest of Rafi's tanks fighting in the American Colony two kilometers south, only these two Shermans were available to guard against any attempt by Jordanian tanks to enter the city from the north. The Shermans took positions on a narrow street running between two hospitals on the east side of the road, flattening several parked cars. Periodically they slipped out into the open and shelled Mivtar Hill, from whose trenches fire was still being directed at the paratroopers on Ammunition Hill. At one point a Jordanian jeep loaded with jerrycans of gasoline sped down the road, but it was hit by small-arms fire and crashed into a stone wall by the hospital.

Paratroopers had mounted the roof of one of the hospitals to observe movement to the north. About 10 A.M. they shouted down to the tank commanders in the street that four tanks were approaching. Sergeant Ben-Gigi, whose tank was nearest the road, was alarmed. Both his and Sergeant Ariel's tanks had been firing all morning and were almost out of ammunition. In addition, the fire superiority of the Pattons, which he presumed were coming, was augmented by a two-to-one superiority in numbers. There was no choice but to attack from ambush.

Ben-Gigi moved his tank to the end of the street, just the front protruding past the corner. He saw the four tanks at five hundred meters and opened fire. Ariel pulled his tank around Ben-Gigi's and began firing.

The four tanks were Natan's. Almost simultaneously with the unexpected tank fire from the front, they were hit by heavy fire from the Jordanian positions on the Mivtar to their immediate right. As if this were not enough, Natan heard the scream of jets, and his radio barked a warning that planes were coming toward him in attack formation. Natan could not see them, but he crouched in his turret and pulled the hatch forward partway. Something struck the front of the tank, and a shower of small shrapnel caromed off the inside of the hatch and ripped into his back. While painful, the wounds were not disabling. Colonel Ben-Ari, following in his own half-track, was injured in the elbow by a stone kicked up by the Israeli jets. He ordered Natan's tanks to pull back to Shuafat.

On Ammunition Hill the wounded had been removed, but the dead—Israeli as well as Jordanian—lay where they had fallen. Almost twenty-five Israelis and more than eighty Jordanians had died on the hill. More than fifty paratroopers had been wounded. Of the fourteen paratroop officers who had been on the hill, four had been killed and six wounded.

A group of paratroopers who sat stunned amid the broken trees were summoned by officers organizing the hill's defense. Dodik had been called away by the battalion commander, and Dedi was in command of the conglomerate force left on the hill. He had Nir organize the men in the main trench on the left side of the hill. Lieutenant Ophir Fenegar, from Gabi's company, took charge of the northern trench facing the Mivtar. Some of the paratroopers in the bunkers had to stand atop the bodies of Legionnaires. Since fire was continuing to come from the Mivtar, the men stayed off the open slope.

Absently scratching his chest, Nir felt something bulky under his shirt. He reached in and pulled out the map of El Arish he had stuck there the day before when the briefing he was giving the men had been interrupted by the news that they were going to Jerusalem. At 10 A.M. he saw several Arabs approach the barbed-wire fence in front of him with their hands raised. They were apparently the small force stopped by Private Kandel in the last moments of the battle, slipping out then through the fence into the wadi. As they approached Nir saw a grenade in one upraised fist. He shouted to his men to open fire and the Arabs were cut down, the grenade blowing the hand off the man holding it. In the northern trench Ophir leapt up to see who was firing and was hit by shots from the Mivtar. Ophir Fenegar— who had written of his wish to be "strong to the point of tears" —was dead, the last man to be killed on Ammunition Hill.

Shortly afterwards Private Nardi looked toward the Mivtar and saw about forty Arabs climbing out of the trenches and running down the slope into the wadi, most of them throwing away their arms. A moment later he saw the reason why—three Israeli tanks pushing over the rear slope onto the crest of the hill.

The tanks were led by Lieutenant Dov, who had been ordered to attack the Mivtar after Natan's tanks had been ambushed. The Arabs fled without firing a shot as the three Shermans started up the rear slope. From the top, Dov looked across to Ammunition Hill and saw the paratroopers come out of the bunkers.

341

The crewmen climbed out and sat on the back of the tanks waiting for further orders. Curious about the Arab defenses, Dov descended into a trench by himself. As he approached a bunker, he heard someone crying. Sitting inside was an Arab youth about eighteen, covered with blood. Dov saw movement beneath a pile of canvas in a corner and fired a burst from his Uzi into the wall. Another youth emerged from beneath the canvas. Dov, who worked in the government's department of Arab Village Planning, told them in Arabic to come out with their hands up.

The youths said they had been taken from their village two weeks before the war. They said they did not know how to fire a weapon and had only been used to carry ammunition for the soldiers, who had all fled the hill. Turning the pair over to his crewmen, Dov continued down the trench and saw a figure duck into a bunker. He yelled, "Come out," and seven youths emerged. The other crewman, meanwhile, had begun to search the other bunkers. Twenty prisoners were collected and taken to a collection point off the main road.

The paratroop engineers who had opened a way through the minefield for Rafi's tanks also found supposedly empty bunkers surprisingly lively. They had entered the trench in front of the Police Training School which Dodik's company had passed through on their way to Ammunition Hill. Several dead Legionnaires lay on the trench floor. But the assault force, moving swiftly up the trench, had not entered the numerous bunkers lining it, merely lobbing grenades into those from which fire came. The bunkers were double-chambered, and any Legionnaire in the far chamber was safe. An hour after the engineers entered the trench, an officer saw a grenade roll out of a bunker. He yelled, and the men nearby dove to safety. The Legionnaire who threw the grenade was killed, and a soldier yelled in Arabic for the others to come out. A single Legionnaire emerged, and at the paratroopers' prompting he in turn called to his comrades in the other bunkers. In a few moments ten Legionnaires had been collected. A religious paratrooper in the trench reached into his pack and pulled out his tefillin. It was time for morning prayers.

While the battle on Ammunition Hill had been raging, the rest of the battalion had pushed beyond to the Sheikh Jarrah quarter. Passing the Spanish Consulate, the paratroopers were fired upon. Captain Giora entered and ordered everyone out. Private Yehuda Amsalam, whose father worked at the Spanish Consulate in Jewish Jerusalem, recognized the consul when he emerged. As with most foreign representatives in Jerusalem, the consul served in both sections of the city. Yehuda gave him a cheerful *"Como esta?"* but the Spaniard didn't recognize him until he took off his helmet. A Legionnaire dashed out from behind the consulate garage and was cut down.

As the men from Heavy Weapons Company started toward Sheikh Jarrah, they met an officer with a white beard and the gentle face of a scholar at the rear gate to the Police Training School compound. It was Colonel Davidi, commander of the paratroop corps. He told the men when they crowded around him that they were making history. The area their battalion had taken, he said, was the most difficult in Jerusalem. Some of the men asked if half-tracks couldn't have been used in the attack to reduce casualties.

There had been almost none available in the city. The evening before at Sur Bahir, Major Yussi, the Jerusalem Reconnaissance Company commander, had received an urgent call to send his half-tracks back in support of the paratroopers. By the time his company had been relieved and made its way back to the city, there were only two half-tracks which had not suffered mechanical breakdowns.

When the Heavy Weapons men reached the Ambassador Hotel, the tallest building in Sheikh Jarrah, most of them turned into the kitchen. Private Biegelman, however, had lived abroad with his father, an official of Zim Shipping Line, and was familiar with large hotels. He turned left into the cocktail lounge. The untouched martini on the bar was warm, and Biegelman made himself another. So did a few other soldiers who wandered in. A sip was enough to satisfy their curiosity, and they soon joined the others in the kitchen.

The hotel staff and two tourist couples from Italy and Mexico found in the rooms were led to the basement. Upstairs, Giora's men exchanged shots from the windows with snipers around the hotel, including some in the nearby Mount Scopus Hotel. One hidden rifleman on the south side of the building wounded several paratroopers, and Giora told him men to stay away from exposed windows. Determined to get the sniper, however, several men continued to look for him from an upper floor. Private Amsalam spotted a Legionnaire wearing an overcoat crouched behind a stone wall three hundred meters away. An Israeli soldier below was on the opposite side of the wall about ten meters from the Arab, but neither had seen the other. The Legionnaire saw Amsalam's window open and started to run. The private fired a single shot, and the Arab fell out of sight.

Giora led a patrol out to make sure the sniper was dead. Passing a house, they heard voices from a basement and flung the door open. Women inside began screaming. A defiant-looking young woman said there weren't any soldiers there. Amsalam motioned a man of about forty outside at the point of his rifle, and the women started screaming again. Giora said to leave him. Farther down the street, the patrol found the body of the sniper.

Captain Gabi's assignment after taking the Police Training School had been to secure the two foreign-built hospitals on the Ramallah road, the northernmost buildings in the city. Entering the French Hospital, Gabi was confronted by a nurse who told him there were no soldiers there. He was suspicious of her promptness in answering a question he hadn't asked. Entering the wards, he found a score of wounded Legionnaires, their uniforms and weapons beneath their beds. The paratroopers took the weapons and left the wounded where they were. In

Saint John's Opthalmic Hospital, the paratroopers braved a tonguelashing from an elderly English nurse for entering the hospital and found other wounded Legionnaires. All unwounded personnel were marched down to the basement.

Late in the morning, Colonel Joseph led a company sweep between Sheikh Jarrah and the Rockefeller Museum to clean remaining pockets of resistance. Noticing military equipment outside a building, a sergeant entered with two men. Pushing a bed aside with his foot, the sergeant found himself looking at a Jordanian officer prone on the floor with his carbine pointed up. The movement of the bed had knocked the barrel aside, and the Israeli got in the first shot. The sergeant threw a grenade into an adjoining room and entered to find the two dead Legionnaires.

On Nablus Road the force reached the blockhouse next to the Nusseibeh house. Elements of the other two battalions had clashed with the Legionnaires here, but the position had still not been cleared. Eight Legionnaires came out and surrendered to Joseph's men. He continued up Saladin toward the museum, a route he presumed had long since been cleared by the Eighth Battalion. In the basement of the Lawrence Hotel on Saladin, where the hotel staff had taken refuge, three Legionnaires suddenly burst in and ripped off their uniforms. "The Jews are coming," they shouted.

On Shmuel Hanavi Street orderlies and doctors at the aid station in the yeshiva courtyard treated an unending stream of wounded well past sunup. Periodically a woman appeared in the window of a house across the street and waved a blanket, signaling the medical staff that a fresh pot of tea was ready. Late in the morning a half-track driver stopped to ask directions to the Police Training School. Esther Zellinger, the ambulance driver who had worked through the night at the aid station as a nurse, was the only Jerusalemite on hand and offered to guide him there.

When the half-track continued on to the Rockefeller, Esther went with it. On a street in Jordanian Jerusalem they passed an Arab woman holding a wounded girl in her arms. The girl was about Esther's daughter's age. The nurse jumped from the half-track to bandage the wounds. The mother ran into her house and emerged with a large box of candy which she tucked into the straps of the medical pack Esther had acquired during the night. The half-track had continued on, so Esther moved toward the museum on foot, staying close to the buildings. She found an Arab woman lying wounded on the sidewalk and stopped to tend her. As she was finishing, a boy of about fourteen came up and spat on her. Esther ran until she reached the museum.

The Scopus garrison, well dug in, had come through a stormy night without a casualty. The hill had been hard hit by shellfire, which uprooted trees and damaged the old university and hospital buildings. The garrison had hit back with a demonstration of firepower which must have surprised its besiegers. From the command post beneath the cupola of the former library, a forward artillery observer in radio contact with gunners in Israeli Jerusalem called down almost three thousand shells on Jordanian positions. Hot meals were provided to the men in their outposts by the garrison cook, who stayed in the kitchen throughout the shelling. Sharing the meals was a UN driver who had been trapped by the outbreak of firing after driving a water truck onto the hill.

At noon three jeeps drew up near the Ambassador. Major Doron, deputy commander of the Sixth, saw Generals Dayan and Narkiss in the lead vehicle. General Weizmann was in another. A year before Doron had been involved in an argument with Narkiss over the loss of equipment during a parachute

346

exercise in the Negev. Narkiss, recognizing him, waggled a mock chastising finger and told him to get a jeep with a recoilless rifle.

"Where are we going?" Doron asked.

"To Mount Scopus," Narkiss said.

Doron pointed out that the road to Scopus hadn't been cleared yet.

"You clear it," replied Narkiss.

A kilometer separated the most advanced paratroop position from the Israeli enclave on Scopus. Doron knew that at two points along the way trench positions covered the approach, which was the regular route used by the bimonthly convoy to Scopus. He did not know if the positions were occupied. Requisitioning a jeep, he told the driver to move up the road as fast as the vehicle could travel. Doron borrowed a couple of grenades from his radioman and climbed in next to the driver, who pressed the gas pedal to the floor. As the jeep rocketed up the rutty road, the driver commented that they weren't "fast-moving" but "low-flying."

Doron, holding on as best he could, noted the empty trenches as they flashed by. The jeeps braked sharply as they reached a road barrier. The barrier swung back, and two members of the Scopus garrison ran toward them. One of them embraced and kissed Doron's driver. The other started toward Doron with similar intent, but Doron stopped him with upraised palm.

"I'm happy you decided to relieve us a day early," the soldier said. The regular bimonthly convoy, Doron remembered, had been scheduled to go up the next day, Wednesday.

He ordered his driver to pull aside and let the jeep bearing Dayan and Narkiss enter first into the enclave. Inside they were greeted by Scharfmann, who led them to the roof of the library for a view of the Old City. They saw how vulnerable the besieging paratroopers would be to fire from the Arab-held portion of the ridge. Dayan ordered the rest of the ridge captured and the Jericho road cut.

The party descended into a basement mess hall for a quick meal and a toast in wine. Someone stopped Doron's radioman at the door and said only officers were allowed inside. Doron introduced the radioman as the battalion communications officer, and the private entered to raise his glass with the defense minister.

## 16  JEWISH JERUSALEM

Tuesday's dawn caught the projector crews on the Histadrut roof by surprise. So absorbed had they been in lighting up the battlefield that no one noticed for some minutes that day was breaking to the east. Although they could hardly have been more conspicuous all night, the crewmen felt naked and vulnerable in the light of day. It was a tense quarter hour before they could disconnect the cables and stow the equipment under cover.

Yusske, the artillery officer who had been shouting directions all night, thanked the projector crews for their help but remained on the roof issuing fire coordinates to the artillery batteries with the endurance of a computer. At 9 A.M. he spotted two Pattons east of the Ramallah road moving toward French Hill, opposite Scopus. The observer on Scopus reported seeing several more. Yusske canceled all other fire missions and brought down a barrage of one hundred heavy mortar shells on the area. When the smoke lifted, the tanks were seen to have fled.

Near Yusske, an air control officer directed the jet strikes against Arab Legion positions on the fringes of the city. (Planes were not used in the city itself except during the attack on the Augusta Victoria trenches.) A chaplain, seeing the two controllers when he mounted the roof shortly after dawn, was reminded of the biblical battle against Amalek, where the enemies of Israel were sent reeling every time Moses, who was standing on a hilltop, raised his hands. Here on the roof the officers had only to speak into their mouthpieces and smoke blossomed on the enemy ridge.

Along the border of Jewish Jerusalem only incoming fire could

349

be felt. On Shivtei Israel Street one could see Jordanian machine-gun tracers oddly gay against the brightening sky as they sailed overhead toward the heart of the city. The border street was tangled with felled utility wires, tree limbs, and broken glass. Cars riddled with shrapnel sagged on flattened tires, and the smell of cooking gas from pierced tanks fouled the air.

Although some civilians had risked sleeping in their beds, the bulk of the population had spent the night in the shelters. On the ground floor of an apartment building next to Notre Dame, a visitor found nine people gathered in a windowless room two meters square. They had been in this oversized closet for twenty hours, and the air was stifling. Most of the time they sat in total darkness, since candles, their only source of illumination, added to the body heat. They had no radio, but despite the furious din outside said they had no fear that the Arabs could cross the border, two hundred meters away.

Farther up the street fifty persons were gathered in a deep basement that looked like a medieval wine cellar. A cheerful woman, an immigrant from France, said they had been up all night swapping jokes and stories. Only the infants had slept, cradled in maternal laps. Among the ultra-Orthodox in nearby Mea Shearim, men and women occupied separate halves of the shelters, just as they were separated in the synagogue.

Haga officials had not anticipated a continuous shelling which would pin much of the population below ground for countless hours at a stretch. One major shortcoming in shelter planning was becoming evident—a lack of adequate toilet facilities. "We're going to win the war," said a dismayed officer, "but we're all going to die of typhus."

Bread and milk were distributed to the shelters by Haga. The Angel Bakery had remained in operation all night, despite shells which exploded all around it. During lulls, civilians made their way on foot or by car to the bakery and the Tnuva Dairy, which had also opened, to pick up supplies for themselves and their neighbors. The three thousand children remaining in school

350

shelters were supplied meals from the central school kitchen, where women workers had stayed the night, sleeping on the floors.

Yussele Weissberg, a cherubic-faced Chassid with beard and sidecurls, had helped carry the wounded at Shaarei Zedek Hospital all night. In the morning he took off his bloodied frock, sterilized his instruments, and—despite the shelling—set out by car on his regular rounds as a mohel (circumciser.) He found most of the eight-day-old infants on his list lying, well wrapped, on benches in shelters. The normally joyous event was marred by the absence of the young fathers and the weeping of mothers uncertain about the fate of their husbands. The traditional schnapps and cake were missing, and the cheerful Yussele reluctantly had to forgo the toast *"Lechayim* (To life)" During his rounds he passed a civilian on the street who had just been hit by shrapnel. Yussele stopped his car and applied sterile gauze to the wound. After transporting the man to the hospital, he started out again to induct another Jew into a noisy world.

Military casualties had begun to reach the hospitals in large numbers shortly after dawn. In Bikur Cholim the scores of cots so hurriedly set up in the corridor less than twenty-four hours before were filled with paratroopers or spattered with blood of men who had been transferred to the operating tables. The soldiers were utterly exhausted, too tired even to lift their heads. The weariness seemed unspeakably deep. A paratrooper wearing a skullcap sat immobile in the corridor, one arm cradling his head which rested on a desk top, the other arm in a sling.

Through the open doors of the makeshift operating room (the hospital had no regular surgical facilities), teams of doctors could be seen clustered in a circle. Only the slight movement of a doctor's shoulder indicated that someone lay in the center. A soldier whose eyes glistened from morphine waited on a stretcher in the corridor for a bullet to be removed from his leg.

351

Although eight operating theaters had been prepared at Hadassah, the flood of wounded was so great—two hundred in one two-hour period alone—that they were soon backed up. A smoothly functioning medical assembly line never left the wounded unattended for a moment. The soldiers' weapons, which lay beside them on the stretcher, were removed as they were carried in the door. Nurses swarmed around the instant the stretcher was set down and stripped off the bloodstained clothing, throwing the garments on the floor, where they were gathered up by high school volunteers. After morphine and anti-tetanus shots were administered, a medical sorting team arrived, composed of the most experienced doctors in the hospital—professors of surgery and medicine. They examined the patient and determined the treatment required and his order of priority to the operating table. So unexpectedly heavy was the flood of wounded that the hospital administration altered its long-standing plans by assigning more of its doctors to sorting and converting a postoperative room to a preoperative room.

Nine hundred casualties were to be brought to Hadassah in fifty-six hours; major operations were performed on three hundred. All but eleven survived. In addition to the speed with which the wounded could be brought from the nearby battlefields to the hospital, much of the credit for this remarkable survival rate was due to the medics in the field, whose efficient first aid, often applied under fire, saved lives and limbs.

The wounded addressed all the nurses as "auntie," even the young and pretty ones whom some were later to marry. One soldier raised no objections to his clothes being stripped off but refused to let the nurses take off his dented helmet, insisting that it had saved his life. Sometimes when a doctor moved a soldier's limb, the wounded man cried out softly, "Gently, fellows." Otherwise, there was hardly a murmur. Several men asked that their officers be treated first.

Outside the hospital a constant stream of ambulances pulled up at the main entrance with loaded stretchers. Helicopters

352

returning from the Harel Brigade area dropped onto the hospital landing pad, and attendants rushed to remove the wounded aboard. In the midst of all this frenzy a bizarre figure in goggles and green surgeon's cap stood on a scaffold beside the Chagall windows patiently cutting away the putty holding the windows to their frames. It was Dan Ben-Dor, unrecognizable now beneath several layers of dust. Working eight hours a day, he was to remove all but three windows before calling a halt to the operations Wednesday night.

Shaarei Zedek Hospital experienced perhaps the closest call of the entire bombardment when a Jordanian shell passed through a large hole blasted in the building exterior and hit an interior wall without exploding. Just on the other side of the wall was a corridor in which eighteen newborn babies had been assembled. Although plaster was knocked off the corridor wall by the impact, the babies were unharmed.

The main burden of bringing the wounded from the battle-fields fell on Magen David Adom, which mustered more than twenty ambulances, including several sent up from Tel Aviv on Tuesday. The ambulances steered unhesitatingly for the front line; three were hit by shrapnel or bullets. Relief teams kept them in operation around the clock. The drivers were women or overage men, and the attendants were often high school boys. One was a thirteen-year-old who ignored his mother's tele-phoned demands to come home. These youths were witness to the grimmest sights of the battle—its shrapnel-torn victims.

One of the ambulance drivers was a blond German girl who had converted to Judaism and changed her first name to Bat-Ami (daughter of my people) after her marriage to Yoram Hamizrachi, the Haga officer who had sounded the air-raid alarm in Jerusalem. Bat-Ami was ordered to drive to Ramat Rachel on Tuesday morning to pick up three wounded. She was fired on as she crossed the kilometer of unsheltered road approaching the kibbutz and as she sped away with her load. She had hardly caught her breath after crossing the last open space

353

and reached Keren Hayesod Street, in the heart of the city, when a shell exploded five meters to her left.

By Tuesday morning Jordanian vehicles were appearing on the streets of Jewish Jerusalem, driven by paratroopers bringing wounded comrades back from the other side of the city. The Arabic markings on the license plates were the first evidence to the civilians that the troops had crossed the border, and small, exultant crowds gathered around the vehicles.

The cutting of communications wire by shrapnel had prevented the news of the paratrooper attack from reaching some of the Jerusalem Brigade troops on the city line. In the Musrara blockhouse shortly after dawn a lookout shouted to Lieutenant Chesin that he saw soldiers running through the streets of the Jordanian sector opposite. Chesin told the man to fire if he had a clean shot. Another man reported seeing soldiers on a roof. Chesin looked out and recognized the familiar shape of Israeli helmets. "Hold your fire," he shouted.

Private Ariel Fisher, the sniper who had been posted in Musrara, had shifted to Notre Dame during the night. At first light he glanced out a firing hole at the Old City wall across the road and saw a helmeted head appear in a perpendicular arrow slit. The Legionnaire saw him and ducked out of sight. Ariel figured he would be coming up for a second look and focused his sights on the slit. A moment later the Arab reappeared, and Ariel squeezed off a shot into the hole. His marksmanship would prove itself again during the final battle in the Old City.

On the roof of the Histadrut Building, Yusske was puzzled by the source of the heavy fire hitting Ramat Rachel. The artillery officer ordered his 120s in the Valley of the Cross to hit likely mortar emplacements to the south, but there was no noticeable slackening of enemy fire. Yusske had requested spotter planes, but the air force had refused to order slow-moving craft over the Jerusalem area bristling with enemy guns. When three Fouga jets arrived to attack the Arab Legion positions at Mar Elias, opposite Ramat Rachel, Yusske raised one of the pilots on the radio and asked him if he could spot any enemy mortars. Yusske could see the plane circling. Suddenly, it went into a steep dive, and the pilot rasped, "I caught it in the stomach." The plane did not pull up.

From the rooftop observation bunker at Ramat Rachel, Private Grover could not see the plane go down. He was looking through a telescope to the southeast, where he had noticed movement in a field just outside Bethlehem. A Jordanian soldier with his hands clasped over his head was doing what looked like a belly dance in a circle of clapping men. Between some foliage Grover sighted the slim barrels of apparent antiaircraft guns. While trying to puzzle out this charade, he heard a shout directly outside. He emerged onto the roof to see a Fouga in flames near the Mar Elias Monastery just across the border. He realized that the belly dancer was the gunner who had downed the plane.

At the Kol Yisrael studios on Queen Helena Street, the Arabic section had a new message now for the Egyptian forces reeling before the triple-edged thrust of the army of the south. Instead of continuing to urge them to surrender and thereby burdening the fast-moving Israeli forces with prisoners, the announcers told the Egyptians they would not be molested if they laid their arms down and made their own way home. "Head for the Suez Canal," they advised.

# 17 ABU TOR

In the field near Ein Kerem west of Jerusalem where they had bivouacked for the night, Colonel Peikes called his officers together early Tuesday morning. The night before he had maneuvered a place for his Jerusalem Brigade unit in Ben-Ari's attack on the Radar position. Today, he told his officers, their own brigade had given them a job. Spreading a map on the ground, he pointed to Abu Tor. General Narkiss, concerned that the UN might order a cease-fire any hour, had ordered the attack in order to gain as much ground as possible in the interim. There was little room for tactical finesse. The four companies in the battalion would hit the four principal Jordanian positions on the hill head on early in the afternoon.

There was time enough for the company commanders to drive to Abu Tor for a look at their sectors. (In no other phase of the battle for Jerusalem would officers have the opportunity for such close-up study of their battle area—but in the end casualties here would be no lower.) Captain Eli, a carpenter in downtown Jerusalem, had drawn the Arye sector on the crest of the hill. The swarthy officer, son of a Kurdistani immigrant, exuded the casual menace of a Caribbean buccaneer. As a teen-ager during the War of Independence, he had been a member of the Stern Gang, his appearance and his fluent Arabic permitting him to pass safely through Arab-held areas. His men knew him as a fearless soldier whose normal good humor could dissolve suddenly in a fierce display of temper.

Reaching the crest of Abu Tor, Eli crawled forward alone to find a breakthrough point for his company. Both sides had their principal blockhouses in this area. Although the opposing positions were only thirty meters apart, they were separated by three barbed-wire fences and a terrace. Eli crawled along the wire for an hour before he found what he was looking for, at the edge of a private garden which came up to the border. The terrace here was partially caved in, making it possible for men to run straight down the slope. The Jordanian building directly opposite seemed to be deserted. The main Arab blockhouse and a secondary position were not far to the left, but only from the latter could the breakthrough point be seen.

Summoning his platoon commanders forward, Eli showed each his target as they lay in the shrubbery behind the wire. They would take less than half their men with them in the attack, he said. In house-to-house combat it was only the men at the front of the line who did the fighting, and Eli felt that there was no need to expose a large number of men needlessly. The first platoon would take the two front-line blockhouses. The second would dash halfway down the hill and block the road, which divided the village laterally. The third platoon would then move through to mop up the area between the blockhouses and the road.

While the officers had gone forward to study their sectors, the troops moved up to Rachel Imenu (Our Mother) Street, a kilometer behind Abu Tor. As the soldiers sat in the street feeding bullets into their magazines, women and children came out of the surrounding houses with trays of tea and cake. The civilians were still mingling with the troops when the officers returned and briefed the men on their mission. Shells suddenly began to hit nearby, and the women and children disappeared into the shelters, leaving the soldiers alone on the street once again. Colonel Peikes, broad shouldered and soft-spoken, looked at the men around him on the street and pronounced the traditional wish for a safe journey: "We leave in peace and we shall return in peace." Forming up on both sides of the street, the men moved out on foot for Abu Tor. (Unlike the men he was leading,

358

Paratroopers crouch by stone wall on road leading to Lion's Gate (background), as tank moves up to provide support. Smoke is from burning bus.

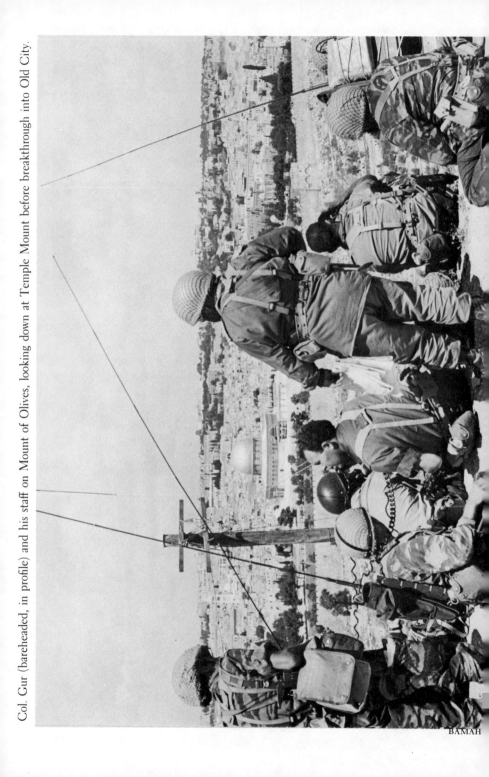

Col. Gur (bareheaded, in profile) and his staff on Mount of Olives, looking down at Temple Mount before breakthrough into Old City.

BAMAH

Smoke billows over Jerusalem during battle for city. Tower on right is YMCA in Israeli Jerusalem. Tower in center is part of church in Old City. Building to right of YMCA with gaping hole in façade is Notre Dame, on border between the two halves of city. In distance, heights of Bait Jalla in Jordanian territory overlook Israeli Jerusalem.

The race for Lion's Gate. Tanks swerve around burnt-out tank on "bridge" above Gethsemane which had been knocked out during aborted attack on Mount of Olives the night before. Smoke beyond mound is from burning bus outside Lion's Gate. Half-track on right, which bears Col. Gur and staff, would be the first to reach gate.

BAMAH.

Colonel Peikes was a professional soldier. In the Sinai campaign he had fought at the Mitla Pass as a company commander. His seventeen-year army career included a stint in Burma as the head of a commando training course.)

Eli kept his company back for ten minutes waiting for the extra bazookas he had requested. He formed the men up and checked their weapons and equipment. Then he addressed them briefly. Their task, he said, might be very difficult. But if they worked well it might be possible to pull it off with no fatalities and only a few wounded. He warned against looting and said he would shoot anybody he caught in the act. It was a threat he had every intention of carrying out. He had killed Arabs in the Old City in 1948 when they had stopped fighting in order to loot, and the memory was still vivid. The company happened to be in front of Eli's own home, and he took the opportunity to drop in for a quick hello.

To catch up with the rest of the battalion after the bazookas arrived, the company was ordered to move forward by bus. Eli was unhappy about this, for one shell would be enough to put the entire company out of action. There wasn't enough room inside the bus for everyone, and some men had to climb onto the roof. Tension had been visible in the men's faces but as the bus started rolling, Eli was surprised to hear them suddenly break into a spirited rendition of *"Havenue Sholom Aleichem* (We Bring You Peace)"* and pound the sides of the bus in rhythm.

Reaching Abu Tor, Eli ordered his men to find shelter from the enemy shelling inside the stone houses behind the crest until the attack order came. However, another company moving up to its position on the left flank was badly mauled by a mortar barrage. The Jordanian shelling was intense and accurate. From the center of the city, ambulances could be seen speeding straight into the shell smoke and emerging minutes later filled with wounded. As one improvised ambulance headed up the slope of Keren Hayesod Street, its tailgate fell open. A supine

363

soldier with almost all his clothing ripped off was prevented from rolling out only by another wounded man who grabbed him and cradled him like a child.

Unaware of the impending attack, the sniper platoon commander, Lieutenant Ben-Moshe, had driven up to Abu Tor to check on his team there. Accompanying him was Colonel Eliraz, the retired founder of the sniper school. The car came under fire as it approached the observation post and crashed into a telephone pole. When Ben-Moshe and Eliraz crawled out and called their snipers by name, they got no response.

The two veterans had seen troops moving up behind the crest and understood that an attempt to crack the enemy line was about to be made. Although they hadn't been invited, they decided to lend the attackers a hand. Working their way uphill, they entered a house overlooking one of the Jordanian strongpoints thirty meters away. Paintings casually stacked against the walls and the smell of oils told them they were inside an artist's home. The snipers placed a stepladder against the rear wall of the studio and climbed partway up the steps on either side of it. Through the window across the room, they could see the Arab Legion post opposite. The dark wall in front of which they themselves stood permitted no silhouette, so they could not be seen. The Legionnaires, however, had made a professional mistake, the snipers saw. They had failed to build a wall behind one of their firing holes, which permitted anyone who appeared at it to be framed against the light coming from behind him. The two Israelis kept their eyes on the opening. When something dark moved into it a few moments later, they both fired, and the figure fell from sight. Machine-gun bursts from the Jordanian position ripped into the studio wall but failed to reach the snipers.

Peikes and a staff officer, Johnnie Hyman, a Jerusalem lawyer, had gone to the Histadrut Building to show the attack plan to Colonel Amitai. From the roof they could see that the Jordanian line north of the city had been smashed. Paratroopers were visible on the roofs of Sheikh Jarrah, and Israeli tanks were moving down the Ramallah road. The brigade commander ordered Peikes to begin his attack at 2:30 P.M. Peikes rejoined his men and at zero hour, from the shrapnel-littered Arye blockhouse, gave the signal for the mortars to begin a fifteen-minute bombardment of the Jordanian positions.

Captain Eli had lost radio contact with Peikes, but as he moved his men up to their line of departure he met the battalion commander coming out of the blockhouse. When Eli said he was ready, Peikes told him to begin. The colonel's radioman, Oscar Sircovich—a Chilean immigrant and a top Jerusalem engineer—had become separated from the battalion commander as they left the blockhouse. He found Peikes outside watching an officer talking to a white-faced soldier who was gripping the bars of a window. The soldier was plainly petrified, and the rest of his unit had halted behind him. The officer's voice was strong but sympathetic. "What's with you?" he said. "You know we have to move." When there was no reaction, the officer slapped the man twice. As if suddenly wakened, the soldier released his grip on the bars and started forward. To encourage the men, Peikes inserted himself among them as they ran toward the wire and shouted, "Faster." An officer asked if he wanted two or three men as bodyguards, but he declined.

The first platoon moved through the hole in the fences blown by Eli's bangalore team and stormed the forward Arab Legion strongpoints. In one they killed six Legionnaires. In the second they found four already dead, apparently killed by fire from the Arye blockhouse. As each platoon passed through the wire, Eli ran forward partway with them and pointed out their target. The second platoon swept unopposed down the slope to the road. Eli told his radioman to inform Peikes that the company's mission was completed. But when he turned he saw that Peikes was coming down the hill right behind him.

The battalion commander said he had ordered the company

on the right wing to cross the road and push on to the house of the village mukhtar (equivalent to the local mayor), near the bottom of the hill. He asked Eli to provide covering fire for their advance. Peikes himself, followed by Oscar and another radio-man, moved forward to find a vantage point from which to observe the right wing. Peikes moved confidently, but it seemed to Oscar that they were getting dangerously ahead of their own lines.

The right wing had run into difficulty. A single hidden sniper had killed five men and pinned down a large part of the attack force. Lieutenant Yonkele Rotblit (he had been watching "The Longest Day" at the university the night he was mobilized) heard someone shout "Yonkele" and crawled forward. The company commander gestured toward the right and told him that Legionnaires had been spotted moving there in an apparent flanking attempt. Yonkele was to take his men and head them off. The lieutenant returned to his men and led them to the right, but the only Legionnaire they encountered was a dead one. When they reached a crossroads, Yonkele deployed his men in defensive positions.

Yonkele was standing in a courtyard when he was suddenly thrown by a mortar explosion. He had heard no whistle of an incoming shell and the explosion itself sounded mild, but he found himself unable to rise. He called to his radioman, who had been standing with him, but there was no answer. Turning his head, he saw the radioman lying dead a few feet away. The lieutenant lay back and waited for death to reach him too. It was not as bad as he had feared. There was no pain; death seemed merely like going to sleep. The young lieutenant was saddened only by the thought of his mother grieving for him. As moments passed and he didn't lose consciousness, it began to occur to him that he might not die. He lifted his head and saw that his right leg was hanging only by a patch of muscle. Well, that one's gone, he said to himself, let's look at the other. The left leg seemed to be all right.

366

A soldier came up and replaced Yonkele's helmet, which had been blown off. "Give me some water and I'll let you have my car to drive," said Yonkele, who felt a calmness he could not understand. The soldier put a canteen to Yonkele's lips and then lit a cigarette for him. A medic came up and stemmed the flow of blood. When Yonkele saw some of his men approaching, he yelled at them to go left. He didn't want them to see the extent of his wound.

Meanwhile, in the adjacent sector Peikes and his two radiomen had crossed the road which marked the limit of Eli's advance and entered a trench about twenty meters downslope. From it, the battalion commander had a good view of the right flank. A house upslope lay between him and the road, its three-meter-high retaining wall rearing up a few meters behind the trench. Unknown to Peikes, several Legionnaires had taken refuge in the house, and he was blocking their escape route.

Lieutenant Johnnie Hyman joined him, and as they spoke they heard a thud behind them. They turned to find a Legionnaire lying on the ground. He had jumped over the retaining wall and injured his leg. He was ordered to lie at the bottom of the trench, where Oscar Sircovich kept him covered. The Legionnaire wore an Australian-type forage hat with its brim turned up, a style also worn by Israeli second-line troops. Remarking with a smile to Johnnie that the Legionnaire looked like one of their own men, Peikes turned back to observe the right flank.

A shot suddenly rang out behind them, and Peikes fell. Before Johnnie could turn, two Jordanians leapt over the trench and escaped downhill. Johnnie knelt beside Peikes, who had been hit in the back. The battalion commander asked him to bandage the wound, but a moment later Peikes said, "That's it." As Johnnie tried to turn the heavyset colonel over, a Legionnaire scrambled down the slope and leapt on the lieutenant's back.

Johnnie, who played basketball regularly with a group of fellow Jerusalem lawyers and academics, was in good physical shape despite the fact that he was only two weeks removed from

367

civilian life. He managed to throw the Legionnaire to the floor of the trench and kneel on his stomach. In tending Peikes, Johnnie had released his hold on his Uzi, which now dangled from a strap around his neck. The Legionnaire, who had abandoned his own weapon, reached up and grabbed the barrel of the Uzi, pointing it away from his own chest. Johnnie tried to swing it downward but could get no leverage on the short weapon. He began beating the Legionnaire's face, meanwhile looking futilely for a stone on the trench floor. The Arab kicked furiously and clawed at Johnnie's face. When the Legionnaire reached for the bayonet in his own belt, Johnnie blocked the move and began choking him. His fingers tightened on the Legionnaire's throat, and the Arab's grip on Johnnie's wrists relaxed as he began to lose consciousness. The officer reached again for his Uzi and fired point blank.

Peikes's deputy, a tax official, was in the Arye blockhouse when he heard Oscar report on the radio that the battalion commander was wounded. A private nearby saw a look of astonishment pass across his face, but an instant later the officer began issuing orders in a matter-of-fact voice. The company on the left wing, cut up by the Jordanian mortars, was just now moving up to the line, more than an hour after the attack was launched. Their target was in plain view from Mount Zion, across the Hinnom Valley. As they moved forward, the Israeli and Jordanian soldiers on Mount Zion stopped shooting at each other and began to hit each others' positions on Abu Tor.

Rabbi Newman, who had lain under fire all night Monday, was inside the building next to the Abu Tor observation point when he saw five soldiers outside looking for shelter. He called to them to enter. As they dashed inside he recognized one of them as a student in an English class he conducted at the university. The soldiers said that fire from the tanks had knocked out the top-floor position in the Jordanian strongpoint downslope. They had to go across now and clear the bottom floor. Newman told his student that if he did the job well he could

368

expect a 9 in English. The soldier didn't recognize the private in the battle-stained uniform as his teacher and stared at him uncomprehendingly. During a lull in the mortaring the five soldiers slipped out. Five minutes later there was a loud explosion downhill. The men returned exuberant. This time Newman's student recognized him.

By late afternoon the fighting on Abu Tor was over. The Israelis had suffered fifteen dead and sixty-five wounded. Eli, whose casualties were few, sent men to help carry up wounded from the right wing, which had been hardest hit. In the aftershock of battle, men's muscles seemed to lock, and sometimes as many as ten men could not lift a single stretcher.

The residents on the Arab side of the village were ordered out of their houses while the Israelis searched for weapons and for Legionnaires in mufti. With the end of the firing, some of the residents on the Jewish side of Abu Tor crossed into the Arab part of the village for the first time in two decades. One Jewish boy looked at a large Arab wearing pajamas and recognized a face he had often seen across the barbed wire. "He's an officer," the boy cried. The Arab blanched and was led away for questioning.

From one house an Arab woman emerged carrying a little girl who had been severely wounded. An officer told a soldier to take the child to a first-aid station and to put her on the first ambulance going out. The child was taken to Shaarei Zedek Hospital. Dr. Schiffman, the head anesthesiologist, was summoned by a nurse from the casualty room. When he took the Arab girl in his arms, she was clinically dead—without heartbeat or breath. Schiffman ran with her to the operating room and began manual massage of her heart. After twenty-five minutes the breath came back to her body.

Lieutenant Yonkele Rotblit was taken to Bikur Cholim Hospital, where his leg was amputated. One of the nurses at his bedside was his pretty sister, Ilana, who had been summoned from Hadassah Hospital, where she had been tending wounded paratroopers.

Colonel Amitai had headed for Abu Tor upon learning that Peikes had been wounded. The shooting was over when he arrived. The slope had been cleared down to the Hinnom Valley, and Amitai ordered a second-line battalion to relieve Peikes's unit on the hill. As he walked along the crest the brigade commander saw a dead soldier being borne up the slope on a stretcher. As it passed, Amitai looked down at the lifeless face of Michael Peikes.

North of the walled city firing had virtually stopped by late morning. In the sturdy stone buildings of East Jerusalem the paratroopers oiled their weapons and lay down to sleep, sprawling on stone floors or downy beds with the indifference of the exhausted.

Losses had been heavy. More than seventy men were dead and three hundred wounded, a substantial part of the brigade's combat strength. The Sixth Battalion, two of its companies ripped on Ammunition Hill, waited on the approaches to Mount Scopus. Gur had decided not to attempt a physical link-up with the Scopus garrison at this stage, since this would have meant leaving the shelter of the built-up area to cross an open stretch of road on which the Jordanian guns were doubtless zeroed in. The Seventh, whose casualties had been lightest, held the line to the east, facing across Wadi Joz toward the fortified heights at Augusta Victoria. The Eighth Battalion, which had suffered the heaviest number of wounded, was in position opposite the wall of the Old City waiting for orders to break through Herod's Gate. That order had not been given because no decision had yet been made at the political level as to whether the attack should be attempted at all. It was the feeling in some high circles that a fight in the labyrinthine alleys of the walled city would exact an enormous toll in casualties and wreak havoc on the ancient city itself. (Such a battle would subsequently be fought by the Americans in the walled Vietnamese city of Hué.) General Dayan believed that the Old City could be squeezed into surrender after the Jericho road was cut. Twice already Narkiss had been given specific orders not to attempt to break in.

Opposite the American Consulate on Nablus Road, men from Company A of the Eighth were breaking into parked cars and using them to evacuate the wounded when two civilians emerged from the consulate carrying between them an enormous American flag. One of them identified himself to Lieutenant Nachshon as the American consul. Pointing to one of the cars under requisition, the consul said it was his. The phrase *a friendly power* passed through Nachshon's mind. He promised the consul, Pierson Hall, that the car would be left alone.

A short time later, Nachshon decided to return the consul's call. Like many others, he believed that shots had come from the consulate's upper story. Approaching with Sergeant Dalit, Nachshon found the consul waiting in the doorway. Although the lieutenant had seen the American flag and the consul had properly identified himself, the fact that the building was a diplomatic establishment with extraterratorial rights had not registered with him. When the consul advised that they could not come in, the paratroopers made it clear they would enter by force if necessary. "This is war," said Dalit. "You're fighting one in Vietnam. We have to do our duty."

At the paratroopers' request, the consul assembled his staff. There were three Arab males among them, but the Israelis were satisfied that they were not soldiers in mufti. The paratroopers winced when they saw the consul's private apartment upstairs. This was the room which had been hit by the tank shell, and it was an utter shambles. (Two young vice-consuls who had slept in the room Monday night had left it just half an hour before the shell hit.) Judging by the position of the window, Dalit concluded that the shots fired at the paratroopers from this direction must have come from the upper floors of the adjacent YMCA Building and not from the consulate. (Some Israelis were later to contend that the shots had come from the roof of the consulate. But the roof was sharply pitched, making it impossible for any Legionnaires to use it as a sniper's perch and remain undetected.) The paratroopers left the building with a wish to the consul that they might meet in better circumstances.

Farther down Nablus Road, inside the Columbia Hotel, Lieutenant Chanoch and Sergeant Natan were feeling more like besieged than besiegers. They were trapped fifty meters from the main entrance into the Old City and could not put their heads out the window without drawing fire. The Legionnaires on the wall above Damascus Gate could even hear their shouts to the rest of the platoon in the Schmidt School across the street and interrupted these exchanges with machine-gun bursts.

The two paratroopers decided to search the hotel and make sure they were alone. Finding no keys at the desk, they jimmied the doors to the rooms with a screwdriver. The beds were disheveled, as if the hotel had been hurriedly vacated, but there was nobody else in the building. Natan wrapped a wound in Chanoch's leg with bandages he found in a doctor's office.

Their survey uncovered four entrances. Unable to guard all, the pair decided to wait in the hotel lounge on the third floor for anybody who might come. They had not slept all the night before, and they desperately fought drowsiness as they sat in the soft lounge chairs. They snapped wide awake when they heard someone step on the broken glass strewn inside a side entrance. They faced toward the staircase with their Uzis, but the stray footfalls retreated. Looking out a rear window, Natan spotted a sole Legionnaire in the yard and dropped a grenade on him. Shouting across to the men in Schmidt, Chanoch said they would wait for darkness before pulling out.

Inside the Schmidt School, the vigil was not as lonely. As Sergeant Oren walked through the corridors he heard the twittering of female voices, and a trio of nuns appeared. They told one of his men who spoke French that there were eighty civilians in the basement. Oren, an accountant from Haifa, asked to see

373

them. The nuns led him down into the basement to reveal a group consisting largely of middle-aged men and schoolgirls. One of the nuns explained that the girls were students at the school who had been trapped by the war before they could leave for their homes, most of them in other Arab countries. She asked if she could lodge the girls in a separate room upstairs, requesting Oren's assurance that the soldiers would not enter. The paratroopers retired to a discreet distance, and the girls ran up the steps hissing at each other to keep quiet. The nun locked the door behind them and handed the keys back to Oren.

In the courtyard of Saint Stephen's Monastery, near the American Consulate, Captain Avidan, commander of Company A, received a radioed order from Colonel Yussi to bring back Chanoch's platoon. Radio contact with Chanoch having been lost, the commanders did not know his awkward situation. Avidan told Sergeant Dalit and two others to fetch the platoon. The three set off gaily in a commandeered minibus, joking with each other as they turned the bend of Nablus Road. A moment later the men at the monastery heard a burst of fire, followed by the blaring of an auto horn sustained as if by a dead weight. The sounds told the story of ambush as clearly as if they had witnessed it. Avidan dispatched a patrol through the courtyard to search for survivors.

When the patrol reached the southern wall of the courtyard, the men heard firing and shouts from the alley on the other side, the alley leading to the Garden Tomb. A rope flipped over the wall, and the men in the patrol hung on as Dalit and his two companions climbed over. They explained that they had driven for one hundred meters straight toward the city wall before realizing what it was. The driver braked, and the men leapt from the vehicle just as the Jordanians opened fire. A bullet had activated the horn. From the alley the trio had fired at the engine in a vain attempt to put an end to the unnerving noise. The horn was to sound the rest of the day.

A number of Dominican fathers were being kept under guard by the paratroopers in the courtyard. Mortar positions had been found behind the monastery, and snipers were thought to have fired from the building. Afraid that snipers might be lurking in the massive building and uncertain whether the priests were in collusion with them, the paratroopers decided to keep several of the Dominicans with them in the courtyard to guarantee that they would not be shot at. Among those held was Père de Vaux, the eminent French archaeologist, whose work on the Dead Sea Scrolls had earned him worldwide acclaim. Tied up to a tree nearby was a Legionnaire who had been taken prisoner.

While Chanoch's platoon was involuntarily standing vigil opposite Damascus Gate, the rest of Company C was poised near Herod's Gate, the point where the breakthrough to the Old City would probably be attempted. While the men rested inside the Rivoli Hotel on Saladin Street, Sergeant Ron stood guard at the entrance with bazookist Rusak. The street itself was open to the Arab Legion positions on the wall seventy-five meters away, but the paratroopers were safe as long as they stayed within the colonnade that extended to the edge of the sidewalk.

It had been quiet since their escape from the cemetery, and Rusak was talking about home. His wife, he said, was now pregnant with their first child. He had not received his mobilization papers but had rejoined his old unit anyway. His reverie was interrupted by the sound of heavy vehicles approaching. Three Egged buses filled with troops were proceeding blissfully down Saladin, straight toward the city wall. The buses contained a company of reinforcements from another paratroop brigade. Their orders being to proceed to the museum, they were simply following the shortest route on the map.

Ron held his Uzi over his head in a desperate signal for them to halt, but the buses kept coming. The first one finally stopped abreast of the hotel just as bullets began to strike it. The firing brought the paratroopers inside the hotel to the windows. The men in the buses and the men in the hotel mistook each other for the enemy and opened fire on each other, but no one was hurt in this brief exchange. The men on the buses leapt through the two narrow doors to the safety of the colonnade as a wind-shield shattered behind them.

Two men were carried into the hotel wounded. A driver said he thought there was another wounded man still aboard the second bus, whose doors were a couple of meters from the colonnade. Rusak jumped through the front and a sergeant through the rear, but they found nobody inside. The Legion-naires had seen them enter and opened heavy fire. The sergeant tossed a stretcher out the rear door and scrambled to safety as soon as the Arabs stopped firing at it. Standing inside the colon-nade abreast of the bus's front door, Ron could see Rusak next to the driver's seat tense for the jump. The bazookist leapt; in midair two bullets caught him in the side. He fell into the shelter of the colonnade, mortally wounded.

By early afternoon Captain Amnon and his men had de-scended from the battered tower of the Rockefeller Museum for good, and the Arabs ceased firing from the wall opposite. Hun-dreds of soldiers filled the museum's galleries and spilled over into the courtyard. Outside Amnon saw an officer with thick glasses, beard, and the pips of a general. He was telling some men that they would be in the Old City the next day. Amnon doubted it. He assumed it was political considerations—some-thing to do with the UN—which had thus far kept them from attacking the Old City. He could think of no reason why the same considerations would not prevail tomorrow.

The bearded general was Rabbi Shlomo Goren, chief chaplain of the Israeli Army and one of its most colorful figures. An acknowledged scholar, he had earned his paratroop wings when he was in his forties, breaking a leg in the process. In time of war he was the servant of an angry God, calling upon his uni-formed congregation with the passion of the ancient prophets to destroy Israel's enemies.

On Monday morning he had learned at 7 A.M. about the pending air strike and hurried to his office. "Blessed be the Lord," he said in Yiddish to his assistant, "it's begun." The two of them had driven to kibbutz Nahal Oz and joined the troops preparing to attack the Gaza Strip. Goren carried a small Torah, and the soldiers kissed it as he moved among them. At his insistence he was permitted to go in with the attacking force.

Heavy fire mauled the unit and a shell hit the half-track in which Goren was riding, killing the driver next to him. In a nearby half-track a *Life* photographer was killed. Goren and his assistant were rescued after lying in the fire-swept field for two hours, but the shofar (ram's horn) which he had blown on Mount Sinai during the Sinai campaign had been lost in the half-track. That night General Gavish, commander of the Southern Front, told him that something might be happening in Jerusalem, and Goren had promptly driven to the city.

Now, in the Rockefeller, Goren called for men to participate in the first minyan on this side of Jerusalem in nineteen years. Dozens of paratroopers assembled in the yard for the mincha service. A nonreligious kibbutznik asked Dr. Jack what one had to do during the prayers, and Jack assured him he simply had to stand there. That morning Jack, a religious immigrant from Rhodesia, had been putting on his tefillin when another kibbutz youth said, "Show me how." When Jack asked if he hadn't worn tefillin when he was bar mitzvah, the youth explained that he had never had a bar mitzvah ceremony at his kibbutz.

Inside the museum some men entered their names in the guest registry near the main entrance. The first soldier followed the style of the previous visitors, writing his name on the left side of the page in Latin letters beneath that of the last visitor to sign, a Senora Bacigalup from Lima, Peru. But the soldier who followed inscribed his name in Hebrew on the right side of the page as if asserting that he was not a tourist in a foreign land. The rest of the soldiers followed suit, sometimes adding comments on the museum itself. These ranged from enthusiastic ("What beauty, fantastic") to polite ("It was pleasant"). Some of the

377

notes indicated that the soldiers had learned things on their visit to the museum that they would rather not know. "Believe me, it hurts to see dead, even theirs," wrote one; another, "If only we could have visited here without war."

Fatigue and bitter sadness dogged Nir as he quit Ammunition Hill in the early afternoon. Only a handful of men from the company were still with him; he presumed the rest were either dead or wounded. Convinced that Dodik was dead, Nir was plagued by the thought that if he had managed to stay at Dodik's side, the company commander would still be alive. Nir was directed to a school opposite the Spanish Consulate, where he found many of the missing men asleep on the floor. Igal Arad, the medic, looked up at Nir and said, "Are you still alive?"

Propped against a wall with his eyes closed was Dodik. Nir ran to him and shook him by the shoulders. Dodik, utterly exhausted, opened his eyes and stared blankly at Nir for a moment; then his lids shut again. (Dodik had also been sure Nir was dead. When he woke, he said he had just dreamed that he had seen Nir alive.)

In the afternoon a young lieutenant arrived, and the men who recognized him shifted awkwardly. It was Udi Tsuri, younger brother of Yoav, whose charge had opened the way for the final thrust on Ammunition Hill. Udi had gotten permission to come up to Jerusalem and had hitched a ride with General Chaim Herzog. Learning that the Sixth was at Ammunition Hill, he came looking for Yoav. The officers exchanged glances, and it was Colonel Joseph who finally took Udi aside and told him his brother was dead. Udi begged permission to take over his brother's platoon, but Joseph told the distraught young officer it wasn't possible. He did not want to risk having both brothers killed.

Poet Chaim Guri's second-line company, which had taken a severe pounding the day before at Pagi, was ordered to relieve the paratroopers on Ammunition Hill Tuesday afternoon. The men assembled the dead Legionnaires and buried them in temporary mass graves. Mike Ronen, the acting gunnery sergeant, was a political cartoonist for one of the afternoon papers and had carried a felt-tipped pen to war. There had been no opportunity for sketching since the shooting started, but he used the pen now to inscribe an epitaph for one group of Legionnaires on a piece of cardboard he found in the NCO barracks on the hill: "Here lie seventeen brave Jordanians." He impaled the card on the bayonet of a Jordanian carbine, which he thrust into the ground. The hill was quiet, but looking across at Jewish Jerusalem Ronen saw shells hitting around his home on Street of the Prophets, where his wife and two daughters were taking shelter.

Guri's men discovered that not all the Legionnaires on the hill were dead. Arabic voices were heard coming from two ventilator shafts in the middle of the hill. The Israelis shouted, "Come out," and seven Legionnaires emerged from the command bunker. One of them was wounded, apparently from the grenade thrown by Corporal Eylan during the night. In the bunker the paratroopers found three dead Legionnaires.

"We fought well, but you fought better," one of the prisoners said.

Another, who seemed dazed, tried to take his rifle back when it was taken from him. He said King Hussein, on a visit just before the war, had made the soldiers pledge not to part with their weapons as long as they were alive. "I'm still alive," he said.

While the Sixth in Sheikh Jarrah and the Eighth in the American Colony were bivouacking in uninhabited schools and hotels, the Seventh was concentrated in the residential area of Wadi Joz hamlet, and the men were distributed among private homes. Some, attempting to converse with the Arab occupants, found the older men willing to talk, occasionally even in remembered Hebrew; but the young men were silent and sullen. Many of the older Arabs recalled Jewish acquaintances they knew prior to the splitting of the city and asked the paratroopers if they

379

knew them. Private Elisha, a Jerusalem native, found that he did indeed share a mutual acquaintance with the owner of the house in which he was bivouacked. The Arab had owned a shop on Jaffa Road in Jewish Jerusalem twenty years before and knew one of the Angel brothers who owned the bakery.

The paratroopers helped themselves to food and slept on beds when they could, but for the most part were scrupulous in avoiding looting. (Second-line troops arriving later were to prove less scrupulous. There was, however, to be no instance of rape, molestation, or murder on the part of the Israeli troops.)

In houses where soldiers were bivouacked the Arab families were asked to assemble in one or two rooms and were left alone there. Hananel Mack found himself in the fashionable villa of a man who, according to the diploma on the wall, was an architect. The soldiers took care not to drop ashes on the rug, and when school papers for mathematics and physics homework were found, Hananel, himself a chemist, brought them downstairs to the seventeen-year-old son of the family.

The troops had had nothing substantial to eat in two days, and commanders permitted their men to break into food shops. (Journalists were to find shutters on jewelry shops and camera stores undisturbed.) The most sought-after beverage was not spirits but Pepsi-Cola, which the Arab boycott had succeeded in banning from Israel and which most of the young Israelis had never tasted. In one grocery the starving men wolfed down yogurt, smearing on their sooty faces a white harlequin mask.

Occasionally, Arab hospitality surfaced even toward an occupying army. When the brigade medical staff set up their forward aid station at a villa near the museum, they were greeted by the proprietor with tea. The medical men, ever suspicious of untested beverages, were assured only after their host drank the first cup. At a nearby hotel a group of scouts were offered coffee by the owner, but, finding the gesture obsequious, declined.

Not all civilians accepted the Israeli occupation with resignation. Soldiers from the Seventh were standing on a street in

380

Wadi Joz when a man ran out of a house shouting in Arabic and firing a pistol at them. To Lieutenant Gad, the man seemed old enough to be his father, and for a fraction of a second he wondered if there was a way to stop him without shooting. There wasn't; the man fell in a burst of fire. He knew he was going to die, thought Gad, and he knew what he was dying for.

The only activity during the afternoon was along Wadi Joz, where Companies A and D of the Seventh watched from behind stone walls for signs of counterattack from Augusta Victoria. From time to time Legionnaires were cut down as they attempted to slip out of the occupied part of the city and make their way across the wadi to the ridge. At one point a taxi started down the road from the ridge, and the paratroopers opened fire, sending it crashing into the wadi. A jeep carrying Legionnaires met the same fate. The Israelis could hear an Arab officer directing troops to numbered positions on a walkie-talkie, apparently somewhere up on the ridge. But no movement could be detected in the trenches below Augusta Victoria, and the paratroopers began to doubt if they were still manned.

Captain Zamush, commander of Company A, was studying the ridge through binoculars when his deputy, Lieutenant Malka, saw something move on the roof of an adjoining building. He told the man next to him to check it. Before the soldiers could move, a grenade fell next to him. Instinctively he executed a soccer kick, sending the grenade rolling down the staircase before it exploded. Zamush ordered all residents in front-line houses evacuated to the rear.

Company D, which was holding the Wadi Joz line closer to the Old City, found its front so shallow that there was no rear to which civilians might be sent. Forty Arabs were assembled from the houses in the area and told to walk into the Old City through Lion's Gate, four hundred meters to the south. A lieutenant explained that this was now a front-line area. He was sorry to make them abandon their homes, he said, but Israel had not started the war. The civilians started down the road to Lion's

Gate, nervously looking back toward the paratroopers as if expecting to be shot.

The battle against snipers continued intermittently. Shacham, a sergeant in Kapusta's recon company, went up alone to a roof in the American Colony to search for a sniper firing from another building up the street. In an unfinished room on the roof were four men in pajamas. Assuming they were residents, Shacham brought them to a collection point downstairs. When he went back up, he found four uniforms and rifles on the far side of the roof.

In compliance with Dayan's order to take the ridge, Colonel Gur decided to resume movement late in the afternoon. Uzi's battalion would push across the wadi with Rafi's tanks and storm the heights at Augusta Victoria. A company of tanks from Ben-Ari's brigade was to be made available, and Gur decided to have them supply covering fire from below. Although there had been little sign of the enemy on the ridge all day, the attack would be carried out on the assumption that the Arab Legion was dug in and waiting.

After the morning's battles Rafi had brought his tanks to a large field behind Ammunition Hill for a rendezvous with fuel and ammunition trucks. While the tanks were being rearmed, he and another officer crossed over to Shaarei Zedek Hospital for treatment of their wounds, returning to the unit after being tended.

In midafternoon Rafi proceeded to the Rockefeller after getting orders to meet Gur there. He parked his tank at the rear of the museum and ran into the entrance bent over to avoid sniper fire. Gur told him his tanks would shortly get under way and lead the attack on Augusta Victoria. Rafi informed him that while his Shermans had received shells, they had not yet received ammunition for their machine guns. The Harel Brigade tanks had not yet arrived either, so Gur decided to postpone the attack until dark.

382

Major Kapusta was still trying to get a part in the war for his recon company. They had crossed over on foot after sunrise at the Police Training School, but the battle there was already over. The only job remaining was to stalk the streets on a sniper hunt. At the museum, Kapusta cornered Gur and asked in Yiddish, *"Nu, vaiter?* (Well, what next?)."* Gur told him his company would lead the Seventh in the night attack on Augusta Victoria.

It had been eleven years since Kapusta had received an order from Gur to attack an enemy position. It had been at Mitla Pass during the Sinai campaign, when Gur was a battalion commander. Kapusta was commanding the same company as he was now, with many of the same men. During the battle, Gur, trapped by ambush in the defile with his spearhead force, had seen Kapusta and about forty of his men appear on the crest above the enemy positions. He ordered Kapusta to sweep the slope clean. From Gur's position he could not see the caves and bunkers on the hillside. Kapusta could, but he and his forty attacked. Ten were killed and a dozen, including Kapusta, wounded. Other paratroopers entered the battle, and when it was over two hundred Arabs lay dead on the hillside.

At the Seventh's mortar position in Sanhedria, Raviv's platoon had somehow come through the night without casualties, despite more than one hundred shells that had fallen in the area. (At the nearby position of the Eighth Battalion mortars, Corporal Stolar, who had taken a copy of *The White Nile* with him two weeks before, was wounded and two men next to him killed by a shell when they took shelter in a ditch.) An officer arrived to inform Raviv that he was now in command of the company. The company commander, Captain Bikel, had been wounded, as had a platoon commander; two other platoon leaders had been killed. Join-

383

ing Colonel Uzi at Wadi Joz, Raviv was told to prepare to give supporting fire for the attack on Augusta Victoria. He ranged his mortars in on the trench lines and on A-Tor village on the crest, then settled down to wait for nightfall.

In Jewish Jerusalem the lulls in the shelling Tuesday afternoon lured people out of the shelters, and the sound of whistles echoed off the buildings as wardens shooed them back off the streets. Here and there, units of the Jerusalem Brigade could be seen forming up for movement. Word had spread that Israeli troops were at the gates of the Old City.

"See you tomorrow at the Western Wall," someone on the street shouted.

From a balcony in Musrara, the northern wall of the Old City could be seen, golden in the late afternoon sunlight. An explosion kicked a small cloud of dust off the top of a minaret inside the wall, apparently a bazooka or tank shell aimed at snipers. Nothing could be seen moving. The Mount of Olives never seemed more peaceful as Gur's attack force assembled on its approaches.

The last time a Jewish army had attempted to storm the ridge was during the siege of Jerusalem by Titus nineteen centuries before. The Jews were inside the walled city then and the Romans had brought up four legions, totaling sixty thousand men, to subdue them. The twenty thousand Jewish fighters were divided by a three-way civil war, grudgingly suspended only with the enemy at the walls. One legion had begun constructing its siege camp on the Mount of Olives when a Jewish force sallied from the eastern wall and swept across the wadi, routing the startled Roman legionaries. Only the intervention of Titus halted the flight and permitted the Romans to force the Jews back inside the walls. It was to take the Romans four months to overcome the fanatic resistance of the city's defenders.

Titus, however, didn't have the United Nations to consider. With a UN cease-fire resolution a possibility within hours, the

384

Israeli generals knew they would have to move quickly if they were to return the nation to the Temple Mount. As soon as darkness descended, the paratroopers and tank crews would attempt what their forefathers had failed to achieve two millennia earlier—the placing of a Jewish armed force atop the Mount of Olives.

# 19  TRAPPED

Near King Hussein's still-unfinished summer palace on Tel-el-Foul, three kilometers north of Jerusalem, Major Eytan had been in position with four of his tanks since morning. Eytan, a company commander in the Harel Brigade, had had his command half-track and later a tank blasted out from under him by mines during the previous night's breakthrough near Bidu. He had taken over another tank and led his men in a battle against seven Jordanian Pattons which had taken position among the houses of Shuafat at the foot of Tel-el-Foul.

He was still aboard his borrowed tank when he received an order at 4 P.M. to gather ten tanks and join the paratroopers at the Rockefeller Museum in the city. The force Eytan assembled, a mixed unit from two companies, included Lieutenant Dov's platoon which descended from Mivtar Hill. Darkness was setting in by the time the ten tanks had been fueled and loaded with ammunition.

The road into the city was clogged with the armored brigade's supply trucks, and the tanks wove their way among them with difficulty. When Eytan halted his tank behind the museum, he was hailed by the commander of the fourth tank in line, who reported that he could see no tanks behind him. The six rear tanks had missed a turn in the darkness, but Eytan managed to raise an officer with the rear detachment on his radio. He asked the officer to report his position so that a jeep could be sent to guide him to the museum.

For some reason, however, the officer, who was not in Eytan's company, suspected a Jordanian ruse. He asked Eytan to give his family name and the initials of other officers in the battalion. Eytan, a stoical kibbutznik, patiently answered these and similar questions for several minutes, but in the end the officer refused to reveal where he was. Eytan would have to make do with four tanks. The bizarre tone of the night was set.

Lieutenant Dov had no idea of where he was or what he was supposed to do until a paratroops officer climbed on his tank and explained the mission. "Try to imagine," the paratrooper said. "Before you is a wadi. Beyond that is a ridge. These tanks will stay here and shoot at the ridge. After that we [the paratroopers and the Jerusalem Brigade tanks] will go up and take it." It did not occur to Dov that the ridge he was about to start shelling was the biblical Mount of Olives.

The projectors on the Histadrut Building sprang to life and Augusta Victoria Hospital appeared on the heights with the drama of a Rhine castle in a sound and light presentation. The sound was quickly provided by mortars which opened up on the Arab Legion position next to the hospital and by the tank cannon which fired at the hospital itself. The Israelis operated on the assumption that the massive structure, which dominated the slope, was being used as a defensive position.

The building had been put up as a Protestant hospice at the turn of the century with money donated by Kaiser Wilhelm after his visit to the Holy Land. The British had turned it into a hospital in World War II, and it had continued in that capacity, serving as the principal medical facility for refugees in Jordan. Monday afternoon all thirty-eight patients who had been in the hospital when the war started were evacuated to the shelter at the rear of the building, together with about 170 staff members. In the deep basement they could not even hear the shells blasting the front of the building.

The gunner in one tank, a policeman in Jewish Jerusalem in private life, put white phosphorous shells into the upper-story windows of the hospital, his crewmates shouting "Bullseye" as

388

each explosion sent white smoke foaming out the windows. Eytan fired at the sides of the road leading up to Augusta Victoria and searched the slopes for flashes of counterfire. He could see none.

While Eytan's tanks battered the ridge, the Jerusalem Brigade tanks started forward. Rafi, in the lead, knew he was to make a sharp left turn to reach the Augusta Victoria road. The turn was difficult to spot even in daylight, the road climbing out of the wadi at a steep angle and joining the main road at a traffic circle at an angle of about 150 degrees. It was so dark Rafi couldn't even tell if his tank was traveling on the roadway or the sidewalk. He missed the turn and continued down the road paralleling the eastern wall of the Old City.

Although reassured at first by the road's leftward drift, he became increasingly uneasy about the absence of a sharp left turn. After three hundred meters, machine-gun fire began to come from somewhere near at hand to the right. At this point Rafi was near the road leading to Lion's Gate. Without stopping, he radioed Gur and said he thought he was on the wrong road. Gur told him to turn on his projector to see where he was. Since the projector had been knocked out in the morning's fighting, Rafi ordered the tank behind him to pass to the front and turn on its projector. The tank moved forward, but its projector also failed to operate.

The road now bent to the left at a 90-degree angle as it bridged the wadi. The tanks rumbled across the bridge and turned right. They were now on the site of Gethsemane, where Jesus had spent his last night on earth. The road here widened to four lanes with a traffic island in the middle. Rafi had seen the upper stretch of the Augusta Victoria road from the museum before dark and remembered it to be a two-lane road. He knew now for a certainty that the column was on the wrong road and ordered it to turn back.

As the tanks swung across the traffic island and started toward the rear, fire from the wall quickened. Rafi stopped his tank on

389

the far end of the bridge to give his men cover. From behind the battlements of the city, a flare arced into the sky and fell slowly over the wadi, revealing his tank clearly to the Legionnaires on the Old City wall.

Rafi maneuvered his tank back and forth to avoid presenting a fixed target and fired at the flashes atop the wall. One of his shells hit the Golden Gate which, according to Jewish tradition, is the portal through which the Messiah will enter Jerusalem on Judgment Day. The hour of redemption indeed seemed near at hand as bullets ricocheted off the tanks and antitank guns opened up, apparently from among the olive trees on the slope beneath the Old City wall.

Shrapnel cut Rafi over the eye, and blood from the wound coated his eyeglasses, blinding him. He slid down out of the turret to bandage the cut and told his radioman to take his place and guide the tank back to the museum. It was plain to Rafi that it was only a question of seconds before the antitank guns got his range.

The radioman rose into the turret and found the tank broadside to the roadway, close to the retaining wall above the wadi. To the west, across the wadi, muzzle flashes outlined the top of the Old City wall. The tank gun was pointed in the opposite direction, and the radioman presumed that the front of the tank was pointed in the same direction as the gun. It wasn't. The radioman said, "Forward," but instead of moving in the direction of the gun, the tank moved straight toward the retaining wall. As soon as Rafi heard the order, he shouted, "You made a mistake," but it was too late. The tank crashed through the retaining wall and plummeted to the bottom of Gethsemane, eight meters below. The tank looped in midair, landing on its hatch and throwing the crew violently against its steel walls.

Rafi was knocked unconscious. When he revived he called to his men, but there was no answer. He crawled out of the tank and lay on the ground next to it. His glasses had been broken and he could barely see. In addition to his earlier head wound, his arm had been badly hurt in the fall and seemed to be broken. With his good hand he pulled out his pistol and waited.

The olive grove from which he had seen the antitank fire coming was just up the slope, and he sensed Arabs nearby. There was a sudden movement near him, and Rafi asked in Arabic, *"Minhada?* (Who's there?)." A soldier leapt up and pointed a weapon at him. It was one of his crew. The rest of the men appeared out of the darkness, and Rafi led them to shelter underneath the bridge itself. All were injured. Only one of the crew had taken his Uzi from the tank, and one of the men went back to retrieve the rest of the weapons and maps.

Above them the men could hear a furious fire beating on the roadway. They had no idea of who was up there. Before attempting to make their way back to Israeli lines, they would have to wait until the firing died down.

Kapusta's scout jeeps had been lined up near the museum waiting to follow the tanks to Augusta Victoria when Rafi reported that he was on the wrong road. Gur ordered Kapusta to get under way and attack Augusta Victoria without the tanks.

Sergeant Ishai, a veteran fighter with a shaggy black prophet's beard, was in the lead jeep. Arik, the brigade intelligence officer, came up and briefed him quickly. Two tanks from the Harel Brigade covering force were just up the road. Ishai was to pass them and immediately make a sharp left turn.

The column started forward, Ishai's platoon of four jeeps out in front. Ishai came abreast of the two tanks but could not make out any turning. (One of the tanks was blocking the intersection.) Just as Rafi had done, he continued straight down the road toward the bridge, in fact pulling over to the right to get out of the way of the returning tank column.

Kapusta, in the fifth jeep a little distance behind, told Ishai on the radio that he thought they were on the wrong road. Ishai, who also sensed something wrong, said he wanted to continue a little farther to see what was ahead. His four jeeps were by this time on the bridge. In the light of a flare he saw a tank thirty meters ahead of him. Instinctively, he raked it with the jeep's machine gun but a moment later recognized it as an Israeli Sherman. It was Rafi's tank the moment before it plunged into the wadi.

The jeeps had moved directly into the fire intended for Rafi. Ishai, sitting next to the driver, caught two bullets in his upper right arm; his radioman in the rear slumped forward, fatally wounded. Ishai ordered the driver to turn the jeep around. In one smooth maneuver the driver angled the jeep to the right on the narrow roadway, then swung the wheel left, bringing the jeep about. As they started back, they passed a man rolling on the ground trying to put out the flames on his burning uniform. A jerrycan of gasoline on the back of the second jeep was burning.

Fire raked the entire column. Sergeant Reuven, the driver of the rearmost jeep on the bridge, saw his left hand almost severed by machine-gun bullets, only a patch of skin holding it to the rest of the arm. He got out of the jeep, but with his foot off the brake, it started rolling toward the jeep ahead. He went back and pulled the emergency brake.

Taking shelter in the lee of the jeep, Reuven called the platoon medic, who was sitting in the back seat. As the medic jumped out, he was hit in the leg. On the roadway, a man who lay firing at the wall was wounded in the eye by a ricocheting bullet.

Holding his wounded hand next to his body to keep it from flapping, Reuven ran to the retaining wall, planning to jump over. In falling flarelight, however, he saw deep shadows pulsing below and realized he was on a bridge. He noticed that in the brief intervals between flares the Arabs held their fire. He began moving up the roadway in these patches of darkness. When he drew near the road to Lion's Gate, he saw men from his company coming down to him, and he passed out from loss of blood.

Meanwhile, the jeep commander, Sergeant Uri Levitahan,

Paratroopers from reconnaissance unit mount wall of Old City near Herod's Gate to sweep it clear of Legionnaires. For previous 28 hours, Jordanian troops on this stretch of wall had kept up effective fire from four-centuries-old firing slits, such as those seen here. Israeli troops found large supplies of weapons and ammunition on wall and in chambers beneath it.

Col. Gur's half-track on **Temple Mount** heading for Dome of the Rock.
BAMAHANE

1. Gur (holding map in center) surrounded by staff and radiomen as they reach mosque.

Paratroopers rest before closed entranceway to Dome of Rock on Temple Mount 15 minutes after breakthrough into Old City. Israeli command ordered doors to mosque kept shut to prevent anyone from wandering in. Soldier standing, from kibbutz Kabri, has been slightly wounded in face.

leaned forward in his seat and swung the jeep's machine gun around with one hand to rake the Old City wall at his rear, firing practically over his shoulder. It was a gallant but futile gesture against the fire focusing on the naked jeeps. Uri fired until he was hit. He ran to the edge of the bridge and rolled over the top of the retaining wall, bracing himself for what he thought was a one-meter drop. Instead he plummeted more than seven meters, shattering his jaw.

Kapusta was near the turnoff to Lion's Gate when Ishai's jeep came abreast of him. Ishai was bleeding profusely and the radioman was plainly dying. When Ishai told Kapusta the platoon was badly hung up, the company commander immediately began to organize an operation to rescue the three stranded jeeps.

From their present position on the right side of the road, the second platoon, behind Kapusta, was shielded from the Old City wall by a large mound. By moving to the other edge of the road, however, they would be in view of the Arab Legion positions. Kapusta ordered them to shift left and open fire at the enemy muzzle flashes. Moving up the road to the third platoon, Kapusta ordered its men to dismount from their jeeps and move down onto the bridge to bring back the wounded. The fire from the wall was drumming on the road, but it seemed to Kapusta that his men moved out into it as calmly as on parade.

One of the rescue platoon, Corporal Israel Schindler, carried a wounded man to safety and descended a second time to the bridge. A soldier was lying on the roadway with his clothing on fire, and Schindler beat the flames out with his hands. As he lifted the wounded man, the soldier was shot dead in his arms. Schindler swung over the retaining wall and hung on to the top, suspended over the wadi. His fingers had been badly burnt, and, unable to maintain his grip, he fell to the wadi floor, breaking a leg.

\*        \*        \*

With the four-tank covering force at the museum, Lieutenant Dov could hear heavy firing to the south and see flares rising about every fifteen seconds. A paratroop officer Dov didn't know climbed on the tank. It was Kapusta himself. He told Dov there were three wounded men on the bridge exposed to fire from the Old City wall. A tank was needed as a shield for the rescuers going down. When the wounded had been picked up, the tank would go into reverse, and the paratroopers would follow it up the road.

Dov asked where the bridge was, where the wall was, how long he would be exposed to fire from the wall, whether the Arabs were using antitank weapons. Kapusta answered the questions succinctly. The bridge was half a kilometer down the road. The tank would be exposed to fire from a point three-quarters of the way down where another road turned off to the right (to Lion's Gate). No, there were no antitank guns in evidence. Dov asked him to climb on the tank behind and explain the situation to its commander, Sergeant Chayun, and to tell him to follow.

The two tanks started forward, aided by the light of the flares. Dov found the situation exactly as Kapusta had described. At the turn to Lion's Gate, red tracers started to arc toward him out of a black sky. Most of the red lights fell short. Some passed overhead. Scores, however, tapped against the tank skin as gently and insistently as rain. Dov saw the Uzi at his elbow jump. He picked it up and saw a hole in it. He lit the projector, but it was knocked out almost immediately. Dov ducked into the tank before the red lights could find him. The gunner fired at the Old City wall, but a shell casing jammed the turret, immobilizing the gun.

The tank was about six meters from the wounded men when a recoilless rifle shell exploded one meter away from it. The paratrooper had been wrong about the presence of antitank weapons. The second round was almost certain to hit, and Dov ordered his driver to reverse.

As Dov's tank moved back up the road, it passed Chayun's tank moving down. A paratrooper walking behind the second

398

tank and guiding Chayun on the exterior telephone said, "Forward," and the tank continued down onto the bridge. To shield the wounded from the Old City wall, Chayun ordered the tank driven onto the empty jeeps. Almost immediately a shell hit the fuel tank. There was no perceptible jolt, but flames leapt from the rear to the front, forming a canopy over the tank.

"The tank's on fire," Chayun shouted. "Pull out, fellows." Just before leaping, Chayun swung the tank gun to the rear to permit the two crewmen in the forward compartment to open their hatches. The radioman and Meyer, the gunner, followed Chayun out the turret, leaping blindly onto the dark roadway. The radioman landed badly, breaking his arm.

At the far end of the bridge, about thirty meters away, steps led down to the sunken courtyard of the Tomb of the Blessed Virgin, revered by Christians as the burial site of the mother of Jesus. Chayun led his men there at a gallop, Meyer diving down the steps behind him. When they caught their breath, they realized that the two crewmen in front had not followed them. Chayun tried to remember if he had turned the gun.

The flames had now eaten into the heart of the tank, and the ammunition began to explode. As the more than fifty shells which were still aboard started to go off in volleys, it sounded to Meyer like the whole brigade firing.

Peering over the top of the steps, Chayun saw flames shoot out the two front hatches. The hatches were open, which meant the men must have gotten out. Suddenly, a burst of flame illuminated figures lying in the roadway a few meters from the burning tank. Their faces could not be seen but the escaped crewmen figured they were their two missing comrades. The figures were moving, and between the sounds of the exploding ammunition the trio on the steps heard shouts for help. But to move out onto the road would have meant almost certain death, if not from the Arab Legion fire, then from their own tank's ammunition. In a few moments, the figures stopped moving and the shouts were heard no more.

*　　　　*　　　　*

It was Major Eytan's turn now. Kapusta had asked for two more tanks to be sent onto the bridge, and Eytan started down with the two tanks he had left. Just as he was about to move into the exposed area past Lion's Gate, a paratrooper in the roadway flagged him down. The soldier yelled up to him to have the tanks halt and turn off their motors.

Kapusta had changed his mind. Covering fire and even armor had been of little use against the Legionnaires behind the battlements of the Old City wall. But he reckoned that if there was nothing to shoot at, the Arabs might stop shooting, giving him a chance later to quietly remove the wounded. He ordered his covering platoon to cease their fire and posted a man in the road to halt the two tanks he had asked for before they got in view of the Old City wall.

Fire from the wall slackened but did not die. Accompanied by Meier Harzion and a platoon, Kapusta descended into the wadi and worked his way south. Near the bridge he climbed a pipe and swung back onto the roadway. Occasional bursts of fire still swept the area; when they came Kapusta swung over the retaining wall. As he drew near the still-exploding tank, he saw three charred bodies lying near it. They were beyond rescue, and Kapusta decided there would be no more lives risked on the bridge that night. He led his men back to their assembly point, where he counted his casualties. Of the sixteen men in the four jeeps caught on the bridge, four had been killed and ten wounded. Of the rescuers, one had been killed and fifteen wounded. Kapusta reorganized the survivors and waited for orders to try again.

The traffic circle from which the tanks and scouts had started down to the bridge was itself barely fifty meters from a bastion at the northeast corner of the Old City wall known as the Stork's Nest. The Legionnaires in the position had not fired at the forces as they descended, but as Rafi's tanks came back up, a bazooka shell exploded against the roll of camouflage netting atop a tank commanded by Lieutenant Mordecai. The lieutenant leapt off the tank, badly spraining his ankle but managing to pull off the burning netting.

The fire had spread to the tank's interior, and when the extinguisher was activated the engine was flooded. Mordecai distributed his men among shorthanded crews of other tanks and hobbled up the road in search of an aid station.

Bazooka fire was coming now from the Stork's Nest at every tank coming up the road, and Kapusta ordered a man with a rifle grenade to fire at the next bazooka flash. The grenadier fired, but a moment later fell wounded as a bazooka shell exploded next to him.

Despite the aborted effort on the bridge, Motta Gur decided to press the attack on Augusta Victoria. His operations officer, Amos, climbed on Rafi's tanks at the traffic circle and directed them down the Augusta Victoria turnoff. Uzi's battalion, drawn up near the museum, received the order to advance, and the lead elements began descending the slope into the wadi.

Almost as soon as they started, however, the units were ordered to halt. Lookouts on Mount Scopus had reported sixteen Jordanian Pattons approaching Azariya on the Jericho road south of the city. Lookouts on Abu Tor also reported the faint lights of a convoy on the road rising out of the Judean Desert. Gur decided to wait for the Jordanian tanks in the built-up area of the city, where his foot soldiers would have a greater chance against armor than on the open slope. The battalion commanders were ordered to prepare their men to meet a tank attack in the streets at dawn.

From the Musrara quarter in Jewish Jerusalem, the beams from the Histadrut Building projectors could be seen moving slowly across the slopes of the Mount of Olives. They halted periodically, freezing the landscape in a chilling cone of white light in which nothing dared to move. After the furies of the past two days, the battlefield was wrapped in an eerie silence, broken only by the distant barking of dogs and an occasional round from a tank or a recoilless rifle. In a strange acoustical effect, the sound of these explosions seemed to roll around and around in the surrounding hills, growing in volume until they died in a climactic thunderclap.

The sounds were coming from the area of the bridge, but from Jewish Jerusalem the widely spaced explosions did not hint at the agony of the scouts. Flares shot up from inside the walled city, and sprays of tracer bullets flew over the Old City wall from the east. Beyond the ridge, a great rumbling explosion sounded once in the direction of Jericho.

Dominating the entire scene was a fire raging through Augusta Victoria and the barracks at its feet. From Musrara, the flames seemed to form the outline of a great truncated cross burning silently over Jerusalem.

For the units of the Eighth Battalion close to the Old City wall, darkness had offered the first opportunity to move out on the streets without being cut down by the Legionnaires on the wall.

At the Rivoli Hotel the two men wounded when the buses had blundered up Saladin Street and the body of Rusak were carried to a Jordanian Land Rover parked outside. The vehicle failed to start, and a jeep was brought up without lights. In front of the hotel the jeep swung around with its rear to the Old City wall, seventy-five meters up the street. The driver tapped gently on the brakes, and the dark street was suddenly lit in the garish red of the taillight. The Legionnaires on the wall opened fire, killing a sergeant in the Land Rover. The others leapt for the safety of the colonnaded sidewalk. One of the wounded, forgotten on the Land Rover, cried, "Don't leave us," and men went out to bring them in. When the shooting died, the two wounded were carried out to the jeep and driven to the rear. This time two dead comrades rode with them.

It was 8 P.M. when Lieutenant Chanoch and Sergeant Natan finally stepped out of the Columbia Hotel onto Nablus Road. They had been penned up inside for twelve hours and were famished. Running across the street to the Schmidt School, they called in stage whispers to the rest of the platoon inside the building. Sergeant Oren and his men came out, carrying in a sleeping bag the body of their comrade killed that morning in the school yard. Moving quietly to avoid being heard by the Legionnaires atop Damascus Gate just up the street, they made their way back around the bend of Nablus Road to join A Company. The platoon was directed to a small hotel already filled with soldiers, where they were to spend the night. Chanoch and Natan, who had desperately tried to keep awake all day in a hotel full of empty beds, now could not find a bed to sleep in.

Throughout the two square kilometers of Jordanian Jerusalem they held, the paratroopers prepared for the enemy Pattons. Mines were placed on the perimeter roads, and ambush teams were staked out at strategic corners inside the built-up area. The men prepared explosive charges which would be placed on the tanks when they approached within leaping distance.

At the traffic circle near the museum, Captain Giora—now commanding the Seventh's Heavy Weapons Company—prepared a giant booby trap. If the Arab tanks descended from the ridge and crossed the wadi here, the charge would be set off as the lead tank came abreast. The tank should effectively block the rest of the column.

Inside the museum the front doors were shut and planting pots and chairs piled against them. Men took up positions behind the low walls opposite the barricaded entrance and waited for anyone who might attempt to burst through. Behind the museum a jeep with a recoilless rifle waited out of sight, just inside the entrance to the rear yard. The gate had been blown off during the day to permit the jeep to dart out into the en-

403

tranceway, fire its weapon, and pull back into the shelter of the museum yard.

Dr. Jack shifted the brigade aid station from the museum area to a house a few blocks to the rear.

At the Rivoli Hotel, the company which had arrived in the buses during the day left for the museum shortly after dark, leaving behind only the seventeen soldiers of C Company who had taken the building. Colonel Yussi dispatched twenty men from the museum to reinforce the vital position opposite Herod's Gate. The commander of C Company, Captain Alex, organized the hotel's defenses, placing two machine guns at the street entrance, two on the second floor, and two on the roof.

In the Ambassador Hotel in Sheikh Jarrah, officers woke the men at midnight and assigned them to positions at windows or in street ambushes. They were told to go back to sleep until awakened at dawn.

Sergeant Ariel's tank had been experiencing a protracted breakdown since its battle on Ammunition Hill Tuesday morning. The main gun and one of the two machine guns had become inoperative. The radio had also stopped working, and Ariel had followed the rest of the tanks down to the bridge and back up again with no idea of what was supposed to be happening.

With the rest of the returning tanks, he had turned onto the Augusta Victoria road, which dipped sharply from the traffic circle into the wadi before climbing straight up the face of the ridge to Augusta Victoria. The tank ahead of him stopped before they reached the bottom of the wadi, and Ariel yelled, "Stop." The driver, however, continued forward a few meters, then threw the tank into reverse. Ariel, who by this time was resigned to almost any eventuality, told a crewman sitting near the driver to ask him what was on his mind. The message came back that the gears were malfunctioning and that the tank could not come to rest on an incline. The only way to keep in position was to keep going up and down.

404

The tank commander guided the driver down to a flat area just above a long shed on the wadi floor, the principal fruit and vegetable market for Jordanian Jerusalem. He dismounted and ran to another tank, whose commander informed him that the attack had been called off. The force was to return to the museum. Climbing back onto his tank, Ariel ordered the driver to make a right turn onto the road and move back up to the traffic circle.

The tank started moving, but instead of turning right, it continued straight across the road and fell four meters into the wadi, burying its nose in soft, wet earth. The steering mechanism had failed. The driver opened his hatch and found his face almost in the mud. He stumbled out to the market shed, put his head on an onion sack, and went to sleep. (He had banged his nose in the fall and was suffering a delayed reaction.) Ariel woke him—and wondered what else could happen.

The next event was not long in coming. One of the crewmen, apparently also suffering from delayed shock, found a pile of vegetables and started yelling, "I found a treasure. Apples. Bananas." They were in enemy territory, and Ariel told him to keep still. But the crewman continued to shout. "A treasure . . . I found a treasure." Another crewman slapped him, and the treasure hunter subsided. They were alone in the wadi, and Ariel posted his men with their Uzis in defensive positions around the tank. After an hour Colonel Arik came down and led them up to the main line. The crew bedded down for the night in the house of a gynecologist.

Arik had been ordered by Gur to oversee the withdrawal of the scouts and tanks to the museum area. He climbed on each tank and counted them by crew on his fingers. Only Rafi's tank was unaccounted for, and Arik presumed that Rafi, if he was still alive, was somewhere on the road to Jericho. Of the thirteen tanks on hand when the battle had started, only nine remained.

Scores of soldiers were sprawled on the floors of the darkened museum when Arik and Kapusta entered shortly before 2 A.M. They found Gur asleep in a corridor and woke him briefly to report that the surviving tanks and scouts had all returned from the bridge.

Arik returned to the tanks and placed them all under Major Eytan's command. Three of the tanks were from the Harel Brigade and six from the Jerusalem Brigade; Eytan's first concern was to place the radios of the two units on the same wavelength. Traveling in a confiscated Jordanian taxi, Arik and Eytan split the tanks into three units and placed them in defensive positions above the wadi. Eytan fell asleep as Arik drove. The intelligence officer parked the taxi next to Eytan's tank and told a nearby paratroop sentry to waken the major at four.

The night was nearing its end. On the steps of the Tomb of the Virgin alongside the bridge, Meyer, the gunner in Sergeant Chayun's crew, was convinced that if he, the sergeant, and the radioman were still there at first light they would die there. They were in the middle of enemy territory and their only weapon was a bayonet. Sergeant Chayun used it to pry open the door of a small hut near the tomb, which, despite a strong odor that permeated the cramped space, could serve as a hiding place if a patrol came.

About an hour before dawn the trio decided to try to find their way back to Israeli lines. A path leading off the main road skirted the tomb. As they started toward it they saw the dark outlines of several figures moving across the road in the same direction. It was impossible to tell who they were but one of the men signaled them with a "Psst." At the sound, the figures disappeared behind a stone wall. From behind the wall someone called, "Who's there?" in Hebrew. It was Rafi's crew. Sergeant Chayun spoke the password. As the two groups ran toward each other, Meyer heard someone on the road to his right call his name. Two men were crouching behind the retaining wall around the bend of the road, about twenty meters from the

406

burnt-out tank. They were the two missing crewmen who had been presumed dead.

The two crews found themselves perfectly matched. Rafi and his men were all injured and could walk only with difficulty. They were, however, armed with Uzis. Chayun's men, on the other hand, were capable of walking but were unarmed. The Harel Brigade men took the weapons from the Jerusalem Brigade crew, and each man lent a shoulder to one of Rafi's men as they started into the wadi.

Rafi's men could negotiate the way on the terraced slope only with difficulty. At one point they passed near a house, and a dog barked. It was beginning to turn light when they reached the vegetable market in the wadi. Up the slope they could see Shermans lined up with guns pointed toward Augusta Victoria. The tankmen shouted the password, and soldiers came down the slope to help them up.

In the predawn light Meyer looked at the Jerusalem Brigade man he had been helping for the past hour and recognized him as his best friend in civilian life.

## 20  THE TEMPLE MOUNT

During the night Rabbi Goren had returned to Tel Aviv to arrange burial for the hundreds already fallen on the Egyptian and Jordanian fronts. Starting back to Jerusalem at dawn, he saw a car approach with Dr. Jacob Herzog, political advisor to Prime Minister Eshkol, and flagged it down. Herzog said he was on his way to a conference at General Dayan's office, where a decision about the taking of the Old City was to be made. Goren became agitated. Failure to take Jerusalem, he said, would be an unforgivable sin. He promised Herzog life in the hereafter if he persuaded the others to make the attack. The son of the former chief rabbi laughed and said, "I can't refuse an offer like that."

In Wadi Joz hamlet a paratroop officer scanned the Mount of Olives through binoculars at dawn. There were no signs of tanks or preparations for counterattack. He could see no movement at all in the trenches at Augusta Victoria, but in the village of A-Tor, farther along the crest, a single soldier appeared behind a house. As the officer watched, the Legionnaire stripped off his uniform and changed into civilian clothes.

There would be no counterattack. Israeli jets had gone up to look for the Jordanian Pattons that were reported to be approaching Jerusalem, but their flares discovered only a convoy of artillery on the Jericho road, which they had smashed.

(The night before Menahem Scharfmann, commander of the Scopus garrison, had heard the report of approaching tanks being made by his observer in the "physics" position on the old university grounds overlooking the Jericho road. Skeptical, he had made his way there from the command post on the other side of the hill. He spotted armor at Ma'ale Adumim, the mountain pass halfway down to Jericho, but the tanks did not seem to him to be approaching. By the time his report was received, the night attack on Augusta Victoria had already been called off.)

But if the Jordanians weren't coming down the ridge, the Israelis were going up. Herzog had arrived at Dayan's headquarters to find the decision to take the Old City already made. It was transmitted at 5:30 A.M. to Narkiss by General Bar-Lev, deputy chief of staff.

Concerned over the possibility of a cease-fire agreement at the UN, the High Command urged all possible speed. The ridge would have to be cleared first, and Gur decided to risk a frontal attack by the Seventh up the slope, despite the fact that in daylight they would be exposed to fire from the Old City wall at their right rear as well as from the Augusta Victoria trenches in front of them. The Sixth would simultaneously attack along the crest, from Scopus.

For many of the paratroopers the order to attack Augusta Victoria was the worst moment of the war. Assault on a fortified height in daylight, they had been taught, was a costly business. The Seventh would be exposed for a kilometer as it moved up the slope. The approach of the Sixth was at least as formidable. Their movement would be confined to a narrow road between the Scopus enclave and the enemy positions, the steep slopes on both sides of the road being sown with mines. If the Legionnaires sustained fire on the road, passage would be bloody.

For the men who had fought on Ammunition Hill it seemed that that nightmare was about to be repeated. "Are there trenches up there?" a soldier from Dedi's company asked Major Doron. The deputy battalion commander, trying to reassure him, said scouts had surveyed the defenses and reported that they didn't look too serious. The men cleaned their weapons once more and collected ammunition and grenades. After their

410

experience on the hill they wanted many more grenades, but there was only a limited supply.

Corporal Kreutzmann of the Seventh, who the day before had entered alone the cave from which Lieutenant Dvir (Kushi) had been shot in the throat, felt far more apprehensive now. At the outset of the war, he knew he was plunging into a dark and unfathomable tunnel; it was useless to calculate the chances of emerging alive. This morning, however, the end was clearly visible. One or two more attacks and it would be over. One's chances for survival were suddenly relevant, and looking up at the heights didn't make those chances seem too good. Kreutzmann had stuffed his pocket with candies, which he had expected to nourish him during the day. Now, thinking they would impede his movements, he discarded them. A moment later he told himself it was a cowardly thing to do and picked them up again. Other men fought similar battles with themselves as they prepared for action. Kreutzmann's platoon had been without an officer since the wounding of Kushi, and it was joined now by Lieutenant Arnon, commander of the MAG section which had been shot up accidentally during Tuesday's attack. The men in the platoon didn't know Arnon well, but the lieutenant smiled and his apparent self-assurance lifted morale instantly.

As the Seventh Battalion waited in Wadi Joz hamlet to move out, Kapusta's company rolled by, and men on the sidewalk nudged each other at the sight of a tall figure sitting in one of the jeeps. "That's Meier Harzion," said the man next to grenadier Bower.

In Sheikh Jarrah, where the Sixth prepared to move up to Scopus, Captain Giora asked a private from Jerusalem if he was able to guide them. "I was born up there," the soldier replied. Like dozens of men now besieging the Old City, he had been born in the original Hadassah Hospital on the ridge. (Many also had another personal link to the adjoining Mount of Olives— their relatives were buried in the large Jewish cemetery on the slope.)

411

The Eighth was to concentrate near the Rockefeller, in order to move into the Old City through Lion's Gate in the east wall as soon as the heights overlooking it had been taken. Colonel Yussi ordered Company C to remain opposite Herod's Gate in the north wall in case developments should require a breakthrough there.

The forces near Wadi Joz found themselves confronting Legionnaires even before they moved out. Lieutenant Yair of Kfar Blum heard a rifle bolt slide home and turned to see three Arabs thirty meters away fire at two of his men nearby. The shots missed, and the Arabs disappeared around the corner. Soldiers searching a house directly opposite Seventh Battalion headquarters killed eight Legionnaires. Nearby, seven Legionnaires were taken prisoner on the roof of a building in which a platoon of paratroopers had spent the night.

Sergeant Ariel, whose tank had fallen into the wadi near the vegetable market the night before, felt utterly useless as men all around him prepared for the attack. He had two tank crews—his own and Lieutenant Mordecai's—but no tanks. Two of his men went off to join one of the paratroop companies, and Ariel sought out Gur to explain his dilemma. The colonel, busily synchronizing his battalions with air, artillery, and armored support for the climactic assault, glanced at the sergeant who was asking what to do with his half dozen men and said, "Do whatever you want." As a chastened Ariel was leaving, Lieutenant Colonel Arik overtook him and gently asked him to understand that Gur was in the middle of preparing for the battle.

Ariel went to view Mordecai's tank and discovered that the bazooka shell had damaged little more than the camouflage netting. While the tank's battery was dead, his own tank's was in working order; he decided to transfer it to Mordecai's. He ordered some men to go back to Jewish Jerusalem for tools. They piled into a Volkswagen parked outside a garage, but the engine failed to start. A Jordanian mechanic who was found inside insisted that he couldn't help. An Uzi pointed at his chest changed his mind. In a few minutes the car was sputtering its way toward Jewish Jerusalem.

For two days now the Israelis had scrupulously refrained from shelling the Old City, even though they had sustained dozens of casualties from Jordanian fire coming from within the walls. In the early hours of the war Lieutenant Colonel Amos, the Jerusalem Brigade operations officer, who was incensed at the indiscriminate shelling of Jewish Jerusalem, had given an order that the Old City be hit. The order was heard on the radio by General Narkiss, who rescinded it before any shells were fired. Narkiss was conscious of the likely repercussions if Jewish shells destroyed Christian or Moslem holy places. Now, however, with the units beginning to form up for the assault on the ridge, permission was granted to shell the northeast corner of the walled city just behind the break-in point at Lion's Gate.

Since the target was only twenty-five meters from the Rockefeller Museum compound, all paratroopers in the yards were ordered to take cover inside the museum building. At 6 A.M. the paratroop artillery observer, spotting from the museum itself, called down his first ranging shots two hundred meters inside the walls and then moved the fire steadily closer to the north wall. The 120-mm. mortars emplaced in the Valley of the Cross were spread in a line one hundred meters wide; their salvos accordingly fell across a one hundred-meter front. One salvo straddled the wall and two shells exploded within the museum compound, wounding several soldiers who had either not heard or not heeded the order to come inside. A score of soldiers ran out to pull them in.

The artillery officer got on the radio to the battery commander and barked, "Stop." Seconds later shells crashed among the rescue party outside. A total of nine men lay dead, with many others wounded.

The same fatal double shelling was repeated at Saint Ste-

413

phen's Monastery on Nablus Road, where Company A of the Eighth was concentrated. Captain Avidan, the company commander, had been on the building's tower with a machine-gun crew when Colonel Yussi radioed him that three trucks were on their way to pick up the company and transport it to the museum area. Avidan descended and was assembling the unit when he heard the whistle of incoming shells. Men froze for an instant, then threw themselves flat. A shell crashed into the tower, dismembering two of the machine-gun crew. Another man was killed in the yard. Wounded were being retrieved when a second salvo hit, wounding several more men. Lieutenant Nachshon was next to the mosque across the street from the monastery when he heard the shells. He shouted, "Helmets" to those men near him who had taken theirs off and leapt for the trench next to the mosque, as shells exploded behind him. Expecting the barrage to be followed up by a counterattack, Nachshon sprang from the trench and looked down Nablus Road toward the Old City, but no one was coming.

A call went out to Magen David Adom, and an ambulance arrived with a twenty-year-old girl, a student at Hebrew University, as attendant. The girl, her blond hair tumbling out beneath her helmet, climbed the ladder to the church tower and then quickly descended. She called for blankets and rope with which to bring the dismembered bodies down. She asked that the paratroopers waiting below be cleared from the area. This was no sight for them, she said.

Meanwhile, the assault was getting under way. In the Valley of the Cross the order to prepare for rapid fire—the fastest rate of fire—was given for the first time since the mortars had opened up on Monday. The batteries had been firing without interruption, splaying thousands of shells from Mar Elias in the south to French Hill and beyond in the north. Sergeant Zvi's mortar had become so hot that a sleeping bag nearby caught fire. It made little difference, since there had been no chance to sleep

414

since the war began. When the rapid-fire order came Zvi collected cooks and medics until he had twelve men standing by his mortar. At the signal they began dropping shells down the tube as fast as the lanyard could be pulled. In the three minutes before they ceased fire, eighty-seven shells had been sent arcing toward Augusta Victoria from this one mortar alone.

From a balcony of a hotel behind the museum Gur was orchestrating the preliminary bombardment through the air and artillery controllers at his side. At 8:30 A.M. four jets came low over the trenches of Augusta Victoria, and silver canisters of napalm tumbled away, bursting along the ground in a crimson splash of flame that quickly turned oily black. The planes threw themselves flat against the sky and came in again for strafing runs. Operating on the assumption that the Jordanians were dug in on the ridge with armor support, Gur had wanted three hours of softening up by planes and artillery before making the assault up the open slope. Pressure by the General Staff to begin moving limited this support to twenty minutes. A soldier looking up at Mount Scopus was surprised to see a lively fire being directed at Augusta Victoria from the enclave by at least two recoilless rifles. He had not imagined anything larger than light machine guns up there.

The fire from Scopus was augmented by three tanks which had moved up to the hill with the Sixth Battalion. As the battalion waited for the bombardment to end, Nir, his face black with battle soot, spotted Micha, the deputy commander of Giora's company who had blown the final fence in front of the Police Training School. It was the first time Nir had seen him since that moment when the fate of the battle had seemed to tremble so precariously on the edge of the Arab Legion trench. He grabbed his hand and pumped it. To Micha, still unaware of the searing hours on Ammunition Hill, it seemed that Nir was surprised to find him still alive. From the roof of the Histadrut Building, the men of

415

the Sixth, waiting in line on the road which ran through the enclave, looked to Dennis Silk like a row of newly planted saplings wreathed in drifting smoke.

When the planes had finished their runs, Major Eytan, near the museum, received the order to start his tanks up the road to Augusta Victoria. As he moved up the slope his machine guns fired straight ahead and his cannon fired to the right rear at the city wall. Eytan raked the upper-story windows of buildings along the way with the machine gun mounted on the turret. Halfway up the road, the Old City was blocked from view and the cannon swung forward. Light fire was hitting the road to the front, but Eytan could not tell its source. Behind him came his mixed force of Jerusalem Brigade and Harel Brigade tanks.

When Gur saw the tanks crest the ridge and turn right, he ordered all units to begin moving and raced down to his half-track. Kapusta's scout jeeps moved out in the wake of the tanks, and the Seventh Battalion started up the slope in a broad skirmish line to the left of the road. In an improvisation of his own, Captain Dan collected the battalion's recoilless rifle jeeps and dashed up the road to the crest. Instead of turning right, as Eytan and Kapusta had done, he turned left toward Augusta Victoria to cut off any retreat from the trench positions there. Heavy fire from Scopus on the opposite side of Augusta Victoria was coming directly at him, and he ordered his men to dismount and take cover.

As the Sixth Battalion moved along the crest from the Scopus enclave toward Augusta Victoria, Colonel Joseph walked beside the lead tank. The Sherman had hardly moved twenty yards when it hit a mine. The explosion blew the battalion commander into a ditch, and a cry went back down the line to his deputy: "Doron forward; Joseph's dead."

Doron raced to the head of the column in time to see Joseph, his face blackened, climbing out of the ditch and directing the second tank around the disabled one. This, too, promptly hit a mine, and Joseph was again lifted off his feet. Picking himself

416

out of the ditch once more, he started forward without waiting for the third tank. (It too was to hit a mine. All three mines were Israeli.)

The Scopus garrison force fired furiously over the heads of the paratroopers, but the shots were getting dangerously close to the advancing men. Doron ran back to the firing positions, yelling at them to stop shooting. Inaudible above the din, he ran from position to position rapping the riflemen on their helmets with his Uzi.

Colonel Joseph was nearing the Jordanian line when Captain Giora, at the head of the point company, shouted, "Joseph, why are you going first?" The company commander called to a staff officer running beside Joseph to stop him.

A lieutenant sprinted past Giora with pliers to cut the barbed wire. "Faster, Reuven," shouted Giora. "Faster." They were his last words. Private Amsalam, running beside the company commander, heard bullets skimming overhead and saw Giora fall. He tried to turn him over but saw that he was beyond help.

A sergeant came up, and Amsalam shouted, "Giora's dead."

The sergeant said, "Don't talk about it now. After the battle."

Few of the soldiers glancing down at the body as they raced toward the barbed wire realized that it was their commander.

The men leapt into the trenches and found them empty. Up the slope from the right the Seventh Battalion was sweeping toward the crest. Shouts of "Cease fire" rang across the slope as the two forces swarmed across the abandoned Arab Legion positions. (In a press conference a week after the war, when full details were still not being revealed, Gur said of the attack on Augusta Victoria, "We suffered very heavy casualties in this action, more than were necessary, and the boys who fell were among the best." The only fatality was Captain Giora, but his tragic death in the final moments of the battle weighed heavily on his comrades, who held him in especially high esteem.)

Dedi's company entered Augusta Victoria Hospital and found the beds empty. At the rear of the building Major Doron saw

417

movement at the foot of a staircase leading down to the basement. When he yelled, "Come out," people started emerging in such a flood that he ordered them to stop until more paratroopers arrived. The director of the hospital, an American, assured him that all those present were staff and patients. The major said that patients could be returned to their beds and asked if any medical supplies or assistance was required.

The United Nations flag was lowered from the sixty-meter-high tower, and in its place the soldiers raised a flag sewn Sunday by women from the kibbutz near the paratroop encampment. From Jewish Jerusalem the blue and white flag rising from the highest point on the ridge betokened that the last obstacle before the Old City had fallen.

Eytan's tanks moved briskly south along the top of the Mount of Olives, firing at houses on both sides of the road. They halted beneath the arches of the Intercontinental Hotel, mercifully sparing its huge plate-glass windows despite a few rifle shots coming from a side room. Eytan spotted three Pattons among the houses of Azariya, two kilometers east, and opened fire before noticing in his binoculars that their treads had been blown off, apparently by air attack.

Gur dismounted in front of the hotel with his staff and looked down at the walled city. Directly below him was the vast plaza of the Temple Mount dominated by the golden Dome of the Rock and the silver dome of El Aksa Mosque. The magnificent Dome of the Rock was built around the living stone on which, according to Jewish tradition, Abraham had prepared his son Isaac for sacrifice. On this site Solomon had built the First Temple three thousand years before. It was destroyed by the Babylonians, and the Second Temple was subsequently built, only to be destroyed by the Romans in 70 c. e. during the great Jewish revolt. Except for the brief sway over the Temple Mount six decades later by Bar Kochba's rebels, the holy site had not been in Jewish hands for nineteen centuries.

418

The open space and the almost rectangular lines of the Temple Mount were set off by the formless hive constituting the residential quarters of the Old City. From the ridge it was impossible to distinguish the dividing line between the Jordanian section of the city and Jewish Jerusalem rising beyond it.

From Augusta Victoria, Colonel Joseph radioed that the objective was taken. The High Command informed Gur that he could make use of any artillery or air support he thought necessary to accompany an immediate assault on the Old City. Gur passed up the offer of planes but called down artillery and tank fire on the Moslem quarter, the section of the Old City chosen for the breakthrough. In a few moments the quarter was wreathed in gray smoke. The ten-minute bombardment spared the Temple Mount and the Church of the Holy Sepulcher. The only church structure to be substantially damaged was Saint Anne's, just inside Lion's Gate. Standing on the traditional birthplace of Mary, the Crusader Church received several shells through the roof. (Despite the fact that bitter tank and infantry fighting raged for forty-eight hours in Jerusalem around the holiest places in Christendom, damage to church property was remarkably small. Following a visit to Jerusalem immediately after the war, Monsignor Abrahmo Frescht, president of the Pontifical Aid Organization, reported in Rome that damage "was so minimal it hardly seems possible there was a fierce house-to-house fight." The most notable church damage besides Saint Anne's was the destruction of the massive roof on the Dormition Church on Mount Zion, set afire by a Jordanian shell. Most other damage consisted of chipped masonry and broken windows.)

"To battalion commanders," Gur said into his radio. "We occupy the heights overlooking the Old City. In a little while we will enter it. The ancient city of Jerusalem which for generations we have dreamt of and striven for—we will be the first to enter it. The Jewish nation is awaiting our victory. Israel awaits this historic hour. Be proud. Good luck."

419

He ordered all three battalions to move toward the Old City. "The tanks of Eytan will advance from the left. They will enter Lion's Gate. Move, move. Move to the gate. The final parade will be on the plaza of the Temple Mount. Until then, over."

The decision to make the breakthrough at Lion's Gate in the eastern city wall had been made only that morning. Until the night before Gur had planned to send the Eighth Battalion through Herod's Gate in the north wall, using the main East Jerusalem Post Office, fifty meters opposite, as the jumping-off point, with covering fire being provided from the Rockefeller Museum. The attack on the ridge, however, changed the situation. The paratroop commander had assumed that the armored brigade would be given the job of taking the Mount of Olives, an assumption based on war-game exercises played out over the years. But Ben-Ari's brigade had been sent off to take Ramallah and Jericho, and clearing the ridge fell to Gur. With the bulk of his brigade now assembled on the ridge east of the Old City, the logical entry point had become Lion's Gate.

In contrast to the meticulous battle plans the paratroopers had followed heretofore—in which each battalion, each company, and each platoon had its assigned role—Gur's order turned the momentous assault on the walled city into a race between all the units under his command for Lion's Gate.

One company from the Seventh Battalion—Captain Zamush's—was already halfway there. When the battalion had earlier started up the ridge toward Augusta Victoria, Gur had contacted Colonel Uzi and said, "Remember what you asked about Zamush going into the Old City first? Well, that's an order." The religious company commander halted his men near the Palace Hotel partway up the slope and assembled his officers for a brief conference. He would be provided with two half-tracks, Zamush had been told, and would break in through Lion's Gate with them. He ordered Lieutenant Yair of Kfar Blum, commander of his point platoon, to pick men to ride the vehicles. The rest of the company would follow on foot.

420

The officers didn't know, except from maps, what Lion's Gate or its approaches looked like. They decided that while one half-track gave covering fire, the other, with a demolition charge aboard, would back up to the gate. After an explosive charge had been laid, the half-track would pull clear.

While the officers conferred, Corporal Igal, commander of Yair's point squad, collected explosives from the soldiers to prepare the demolition charges, lashing them together with rope. Suddenly there was a terrifying whine, and two 160-mm. mortar shells landed in the midst of the company. One failed to detonate, and the other bounced forty meters before exploding harmlessly.

Two half-tracks clanked up the hotel driveway, and Yair's men climbed aboard. Zamush himself rode in the lead vehicle, Yair in the second. As they moved forward, the lieutenant saw the walls of the Old City ahead and for the first time realized what a dangerous gantlet they were about to run.

As the two half-tracks approached Lion's Gate from the north, Eytan's tanks were heading toward it from the south. At the foot of the Mount of Olives Eytan detailed several tanks to block the Jericho road and continued with the rest past the bodies of Kapusta's scouts, who had died on the roadway the night before. Nearby, three jeeps lay crushed beneath Sergeant Chayun's burnt-out tank. Fire was coming from the length of the wall and the tanks replied with their machine guns as they moved, refraining from cannon fire in order to avoid accidental damage to the Dome of the Rock.

Zamush's half-tracks arrived first at the junction with the Lion's Gate road, which rose steeply from the main road to the gate, 150 meters away. The lead half-track made the turn, but as it started up the incline, the captain saw heavy fire coming from the slits above the gate. Movement straight forward on the lumbering half-tracks seemed suicidal, and he ordered the driver to drop back down out of sight of the wall.

By this time the tanks had reached the junction. One con-

421

tinued beyond and took a blocking position farther up the main road. The second tank halted and turned its gun toward the gate.

The tank commander was Sergeant Ben-Gigi, who the day before had been involved in the accidental ambush of the Harel Brigade tanks at the Mivtar. To him now had fallen the historic task of hammering open the gates of the Old City. The Moroccan-born tinsmith, whose workshop in Jewish Jerusalem was within two hundred meters of Jaffa Gate, was unmoved by the occasion. He regarded the gate as simply another enemy strongpoint to be reduced, and he ordered his gunner, Moshe Haimovsky, to open fire.

An antiquated bus was parked just outside the gate, and Haimovsky asked what to do about it. "Hit it," ordered Ben-Gigi. Heavy fire was coming from the wall, and Ben-Gigi calculated that if the bus were set aflame, the smoke might shield the paratroopers as they moved up the road. Haimovsky had collected seven shells on his lap for quick firing. He pumped two antitank shells into the bus with little visible result. Then he tried an explosive shell, and the bus caught fire. Black smoke poured out, and an east wind drove it back against the Arab Legion positions on the gate.

Haimovsky, a school administrator, had not been given any specific target except for the bus, but he presumed he should try to open the gate. Magnified in his periscope, the gate was seen to be barred by two large metal-sheathed doors. The right door was partially blocked by the burning bus. Haimovsky aimed for the upper hinge of the left door. The top of the door canted backwards under the impact, permitting him to see through into the Old City itself. He was looking straight up the Via Dolorosa. He thought he could make out a strongpoint inside the gate and put a shell into it. He also hit the firing holes above the gate.

Meanwhile, Gur himself had joined the race for the gates, following the tanks down from the ridge in his half-track. Driving the vehicle was Sergeant Ben-Tsur, a bus driver in civilian life. The heavyset, bearded sergeant had been drafted for the driving assignment just before the morning's attack had gotten under way. The night before, he had been helping evacuate casualties from the Rivoli Hotel when the man sitting next to him in the Land Rover had been shot dead. The brigade commander, who was sitting beside him now, ordered him to pass the tanks. Ben-Tsur swung around them into the Lion's Gate road. The gate was hidden behind a thick column of smoke from the burning bus. The loaded half-track struggled up the incline, Ben-Tsur's foot pressing the accelerator to the floor. He could feel the heat from the bus as he approached. Suddenly, he was through the smoke. Five meters ahead loomed the gate. There was only a fraction of a moment before he would hit, but it was enough to make out two huge doors, the left one hanging partially open. He steered for the center of the gate. The half-track slammed hard and the left door toppled backwards, the right door swinging open. An Arab jumped clear behind the gate, and a shower of small stones from the damaged arch fell into the half-track. They were inside the Old City.

Gur ordered Ben-Tsur to turn sharp left. In that direction lay the Temple Mount, a walled compound with its own gates. A motorcycle stood across the path and the thought that it might be booby-trapped occurred to Ben-Tsur, but he drove the half-track over it and passed through the Tribes' Gate into the Temple compound. The great golden dome rose above the trees, and Ben-Tsur halted at the foot of a platform supporting the mosque. The Israelis leapt out and ran up the steps, Gur in the lead.

Arik ran around the corner of the mosque to see if any Legionnaires were waiting. The platform was empty. Gur raised Narkiss on the radio. "The Temple Mount is in our hands. Repeat, the Temple Mount is in our hands."

The news was soon proclaimed from the top of the mosque itself. Arik entered the dim interior and found a ladder running up the inside of the dome. Outside Lion's Gate, gunner Haimovsky was looking through his tank periscope when he saw a

423

golden plate swing out atop the mosque. A hand reached through the hatch and affixed something to the crescent at the very top of the roof. The wind caught the object and unfurled it into a blue and white flag. Haimovsky looked at his watch. It was 10:21.

Zamush's two half-tracks had swung back into the Lion's Gate road just as Gur's half-track and a command car containing the deputy brigade commander, Stempel, disappeared inside the walls. The driver of the rear half-track hesitated as he approached the burning bus. Lieutenant Yair, sitting behind him, prodded him with his foot and told him to keep moving. Corporal Igal hopped out with a six-kilogram charge of explosives with which to blast open the gate, but swung back on when he saw it wide open.

Instead of turning left when they passed through, the half-tracks moved straight down the Via Dolorosa for two hundred meters before being stopped. The men dismounted and ran back toward the Tribes' Gate. Corporal Igal had his Uzi in one hand and a two-kilogram charge of explosives in the other. But he discovered that this gate too was open. Passing over the crushed motorcycle, the paratroopers found squad tents set up in a small Arab Legion camp just inside the compound. Nearby were shattered mortars.

No Legionnaires were in sight, but the paratroopers fired short bursts among the olive trees on either side as they ran. When they reached the mosque, Gur embraced Zamush and told him to raise the flag on the Western Wall. The company commander, however, was uncertain of just where the Western Wall was. As he and his men descended the staircase on the western side of the mosque platform to look for it, they came under fire. An Arab Legion tender was parked next to a green door—Chain Gate—about fifty meters away, and two Legionnaires were firing from behind the vehicle. A paratrooper fired a rifle grenade from the staircase. The shot was a bad one, landing short, but the grenade skidded under the vehicle where it exploded, killing both Legionnaires.

The paratroopers passed through the green door and found themselves in a narrow street filled with panicky civilians.

An old man in a white jellaba (loose cloak) addressed them in broken Hebrew. "I am good," Lieutenant Yair heard him say.

Zamush asked him, "Where is the wall of the Jews?"

The old man understood immediately and led them back through the Temple compound to the Moors' Gate, one hundred meters to the south. He pointed up the alley beyond to a metal door about twenty meters on the right side. Zamush pushed it open and shouted, *"Hakotel!* (The wall!)."

Looking through the door, the men saw that they were nearly level with the top of a high wall to their right, bare except for tufts of vegetation growing between the upper courses of stones. Hemmed in by low hovels at its feet and matched in height on both sides by tiers of structures running at right angles to it, the wall seemed at first glance like part of an enclosure rather than an entity unto itself. Only the unusually large stones, fitted into place under King Herod two thousand years before, set it apart from the clutter of its surroundings. These stones, part of the massive retaining wall of the Temple Mount, had become— following the destruction of the Temple—the most sacred site in Judaism.

With the men following close behind, Zamush descended two staircases and reached the narrow alley in front of the wall. They stood silently a few seconds and then headed back up to the Temple Mount to find a place where they could raise the flag above the wall.

Inside Chain Gate they entered the first building on the left. Descending the stairs was a tall young man in Arab dress who in English identified himself as an American. Lieutenant Yair assured him he wouldn't be harmed. The man was Abdullah Schleiffer, a New York Jew—born Mark David Schleiffer—who had converted to Islam, married a pretty Negro girl from

425

Jamaica, and worked on the staff of an English-language newspaper in Jordanian Jerusalem. He was an odd witness to this moment of Jewish history.

On the roof Zamush drew from his shirt the flag given him in Bait Hakerem by Mrs. Cohen. He tied one end to a metal fence overlooking the Western Wall. Yair held the other end. When he released it, a strong breeze caught the flag and held it open. At the command of Colonel Stempel the men fired three bursts from their Uzis into the air.

Zamush descended again to the Western Wall with four men. They passed two dwellings on the way down, and the captain sent a search team into each. When he reached the bottom of the staircase, he was alone. He stood silently before the wall, conscious that he and his men had been the first soldiers of a Jewish army to reach it since the Romans had overwhelmed Bar Kochba's men eighteen centuries before. He reached out to touch one of the stones. It felt, he was later to explain, "as if millions of Jews had been crying there." The account with the Romans, he felt, had been settled.

Meanwhile, the rear of Zamush's company—the men who had not ridden the half-tracks—had made their way on foot to Lion's Gate. Commanding the rump force was Zamush's deputy, Lieutenant Malka. As they approached the gate they found the entrance blocked by a tank which had to back out to allow them passage. A smiling Gur greeted them when they reached the mosque. "Hurry, Malka," the colonel said, "get your men out there."

The lieutenant knew that Zamush had headed for the Western Wall and searched for a position from which he could cover him. Passing through Chain Gate he came upon a swarm of civilians, some of them armed. His orders were not to shoot unless fired upon. Malka, born in Morocco, yelled at them in Arabic to get inside the houses and fired a warning burst.

Turning down an alley to his left in the general direction of the Western Wall, he saw an Arab ahead of him. Malka fired

426

a warning burst, but the Arab stood his ground, gesturing down a side alley. Zamush emerged from it and led Malka's men to the wall. Along with another religious soldier from his unit, Zamush drew his tefillin from a pouch and began the first morning prayer at the Western Wall in nineteen years.

The tank which Malka had found blocking his way at Lion's Gate was commanded by Lieutenant Dov, the Harel Brigade platoon commander who had taken the Mivtar the day before and descended to the bridge during the night. After Zamush's half-tracks had entered, Major Eytan, in his command tank at the road intersection, had decided to see if it was possible to get a tank through the gate to assist the paratroopers. With a wave of the arm, Eytan signaled Dov, who was next in line behind him, to pass him and move up to the gate.

As he approached, Dov saw that the arch above the entrance-way, having been hit by one of Haimovsky's shells, was about to fall. Pulling the hatch over him, he ordered the driver to take the tank through. The gate was barely wide enough, and Dov could hear the sound of metal scraping on stone. As soon as the scraping stopped, he ordered the driver to halt and threw open the hatch. He was inside the gate. The occasion, he felt, called for a few words.

"For all of you," he said to the crew on the intercom, "this is one of the most important moments in your life. You are now in the Old City. This is the first tank in Jewish history to be inside the Old City."

The radioman, the only religious member of the crew, pronounced a blessing.

Looking around him, Dov saw an amazing scene. Jordanian soldiers and civilians were milling frantically, apparently unnerved by the sight of a tank within the walls. Some were throwing weapons away and running toward him. Others were throwing weapons away and running from him. Dov had no specific orders, just Eytan's arm wave, and he chose to ignore the

427

Jordanians. The first Jewish tank inside the Old City, he felt, should be the first Jewish tank at the Western Wall. He had no idea of the narrow alleys and winding staircases that lay between him and the wall, but, responding to the call of history, he ordered the driver to press on.

The tank had moved just a few meters when it entered another archway. This time a jerrycan tied on its side was crushed against the stones. Fuel poured out of the can, and Dov ordered the motor shut off immediately, before the gasoline reached the engine. If the tank caught fire and its ammunition started to explode, it would be disastrous; for at this moment the bulk of the brigade was approaching the blocked gateway.

The two battalions on the ridge had descended the Augusta Victoria road at a near run, the men shouting at each other in excitement, "Be careful. . . . Watch for snipers." From the Rockefeller, the third battalion—the Eighth—started down into the wadi. Colonel Yussi intended to start working his way around to Lion's Gate well below the road to avoid fire from the Stork's Nest. As he moved, however, he heard on his radio Gur's exultant cry from the Temple Mount. With the Old City having apparently capitulated, he ordered his battalion back up on the road. They met the men of the Seventh coming down from the ridge, and the two units fell in side by side.

Yussi's initial instinct about the Stork's Nest quickly proved correct. Fire opened up from the position as the paratroopers passed, and one man fell wounded. Captain Eilat, who had led the Seventh's fence-busting team during Tuesday morning's breakthrough, found himself next to Heavy Weapons Company of the Eighth, the men who had taken the Rockefeller. Borrowing a bazooka from one of them, he fired a shell into the Arab Legion position. The line resumed movement, but more shots came from the wall and a paratrooper slumped dead to the ground. Eilat put another shell into the Arab Legion firing hole, finally silencing it.

ratroopers get their first glimpse of Western Wall (right).

Two Arabs are taken prisoner as the first paratroopers descend to wall.
BAMAHANE

Capt. Zamush (atop wall, right), after fixing flag to fence above Western Wall.

Orthodox paratroopers with *kipot* on their heads stand before Western wall.
BAMAHANE

At Lion's Gate the men scrambled over Dov's tank, whose crew stood on top helping the paratroopers up. After giving a hand to a dozen men, Dov saw Rabbi Goren standing below. The chaplain was carrying a Torah in one hand and a shofar in the other. Dov and a crewman bent down and lifted the rabbi by his arms. From atop the tank Goren sounded a shofar blast, his first within the walls of the ancient city.

The rabbi continued to blow the shofar as he ran to the Temple Mount. At the mosque he kissed Gur and called for spirits for the sacramental kiddush. Sergeant Ben-Tsur produced a flask of whiskey from a belt pouch. Clutching the Torah, Goren led forty paratroopers in a Chassidic dance, the men moving in a circle, their arms on each other's shoulders. Beneath the golden dome, soldiers began singing Naomi Shemer's new song about Jerusalem, which already sounded like an ancient spiritual.

Captain Zamush received a radio summons from Colonel Uzi to come up and escort Rabbi Goren to the Western Wall. On the way the jubilant rabbi recited psalms, pausing only for periodic blasts on the shofar. Scores of soldiers filled the narrow space before the wall. Those who were bareheaded now donned their helmets. The sweat of battle still upon them, the paratroopers repeated after Goren the shehecheyanu prayer: "Blessed art Thou, O Lord our God, King of the universe, who hast kept us in life, and hast preserved us, and enabled us to reach this moment."

After reciting yizkor for the men who had fallen in the battle, Goren began singing the national anthem in his gravelly voice. Standing at attention and saluting the wall, the paratroopers joined in, many of them weeping openly. Amidst the press of bodies before the wall, each man was left to his own thoughts. Dr. Jack, the brigade medical officer, remembered that this was the place where Abraham had been ready to sacrifice his son, and he thought of the men who had been sacrificed in the last two days to reach it. He sensed a mood of "From here we don't

433

move"—that the return of the Western Wall to the Jewish people was a matter of destiny in which the United Nations and other worldly bodies were totally irrelevant. He remembered a phrase of the Jewish nationalist Jabotinsky: "In blood and fire Judea fell and in blood and fire Judea will arise." Soldiers pressed their faces against the wall. There were others, however, who stared at the stones in search of an emotion that wasn't there. For two days they had moved on command from one place to another, and now they were here. They had struggled with fear and they had seen men die and they were far beyond tears.

For many of these men the most forceful impact had come on the Temple Mount, where for the first time since the battle began they had seen men from the other battalions. They would learn later who was killed, but now they saw only those who were alive. Men from the same kibbutz and village embraced each other, and brothers anxiously sought each other out.

But the battle was not yet over, not even on the Temple Mount. Lieutenant Gad of the Seventh, whose company was one of the last to enter, was approaching the steps to the mosque when a soldier behind him yelled, "Watch out. They're firing from there." The soldier was motioning toward Golden Gate in the eastern wall through which, tradition holds, the Messiah will arrive. Gad saw movement within the massive gate and ordered two men to mount the wall and charge it along the parapets. Gad and another soldier ran straight toward the entrance. The lieutenant leapt inside and killed two Legionnaires before they could fire.

Lieutenant David was lost again. His platoon had separated from the rest of the battalion after entering Lion's Gate and found itself in a maze of alleys. The redhead and his men cautiously watched the windows overhead. Rounding a corner, they were confronted by an incongruous scene—two Jordanian policemen holding a drunk who could barely stand. The policemen were ordered to leave the drunk and lead the way to the

434

Western Wall. As they walked, four Arabs in civilian dress emerged from a side alley carrying a bandaged man on a stretcher. Sighting the paratroopers, the Arabs bolted, dropping the stretcher. It no sooner hit the ground than the wounded man leapt to his feet and disappeared after them. The comedy ended when one of the policemen attempted to escape and was brought down by a burst from an Uzi.

A reconnaissance unit swept the northeast corner of the walled city, from whose ramparts the Jordanians had been keeping up a deadly fire for more than twenty-four hours. The paratroopers found prodigious amounts of ammunition on the wall and in the chambers beneath, but no soldiers. Abutting the wall was a large open area in which the Jordanians had set up a mortar position and a small camp. The Israeli shelling prior to the breakthrough had hit the position on dead center, smashing the mortar pieces and ripping the tents. Fringing the open space was a shantytown of small huts which had also been hit by the shelling, accounting for many of the civilian casualties suffered on this side of the line.

On his tank just inside Lion's Gate, Lieutenant Dov told the driver to start the engine again. The fuel from the jerrycan had run off, and it was safe to move. As the engine caught, an officer with white hair and a black beret called up to Dov in the turret and politely asked where he was going.

The young officer recognized General Bar-Lev, deputy chief of staff. "I'm going where everybody is going," said Dov, a bit petulantly. "To the Western Wall."

"I'm afraid the tank wouldn't be able to get much farther," said Bar-Lev. "I'll ask you to take a position over there." He pointed to an open area between the gate and the Temple Mount. Spasmodic fire could still be heard, and Bar-Lev said the tank might help suppress snipers. Dov was unhappy about the order, but he touched his hand to his forehead in what he interpreted as "a sort of salute" and ordered the driver to move

435

into the open area. Arabs, some of them armed, were still moving around, but the paratroopers had paid no attention to them as they rushed to the Temple Mount. Dov motioned the Arabs forward and had them lie down around the tank in a circle to dissuade anyone from lobbing a grenade at it.

Outside the gate Sergeant Ishai, who had led the sweep through the museum back yard Tuesday, sat in a jeep waiting for Dov's tank to unblock the entrance. Glancing up at one of the firing holes above the gate, he saw a Legionnaire waving his hands in surrender. The sergeant obligingly covered him with the jeep's machine gun. But when the tank moved out of the gateway, Ishai ordered his driver to enter, leaving the Jordanian to find someone else to surrender to. The jeep drove down the Via Dolorosa for five hundred meters to the junction with a narrow lane leading to Damascus Gate. The sergeant assumed his battalion had already gone this way, so when he saw an Arab with a light machine gun on the road he thought he had another Legionnaire trying to surrender. Ishai said, "Hands up" in Arabic, but the Legionnaire leapt for cover and opened fire. The men in the jeep returned fire as the driver hurriedly turned and made off. Ishai found the rest of the battalion still at the mosque.

While the main force was entering Lion's Gate in the eastern wall, Captain Dan led a column from the Seventh Battalion around the outside of the city wall toward Dung Gate in the southern wall. The men stared like tourists at the part of Jerusalem which had been hidden from them all these years—the onion domes of the Russian Church in Gethsemane, the conical Tomb of Absalom, cut from the living rock in the Kidron Valley, the vandalized tombstones of the Jewish cemetery on the slopes of the Mount of Olives. Corporal Kreutzmann was so fascinated by the view to his left that he did not realize the stones rising to his right formed the wall of the Old City.

At Dung Gate, Dan found the entranceway barred by a metal door, which he slid open. On the high ground to his left half a dozen men in uniform—either police or Legionnaires—looked down from the Jewish quarter. They disappeared quickly when the paratroopers snapped a few shots at them. Turning right, Dan led the column onto the Temple Mount.

Outside the door to El Aksa Mosque, opposite the Dome of the Rock at the southern end of the compound, the paratroopers found half a dozen Arab Legion knapsacks. They tried the mosque door and found it locked. A lieutenant ordered the lock blown open. No Legionnaires were found inside. (A few days after the war a cache of weapons and ammunition was found in the mosque's basement.) An officer from the brigade staff, incensed by the explosion at a holy place, upbraided the officer who had ordered it. A guard was posted at the blasted entrance-way to keep out all persons, including soldiers.

From a rooftop in Abu Tor, a Jerusalem Brigade private saw sudden movement in the Arab village of Silwan just south of the Old City walls. He could detect no one at the windows, but white flags seemed to emerge from every house simultaneously. The inhabitants were heeding the direction of Kol Yisrael's Arabic network. Haazma's men, who for two sleepless days had been addressing themselves to Arab communities and units from Gaza to the Suez Canal, were now talking to an audience they could almost reach with a megaphone. Because of the topography they couldn't see it, but the flags were going up about a kilometer and a half from their studio windows.

The Jerusalem battalion which captured Abu Tor had spent Tuesday night in a grove near the university. In the morning Captain Eli was ordered to leave his men there and proceed to Mount Zion with Lieutenant Colonel Brush, the battalion commander who had replaced Colonel Peikes. Eli sensed that the day's mission might involve the Old City, and he told his deputy to assemble the company and bring it up immediately to Yemin Moshe, across the valley from Mount Zion.

437

Colonel Amitai had indeed asked Central Front Command for permission to send his men into the Old City through Dung Gate simultaneously with the paratrooper attack, but was told that the chances of the two units firing at each other accidentally made it too dangerous. Amitai ordered Brush to break through the Legion positions on the eastern slope of Mount Zion and halt at Gallicantos Church, four hundred meters from the gate. (The church was built on the site believed by some Christians to be where Peter thrice denied Jesus before the cock crowed.)

Eli's company had been slated to wait in reserve while another company made the attack; but when Eli informed Brush that his men were already on hand at Yemin Moshe, he won the breakthrough assignment. Eli's first problem was getting across the enemy minefield. Picking a stretch of blackened scrub in the hope that a brush fire might have set off any mines that were there, Eli led the company across without a casualty. They found the Arab Legion bunkers abandoned.

Meanwhile, Brush had received orders from brigade to continue to Dung Gate. When Eli informed him that he was at Gallicantos, the battalion commander told him to continue forward.

Eli asked, "Forward to where?"

The answer came back, "Forward."

Eli didn't ask again. He told his men they were going to pass through Dung Gate into the Old City. On the final part of their approach, he said, they would be exposed to fire from the wall for more than two hundred meters. They would move at the run and would not stop to pick up wounded or return fire. Eli turned and started down the hill.

It had been nineteen years since he last entered the walled city. During the darkest days of the 1948 war, he had passed through Jaffa Gate barefoot, disguised as an Arab youth. For half a year Eli, then sixteen, had been employed on missions by the Stern Gang, often in Arab-held territory. He had watched Arab irregulars plunder a Haganah convoy ambushed on its way from

438

the Etzion bloc of kibbutzim in the Hebron Hills, south of Jerusalem—the frenzied raiders slashing repeatedly at the dead bodies and waving severed heads aloft.

He had returned to the besieged Jewish quarter to be with his family. In one of the final skirmishes he was wounded, but he left the improvised hospital after twelve hours when word came that the Arabs had overrun one of the major synagogues. With a yeshiva student, he slipped into the building through the women's entrance. Several Arabs were cavorting in the synagogue, their weapons set down. They had broken open the holy ark, and one of them was draping himself in the parchment scrolls of a Torah while the others smashed ornaments and scattered prayer books. Telling the yeshiva student to do whatever he did, Eli flung a grenade and opened fire. The two youths fired until the last Legionnaire lay still on the floor. When the quarter capitulated, Eli and his father spent nine months in a Jordanian prison before being repatriated.

Now, as Eli approached the walls there was a company of armed men at his back. Looking up at the firing slits, he estimated that if Legionnaires were waiting up there he would lose half his men before he reached the gate. He did not know that Dan's force of paratroopers had passed through the gate a short time before. Indeed, so fast had events been moving that he did not even know that paratroopers had been fighting in Jerusalem for the past thirty hours.

Eli did not look back as he sprinted toward the gate. Reaching the metal door, he pulled it slightly ajar and looked through the gap with his binoculars, scanning windows for rifle barrels or movement. He was so intent on signs of ambush that he failed for some second to notice the most striking part of the scene— the white flags hanging from every building. When he did, the impact reached him with a delirious rush. Stepping through the gate, he threw back his head and shouted a wild phrase of triumph and thanksgiving, *"Ani ohaiv Elohim"* (I love God)."

# 21  THE JERICHO ROAD

Four Arabs strode across the Temple Mount to the knot of officers beside the Dome of the Rock and asked in English whom they could speak to. Colonel Gur replied that he was in command. The Arab spokesman was the Jordanian governor of Jerusalem, Anwar El Khatib. He declared that the Arab Legion had left the city and that there would be no organized resistance. If no one resists, said Gur, peace will fall on the city. El Khatib said that the people of Jerusalem didn't want to fight but put in a disclaimer as to young hotheads who might attempt to shoot. Gur said his men would start the mopping up without firing and would shoot only if they met resistance.

The Old City had, in fact, not yet fallen. The paratroopers had poured onto the Temple Mount, but the residential quarters, constituting five-sixths of the walled city, still remained to be cleared. The bulk of the Arab Legion force in the city had pulled out during the night, after word was received from Amman that reinforcements destined for the city had been destroyed by air attacks. About 150 Palestinian soldiers, however, had refused to leave. Following the morning's shelling of the Lion's Gate area and the low buzzing by jet planes, some of the soldiers had discarded their weapons and changed into civilian clothing. Others, however, were still abroad, armed and prepared to fight.

Gur briefed his three battalion commanders near the mosque on the areas to be secured. Yussi would take his Eighth Battalion to Nablus Gate in the northern wall and clear a safe route through the Moslem quarter for Prime Minister Eshkol, who

441

was expected to arrive at noon. Uzi's Seventh Battalion would clear the western city wall, the one facing Jewish Jerusalem. Joseph's Sixth Battalion would move to Dung Gate in the southern wall on the fringe of the Jewish quarter, where no Jew had lived for nineteen years.

The Eighth moved out toward the north wall with Chagai's Company D in the lead—that half of it which had come through the shelling in Bait Yisrael prior to Tuesday's breakthrough. Turning a corner, the men at the point came under fire. They returned it and charged forward to find three abandoned Bren guns. Filing through a narrow, roofed-over marketplace, the men emerged at the foot of a broad stone staircase leading to a closed gate.

A sign in English read DAMASCUS GATE, but the paratroopers were looking for Nablus Gate. Unknown to them, both gates were the same. All the gates of the Old City had accumulated several names over the centuries. The road to Nablus, sixty-seven kilometers to the north, began at the gate, and the Jews had always called it Nablus (in Hebrew, Shechem) Gate. But the same road continued on to Syria, and the gate had thus acquired the English designation of Damascus Gate. (To the Arabs, it was Bab El Amud—Gate of the Pillar.) An Arab civilian was found nearby and one of the paratroopers asked him in English if this was Nablus Gate. He said it was. Then why was DAMASCUS GATE written on the sign? It's called that too, he said. The officers believed the Arab to be either ignorant or lying. A "New Gate" was indicated on the map four hundred meters farther along the north wall, and Yussi asked the Arab to guide them there, believing that this might turn out to be Nablus Gate.

Once again, as on Nablus Road the day before, the Eighth was to find itself on the wrong road—with fatal consequences. Lieutenant Dan Drorr was in the lead as the battalion wound through the alleys. It was his pack which had mysteriously caught fire Monday in camp prior to coming to Jerusalem but no one had considered it an omen. As Drorr and his point element crossed an intersection, two Arabs in khaki uniforms pitched grenades from up ahead and opened fire. Drorr fell dead. Three other soldiers were hit. One of the wounded, convinced they had been led into a trap, shot and killed the Arab guide. The fallen were retrieved and carried back to Damascus Gate.

After passing through Dung Gate, one of Captain Eli's men had suggested turning right toward the Western Wall. "First we're going to see my house," the Jerusalem company commander said, turning toward the Jewish quarter. Much of the quarter lay in ruins. The few synagogues which had not been destroyed had been turned into stables. Continuing past the Armenian quarter toward Jaffa Gate, the Jerusalem Brigade troops heard men approaching. A group of paratroopers rounded a corner, and the two sides ran to each other and embraced. Eli, who thought his company was the only Israeli unit in the Old City, asked what they were doing there.

The paratroopers were from a company of the Seventh Battalion whose objective was the Citadel, next to Jaffa Gate. Surrounded by a dry moat and marked by a graceful minaret known as David's Tower, the Citadel was built on the remains of a Herodian fortress. It was still a military position, serving as the main Arab Legion camp in the Old City. Abutting on the south was the Kishle compound, a prison since Turkish times. A priest from a nearby mission told a paratroop officer that the Legionnaires had freed all prisoners the night before and given them weapons.

The moat girdling the Citadel was crossed by a short stone bridge with a gate. An officer who mistakenly thought it locked ordered Corporal Kreutzmann and another soldier to blow it open. (The same officer had ordered the lock on El Aksa Mosque blown.) The charge laid was too heavy, however, and falling rubble completely buried the two men. The other soldier was quickly retrieved, but no one noticed that Kreutzmann was

443

missing until a pack was seen sticking out of the debris. The corporal's eyes were open and covered with dust when he was dug out, and he was accounted dead. He soon regained consciousness, however, and was driven to a hospital.

Captain Zamush mounted the city wall below David's Tower and encountered an armed Legionnaire, who surrendered meekly. The Jordanian seemed stunned. "Aren't you from the Iraqi Army?" he asked. An officer who spoke Arabic asked why he hadn't fled with the rest of his comrades. The Legionnaire said he couldn't believe the Israelis would come. Inside the Arab Legion barracks the paratroopers found clothing neatly laid out for inspection on tightly made beds. Lieutenant Yair changed into a pair of clean Jordanian socks. Private Yaacov found a large drum which he hauled up the narrow stairways to the top of the city wall. The day before, his weapon had stopped a Jordanian bullet that would have hit him in the chest, and he sounded out his joy now with a vigorous beat.

With the Arab prisoner in front to thwart ambush from any of the pillboxes on top of the wall, Zamush and half his company started moving along the ramparts toward Zion Gate. The paratroopers were amazed at the amount of ammunition stacked beside the firing holes facing Jewish Jerusalem. Most of the weapons had been removed, but mortars were still in place.

From the border areas across the Hinnom Valley, where residents had been eagerly watching the walled city since dawn, the paratroopers could be clearly seen as they mounted the ramparts. Hundreds of civilians poured out into the streets. Zamush could see them coming out of the old stone houses of Yemin Moshe and the Mamilla quarter. Others appeared at the windows of the luxurious King David Hotel and filled the balconies of apartment buildings. Youngsters began running toward no-man's-land, and Haga wardens, fearful of mines, tried to keep them back. As in the climactic moment of a pageant, the Arab prisoner stood silhouetted atop an Arab Legion pillbox at the southwest corner of the city wall, his hands on his head, while a paratrooper beside

444

him unfurled a Jordanian flag, taken from the Kishle. Above the shouts of the crowds below could be heard the triumphant tattoo of Yaacov's drum.

Many of the soldiers who had stood dry-eyed at the Western Wall shed tears now. Looking down at the cheering citizens of Jerusalem from the firing positions which had dominated them all these years, the paratroopers had the feeling of deliverers. Lieutenant Yair, who had remained on the wall near David's Tower, could hear the Jerusalemites singing the *Hatikva*. Civilians approaching close to the wall yelled for a flag to be raised. Yair turned to Lieutenant Bitan, who had awakened him three weeks before at Kfar Blum with the mobilization order, and told him to raise a flag atop David's Tower.

Bitan descended from the wall and raced up the tower's spiral staircase. Emerging on a narrow balcony near the top, he climbed a metal railing to afix the flag to the tower's peak, teetering over a sheer drop as he did. Of all the flags raised that day, none had a more dramatic impact than this, proclaiming to the Jews of Jerusalem that the Old City was theirs.

While Zamush's company cleared the wall south of Jaffa Gate, the rest of the Seventh turned north. Men from Company D mounted the wall next to the gate and killed two Legionnaires on the ramparts. In the narrow streets of the Christian quarter below, Companies B and C felt their way toward the New Gate behind Captain Eilat. During Tuesday's breakthrough, Eilat had been uncertain of the number of fences that had to be penetrated. He was no more enlightened now about this area of operations. He was without a map of the Old City and was not quite sure where he was. He had borrowed a map from another company commander earlier and had tried to pocket it, but the other officer sent a runner to bring it back.

From the Temple Mount he had proceeded in a relatively straight line until he reached a large gate, but was disappointed to learn from a street sign that it was Jaffa Gate. Working from memory, he turned right. The two companies passed the low

445

entranceway to the Santa Rosa Convent. Inside, eighty Arab Legionnaires were taking shelter. (They were to surrender a few days after the war.) As the column passed the Knights Palace Hotel, a shot rang out and a soldier slid dead to the ground.

The possibility of getting killed at this stage, when the battle was virtually over, was so unattractive that officers of the two companies in the column debated whose job it was to clear the building. It finally was delegated to David's platoon. The ubiquitous redhead, who had drawn the heaviest share of the fighting during the breakthrough stage, threw Pach-Pach a sidelong glance of exasperation that the corporal well knew by now. *They're trying to kill me,* it said.

A narrow ditch, apparently intended to represent a moat, separated the Knights Palace from the street. David made his way across a glass-enclosed "bridge" but found the front door of the hotel locked. It was blown open with a demolition charge.

As the paratroopers entered, they heard the terrified cries of women and children from the basement. A mosaic madonna looked down from a wall, and the Israelis thought they were in some sort of monastery. (The building had once been part of the adjoining Latin Patriarchate.) David started up the staircase but hastily backed down when bullets hit the steps in front of him. Spraying the flight of stairs with his Uzi, he tried again to mount but was driven down once more by fire. He tried throwing grenades around the bend of the staircase and rushing. Each time he was stopped.

After a quarter hour David received some unexpected reinforcements—the battalion commander and his deputy. Colonel Uzi and Captain Dan, hearing of the shooting, had commandeered a platoon and rushed to the hotel. David explained the situation to Uzi in the lobby.

"All right," said the colonel, "I'm going up."

David said he wouldn't get past the third step. Uzi reached the third step, and bullets hit inches in front of him. He descended abruptly.

446

In the discussion which followed, Private Bower, the grenadier, found himself, to his own considerable surprise, offering
tactical advice to the battalion commander. Uzi heard him out
but the assignment given to grenadier Bower was not one the
private had suggested. He was to enter the exposed rear yard of
the hotel and fire grenades through the second-story windows in
the hope of driving the Legionnaires away from the staircase.
Feeling like an insect at the bottom of a bottle, Bower dropped
into the yard from a window. Walls bristling with windows
hemmed him in on three sides. The fourth side was open to the
Old City wall forty yards away. Bower dashed across the yard to
a small shack. To his relief, he drew no fire on the way. Bit by
bit, his head emerged from his shelter. Encouraged by the silence, he set to work, methodically firing grenades into every
window on the second floor.

Captain Dan, meanwhile, had taken ten men and begun
probing for a way to get to the roof of an adjoining building. The
men opened fire on a door around the corner from the hotel, but
it failed to buckle. "Why don't you try turning the knob?"
suggested Dan. One of the men did and found the door open.
The soldiers clambered over courtyard walls and roofs until they
reached the roof abutting the Knights Palace. They found that
it was seven meters lower than the hotel.

The building the men were on was the Latin Patriarchate,
seat of the Vatican in the Holy Land. A robed figure Dan took
to be a monk apppeared and told the captain that the archbishop
wanted to see him. The kibbutznik, who had never met an
archbishop before, followed. He was led through a room
crowded with civilians into the clergyman's presence. Asked
what he wanted, Dan said he wished to get to the Old City wall.
The paratroopers were led to the building's rear gate, which was
shut after they passed through. The city wall loomed above
them, and the men scrambled up a ladder to the parapet.

From a downstairs window in the hotel Uzi leaned out and
shouted to Dan that the Legionnaires were still on the second

447

floor. Dan assigned men to each of the six windows on the floor which was level with the parapet. At his command, a fusillade of bazooka and small-arms fire ripped into the hotel.

Inside the building David pulled the pin of a grenade and tossed it up the staircase, but it bounced back toward him. He dove out the front door, but instead of landing on the "bridge," he fell to the bottom of the two-meter-deep moat. The bridge, weakened by the demolition charge placed against the hotel door, had collapsed seconds earlier under the weight of several soldiers. The long-suffering redhead dusted himself off and climbed back into the hotel.

Trying the staircase again David placed his foot on the fourth step, and for the first time nothing happened. The Legionnaires had apparently been driven away from the staircase. David bolted up the steps, firing around the bend. Halfway up he fell through a hole in the staircase blasted by his own grenades, falling with a thud to the landing below. It was his second involuntary airdrop in minutes. Running back up to the second floor, he found Uzi. The colonel had climbed to the second floor through a side window and had fired at the Legionnaires down the corridor. The combined attack drove the Legionnaires to the roof.

From the city wall Dan's men could no longer bring fire to bear, since the roof was higher than they were. The captain descended alone and passed through the hotel to the street. Immediately opposite was a building the same height as the hotel. Dan crossed the narrow roadway and tried the building's door but found it locked. Shots suddenly chipped the stone lintel above his head. Before he could move, bullets tore into his arm and leg. He turned his head and saw a Legionnaire firing at him from the hotel roof across the way. The captain managed to leap across the roadway to the shelter of the hotel wall.

At this point Captain Eilat returned from New Gate. His troops had brushed there with half a dozen Legionnaires on the wall who managed to escape. The war had seemed about over,

448

but he now discovered a battle in progress, with the battalion commander inside fighting like a rifleman and the deputy battalion commander outside bleeding from fresh wounds. Dan told him to find a way into the building across the street and to put grenades from there onto the hotel roof.

Inside the hotel Colonel Uzi prepared to rush the roof. He called for men with Uzis, and David and Lieutenant Zeev, the battalion operations officer, stepped forward. The colonel started up the staircase.

The door at the top was held by a wire. Through a crack he could see three Legionnaires on the other side. He called forward a man with an automatic rifle, who fired a burst through the door. Now there was no more room to maneuver. To get whoever was on the roof—and the paratroopers had no idea how many were up there—they would have to move through the door at the top of the staircase one at a time and face whatever guns were waiting for them. David pushed to the front and moved toward the door.

In Notre Dame, Ariel Fisher and three other Jerusalem Brigade snipers were eating lunch on the second floor when someone ran down from the roof shouting that he could see Legionnaires. The snipers had seen the Israeli flag go up on David's Tower more than an hour before and had assumed that the war was over. They went up to the roof and saw soldiers on top of a building 150 meters away, inside the Old City. There were five of them, and they seemed to be firing periodically down the stairwell. The snipers could not tell if they were Legionnaires or paratroopers.

Ariel borrowed a 60-power telescope from his partner, a shooting instructor at a sports club who had brought his personal telescopes to war with him. The five on the Old City roof wore dish helmets, but that was not conclusive evidence that they were Legionnaires. However, he noted too that their canteens were not hung from the belt, as in the Israeli Army, but from

449

their equipment webbing. His eye was drawn to their rifles, all of them with fixed bayonets. The weapons were British and unlike any in service in the Israeli Army. Ariel was now convinced that they were Legionnaires, especially since they were plainly besieged. The paratroopers would be attacking, not defending.

There were strict orders not to fire into the Old City for fear of hitting the paratroopers, and one of the snipers contacted brigade headquarters on the telephone. When he insisted he saw Legionnaires on the roof, he was given permission to fire.

One of the snipers was still not certain the men were Arabs and refused to shoot. Ariel, however, had no doubts. Looking through the telescope, he saw a heavyset soldier gesticulating and shouting at the other men on the roof. The soldier, evidently the unit commander, was the only one not wearing a helmet. He had graying, crew-cut hair. Ariel, who had received his first sniper instruction as a high school youth in Gadna, was not particularly well armed for his mission. He had an ordinary rifle, not the more precise Lee-Enfield that the other snipers used, and he had no telescopic sight mounted on the weapon itself.

He aimed at the head of the crew-cut soldier and fired. Looking through the telescope, he saw that the Legionnaire, still on his feet, was holding a hand on his bloody cheek and giving orders to his men. Ariel aimed for the chest and squeezed off another shot. This time the soldier went down. Two other snipers alongside Ariel opened fire, and two more Legionnaires fell. But it was difficult to know if these had been hit by the snipers or a burst of automatic fire which could be seen coming through the roof door from the staircase. Ariel hit the two men remaining. A low wall on the roof of the building in the Old City masked the fallen Arabs from view, but Ariel was certain all five were at least wounded, if not dead.

In the hotel Lieutenant David pushed open the roof door and saw two Legionnaires lying directly opposite him, one of them

450

a big man with a crew cut. He fired from the head of the stairs. "It's over," he yelled. Stepping out onto the roof he saw three more Legionnaires a few feet away and emptied his weapon into them. He had no idea that the Legionnaires who had been producing such a lively fire just a few moments before had already been wounded or dead when he came out on the roof. Nor did he know that a sixth Legionnaire, still quite alive, was just a few meters away.

Captain Eilat had reached the roof of the house opposite the hotel just after Ariel had hit his first man. As Eilat stepped out of the stairway housing, he saw four Legionnaires lined up at the edge of the hotel roof, twenty meters away. They fired at him, and he ducked back to the shelter of the stairway, where he pulled the pin on a grenade. He was bracing himself to step into the open and fling it when he heard a burst of fire on the hotel roof. Looking over, he saw paratroopers streaming through the door. Colonel Uzi yelled to Eilat that there might be a Legionnaire behind the hotel water tank. Happy to get rid of the live grenade in hand, Eilat tossed it there. David and Uzi ran behind the tank and killed a Legionnaire trying to take cover. Ricochets off the concrete tank wounded Uzi in the hand.

David searched the dead Legionnaires. They had put up a brave fight, and he wanted to know if there had been an officer among them. In the crew-cut soldier's pocket he found a lieutenant's insignia. (Officers on both sides had removed marks of rank to make themselves less conspicuous targets.)

When men from Company B came to carry away the body of the soldier killed in front of the hotel, nobody at first knew who he was. Instead of camouflage uniform and helmet, he was wearing a khaki dress uniform and red beret. He was finally recognized as a young soldier on regular service who had been with a group of reinforcements from another paratroop brigade at the Temple Mount. He had told Lieutenant Oded there that he had lost his unit and asked to join Company B on its sweep to New Gate. He had apparently been picked out by the sniper

451

because of his beret. The soldier, Itzak Weiss, was the last Israeli to die in the battle.

(In all, 179 Israeli soldiers were killed in the battle. Civilian dead brought the total to about 200. One thousand soldiers had been wounded. More than half the battle casualties were sustained by the paratroop brigade. On the Jordanian side of the city, 330 soldiers and 100 civilians are estimated to have been killed.)

Although mopping up still remained, the action at the Knights Palace Hotel was the final fire fight in the battle of Jerusalem. The hotel was located in the northwest corner of the Old City which thrust into the heart of Jewish Jerusalem. The two-day battle which had enveloped Jerusalem from Sur Bahir in the south to Ammunition Hill on the north had ended three hundred meters from Mayor Kollek's office in City Hall.

Itzak Weiss was not the only volunteer who joined Gur's men that morning. Yoram Hamizrachi, the civil-defense officer who had sounded the air-raid alarm in Jerusalem Monday morning, had crossed over to the Jordanian section in search of the war he had so dramatically announced. The spade-bearded Jerusalemite had been a paratroop officer until wounded in a clash with Arab raiders.

On Nablus Road he found soldiers from the Eighth Battalion's Company A and recognized Lieutenant Nachshon, with whom he had taken basic training. Captain Avidan, the company commander, was sitting outside Saint Stephen's Monastery following on his radio the progress of the units moving through the walled city. He looked tired.

"How do you feel?" asked Yoram.

"How can I feel?" replied Avidan. "We've had a lot of casualties."

Half the company was wounded or dead, and the heart seemed to have been knocked out of it by the morning's shelling, which the men suspected came from Israeli lines.

Avidan granted Yoram's request to stay with the company. The former paratrooper provided himself with a weapon taken from one of the wounded and joined a patrol searching houses across from the monastery, where suspicious movements had been spotted. In one house they came upon ammunition and discarded uniforms. Hearing whispering from a basement, Yoram called out in Arabic, "Come out or we'll blow up the house on you." Women and children emerged, then several men —one in uniform, others in pajamas or underwear. They were taken for identification.

As Nachshon and Yoram walked together down an alley, the paratrooper remarked that it finally seemed to be over. An armed Legionnaire suddenly stepped out of a doorway directly in front of them. The Jordanian's rifle was pointed toward the ground, but Nachshon's Uzi was aimed directly at him. Yoram, who was slightly behind Nachshon, yelled, "Shoot!" Nachshon, his eyes fixed on the Legionnaire, quietly asked Yoram to tell the Jordanian in Arabic to drop the weapon. Nachshon knew he was supposed to shoot, but he felt there had already been a surfeit of blood.

Yoram translated the order but the Legionnaire hesitated, apparently weighing the chances of trying to beat Nachshon. Then, still maintaining a grip on the rifle with one hand, he raised the other. Yoram stepped forward and took the weapon. The Legionnaire's hands, released from the weight of the rifle, started shaking uncontrollably. Yoram offered him a cigarette and asked where he was from. The soldier said Jenin. His officers, he said, had fled the day before.

As the paratroopers moved through the surrounding alleys, windows began to open, and the residents put their heads out for the first time in two days. "I'm an Ethiopian," shouted one man, to the bafflement of the soldiers. From another window came the cry of *"Viva Eshkol."* A paratrooper, joining in the spirit, shouted back, "Say *Viva Dayan.*"

*        *        *

The Jerusalem sniper platoon sat glumly in the park in front of City Hall. Since early morning they had waited for orders, and it had begun to appear that they would be given no part in the capture of the Old City. Shortly after noon Lieutenant Ben-Moshe drove to brigade headquarters and informed a staff officer that the platoon was waiting for something to do. He was told that there were many units waiting for orders and that he would keep on waiting until he was called.

Although Ben-Moshe was new to his veteran platoon, he had adjusted to its egalitarian ways. Returning to the park, he told the men he would put it to a vote whether to await orders to enter the Old City—an unlikely eventuality—or to move on their own. In a moment, the men were in their cars heading for Mount Zion—the jumping-off point to Dung Gate.

Half a dozen snipers crowded into Private Joseph Epstein's big red Impala. The husky electrician (a second cousin of Zerach Epstein, the Tsalash winner from the Jerusalem Reconnaissance Company) had been born in the Old City and had fought there in 1948. His father had been the chief Ashkenazic rabbi of the community, and young Joseph had worn the sidecurls and black robes of the ultra-Orthodox.

He had been part of a serene and courtly world that belonged to another century. Each morning at 2 A.M. his father had risen to begin the study of the Talmud. In the two weeks before the Jewish New Year, when the Orthodox rise early to read special prayers of repentance—selichot—the rabbi had paused in his studies to waken Joseph just before dawn. The sleepy boy had walked through the quarter chanting to a melody of his own making the traditional words, "Israel, holy people, rise for selichot, rise for selichot, rise to God's work." Epstein particularly remembered Friday afternoons, when the community prepared for the Sabbath—housewives washing their front steps and lowering cans of gefilte fish into the ancient cisterns from where they would be pulled up on the Sabbath, ice cold.

That world had ended, seemingly forever, early in 1948, when

454

the Arabs began to mount sustained attacks on the Jewish quarter. Joseph's father had believed that the fifteen-year-old boy was studying in his yeshiva and was incensed to discover that he had instead been making crude bombs for the Irgun and serving as a runner. The rabbi left the quarter before the siege was drawn, but Joseph remained behind, turning the house over to the Irgun. He fought with them until the quarter fell and spent nine months as a prisoner across the Jordan. Nineteen years had now passed. He had lost his sidecurls and the customs of the Orthodox, but as he drove he wept until it was difficult for him to see.

On Mount Zion, Lieutenant Ben-Moshe raised Colonel Brush inside Dung Gate and told him that the sniper platoon was reporting for duty. The battalion commander told the lieutenant to bring his men in and post them on the rooftops.

In the alleys leading away from the Western Wall, hundreds of weary paratroopers sprawled on the paving stones. Singer Yaffa Yarkoni, who had performed for the men of the Haganah twenty years before, moved among the men, leading them in song. Most of the soldiers, however, lay with their eyes shut, their weapons and bandoliers of ammunition beside them.

Late in the afternoon sober dark suits and homburgs mixed with battle dress, as the leaders of the nation began to arrive at the Western Wall, most of them looking dazed. The paratroopers were for the most part too young to have seen the wall before, yet young enough to have expected that one day they would— through peace or war. On the other hand, few of the veteran political and religious leaders had felt they would live to see it again.

With shots still ringing out periodically, the plan to bring Eshkol through Damascus Gate and the Moslem quarter had been dropped. Instead, the dignitaries were led in through Lion's Gate and across the Temple Mount, the same route the paratroopers had taken. Eshkol was accompanied by the two chief rabbis. The Ashkenazic rabbi, representing Jews from

Western communities, wore his traditional top hat; the Sephardic rabbi, representing the Eastern communities, wore a turban.

The two men who had led Jerusalem through the siege of 1948 (not always amicably) were seen standing together at the wall—Dov Joseph, the former governor of the city and David Shaltiel, the former military commander. The Haga district chiefs who had shepherded the city's population through the current battle arrived together. The one religious officer among them, David of the western district, led them in prayer. All of them were weeping—even the tough ex-cop in charge of the northern district. (His son was fighting with paratroopers in the Sinai, and he prayed for his safe return.)

Two venerable rabbis arrived on the Temple Mount in a recoilless rifle jeep, their white beards bending in the wind as they clung to the speeding vehicle. The pair were Rabbi Zvi Yehuda Kook, son of the former chief rabbi of Israel, and Rabbi David Cohen, better known as the Nazir. Captain Zamush had studied with them when he was a yeshiva student in Jerusalem, and the paratrooper had asked Goren's assistant, Major Menahem Hacohen, to pick them up at their homes.

Hacohen had found Rabbi Kook studying when he arrived. "I've come to take you to the Western Wall," the chaplain said. The rabbi didn't seem to understand, and Hacohen led him out to the jeep by the arm. The Nazir, who was Rabbi Goren's father-in-law, immediately grasped the message. It was, in fact, his shofar which Rabbi Goren had blown in the Old City. Goren had stopped by his father-in-law's house the night before to borrow it to replace the shofar blown on Mount Sinai, which had been lost in the half-track wrecked on the attack on the Gaza Strip Monday.

The Nazir had years before made a vow not to leave his house and his studies for the outside world. The vow could be waived on infrequent occasions such as funerals or weddings, but three persons—adult Jewish males—were needed to grant permission. A young man present in the Nazir's apartment when Hacohen

456

arrived was eligible to serve as one of the three. Hacohen himself made a second, and a neighbor was collected for the third. (Hacohen had left Rabbi Kook downstairs in the jeep.) The Nazir asked the three if he could leave. In unison, they repeated, "You may, you may, you may," and Hacohen hurried the rabbi downstairs.

At the wall the Nazir went immediately to the stones and began a solitary prayer, but Rabbi Kook still didn't seem to grasp the situation. He stood in the midst of the crowd, chatting absently with Hacohen, to the major's astonishment, asking the address of a mutual acquaintance and commenting on a book he had just written. Suddenly, as if a door in his mind had just opened, the rabbi burst into tears and threw himself at the wall, spreading his arms to embrace the stones.

While piety marked the scene at the cramped alley before the Western Wall, power dominated the monumental stage of the Temple Mount above. Long lines of Arabs were silhouetted against the sky as they moved across the platform of the Dome of the Rock guarded by helmeted paratroopers cradling Uzis. The Arabs, in civilian dress, were ordered to kneel in a line facing a stone wall, their hands on their heads, until they were called individually for interrogation. Some of the prisoners were older men, but young men with military bearing could be seen stiff-backed among the rest. Several were identified as soldiers by dog tags or compass straps, which for some reason they retained after discarding their uniforms.

When one Arab put his hands down, a paratrooper barked at him and motioned with his Uzi to get them back up. A swarthy sergeant major commanding the guard detail cautioned his men, "They're prisoners, but they're also human beings." The Arabs seemed completely stunned by the display of might casually bristling about them. Intelligent Jordanian citizens had believed the Arab Legion by itself could defeat the Israeli Army, and the present debacle was as incomprehensible as it was humiliating.

One of the prisoners slumped against a tree with his eyes

closed as if hoping the scene would disappear when he opened them. As a plane roared overhead, tears flowed through his closed lids and his hands trembled. "They're afraid," said a young soldier looking down at him, "but we won't harm them." (Colonel Daoud, the Jordanian liaison officer to the Mixed Armistice Commission, had been captured the day before outside the walled city. It was he who had filed the protest against the Independence Day parade in Jerusalem three weeks before. Shaul Ramati, the Foreign Ministry official who had sat opposite him at the meeting, contemplated visiting him now but decided that it would embarrass his old acquaintance. The colonel was released after a short time. Three years later he was to become prime minister of Jordan.)

Behind the mass of detainees a score of dignitaries had been seated, including Governor El Khatib, the cadi (chief judge) and the police chief of East Jerusalem. They were not obliged to keep their hands on their heads. The Arabs had been rounded up from houses in the area, most of them expecting to be shot as they were led away. It was commonly believed in Jordan that in 1956 the Israelis had rounded up all the males in Gaza and shot them. They expected a similar fate. Instead, soldiers offered them water from their canteens and cigarettes, which they lit for them. "It's your king who started this," a soldier said to one of the dignitaries.

The paratroopers were bronzed and unshaven and many wore captured Arab *khefiyas* on their heads or around their necks. On the mosque platform a group of officers surrounded by the antennas of their radiomen watched jet planes circling beyond the Mount of Olives and darting down somewhere above the Jericho road. Supply vehicles, including a mobilized milk truck laden with military equipment, were parked between the mosques, and some soldiers had climbed into the cabs to sleep. Across the vast plaza cheers went up from a company of paratroopers gathered around an officer who had just finished addressing them.

In Arab Legion storerooms at the northern end of the compound a dozen soldiers poked through crates of weapons until they uncovered boxes of soda pop. As they sat drinking on the terrace outside they spoke to a foreign reporter about the Legionnaires they had met in battle. "They were good," said one, "but we were better."

Despite the bewildering speed of events, the soldiers had obviously given thought to the political implications of the battle. "They can have all the rest back," said one, "but not our Holy City." Others spoke of keeping all or part of the territory captured on the other fronts. Only one soldier advocated returning everything. In this offhand discussion on the Temple Mount before the last shots were heard, virtually all the major positions that would occupy the Israeli political scene in the coming years were outlined.

Soldiers roamed the compound like tourists but were barred by sentries from entering the mosques. The flag which had been raised on the golden dome was taken down after an hour, in deference to the religious nature of the buildings. Two privates happened to find the door to the Dome of the Rock temporarily unguarded when they arrived late in the afternoon. They made their way to a balcony beneath the dome and tested the acoustics by speaking to each other from opposite ends. A third voice drifted up from the mosque floor. It was Colonel Gur summoning them down.

Colonel Amitai had begun massing a substantial part of his brigade near Ramat Rachel early in the morning. At 10 A.M. he saw through binoculars an Arab Legion convoy moving east on a dirt track leading past the flat-topped Mount Herodium, which had served as King Herod's administrative center twenty centuries before. The convoy disappeared into the Judean Desert heading for the Jordan River. Late in the morning, Amitai received the order to cross the frontier and begin moving south toward Bethlehem and Hebron.

      \*          \*          \*

Private Yussi Goell's battalion at Ramat Rachel assembled in a sheltered grove. "If you were afraid we weren't going to see action," the battalion commander told his men, "I can tell you we're going in now." They would move into the wadi, he said, and attack the Arab Legion trenches on the opposite slope, below Mar Elias Monastery. "If you do it quickly and well, our casualties will be kept to a minimum. Of course, wounded will be taken care of as quickly as possible. Stick by your officers and noncoms, and do what they tell you."

Though he had led an eventful life as a newspaperman, the American-born Goell had never yet charged an enemy trench, and he looked forward to the experience with some reservations. It was a mistake for him to be here at all. He had reached thirty-nine, the age when he was supposed to have been transferred to a second-line unit. But the crisis had frozen him in his old first-line battalion. What concerned him most was whether he would be able to make it up the hill, regardless of mines or bullets. He weighed two hundred and twenty pounds, and in addition to his own paunch he carried a double load of ammunition as well as bazooka shells and a bangalore. It would be embarrassing if he ran out of wind halfway up. As two tanks moved out into the open and began to shell the enemy bunkers, a soldier marched up and down with a prayer book reciting psalms at the top of his voice. The companies formed up and started into the wadi in single file, officers shouting, "Don't bunch up." Goell felt surprisingly detached. Looking behind him at the line winding down the slope, he was reminded of a scene from Eisenstein's *Ivan the Terrible,* depicting the flight from Moscow. Sappers exploded bangalores beneath the barbed-wire fences, and the infantrymen scrambled through into the trenches. Goell made it to the top and discovered that the enemy had fled.

On an adjacent hill the Jerusalem Reconnaissance Company filed into similarly abandoned trenches and looked across the rolling country to Bethlehem, five kilometers to the south. The

460

men were tense. They would be the spearhead of the attack on the city, and if the Arabs made a determined stand in the narrow streets, it would be grim. As they watched, white flags began to appear in the windows. There would be no dying in Bethlehem. Someone in the trenches started singing "Jerusalem of Gold," and the entire company on the hillside joined in.

Colonel Amitai ordered the battalion at Government House to move to Bethlehem on foot, down the winding road the Jordanians had built between Bethlehem and the Old City after 1948. The battalion at Mar Elias—using the direct, pre-1948 road—would march past Bethlehem and seize the Khadr crossroads, several kilometers to the south.

Amitai himself joined the tanks and the reconnaissance company which moved ahead of the rest of the brigade.

As the force started south, the sky was rent by a deep roaring. The noise could be heard throughout the city, and people stopped in their tracks to gaze upward. It sounded as if jet planes overhead were engaging in a violent dogfight but at an altitude so high that they were impossible to see. As if to confirm this speculation, wisps of white smoke like jet contrails could be made out.

The noise, however, was not produced by planes but by special mortar shells devised in Israel's military workshops. The shells could reach far beyond conventional range, providing extended cover for Amitai's force on its drive south. Their awesome sound added substantially to their effectiveness in much the same way as the homemade Davidka mortars had served for the Israelis during the 1948 battle for Jerusalem. The current battle for the city, which had seen the Israelis unleash a secret weapon in the opening moments of the battle—Colonel L's blockhouse buster—was concluding now with another.

At sunset, Amitai's force rolled into Kfar Etzion, the largest of the four kibbutzim which had formed the Etzion bloc overrun by the Arab Legion in 1948. Two hundred forty of the defenders had died in that fight and subsequent massacre, and the kibbutz

461

had been converted by the legion into an army camp. It was now deserted. Passing beneath the royal Hashemite arch, Amitai's force found that all kibbutz buildings except for one small barracks had been razed and quonset huts erected on their foundations. Amitai raised Narkiss's headquarters on the radio. "The Etzion bloc is in my hands." Headquarters asked him to repeat. Amitai gladly did.

Late in the afternoon a paratroop officer approached the Arab detainees being held near the Dome of the Rock and said, "All right. You can go home now." Those suspected of being soldiers had already been weeded out. A dignitary found the officer's casual dismissal difficult to believe. He had been sure they would, at best, be taken away to a concentration camp or prison. An officer escorted him and several others to one of the exits from the Temple Mount. With patrols hunting snipers and soldiers in mufti, it was too dangerous for civilians to wander through the streets. The officer inquired where they lived. When several said they lived some distance outside the walls, the officer asked the dignitary who had mentioned that his home was nearby if he would mind putting them up for the night. "I would tell the king himself," the dignitary would say later, 'These are not ordinary conquerers.'"

In the last minutes of sunlight Lieutenant Ben-Moshe led his sniper platoon back out through Dung Gate. The village of Silwan in the Kidron Valley had not yet been combed, and the lieutenant told his men to keep their eyes on the windows as they passed above it. A reporter who walked with them found it impossible not to keep one's eyes on the village. The view was hypnotic. The stone houses—the same dun color as the rocks covering the slopes behind—seemed to disappear into the hillside in the incredibly golden light. Beyond was the great cleft of the Jordan Valley and, half hidden in a purplish mist, the mountains of Moab.

The snipers climbed the eastern slope of Mount Zion, which was covered with soldiers. Groups of men crowded around transistors as high-pitched beeps signaled a news bulletin. Cheers marked each announcement of the war's progress. Soldiers of the Southern Command were already reported at the Suez Canal. One group sat in a circle singing Chassidic songs. At the parking area on top of the hill Ben-Moshe told his men where they would meet in the morning. There would be no need for snipers that night, so they could go home and sleep in their own beds. Driving into Jewish Jerusalem, they saw that the lights of the city were on for the first time since Sunday night.

Inside the Old City the darkness was absolute. The visiting dignitaries had left, the inhabitants were silent behind closed shutters, and for the moment the city belonged to the paratroopers alone. Against orders, a number of them slipped from their posts and made their way through the dark alleys to the Western Wall.

At the aid station which had been set up on the Temple Mount, Esther Zellinger took leave of the medical team. The men asked her to call and reassure their families. She had sixty-three telephone numbers when she passed out of Lion's Gate, many of them written on candy wrappers and cigarette paper. Hitchhiking rides in military vehicles, Esther reached the school where she had left her two children two-and-a-half days before. The school's shelter was empty when she entered except for a boy and girl in the far corner and a teacher who had remained to look after them. The children were half asleep when Esther knelt to embrace them.

It was cold at Kfar Etzion when the Jerusalem Reconnaissance Company woke early Thursday, and fog had turned the dawn to murk. Ahead of them lay their final target—Hebron. The burial place of Abraham, Isaac, and Jacob, Hebron was second in holiness only to Jerusalem, but no Jew had lived there for decades. In 1929 a long tradition of friendly relations between local Arabs and Jews had been broken by a massacre of sixty members of the Jewish community and the wounding of many more. The city was considered fanatical, even by Arabs. Its religious conservatism obliged local youth to travel to Bethlehem or Jerusalem if they wanted to see a movie, because no cinema was permitted there. Among the cities on the west bank, only Hebron enforced Moslem injunction against liquor so strictly that a non-Moslem visitor could not get so much as a beer. The Hebronites' penchant for vendettas and bloodletting was unmatched in Palestine.

Fierce resistance was anticipated—if not from the Arab Legion itself, then from irregulars operating from rooftops and windows. During the night Amitai brought up two battalions of heavy mortars to cover the town and its approaches. In addition, two extra platoons of tanks had joined him. As the recon men prepared to move out, a bearded figure climbed onto a jeep and called on the men to gather around him. It was Rabbi Goren. The rabbi reminded the soldiers of the 1929 massacre. "Don't forget what the Amalekites did to us." (Amalek, the tribe that attacked the Israelites during their wandering in the desert, serves as the eternal, traditional symbol of the enemy of the Jews.)

There was a blood debt, and the Israelis were prepared to claim it as they started south, the recon company and tanks in the lead. But the Hebronites, guided by a prudent mayor, declined to offer provocation. The streets were deserted when the troops rolled in, and white flags hung from every building. Not a single shot disturbed the morning calm. Goren swerved around the lead scout jeep and pulled to a stop in front of the Tomb of the Patriarchs.

Leaving the chaplain to blow his shofar, Amitai continued south, passing through Samua, the scene of a major Israeli retaliatory raid a year before. South of the village of Dhahiriya Amitai halted his force and sent two scout jeeps forward to the

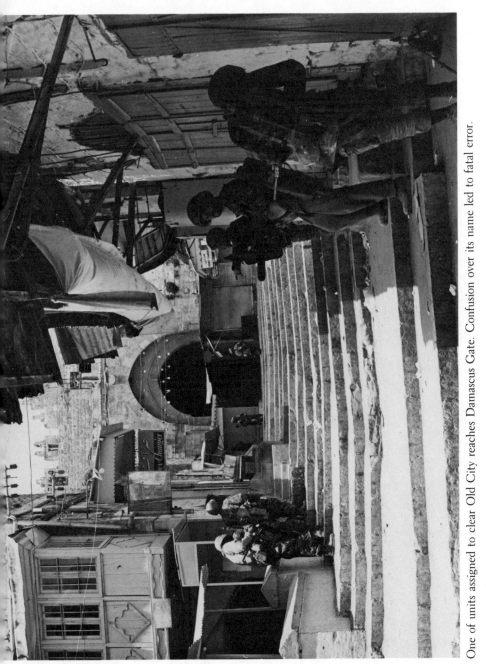

One of units assigned to clear Old City reaches Damascus Gate. Confusion over its name led to fatal error.

BAMAHANE

Arab prisoners on Temple Mount; Mount of Olives in background. Many Legionnaires remaining in Old City changed to civilian clothing.

JOSEPH BEN-OR

Men from Seventh Battalion on Temple Mount look east beyond Mount of Olives at Israeli planes attacking retreating Jordanian vehicles on the Jericho road. Bareheaded in center (next to man with bandaged wrist) is Col. Uzi, battalion commander. In left foreground is Lt. Raviv, commander of mortar platoon. Dark-skinned youth to his right is Pvt. Yaacov Hai, Indian-born runner later cited for bravery.

Jubilant troops surround Rabbi Goren, chief army chaplain, blowing shofar on Temple Mount.

border, five kilometers to the south. Half an hour later the jeep returned with the commander of a battalion guarding the Beersheba road. The officer and Amitai shook hands. The Jerusalem Brigade had linked up with the Southern Command.

In Shuafat, north of Jerusalem, the staff of the Sixth Battalion had spent the night in a posh villa, where Colonel Joseph and Major Doron had collapsed on an oversized bed upstairs. In the morning an Arab doctor who lived in a neighboring house came to ask permission to visit his patients during the curfew which had been imposed. Permission was granted, and the doctor asked if it would be all right, as long as he was there, to have a look at the villa. The doctor said he hadn't been inside before. It had served as King Hussein's summer dwelling, he explained, while his summer palace was being built on the hill above. Joseph and Doron realized they had spent the night in the king's bed. The two farmers fell into an argument over who had been sleeping on the king's side and who on the queen's.

Private Arye Comay also had a surprise when he woke that morning. His Jerusalem unit had taken over an abandoned house on the Hebron road, and the officers had invited the convivial Chilean to their room the night before. Comay had sat propped up on his platoon commander's bed drinking coffee and talking late into the night until he became drowsy. When he awoke he found it was morning. He was still lying on his officer's bed. The lieutenant had not roused him but had lain down instead on the bare floor, where he was still asleep.

Most of the paratroop units were withdrawn from the Old City during the day, as the brigade prepared to move to the Syrian front, where the final chapter of the war was about to get under way. Captain Zamush's company marched toward Lion's Gate, through which they had been the first to enter the day before, to the beat of the Arab Legion drum that Private Yaacov

469

had captured. Lieutenant Malka, the deputy company commander, tried to persuade Yaacov to get rid of the heavy drum, but gave up when Arabs on the street began applauding the impromptu parade. The private kept up the beat as the company marched out of the walled city.

On Jebel Mukaber, south of the Old City, Corporal Paz walked out by himself to the Lonely House. It had been his report from there three days earlier—that Legionnaires had entered the adjacent Government House compound—which in effect had triggered all-out war on the Jordanian front. The Arabs had occupied the house just a few hours, but Paz noted with chagrin that they had had time enough not only to install a telephone but to finish off his bottle of cognac.

In Hebron that night the Jerusalem Reconnaissance Company was visited again by composer Naomi Shemer. She had seen them in camp only two weeks before, but they looked immeasurably older. Their faces were black and drained by exhaustion. Naomi had been with the desert forces in El Arish on Wednesday when she learned about the capture of the Old City. She had immediately rewritten the concluding stanza to her "Jerusalem of Gold." In her original song she had written:

> How your cisterns have dried up;
> How desolate is the marketplace.
> No Jew visits the Temple Mount;
> And the caves in the rock
> Keen the winds.
> No Jew goes down to the Dead Sea
> By the Jericho road.

Now, by the light of a campfire in Hebron, she sang her new verse to the men gathered around her:

> We have returned to the cisterns,
> To the marketplace and square.

470

*A shofar sounds on the Temple Mount;*
*In the caves in the rock*
*Thousands of suns rise.*
*We shall go down to the Dead Sea again*
*By the Jericho road.*

## DATE DUE